RE-IMAGINING CAPITALISM

Re-Imagining Capitalism

Edited By
DOMINIC BARTON, DEZSÖ HORVÁTH,
AND MATTHIAS KIPPING

OXFORD
UNIVERSITY PRESS

OXFORD
UNIVERSITY PRESS

Great Clarendon Street, Oxford, OX2 6DP,
United Kingdom

Oxford University Press is a department of the University of Oxford.
It furthers the University's objective of excellence in research, scholarship,
and education by publishing worldwide. Oxford is a registered trade mark of
Oxford University Press in the UK and in certain other countries

© Oxford University Press 2016
Chapter 8 © John Kay
Chapter 3 © Kathleen McLaughlin and Doug McMillon

The moral rights of the authors have been asserted

First Edition published in 2016

Impression: 1

Published in the United States of America by Oxford University Press
198 Madison Avenue, New York, NY 10016, United States of America

British Library Cataloguing in Publication Data
Data available

Library of Congress Control Number: 2016945379

ISBN 978-0-19-878545-3 (hbk.)
978-0-19-878546-0 (pbk.)

Printed in Great Britain by
Clays Ltd, St Ives plc

Contents

List of Figures

List of Tables

List of Contributors

Dominic Barton is Global Managing Director of McKinsey & Company. He leads the firm's focus on the future of capitalism and the role business leadership can play in creating long-term social and economic value. In his 25 years with the firm, Dominic has advised clients in a wide range of industries, helping transform institutions from local and regional players into global leaders. Before becoming managing director, he served as McKinsey's chairman in Asia from 2004 to 2009 and headed its office in Korea from 2000 to 2004.

Shawn Bohen serves on the executive leadership team at Year Up, responsible for leading the social enterprise's systems change strategy and research and development efforts. Shawn has made a career as a collaborative strategist, creating, growing, and strategically managing mission-driven organizations. Prior to Year Up, Shawn spent 14 years working at Harvard University in a series of leadership roles facilitating interdisciplinary collaboration to tackle some of society's most challenging social, political, and economic dilemmas. Shawn began her career conducting grassroots environmental and consumer affairs campaigns for the public interest research groups in Connecticut and Massachusetts.

Gerald Chertavian is CEO and Founder of Year Up, an innovative program that empowers urban young adults to enter the economic mainstream. With its annual operating budget of approximately $100 million, Year Up is the largest youth-serving non-profit founded since 2000. Gerald has received numerous awards for social entrepreneurship and youth development, and serves on the Board of Advisors for the Harvard Business School Social Enterprise Initiative. In 2013 he was appointed to serve as Chairman of Roxbury Community College by Massachusetts Governor Deval Patrick. Gerald is a graduate of Bowdoin College and Harvard Business School.

Gordon L. Clark is Professor and Director of the Smith School of Enterprise and Environment at Oxford University, Professorial Fellow at St Edmund Hall, the Sir Louis Matheson Distinguished Visiting Professor at Monash University, and a Visiting Professor at Stanford University. His research focuses on the governance and management of institutional investors and the behavior of participants in pension and retirement income funds. Recent publications include *Sovereign Wealth Funds: Legitimacy, Governance and*

Global Power with Adam Dixon and Ashby Monk and *Saving for Retirement* with Kendra Strauss and Janelle Knox-Hayes.

Andrew Crane is the George R. Gardiner Professor of Business Ethics and Director of the Centre of Excellence in Responsible Business at the Schulich School of Business, York University. He is the author or editor of 12 books, including an award-winning textbook on *Business Ethics* and *The Oxford Handbook of Corporate Social Responsibility*. His latest book is *Social Partnerships and Responsible Business: A Research Handbook*. He has published widely on business ethics and corporate social responsibility in scholarly management journals, and is Co-editor of the journal *Business and Society*. He is a frequent contributor to the media, and is the co-author of the Crane and Matten blog.

Robert G. Eccles is Professor of Management Practice at the Harvard Business School. He first joined the faculty at the Harvard Business School in 1979 and received tenure in 1989. He left in 1993 to work in the private sector and rejoined the faculty in 2007. His most recent book is *The Integrated Reporting Movement: Meaning, Momentum, Motives, and Materiality* (with Michael P. Krzus and Sydney Ribot). He is a member of the Steering Committee of the International Integrated Reporting Council (<http://www.integratedreporting.org/>) and on the Board of Directors of the Sustainability Accounting Standards Board (<http://www.sasb.org>).

R. Edward "Ed" Freeman is a prolific educator, consultant, and speaker, best known for his work on the topics of stakeholder management and business ethics. Freeman is the author of the award-winning book *Strategic Management: A Stakeholder Approach*, first published in 1984. It is a landmark book, said to have helped to define and shape our understanding of how good management practice really is based on relationships. Freeman joined the Darden Graduate School of Business Administration in 1987, where he is currently University Professor and Elis and Signe Olsson Professor of Business Administration.

Dezsö Horváth is Dean and Tanna H. Schulich Chair in Strategic Management at the Schulich School of Business, York University in Toronto. Under his leadership, the School internationalized extensively, including a campus in India, and became widely recognized as a global leader in responsible business. Horváth is a director of several companies and organizations and serves on the advisory board of various business schools around the world. He was named 2004 Dean of the Year by the Academy of International Business and, in 2008, was made a Member of the Order of Canada for his academic leadership and sustained commitment to business education.

Bryan W. Husted is Professor of Management at the EGADE Business School of the Tecnológico de Monterrey, Mexico. His research interests include corporate social responsibility, international business, governance, and sustainability. He is past president of the Society for Business Ethics and the International Association for Business and Society and is currently Co-editor of *Business and Society*.

John Kay is one of Britain's leading economists. He is a Visiting Professor at the London School of Economics, Fellow of St John's College, Oxford, Fellow of the British Academy, and Fellow of the Royal Society of Edinburgh. He is a director of several public companies and contributes a weekly column to the *Financial Times*. In 2012, he chaired the Review of UK Equity Markets and Long-Term Decision-Making for the British government. He is the author of many books, including *The Truth about Markets, Obliquity*, and *Other People's Money*.

Matthias Kipping is Professor of Policy and Richard E. Waugh Chair in Business History at the Schulich School of Business, York University in Toronto. He held previous positions in the UK and Spain and has been a visiting professor in France, Italy, and Japan. He has published widely on the history of management, management knowledge, and its diffusion, including *The Oxford Handbook of Management Consulting* (co-edited with T. Clark) and *Defining Management* (co-authored with L. Engwall and B. Üsdiken).

Monique Leroux is President of the International Cooperative Alliance. She was Chair of the Board, President, and Chief Executive Officer of the Desjardins Group, the fifth largest cooperative financial group in the world from 2008 to 2016. Under her leadership, Desjardins defined a strategic vision that is strongly rooted in its cooperative mission and values and focuses on growth, service, and efficiency for the benefit of its members and clients. In order to promote cooperative values and their contemporary relevance, in 2012 she published *Alphonse Desjardins: A Vision for Today's World*, and became a founding partner of the International Summit of Cooperatives, which elected her as president in 2015.

Nick Lovegrove is US Managing Partner of the Brunswick Group, a business communications firm, after working for more than 30 years with McKinsey & Company in London and Washington, DC. He co-published his research in the *Harvard Business Review* ("Triple Strength Leadership") and *Global-Is-Asian* ("The Tri-Sector Athlete"), and has authored a forthcoming book entitled *The Mosaic Principle*. Nick recently served as a senior fellow at Harvard's Kennedy School, and graduated with master's degrees in modern history, public policy, and business administration from Oxford University, Harvard University, and INSEAD, respectively.

Kirsten E. Martin is Assistant Professor of Strategic Management and Public Policy at the George Washington University's School of Business. She is the principle investigator on a three-year grant from the National Science Foundation to study online privacy. Martin is also a member of the advisory board of the *Future Privacy Forum* and the Census Bureau's National Advisory Committee for her work on privacy and the ethics of "big data." She is regularly asked to speak on privacy and the ethics of big data. Her research interests center on online privacy, corporate responsibility, and stakeholder theory.

Dirk Matten is the Hewlett-Packard Chair in Corporate Social Responsibility and Professor at the Schulich School of Business, York University in Toronto. He holds a doctoral degree and the habilitation from Heinrich-Heine-Universität Düsseldorf, Germany. He is also Visiting Professor at the University of London, the University of Nottingham, and Sabancı University in Istanbul. His research interests are in business ethics, corporate social responsibility, and global governance. He has published 23 books and edited collections as well as over 80 articles and book chapters.

Kathleen McLaughlin is the Chief Sustainability Officer for Walmart, and the President of the Walmart Foundation. Last year, in addition to business initiatives investing in people and businesses in supply chains, the company surpassed $1.4 billion in giving worldwide, including $1 billion of food donations. McLaughlin joined Walmart in 2013. Before that, she spent over 20 years with the global consulting firm McKinsey & Company. McLaughlin earned a Bachelor of Science from Boston University, and a Master of Arts from Oxford University, where she was a Rhodes Scholar.

Doug McMillon is President and CEO of Wal-Mart Stores, Inc. (Walmart). He oversees the world's largest company, including its more than 11,000 retail units and 2.3 million associates in 28 countries, and its eCommerce websites in 11 countries. Doug first worked for Walmart in 1984 as an hourly summer associate in a distribution center. He rejoined the company in 1990, as an assistant manager in a Tulsa, Oklahoma Walmart store before moving to merchandising as a buyer trainee. He went on to serve in senior leadership roles in all of Walmart's business segments, including Sam's Club and Wal-mart International.

Bidhan "Bobby" L. Parmar is Assistant Professor at the Darden School of Business. Parmar's research interests focus on how managers make decisions and collaborate in uncertain and changing environments to create value for stakeholders. His work helps executives better handle ambiguity in their decision-making. Parmar is a Fellow at the Business Roundtable Institute for Corporate Ethics and the Olsson Center for Applied Ethics, and the Safra Center for Ethics at Harvard University.

Paul Polman has been Chief Executive of Unilever since 2009. Under his leadership the company has set out an ambitious vision to decouple its growth from environmental impact while increasing its positive role in society. Paul is Chairman of the World Business Council for Sustainable Development and serves on the board of the UN Global Compact. He has been closely involved in action to tackle climate change and served as a member of the High Level Panel on the post-2015 development agenda. In recognition of his contribution to responsible business, Paul has received numerous awards and accolades including the UN Environment Programme's Champion of the Earth Award.

Richard A. Ross has 35 years of progressive experience in the mining industry. He was the chairman and CEO of Inmet Mining Corporation until December 31, 2009. Mr. Ross has also held a number of board of directors' positions in both public and non-profit organizations including the chairman of the Mining Association of Canada and chairman of the St. Joseph's Health Centre in Toronto. He is now devoting his time, energy, and passion for the mining industry to the development and direction of the Global Mining Management MBA Program at York University's Schulich School of Business.

Douglas Sarro is Associate at Sullivan and Cromwell LLP in New York. He holds an Honours BA from the University of Toronto and a JD from Osgoode Hall Law School.

Bruce Simpson is Director, and 29-year veteran, of McKinsey starting in New York, then Paris, and now Canada. He led McKinsey's Canadian Practice, then convened the Global Operations Practice, and served on McKinsey's global board. Bruce advocates for capitalism to focus on the long term, fully integrating corporate social responsibility into strategy and corporate culture. Bruce is on the Boards of Human Rights Watch, Catalyst, and the Trans Canada Trail. He holds two law degrees from Cambridge University and an MBA/MA from Wharton Business School and the Lauder Institute at the University of Pennsylvania.

Birgit Spiesshofer is Of Counsel at Dentons. Before, she was partner at Hengeler Mueller. She was educated at New York University (MCJ) and the Universities of Heidelberg (Dr. iur.), Freiburg, and Tübingen and worked as foreign associate in Washington, DC and at the European Commission. Her focus is on corporate social responsibility (CSR), compliance, international, European, public, and environmental law. She is Chair of the CSR Committees of the Council of Bars and Law Societies of Europe and the German Lawyers Association. She is a member of the Advisory Board of Generali Zukunfts-fonds. She publishes and speaks frequently on CSR.

John Stackhouse is Senior Vice President in the Office of the CEO of Royal Bank of Canada, serving as an adviser to the senior executive and board on social, economic, and political issues. He was previously editor-in-chief of the *Globe and Mail*, Canada's national newspaper, where he also served during his 25-year career at the paper as business, national, and foreign editor, correspondent-at-large and, from 1992 to 1999, foreign correspondent in New Delhi. He is the author of three books, *Mass Disruption* (2015), *Timbit Nation* (2002), and *Out of Poverty* (2000). Stackhouse is also a Senior Fellow at both the CD Howe Institute and the University of Toronto's Munk School of Global Affairs.

Lynn Stout is Distinguished Professor of Corporate and Business Law at Cornell University. An internationally recognized expert in corporate govern-ance, financial regulation, and ethical behavior, she has published numerous books and articles and lectures widely. She currently serves on the Board of Governors of the CFA Institute, the Board of Advisors for the Aspen Insti-tute's Business and Society Program, and the Advisory Committee to the US Treasury's Office of Financial Research. Her most recent book, *The Share-holder Value Myth*, was named 2012 Governance Book of the Year. In 2014, Ethisphere Institute listed her among the 100 Most Influential in Business Ethics.

Ratan N. Tata was the Chairman of Tata Sons from 1991 to 2012. Under his leadership the Tata Group developed from a largely Indian player to a global business group with 65 percent of revenue coming from overseas. Tata continues to be the Chairman of the Tata charitable trusts and has built a reputation for showcase community engagement over the years of his career as a businessman. He holds a degree from Cornell University and has completed the Advanced Management Program at Harvard Business School. He has received several honorary degrees, including a doctorate from York University in Toronto.

Matthew Thomas is Founder and Chief Executive of Paddle, a non-linear career development platform. He has co-published his research in the *Harvard Business Review* ("Triple Strength Leadership") and *Global-Is-Asian* ("The Tri-Sector Athlete"), and serves as a David Rockefeller Fellow of the Trilateral Commission, and Global Shaper of the World Economic Forum. He previ-ously founded and led The Intersector Project and worked at McKinsey & Company, Department of Finance Canada, and Morgan Stanley. Matthew graduated with a bachelor's degree in business administration with distinction from the Schulich School of Business at York University.

Michael Viehs is Research Director at the Smith School of Enterprise and the Environment at the University of Oxford. He was Visiting Assistant Professor at the School of Business and Economics at Maastricht University and is currently a research affiliate with the European Centre for Corporate Engage-ment. Michael's research on sustainability and environmental, social, and corporate governance was featured in several newspapers and magazines such as the *Financial Times* and *Forbes*. His academic work on corporate governance and shareholder engagement is published in *Corporate Governance: An International Review* and *Annals in Social Responsibility*.

Tiffany Vogel is Associate Principal at McKinsey in Toronto and has been with the firm since 2011. She leads large-scale performance transformations for multilateral institutions, non-profits, and private sector clients. At the Oxford Martin School, she wrote extensively on global governance and systemic risk in the 21st century, co-authoring a journal article in *Global Policy*, and a chapter in *The Butterfly Defect*, published by Princeton University Press. Tiffany completed her environmental policy MSc at the University of Oxford as a Commonwealth Scholar and Rotary Ambassadorial Scholar, and she also holds an Honours BSc and BA from the University of Western Ontario.

Edward Waitzer is former chair of Stikeman Elliott LLP and remains a senior partner. He is a professor, the Jarislowsky Dimma Mooney Chair in Corporate Governance and Director of the Hennick Centre for Business and Law at York University. He served as chair of the Ontario Securities Commission and as vice president of the Toronto Stock Exchange. He is Chair of the Liquor Control Board of Ontario and Vice Chair of Sociedad Quimica y Minera de Chile. He has written extensively on a variety of legal and public policy issues and served as director of a number of corporations, foundations, and community organizations.

D. Eleanor Westney is Professor Emerita at the Schulich School of Business and at the MIT Sloan School of Management, and Visiting Professor of International Business at Aalto University in Helsinki. She has written extensively on the organization theory and the study of multinational corporations, on cross-border learning, on the Japanese business system and Japanese multinational corporations, and on the internationalization of research and development.

Galen G. Weston is the fourth generation of Weston family leaders, now Deputy Chairman of George Weston Limited and Executive Chairman of Loblaw Companies Limited, a portfolio of businesses including food and pharmacy retailing, fashion, real estate, and financial services. Mr. Weston holds a BA from Harvard University and an MBA from Columbia University. At Loblaw, he has taken a strategic, values-based approach to doing business. He has advocated, in particular, food sustainability and diet as a solution to health-related issues and introduced a range of initiatives that include an industry-leading sustainable seafood policy and action on ingredients of concern in two of Canada's largest brands, President's Choice and Life Brand.

Simon Zadek is Co-director of the UN Environment Programme Inquiry into Design Options for a Sustainable Financial System, Senior Fellow at the Tsinghua School of Economics and Management, the Singapore Management University, and Distinguished Senior Fellow at the Academy of Business in Society. He was the founder and chief executive of AccountAbility, and is on the Advisory Board of Generation Investment Management. He is the author of the prize-winning book *The Civil Corporation* and the much used *Harvard Business Review* article "Pathways to Corporate Responsibility."

1

Re-Imagining Capitalism for the Long Term

Situating the Volume

Dominic Barton, Dezső Horváth, and Matthias Kipping

INTRODUCTION: THIS TIME IS DIFFERENT... BECAUSE IT HAS TO BE

This time is different is the title of a book by economists Carmen Reinhardt and Kenneth Rogoff (2009), which puts the 2008 financial and economic crisis—now widely referred to as the "Great Recession"—into a long-term, historical perspective by examining what they call "eight centuries of financial folly." One does not have to agree with their argument that (excessive) government borrowing is largely to blame for the recurrent cycles of boom and bust—and others have pointed to more varied and complex origins of the most recent and previous crises (e.g., Coffee, 2009; McLean and Nocera, 2010; Krugman, 2008). What they do show quite clearly, however, is a concurrent pattern of denial, short-term memory, and, most importantly, a failure to learn from the past to prevent future crises. Let's examine our own thinking: does the 2007–9 crisis not seem far away today, with most of its negative consequences already behind us? Probably. And since many believe these recent challenges have been overcome, why not go back to business as usual?

Capitalism has indeed survived much more daunting challenges. Take the Great Depression of the 1930s, when large parts of the population even in the most developed economies faced not only unemployment but widespread poverty and even starvation. Or, more fundamentally, the emergence of a system diametrically opposed to capitalism in the Soviet Union after 1917: with collective or state rather than private ownership, no individual incentives, and central planning instead of market exchanges. It spread to half of the globe after World War II, prompting Nikita Khrushchev to famously predict in 1956 that communism would eventually "bury" capitalism. But it did not: with very few and largely marginal exceptions, capitalism has actually triumphed around the world: market-based reforms in China from 1978 onwards, the end of the Soviet bloc and its planned economy, symbolized by the fall of the Berlin Wall in 1989, and the liberalization of the Indian economy since 1991.

However, this time, we believe, *needs* to be different; not because of the recent "Great Recession," but because of a confluence of many factors that provide humanity with rather unprecedented challenges, which, if left unresolved, might threaten not just the capitalist system but prosperity and global order. There is no doubt that capitalism has been an engine of wealth creation since the first Industrial Revolution in the 18th century. It has led to sustained productivity gains and long-term growth, lifted an increasing part of humanity out of poverty and subsistence, and, consequently, spread around the globe from its origins in the Atlantic economy (Maddison, 2001; McCraw, 2011). But today, there are fundamental questions about the consequences of capitalism and, hence, its future: is capitalism still improving the wealth and well-being for the many? Or, as some have suggested, has it become detrimental not only for the economy, where long-term value creation is being sacrificed to the pressures of short termism, but also for society, where the gap between rich and poor has increased—often significantly—and opportunities to lift oneself out of poverty have decreased (e.g., OECD, 2011, 2015; Piketty, 2014; Wilkinson and Pickett 2009). And what about the natural environment, which seems increasingly under threat in ways that could have unforeseen consequences for centuries? Moreover, are those entrusted with its functioning, namely business and political leaders, able—and willing—to put the interests of a broader set of stakeholders before short-term, sometimes personal gains?

We also believe that this time *can* be different, because there is a widespread recognition that "business as usual"—in the broadest sense of the term—is no longer an option. Concerns about the consequences and future of capitalism are not a question of political left or right. In this respect, in the US for instance, the Tea Party and Occupy Wall Street or the popular support for the rather different positions taken by Donald Trump and Bernie Sanders reflect two sides of the same coin—whether their proponents like it or not. And worrying about the consequences of climate change or the water supply is no longer the exclusive domain of governments, the United Nations or non-government organizations (NGOs), but has become a matter for the C-suite.

This volume reflects both the urgency of the needed action and the opportunity to achieve a wide-ranging agreement and lasting movement towards a more responsible, equitable, and sustainable model of capitalism in order to generate long-term value—even if questions remain regarding what exactly the necessary reforms should be and who should drive them. The volume is unique in that it brings together many of the leading proponents for a reformed, re-imagined capitalism from the fields of academia, business, and NGOs. Its contributors have been at the forefront of thought and action in regard to the future of capitalism. Both individually and collectively, they provide powerful suggestions of what such a long-term oriented model of capitalism should look like and how it can be achieved. Drawing on their research and/or professional experience, they write in an accessible way aiming to reach the broad audiences required to turn a re-imagined capitalism into a reality.

The remainder of this introductory chapter first provides an overview of the debates about capitalism and its future from the late 18th century until the present day. This will help to situate the contributions made by the various chapters in the volume, which are briefly summarized later in this chapter.

CONTEXT: CAPITALISM AS A DYNAMIC—AND DEBATED—SYSTEM

Capitalism—short for a system based predominantly on private ownership, individual incentives and rewards, and exchanges through markets—has never been of a single uniform type. And since, as Dore (2002: 116) succinctly put it, "[t]ypes of capitalism are not static," capitalism has seen many changes over time—sometimes significant ones—and there have always been debates about what capitalism *should* look like. We will outline these debates and changes in the remainder of this section, showing how they gradually became more organized and comprehensive—reflecting both the spread of capitalism itself and a growing recognition of the need for reform to make it more sustainable. What has to be noted is that there were also those, like Karl Marx, who rejected capitalism completely or saw it, at best, as a stage in the evolution towards other, supposedly more productive and equitable forms of economic organization. We will leave them aside here, since their predictions and the efforts to turn them into reality ultimately proved unsuccessful and capitalism prevailed.

A Patchwork of Reforms since the Late 18th Century

Efforts to reform capitalism started with what is now called the first Industrial Revolution, which originated in parts of England in the late 18th century and then quickly spread through much of Europe and across the North Atlantic (e.g., Pollard, 1981; Stearns, 1998). It saw significant increases in output and productivity based on new sources of energy (the steam engine), the development of increasingly sophisticated machinery (in particular in the textile industry), and the introduction of new forms of organization (the factory), which brought together hundreds, at times thousands of workers under a single roof. While contributing to economic growth and, ultimately, the improvement of living standards across an increasingly industrialized world, these developments also created hardships for many, namely those working in the new factories, which included many children. From the outset, attempts were therefore made to reform the emerging capitalist system to alleviate these hardships and share capitalism's benefits among all those involved. In general, these efforts remained piecemeal, largely based on individual initiatives, but they did create "pockets" of alternatives, i.e., more socially responsible and equitable capitalist models, some of which lasted or even expanded over time, and, occasionally, turned into the foundation for broader reforms.

Many of these initiatives were "bottom-up," with visionary business leaders playing a significant and visible role. One of the most prominent among them was Robert Owen (1771–1858), who turned a cotton mill at New Lanark in Scotland into a social experiment that was both commercially successful and significantly improved conditions for workers and their families and, therefore, became an exemplar for many social reformers at the time. In order to improve both the productivity and well-being of their workers, other industrialists also adopted social policies, generally subsumed under the "paternalism" label with the efforts by the German steel producer Alfred Krupp in the 19th century described as being "among the first steps towards industrial social responsibility" (McCreary, 1968: 24–5; for a more comprehensive overview see Husted, 2015). At around the same time, other German industrialists went even further, collectively suggesting the regulation of working hours and wages as well as the introduction of pension schemes funded by employers and workers—decades before the German government actually took such steps. These suggestions, it should be noted, were primarily motivated by the recognition that a sharing of the gains from industrialization would benefit all and make the capitalist system itself more acceptable (Reckendrees, 2014).

There were also bottom-up collective endeavors, many of them self-help initiatives, notably in the form of mutual societies or cooperatives. Among them, the consumer cooperative established in Rochdale, England in 1844 as the Rochdale Society of Equitable Pioneers served as a model for subsequent efforts and its explicit "principles," including open membership and democratic control, were adopted formally by the international cooperative movement in 1937. Cooperatives form another "pocket" of stakeholder-driven organizations to this day—operating alongside, often in the shadow of, privately owned or publicly traded companies (for an overview see Birchall, 1997). More prevalent in certain sectors, such as agriculture and housing for instance, they have also thrived in financial services—and continue to do so.

And so do mutuals, i.e., policyholder-owned insurance companies, with State Farm and Nationwide as two prominent US examples (Borruso, 2012).

Under pressure from an emerging civil society, an increasingly vocal press, as well as the growing labor movement and its affiliated political parties, governments eventually started adopting broader reforms. In Britain, for example, the Factory Acts of the 1830s and 1840s outlawed child labor, which, nevertheless, persisted longer in other countries and continues until this day in parts of the developing world. And in the late 19th century, Germany was among the pioneers in introducing compulsory social insurance—a practice gradually adopted elsewhere throughout the 20th century. In general, the late 19th and early 20th century saw more organized and sustained efforts to improve various aspects of the capitalist system.

More Systematic Attempts to Improve Capitalism

Capitalism developed further with the so-called second Industrial Revolution in the late 19th and early 20th century, which, first in the United States and then elsewhere, saw the creation of large-scale organizations supplying fast-growing urban markets with packaged consumer goods as well as automobiles and also producing the necessary inputs, including steel, chemicals, and machinery (see, e.g., Chandler, 1990). As a result, the benefits of capitalism became more wide ranging and widespread, but so did the challenges—not surprising given that many companies now had tens or hundreds of thousands of employees. Efforts to address these challenges also became more pronounced and increasingly organized, though trailblazing individual initiatives persisted as well.

Examples for the latter include, quite prominently, Henry Ford (1863–1947), who dramatically improved productivity and output through the introduction of the moving assembly line in the production of his Model T automobile. He transferred part of the gains to consumers in the form of lower prices and also shared the resulting profits with his workers by reducing working hours from nine to eight per day and by more than doubling wages to $5 per hour—a significant amount for the early 20th century—famously aiming to enable these workers to buy the cars they helped produce. In a kind of virtuous circle, the higher wages attracted better workers and reduced turnover and absenteeism, resulting in even higher efficiency (see, e.g., Brinkley, 2003). Another important, albeit less well-known individual pioneer was the Boston-based department store owner Edward A. Filene (1860–1937) (Stillman, 2004), who in 1916 created an international association to spread more social business practices among retailers worldwide and, in 1919, established a foundation—originally called the Twentieth Century Fund in 1922 and today known as the Century Foundation—to more widely promote his ideas of a socially responsible capitalism. Foundations set up by other successful industrialists, including Ford, Carnegie, and Rockefeller, pursued similar aims, "promoting the well-being of humanity throughout the world" as the latter puts it today (<https://www.rockefellerfoundation.org/our-work/>)—even if they were originally also intended to deflect critiques of these entrepreneurs as "robber barons."

Overall, these initiatives were part of more comprehensive efforts in the United States to reform its capitalist system during what is now referred to as the Progressive Era between the 1890s and the 1920s (for an overview, see Gould, 2001; for the connections with Europe, Rodgers, 1998). The initiatives aimed at limiting excessive concentrations of economic power, notably through anti-trust legislation; reducing corruption and inefficiencies in local government; furthering women's rights including universal suffrage; and improving public education, widely seen as the "grand solution" to society's troubles. These changes were precursors to a more systematic, government-led effort to improve the capitalist system following the stock market crash of 1929 and the ensuing Great Depression—reforms initiated by US president Franklin D. Roosevelt beginning in 1933 and generally subsumed under the "New Deal" label (for an overview, see Kennedy, 2009). They comprised, among others, banking and financial regulation, including the creation of the Securities and Exchange Commission, the introduction of labor standards and union rights, the inception of social security, initially for the unemployed and retirees, as well as large, publicly funded infrastructure projects.

Opposed by some, many of these measures found the support of forward-looking business leaders—among the most prominent being Thomas Watson Sr., who came to think of IBM "as more than a company . . . an institution that would improve the world and promote peace, capitalism and democracy" (Maney, 2003: 174). Similar ideas were also espoused by the emerging business schools, many of which were promoting a wide-ranging social role for managers (see for details Khurana, 2007; Engwall et al., 2016). This is perhaps most succinctly expressed by the then dean of the Harvard Business School (HBS), Donald K. David, in the introduction to a book on *The Responsibilities of Business Leadership* (Merrill, 1948: xiv), which reproduced the presentations of leading US managers at HBS:

> The competent business administrator must know that in a free society his enterprise can maintain profits over any considerable period of time only by serving the public and by achieving a proper balance among the real long-term interests of employees, stockholders, suppliers, customers, and all others directly affected by the activities of the business.

By the end of World War II, these ideas, which we would today subsume under the notion of a "stakeholder model" of capitalism (e.g., Freeman and Reed, 1983; Aguilera and Jackson, 2010), had become widely accepted within the US, where they were enshrined for instance by Peter Drucker (1954) in *The Practice of Management*, and inspired further reforms under presidents Eisenhower and Johnson during the 1950s and 1960s. Often, building on earlier home-grown efforts, they also drove similar changes towards a more socially responsible capitalism in many Western European countries and in Japan—usually with the active engagement of domestic modernizing elites in both business and politics, wide-ranging intellectual and material support from the US government and businesses, as well as some of the above-mentioned foundations and institutions (see, among others, Djelic, 1998; Kipping and Bjarnar, 1998; Kudo et al., 2004). While difficult to establish a singular causal link, it is nevertheless notable that during the ensuing decades all these countries, including the US, saw unprecedented economic growth leading to unrivalled prosperity for large parts of their populations—a period referred to as an "economic miracle" (*Wirtschaftswunder*) in Germany or "the thirty glorious years" (*les trente glorieuses*) in France. And it should not be forgotten either that the opportunities opened for many by this stakeholder model helped contain and eventually push back the sway communist ideas and parties held in many of these countries.

Thus, between the 1930s and the 1960s, socially responsible, long-term-oriented capitalism moved from isolated "pockets" during the earlier period to the mainstream and became commonplace and widely accepted—at least in the most developed parts of the world. But, as it turned out, despite its undeniable successes, the hold of the "stakeholder model" on capitalism was tenuous, especially in the US, where a different model, focusing more on shareholders, started to emerge in the 1970s—in turn shaping developments elsewhere.

From Revival (and Triumph) to a Quest for Fundamental Renewal

It is difficult to ascertain why what appeared like a successful model of socially responsible, stakeholder-oriented, and long-term-focused capitalism became increasingly questioned. Part of the problem might have resulted from the stakeholders' own doings, with each group putting their specific interests over those of others; part might have been external pressures, including the uncertainty and turmoil created by the Vietnam War, the demise of the Bretton Woods system and the resulting currency fluctuations, the oil crises and skyrocketing prices in the 1970s; another part emanated from ideas questioning the role of government in the economy, later often summarized as "neo-liberalism" (Krugman, 2007)—altogether creating what historian Charles Maier (2010) has referred to as a profound "malaise." This in turn opened the door to a fundamental rethinking and reshaping of the capitalist system in the US toward the interest of a single stakeholder, those owning company shares—with the rationale for this shift probably best summarized by Milton Friedman (1970), who argued that the corporate executive was only appointed by the stockholders as "an agent serving the interests of his principal" and that the "social responsibility of business is to increase its profits."

US capitalism did revive during the 1980s and 1990s and it did triumph over the communist economic system. It is not clear whether this was a consequence of the focus on "shareholder value" as it came to be called, or resulted from other factors, including, first and foremost, the information and technology revolution. In any case, US growth rates during this period never approached those the country experienced in the post World War II decades. Not only did the US evolve but so did other countries, in particular those in Northern Europe, which modernized their own version of capitalism, retaining its more responsible and inclusive nature, while making it more competitive (see, e.g., Fellman et al., 2008). The increasing divergence between capitalist systems became the subject of more intense scholarly research, which examined the respective features of what tended to be referred to as "shareholder" and "stakeholder" models or, quite influentially, as "liberal" and "coordinated" market economies (Hall and Soskice, 2001).

There was also a growing chorus of critical voices, warning about the consequences of what one of its earliest critics, Michel Albert (1993), referred to as the "neo-American model" and its "obsession with individual achievement and short-term profit." Albert not only exhorted his native France to espouse the alternative "Rhine model" exemplified by Germany, Switzerland, and the Netherlands, but also highlighted the dangers of exclusion and short termism for the US itself. Similarly, Dore (2000) defended the merits of what he termed "welfare capitalism" and voiced concern about companies even in countries like Germany and Japan that favored "stockholder capitalism" and its features such as stock options or an obsession with quarterly results.

Rather than these warnings, it was ultimately the excesses and resulting crises from *within* the shareholder model of capitalism that prompted more widespread reflection and growing calls for reform: the dot com-fueled stock market boom and its eventual bust in 2000, the major corporate scandals of the early 21st century, including Enron, Worldcom, and Bernie Madoff, and, last but not least, the "Great Recession" from 2007 to 2009, triggered by certain financial practices, in particular the so-called subprime mortgages and their securitization (see e.g., above, also Lewis 2010). Critics of "quarterly capitalism" (Barton, 2011) and proponents for reform now increasingly came from a wider range of academic disciplines, press outlets, and, most importantly, from the business community itself—with a growing number of leaders pointing not only to the consequences of the Great Recession as a reason for re-imagining capitalism but also highlighting even broader challenges such as climate change and the growing threats to our water and food supply. Many of the most prominent among this growing chorus of voices advocating and promoting change to the capitalist system are assembled in this volume.

IMPROVING CAPITALISM FROM WITHIN

Taken together, the chapters in this volume aim at moving capitalism forward, re-imagining a capitalism that lives up to its promise as an engine of innovation and wealth creation and allows us to successfully face current and future societal and environmental challenges. The book stands in the long tradition of those from inside capitalism who espoused its tremendous benefits, while recognizing its shortcomings and developing ways to overcome them. It brings together many of the leading thinkers and actors pioneering and pursuing similar goals.

Their contributions are subdivided into three parts. The first part looks at those individual leaders who have, through their actions, become *trailblazers* and can serve as examples for a re-imagined capitalism. The second part provides *in-depth analyses* from various perspectives on capitalism's weaknesses and, more importantly, how it can be made better, focusing in particular on the role business can play in this respect. The third part offers *suggestions* about the specific steps that should be adopted to move toward such a responsible and sustainable capitalism for the long term, capped by a concluding chapter outlining what it might look like.

The first part opens with a chapter by *Paul Polman*, who presents the steps Unilever has taken to move beyond the short term and adopt policies that lead to shared prosperity and protect the planet. Conscious of the limitations of what a single company can achieve, he forcefully argues for collective action, which in his view can only succeed if business manages to regain the trust of society through a renewed sense of purpose. In their chapter, *Kathleen McLaughlin* and *Doug McMillon* show how a company that has sufficient reach and scale (and is prepared to work with multiple stakeholders) can influence and even reshape global systems in ways that benefit both business and society, illustrating their argument with Walmart's efforts towards food sustainability. The next two chapters deal with organizations that have a built-in long-term focus. First, there are family firms that, as *Galen G. Weston* explains, aim to create value for all stakeholders over decades rather than quarters by espousing long-term-oriented, and sometimes unconventional policies—a characteristic often summarized under the label of "patient capital" and illustrated here with examples from a variety of family businesses including the author's own, Loblaw. Cooperatives are another such long-term-oriented type of organization, and their functioning is discussed in detail by

Monique Leroux based on her experience at Desjardins. The resilience of cooperatives, which became apparent during the recent financial crisis, is based on a democratic governance model leading to much greater focus on the main stakeholders. One important stakeholder, the community, is at the center of the chapter by *Ratan N. Tata*, who shows that throughout his own organization's history, serving the communities where it operated was seen as the very purpose of its existence. While this might have been originally driven by the less-developed context in which the Tata organization evolved, he argues that an engagement with local and broader communities can be a way for companies to contribute to building better societies in the 21st century. In the final chapter of this section, *Nick Lovegrove* and *Matthew Thomas* build on a study of many responsible leaders to argue that those who have a broad set of experiences covering multiple sectors, disciplines, and cultures are best equipped to deal with the complex challenges facing business and society today and in the future—ultimately suggesting a need to rethink the notion that excellence requires only specialization.

The second part of the volume starts with a reflection by *John Kay* about which aspects of capitalism are behind its triumphs, highlighting that markets are excellent in providing honest feedback but are also prone to rent seeking, with actors trying to increase their share of existing wealth rather than creating new wealth. The success of modern business, he therefore argues, cannot only rely on individual initiatives but depends equally on cooperative activities and an embeddedness in social institutions and the community. *Andrew Crane* and *Dirk Matten* explain in more detail the broader role of business in society today, including the protection of human rights, the provision of public services, and the participation in public policy—all of which, they suggest, require a careful reconsideration of corporate purpose, performance, and partnerships. From a more normative point of view, the chapter by *R. Edward Freeman, Bidhan L. Parmar*, and *Kirsten E. Martin* also suggests that capitalism in the 21st century has little alternative to being responsible, which requires revising some fundamental assumptions about business and value creation, including the relevance and interdependence of *all* stakeholders. *Bryan W. Husted* points out that, depending on the conditions, doing well financially *and* being good towards society and the planet might not always be feasible. This might require managers to make certain trade-offs between the two—trade-offs which should be made with an explicit consideration of all consequences. *Lynn Stout*'s chapter dismantles the myth that maximizing shareholder value should be the only corporate objective. In the final chapter of this second part of the volume, *John Stackhouse* looks beyond the corporation at the role of public opinion and the press as a force for the reform of capitalism. Their influence, which, as seen above, was quite considerable in the past, has been diminished by technological innovation. While increasing the accessibility and ubiquity of information, technology has also reduced attention span, fragmented dialogue, and made transformative collective action more challenging.

Contributions in the third part of the volume focus on how, within this context and beyond individual leadership, capitalism can be re-imagined and reformed more profoundly and broadly. Drawing on a multi-year inquiry into the development of a more sustainable economy by the United Nations Environment Programme, *Simon Zadek* outlines a financial system that would favor an inclusive and balanced economic development. A similar role at the corporate level could be played by the adoption of so-called "integrated reporting," which is discussed in the chapter by *Robert G. Eccles* and *Birgit Spiesshofer*. It re-orients companies away from their current short-term focus by allowing them to account for the material issues that affect their ability to create value over multiple time horizons. Drawing in particular on Canadian and US cases, *Edward Waitzer* and *Douglas Sarro* highlight the powerful role that legal systems are starting to play in requiring corporations to consider all stakeholders and the long-term consequences of their actions. Another powerful actor, institutional investors, is at the center of the chapter by *Gordon L. Clark* and *Michael Viehs*, who forcefully argue in favor of more active ownership and effective stewardship by these investors toward corporate social responsibility (CSR) based on their survey of extant studies showing a positive correlation between CSR and financial performance. In their chapter, *Bruce Simpson* and *Tiffany Vogel* put the onus for more responsible behavior squarely on corporations and their leaders, suggesting that CSR is most effective when based on what they call the "trinity" of visionary leadership, mindful strategy, and flawless execution. The following two chapters in this part examine two specific examples of how the challenges to a transformation of current systems can be overcome in practice. Focusing on the mining industry, *Richard A. Ross* and *D. Eleanor Westney* argue that to limit environmental impact and make wealth distribution more equitable require a recognition of the diversity of stakeholders and of the values underpinning their various expectations—pointing in particular to the role of boards in finding the necessary balance. In a more bottom-up approach and focusing in particular on the US case, *Shawn Bohen* and *Gerald Chertavian* highlight the need to provide disengaged and disadvantaged young people with economic opportunities in the labor market to restore their faith in the capitalist system *and* help companies fill the skills gap.

To conclude the volume, *Dezső Horváth* and *Dominic Barton* go beyond the suggestions made in the various chapters to outline their vision for what a re-imagined capitalism should look like. At the macro level, they see it as evolving from a narrowly defined shareholder capitalism to a focus on long-term value creation and prioritization of a broader set of stakeholders. Similarly, at the micro level, they exhort asset managers, executives, and board members to move away from "quarterly capitalism" and act like owners, using longer time horizons to invest and create sustained value.

ACKNOWLEDGMENTS

A book like this is a collective endeavor, which can only succeed with the contributions from many people. This includes all the authors, who positively responded to our call for inclusion in this volume and our editorial suggestions for their chapters; our publishers at Oxford University Press, David Musson and Clare Kennedy, who patiently waited for the completed manuscript and expertly guided us through the publishing process; and the many people providing support behind the scenes by contributing intensive feedback and constructive comments, helping with copy-editing, identifying and checking references, and assuring the smooth flow of communications between all those involved, whose invaluable input we gratefully acknowledge (in alphabetical order): Lisa Andrews, Katharine Bowerman, Andrew Cedar, Yvonne Massop, Paul Pivato, Deanna Schmidt, JoAnne Stein, and Lily Shuk Man Wong. As usual, the ultimate responsibility remains ours.

REFERENCES

Aguilera, R. V. and Jackson, G. (2010). "Comparative and International Corporate Governance," *Academy of Management Annals*, 4(1): 485–556.
Albert, M. (1993). *Capitalism vs. Capitalism*. New York: Four Walls Eight Windows (French original: *Capitalisme contre capitalisme*. Paris: Le Seuil, 1991).
Barton, D. (2011). "Capitalism for the Long Term," *Harvard Business Review*, 89(3): 84–91.
Birchall, J. (1997). *The International Co-operative Movement*. Manchester: Manchester University Press.
Borruso, M. T. (ed.) (2012). "McKinsey on Cooperatives." Available at: <http://www.mckinsey.com/client_service/strategy/latest_thinking/mckinsey_on_cooperatives>.
Brinkley, D. G. (2003). *Wheels for the World: Henry Ford, His Company, and a Century of Progress*. New York: Penguin.
Chandler, A. D., Jr. (1990). *Scale and Scope: The Dynamics of Industrial Capitalism*. Cambridge, MA: Belknap Press of Harvard University Press.
Coffee, J. C. (2009). "What Went Wrong? An Initial Inquiry into the Causes of the 2008 Financial Crisis." *Journal of Corporate Law Studies*, 9(1): 1–22.
Djelic, M.-L. (1998). *Exporting the American Model: The Post-War Transformation of European Business*. Oxford: Oxford University Press.
Dore, R. (2000). *Stock Market Capitalism: Welfare Capitalism—Japan and Germany versus the Anglo-Saxons*. Oxford: Oxford University Press.
Dore, R. (2002). "Stock Market Capitalism and Its Diffusion," *New Political Economy*, 7(1): 115–27.

Drucker, P. F. (1954). *The Practice of Management*. New York: Harper and Row.

Engwall, L., Kipping, M., and Üsdiken, B. (2016). *Defining Management: Business Schools, Consultants, Media*. New York: Routledge.

Fellman, S., Iversen, M. J., Sjogren, H., and Thue, L. (eds) (2008). *Creating Nordic Capitalism: The Business History of a Competitive Periphery*. Basingstoke: Palgrave Macmillan.

Freeman, R. E. and Reed, D. L. (1983). "Stockholders and Stakeholders: A New Perspective on Corporate Governance," *California Management Review*, 25(3): 88–106.

Friedman, M. (1970). "A Friedman Doctrine: The Social Responsibility of Business Is to Increase Its Profits," *New York Times*, September 13.

Gould, L. L. (2001). *America in the Progressive Era, 1890–1914*. New York: Longman.

Hall, P. A. and Soskice, D. (eds) (2001). *Varieties of Capitalism: Institutional Foundations of Comparative Advantage*. Oxford: Oxford University Press.

Husted, B. W. (2015). "Corporate Social Responsibility Practice from 1800–1914: Past Initiatives and Current Debates," *Business Ethics Quarterly*, 25(1): 125–41.

Kennedy, D. M. (2009). "What the New Deal Did," *Political Science Quarterly*, 124(2): 251–68.

Khurana, R. (2007). *From Higher Aims to Hired Hands: The Social Transformation of American Business Schools and the Unfulfilled Promise of Management as a Profession*. Princeton, NJ: Princeton University Press.

Kipping, M. and Bjarnar, O. (eds) (1998). *The Americanisation of European Business*. London: Routledge.

Krugman, P. (2007). *The Conscience of a Liberal*. New York: W. W. Norton.

Krugman, P. (2008). *The Return of Depression Economics and the Crisis of 2008*. New York: W. W. Norton.

Kudo, A., Kipping, M., and Schröter, H. G. (eds) (2004). *German and Japanese Business in the Boom Years: Transforming American Management and Technology Models*. London: Routledge.

Lewis, M. (2010). *The Big Short: Inside the Doomsday Machine*. New York: W. W. Norton.

McCraw, T. K. (2011). "The Current Crisis and the Essence of Capitalism," *Montréal Review*, August. Available at: <http://www.themontrealreview.com/2009/The-current-crisis-and-the-essence-of-capitalism.php> (accessed April 18, 2013).

McCreary, E. C. (1968). "Social Welfare and Business: The Krupp Welfare Program, 1860–1914," *Business History Review*, 42(1): 24–49.

McLean, B. and Nocera, J. (2010). *All the Devils Are Here: The Hidden History of the Financial Crisis*. New York: Portfolio/Penguin.

Maddison, A. (2001). *The World Economy: A Millennial Perspective*. Paris: OECD.

Maier, C. S. (2010). "'Malaise': The Crisis of Capitalism in the 1970s," in N. Ferguson, C. S. Maier, E. Manela, and D. J. Sargent (eds), *The Shock of the Global: The 1970s in Perspective*. Cambridge, MA: Belknap Press of Harvard University Press, pp. 25–48.

Maney, K. (2003). *The Maverick and His Machine: Thomas Watson, Sr. and the Making of IBM*. New York: Wiley.

Merrill, H. F. (ed.) (1948). *The Responsibilities of Business Leadership*. Cambridge, MA: Harvard University Press.

OECD (2011). *Divided We Stand: Why Inequality Keeps Rising*. Paris: OECD Publishing.

OECD (2015). *In It Together: Why Less Inequality Benefits All*. Paris: OECD Publishing.

Piketty, T. (2014). *Capital in the Twenty-First Century*. Cambridge, MA: Belknap Press of Harvard University Press.

Pollard, S. (1981). *Peaceful Conquest: The Industrialization of Europe, 1760–1970*. Oxford: Oxford University Press.

Reckendrees, A. (2014). "Why Did Early Industrial Capitalists Suggest Minimum Wages and Social Insurance?" Munich Personal RePEc Archive (MPRA) Paper No. 58186. Available at: <https://mpra.ub.uni-muenchen.de/58186/>.

Reinhart, C. M. and Rogoff, K. S. (2009). *This Time Is Different: Eight Centuries of Financial Folly*. Princeton, NJ: Princeton University Press.

Rodgers, D. T. (1998). *Atlantic Crossings: Social Politics in a Progressive Age*. Cambridge, MA: Belknap Press of Harvard University Press.

Stearns, P. N. (1998). *The Industrial Revolution in World History*, 2nd ed. Boulder, CO: Westview Press.

Stillman, Y. (2004). "Edward Filene: Pioneer of Social Responsibility," *Jewish Currents*, September. Available at: <http://www.jewishcurrents.org/2004-sept-stillman.htm>.

Wilkinson, R. and Pickett, K. (2009). *The Spirit Level: Why Greater Equality Makes Societies Stronger*. London: Allen Lane.

Part I

Trailblazing: The Role of Exemplary Leadership

2

Re-Establishing Trust

Making Business with Purpose the Purpose of Business

Paul Polman

INTRODUCTION: THE NEED FOR ACTION

Winston Churchill once famously observed that democracy was the worst form of governance—apart from all the others that had been tried! If he were alive today he might say the same about capitalism as an economic system. For all its failings, no other system has approached its efficiency in bringing unprecedented growth and prosperity to billions of people. Capitalism is the best we have at marrying solutions with needs, funneling capital to worthy ideas, and matching people with necessary work. But the "best we have" is no longer good enough, as capitalism is also failing us on many levels. The system includes deep flaws, both in theory and in outcomes (see also Chapters 8 and 20, this volume). Perhaps the core failing is an inability to deal with what economists coldly call "externalities"—those impacts, sometimes positive, but also dramatically negative, that fall outside the marketplace (Helbling, 2010). Pollution is the classic externality, but that's only one example of a general disregard for all the critical assets the planet provides to society and economies—mostly free of charge. The theoretical failings of our current system also include a range of other ills: a consistent bias against the future—through the use of discount rates that make future benefits worthless—and a general obsession with short-term performance (Barton, 2011); an inability to put numbers on things that are clearly valuable to society and business, such as people's skills and knowledge; and a focus on maximizing growth above all else.

The outcomes of these structural deficits are predictable. On the environmental side, we are pushing the limits of "planetary boundaries" as growth has come at an enormous cost. We are depleting our stocks and inventories of critical natural resources from a stable climate and abundant clean air and water, to rich stocks of food, fiber, and minerals. These things are not "nice to haves" or luxuries, but critical assets for a thriving society and economy (see also Chapter 19, this volume). We are at the precipice—or already over it—of what the latest science warns will be "severe, pervasive and irreversible impacts for people and ecosystems" (IPCC, 2014: 8). Extreme weather is on the rise, from floods in Pakistan, Russia, Thailand, and the Philippines, to prolonged droughts in Africa, Australia, Southern Europe, Latin America, and record— possibly permanent—dry spells across wide swaths of the western United States (Carrington, 2014). A few years earlier, the group of the world's leading climate scientists assembled by the United Nations cautioned that "extreme weather events will wipe billions off national economies and destroy lives" (Harvey, 2011).

In total, our current economic system is inflicting tremendous biophysical damage that is threatening our 10,000-year-old experiment in human society. But even this extensive cost of our progress would be somewhat forgivable if capitalism were bringing *everyone* more prosperity. But in truth, the system is failing many people and creating growing disparities between the rich and the poor. The 1.2 billion poorest people on the planet account for only 1 percent of global consumption, while the 1 billion richest consume nearly three-quarters of the world's economic output. In a measure of extreme absurdity, the 62 richest people in the world have amassed the same wealth as the poorest 3.6 *billion* (Oxfam, 2016). Oxfam's executive director, Winnie Byanyima, agreeably framed the situation when she said "it is staggering that in the 21st century, half of the world's population own[s] no more than a tiny elite whose numbers could all sit comfortably in a single train carriage" (Puzzanghera, 2014). Those at the bottom of the pyramid are struggling to meet basic needs. Over 3 billion people die each year from water, sanitation, and hygiene-related causes, with more than 2 billion living without access to basic sanitation (Water.org, 2015). And while a billion people struggle with health problems from being overweight, another billion go to bed hungry every night, unsure if they will wake up in the morning (Nierenberg and Small, 2014).

Hence, capitalism is in essence a complicated system of equations, solving very well for some outcomes, like efficiency, but not for equity or prosperity. And while the system can extract and maximize economic value, it does not address the values that really matter in life—well-being, shared prosperity, community, trust, and, perhaps greatest of all, purpose. What this chapter argues is that business has to play a fundamental role in addressing these challenges and make sure capitalism actually helps to provide what matters. It is structured as follows. The next section shows that the failings of capitalism not only impose a tremendous cost on our planet and on its most vulnerable people, but that they are also very costly to business and our economies as a whole. The main section of the chapter then discusses how business should and can become an agent for change helping to address these challenges. It first stresses the fundamental necessity to regain the trust of society; then provides examples of what a single company can do, drawing on the Unilever case (see, for other examples, Chapters 3, 4, and 5, this volume); and finally highlights the need for collective action given the magnitude of the challenges. A brief conclusion lays out a vision of business as a "force for good."

THE COSTS FOR BUSINESSES AND ECONOMIES

All of these systemic flaws in capitalism result in very real and growing costs to business and our economies. According to former New York mayor Michael Bloomberg extreme weather is "already costing local economies billions of dollars" (quoted in Risky Business, 2014: 2). Bloomberg and his two co-chairs of the *Risky Business* project, former US treasury secretary Henry Paulson and Tom Steyer, the retired founder of Farallon Capital Management, commissioned a research report on "The Economic Risks of Climate Change in the United States," which points for instance to the distinct possibility of $700 billion worth of coastal property falling below sea level in the coming decades. In response, the report supports a price on carbon, which provides a regulatory or, in the case of cap-and-trade, a market-based solution to make these shared costs of climate change apparent.

The *Risky Business* project co-chairs are not alone. A group of powerful institutional investors representing $24 trillion in assets have also called for "stable, reliable and economically meaningful carbon pricing that helps redirect investment commensurate with the scale of the climate change challenge, as well as plans to phase out subsidies for fossil fuels" (UNEP, 2014). Adding to the new sea of voices, the World Bank issued a Price on Carbon Statement signed by 73 countries and over 1,000 companies. When powerful and mainstream financial institutions, representing so many trillions of assets, and countries representing 52 percent of global GDP are on board, you know things are changing (World Bank, 2014). These investors and businesses are pushing for carbon pricing because, as the *Risky Business* report makes clear, the costs to our economies are real and growing. The world has already witnessed entire economies and livelihoods wiped out in regions where geopolitical disasters are closely linked to environmental threats.

The global economic damage that we can directly measure is astounding—in the last decade alone, the world spent $2.7 trillion more on natural disasters than usual (Our Planet, 2014). We have seen the additional costs that arise from a volatile world first hand at Unilever, where the annual cost of natural disasters and geopolitical instability is already around €300 million a year. We have seen impacts around the world, from shipping routes cancelled due to hurricanes in the Philippines to distribution networks in disarray from floods in the United Kingdom. And our experiences are not unusual, as companies everywhere are now frequently dealing with expensive disruptions in supply chains. In 2011, floods in Thailand crippled the production of hard drives and cars for months. In some regions, big food and agriculture companies have had to shut down production for many days, or even permanently. Severe weather swings and drought conditions are hurting farmers and world food supplies, costing the US economy alone hundreds of billions of dollars. The prices of commodities are rising fast, sometimes doubling or tripling in a couple years, driven partly by ever rising demand as a billion people enter the middle class, but also by extreme weather threatening supplies (Gober, 2008).

In sum, we have reached a tipping point where we cannot continue on the current path. No business can prosper in a world of runaway climate change, or one with rampant inequality and poverty. Business leaders are starting to recognize, perhaps for the first time in large numbers, that the cost of inaction is now greater than the cost of action. As the world heads toward what may be 10 or 11 billion people—all aspiring to a higher standard of living—something profound needs to change in how we live, eat, get around, and do business (Kunzig, 2014). This has become the core question of our times: how can we provide prosperity to billions more people without undermining the ability of the planet to support us? Business, run in new ways, will be a key part of the answer.

HOW BUSINESS SHOULD AND CAN ADDRESS THESE CHALLENGES

Global-scale problems of course require collective action, and that does mean government, working in conjunction with the other major sectors of society. But governments and international bodies are themselves struggling to address many of the biggest global challenges. There are many reasons why governments have been preoccupied, such as the recurring financial crises and the budget constraints they bring, or in dealing with fundamental structural problems—like the "checks and balances" that have been overworked and now grind governing to a halt in the West. It was telling that Narendra Modi came to office pledging to give India, "minimum government and maximum governance" (<http://www.narendramodi.in/minimum-government-maximum-governance-3162>). More broadly, the fact is our global institutions were designed in a previous era, in the days of Bretton Woods, when the world economy was dominated mainly by the United States and Europe. Today, the so-called BRIC countries (Brazil, Russia, India, and China) are as large, but with institutions that are not adjusted to the magnitude of our problems. And neither is compromise and negotiations with 200 countries in a room a workable solution—given the urgent need for action.

So, we need business to step up and help fill the void—albeit not alone. Our serious and global-scale challenges require partnerships across societal lines, with civil society, governments, academia, and business working together— though business is clearly a large component of the response. In developing countries, for instance, business represents 60 percent of GDP, 80 percent of financial flows, and 90 percent of new jobs (UN, 2014). World Bank President Jim Yong Kim made this situation clear when he expressed that "it's critical that governments work well with the private sector [as it] accounts for 90 percent of all jobs." Business can play a critical role in society. Companies bring to the table tremendous resources, including trillions in capital and enormous capacity for innovation and fast action. After many natural disasters, companies have discovered that they could reach people with critical aid in a more organized and consistent way than most of the government agencies around them. Shouldn't we use those organizational skills to help our businesses and communities avoid these issues before they turn into disasters?

But to change how and why business operates in a fundamental way, our leaders need to make a fundamental turning point in both strategy and tactics to rethink the way they do business (Winston, 2014). This new form of responsible capitalism goes well beyond traditional definitions of "corporate social responsibility" or "sustainability," moving from a simple license to operate to creating a *license to lead.* We, as business leaders, need to change our perspective and vision of the world and focus on long-term, real value creation, not just quarterly earnings. This new vision will allow business to serve the needs of citizens and communities with the same vigor with which it has served the needs of shareholders over many years. And it will allow business to see itself as a part of society, not separate from it. With the right lens, we can see clearly that it has always been absurd to treat environmental and social issues as a subset of the business agenda. It is obviously the other way around—business is a part of society and one of its most important expressions (see also Chapters 9 and 10, this volume). But as we change to take into account all of society's needs, we face a big challenge: overcoming a lack of trust.

Restoring Trust in Business through Purpose

The level of action our global problems demand will require a very high level of cooperation, which of course requires trust. But trust in all of society's institutions is something that is in short supply today. According to the global survey by PR firm Edelman, less than half of the general population trusts their government. And faith in business leaders is even lower—just 20 percent believe they can be trusted to tell the truth or make ethical decisions (Adams, 2014). The public can be forgiven for being skeptical of business intentions. Seemingly daily scandals—corruption charges, oil spills, being caught replacing ingredients with dangerous substitutes, or big financial institutions fixing base bank rates or manipulating exchange rates—have done little to help. Such a lack of trust undermines business and our credibility when we make commitments to customers, employees, and communities. Without buy-in from our stakeholders, we have to work even harder to make a difference and to succeed in traditional financial terms. This deficit of trust means that we are beginning our journey from behind the starting line.

The lack of trust combined with the seriousness and urgency of the challenges make these dangerous times for those businesses that do not take the larger societal interest into their thinking in a real way. Empowered by new technologies and rising transparency, people can take matters into their own hands. They can create communities of interest quickly and share information faster to drive action. For instance, a 17-year-old girl started a Change. org petition about the ingredients in soda, and the world's largest beverage companies agreed to eliminate a chemical of concern. Others have pushed companies to answer questions about their products' recyclability or availability to underserved populations. People are even coming together to create their own solutions and business models, going around big business. They are using collaborative consumption to challenge the normal operating model of everything from cars to hotels to apparel.

Companies that understand these new realities can rebuild trust and become part of the solution. They will have a bright future. Those that don't will become dinosaurs—outdated, outmoded, and out of business. So, the key question is how do we create a new form of capitalism that rebuilds trust in business. Let us start with describing the people in our lives who we trust. Reliable, as in they do what they say they will. Fair and equitable. Responsible. In sum, those we trust have *our* best interests at heart. In the most famous of trust exercises, we gladly fall backward blindly, knowing they will catch us. But can citizens trust business to catch those among us who fall? Business—and the capitalist system it is at the heart of—is in most regards amoral. Capitalism will optimize many outcomes, but will do so regardless of the larger implications. We can use the tools of capitalism to maximize production of cigarettes or nuclear weapons as well—or poorly—as we can produce apples or affordable health care.

So, how can citizens develop the trust that companies will *not* continue on their hitherto predictable path: do whatever they can to maximize short-term earnings at the expense of larger well-being and even a company's own longer-term interests? Rebuilding such trust will require business to change in both principle and action. Our core operating values must include new commitments to the larger world such as:

- *Authenticity, driven by a sense of larger purpose*: we must bring to bear all sides of ourselves and our organizations, combining the powerful business tools of the "head"—analyses, structure, and efficient management of capitals of all forms—and the "heart," the passion and creativity that business uses to solve problems and inspire people.
- *Transparency about our products and processes*: this openness will do the most to create trust. We should be sharing information about what is in everything and who made it, and be honest about what is *not* going well and needs improvement.
- *A systemic, longer-term perspective*: this means we should not sacrifice the greater good on the altar of short-term profit. In a world where the majority of stock shares are bought and sold in milliseconds, and with relentless pressure on public companies to perform on a quarterly basis, this last principle is challenging.

To bring these core principles to life, the list of actions business should, and must, undertake is long and sometimes daunting but also inspiring and exciting. There are a few key tactical areas:

- *The setting of bold goals* based on science and external thresholds, benchmarks, and realities, such as the dire need for the world to control carbon emissions very quickly. This means, for instance, to commit to keeping greenhouse gas emissions declining at the pace that science demands.
- *The open tracking of measurements and metrics* to build accountability. This drives a deeper understanding of and ability to manage our impacts up and down the value chain.
- *The use of deep partnerships and radical collaborations* across traditional lines. Our problems have become enormously complex, and neither governments nor business or non-government organizations (NGOs) have shown the capabilities to tackle them alone. We must work together to create broad movements and tipping points.

These principles and tactics create more transparency and trust in a company's actions. They represent a better path, but also a clear choice. We can accept the current state of affairs—one that is losing touch with our humanity—and bury our heads in the sand, hoping that the storms of rising public indignation will pass. Or we can make a conscious choice to, in the words of poet Robert Frost, take the road "less traveled by." We can choose to be givers and not takers from the system that gives us life in the first place. Let us look at what Unilever has done in this respect.

The Power of One: What a Single Company Can Do

Unilever has by no means figured out the perfect answers on how to operate with these principles at the heart of our business. But we have chosen a less traveled path. Our approach was, first, to give ourselves the space to operate in the best long-term interests of *all* our stakeholders, including shareholders—or at least those with an interest in real value creation. We abandoned the "guidance" game and moved away from quarterly profit reporting—beyond what is legally required. And in a critical internal step, we changed our compensation system to incentivize longer-term thinking. And then, we have set out a clear and audacious goal to decouple our growth from environmental impact while increasing our positive role in society. We call this the Unilever Sustainable Living Plan (USLP). It is a total value chain approach: from sustainable sourcing to sustainable living. It has never been attempted before by a company of our scale.

The USLP is founded on three big goals. By 2020 we want to: help more than a billion people take action to improve their health and well-being; halve the environmental footprint of the making and use of our products; and enhance the livelihoods of millions of people across our supply chain. Underpinning these goals are over 50 specific, time-bound targets (Coalition for Inclusive Capitalism, 2014: 115). And so far we are making real progress. We have added around €10 billion to our revenues—growth that is directly supported by the USLP. Around 50 percent of our growth in 2014 came from what we are now defining as "sustainable living brands," tied to a sense of purpose, such as Dove, Lifebuoy, Ben and Jerry's, and Comfort. These brands delivered nearly half our growth last year, and grew significantly faster than the rest of the business—answering to critics who claim or assume that sustainability costs companies money.

Unilever is moving towards a circular economy model, which reduces business risk and is good for the planet. We have lowered costs by more than €600 million through a range of initiatives. Across our manufacturing network, we have reduced our energy consumption by 20 percent, saving 1 million tons of CO_2 since 2008, and we now send zero waste to landfill in over 600 sites in 70 countries. We are reducing the risks from extreme weather and climate change by shifting to more renewable energy. We will become carbon positive in our operations by 2030—with markets like Japan and Germany already achieving 100 percent renewable power. We have also announced a one-year, international partnership with the World Wildlife Fund (WWF) to engage consumers in the fight against deforestation—one of the key drivers of climate change—and help protect a million trees in Brazil and Indonesia. We are making our supply chains more resilient and stable by working with small-holder farmers to improve their farming practices and livelihoods. We have already helped or trained over 800,000 additional smallholders, from tea farmers in Turkey to vanilla farmers in Madagascar.

And we have already achieved real change in the life of people in many of the countries we operate in. Take infant mortality, for instance. It is morally repugnant that 6.3 million children die before their fifth birthday, including 2 million from easily preventable diseases and ailments like diarrhea (UNICEF, 2014: 5). That is the equivalent of a jumbo jet of children crashing every hour, every day! The most basic of health practices, hand washing, can significantly reduce the number of deaths. Lifebuoy soap, one of Unilever's oldest and proudest brands, has made awareness and practice of hand washing a mission. We employ the only known PhD in the world with a specialty in public health and hand washing. Our programs have already reached millions of people across Asia, Africa, and Latin America. Just a single event, Global Hand Washing Day, touches 200 million people in 100 countries. These efforts are working—in one of the poorest areas of India, the incidence of diarrhea among children fell from 36 percent to just 5 percent. The work has also been remarkable in driving the success of the Lifebuoy brand and business. A beautiful video featuring an Indian boy surviving to age five has reached tens of millions of views on YouTube. The Facebook page for Lifebuoy has more than 4.2 million likes—for hand soap! And this once dated, 100-year-old product is now one of the company's fastest growing brands.

The USLP is also helping us motivate and attract the best talent. Employees are highly engaged by our efforts to make sustainable living commonplace as they look increasingly for meaning at work in a turbulent world. Engagement and being an "employer of choice" is hard to measure, but we have some solid evidence of progress. We are now the number one employer of choice in 34 of the 50 markets in which we measure our performance. We are also—for the second year running—the third most "in-demand" employer among jobseekers on the global networking site, LinkedIn, behind only tech giants Google and Apple, and the first fast-moving consumer goods company to reach 2 million followers. Not bad for a "soup and soap" company going back 130 years. We have found that the USLP is a key driver of recruitment, employee satisfaction, and retention. Half of graduate entrants cite our ethical and sustainability policies as the primary reason for wanting to join us, and more than 75 percent of our employees feel they contribute to the USLP in their roles and help realize our vision. People come to us and stay with us in large part because of our purpose, and they demand that we live up to our goals.

All of these business benefits stem from a concerted effort across the company to bring the principles of responsible capitalism to every part of the business. We have had significant success building both our business and helping solve larger global challenges. But while we can and should be proud of what Unilever has achieved so far, a single company cannot change capitalism as a whole.

Driving Transformational Change: The Need for Collective Action

While there is a lot we can do—and are doing—the challenges are too big for any one organization to solve alone. Real transformational change is only possible with new and innovative partnerships. We have to act together to address challenges as large and complex as climate change, inequity, or poverty. Take an issue like deforestation, requiring complex coalitions, extensive resources, and big ambitions. The burning of trees—to clear the way for soy and oil palm plantations, cattle grazing, paper and fiber production, or other human needs—accounts for 17 percent of all greenhouse gas emissions (Friedman, 2009). That is about the same as the emissions from all the cars, trucks, and planes combined.

All big buyers of food and agriculture inputs have a responsibility to protect these natural resources for our own business resilience and for humanity. So we have led the way in building a vast industrial coalition made up of most of the largest retail and consumer goods companies in the world. With a combined $3 trillion in revenues and purchasing power behind us, we have committed to eliminating deforestation from supply chains by 2020. We have also joined the New York Declaration on Forests, an agreement signed by more than 30 countries, many subnational governments in critical forest areas such as Brazil and Indonesia, 40 multinationals with extensive supply chains, and many groups of indigenous peoples and NGOs. This global coalition is pledging to halt all deforestation by 2030. It is only by getting whole sectors to come together in a common cause like this that we can reach the kind of tipping points to drive the kind of wholesale changes that are needed. Hopefully, we are close to reaching that point on deforestation.

More specifically, it is not the companies but the relatively small pool of multinational CEOs and corporate leaders that has an unusual opportunity –one might say, obligation—to promote deep change. Along with the role should come a deep sense of responsibility. We certainly have leverage to change the way business and the world work—just the largest 200 public companies have revenues over $20 trillion, or 29 percent of the world's economic output (Winston, 2014). As one of these CEOs, I have had the opportunity and privilege to bring the leverage and reach of Unilever to a number of important initiatives. These programs are opportunities to help shape the policy environment. For instance, because of Unilever's willingness to play a leadership role in tackling issues of global poverty and development, I was asked to serve on the UN Secretary General's High Level Panel on Post-2015 Millennium Development Goals (MDGs). It was my honor to sit with a group of leaders from all over the world, exploring how we can eradicate extreme poverty and improve the lives of the 2 billion people at the bottom of the pyramid. Progress on the MDGs is real. Global poverty has been halved, but the challenges remain. Submitted in 2013, the High Level Panel's report included the proposal to replace the MDGs with broader Sustainable Development Goals—which were indeed adopted as "Agenda 2030" at the UN Sustainable Development Summit in September 2015 (<https://sustainabledevelopment. un.org/post2015/summit>).

Overall, there is reason for optimism. The role of business in moving the world in a new direction is becoming clearer. The post-2015 MDGs agenda will not end extreme poverty without the resources and skills of business brought to bear. Companies like Unilever have extraordinary reach—we are present in more than half the households on the planet and, every day, 2 billion people in 200 countries use one of our products. This reach gives us the opportunity to improve the lives of millions by offering them the fundamentals of a decent life—clean drinking water, basic hygiene, and good nutrition. And the broader business community seems headed in the same direction on our biggest challenges—despite the continuation of some high profile lapses (see above, "Restoring Trust in Business through Purpose"). Of the world's 200 largest companies, 75 percent have specific, publicly stated social and environmental targets in place—and 50 of these companies have a goal for carbon reduction for a large part of their business that reflects the pace of change the science demands (Gowdy, 2014). PwC's global CEO survey found that CEOs were five times more likely to be increasing rather than lowering their priorities on reducing environmental impacts.

Business is organizing and mobilizing in many different ways. Take the "B Team," for instance, launched, among others, by Sir Richard Branson. It is bringing innovators and business leaders from around the world together with a goal to "catalyze a better way of doing business for the well-being of people and the planet" (<https://www.facebook.com/TheBTeamHQ/info?tab=page_ info>). Or, the World Business Council for Sustainable Development, which I have the honor of chairing, is using its Action 2020 Roadmap to champion an ambitious message of opportunity rather than mitigation. This was also the message coming from the New Climate Economy's second report, *Seizing the Global Opportunity*, published in June 2015 by the Global Commission on the Economy and Climate, chaired by the former president of Mexico, Felipe Calderón. This report makes a compelling case on how better economic growth can close the emissions gap, with the global market of low carbon services now worth more than US$5.5 trillion and growing at over 3 percent per year. It also shows that sustainable companies outperform their peers in financial performance, with 53 of the Fortune 100 companies already saving around $1.1 billion per year from emissions-reduction initiatives (<http://newclimateeconomy.report>). In short, the tradeoff between economic development and environmental protection is false.

CONCLUSION: PURPOSE-DRIVEN BUSINESS AS A FORCE FOR GOOD

Many in business have lost track of why companies exist in the first place: at its most basic, a company is meant to solve a problem for a customer. But taking that beyond face value requires putting a moral, purpose-driven center at the heart of that quest. A company should not fill just any need, but the ones worth filling and the ones most needed. It should solve real problems, not create new ones. Purpose-driven business is an old idea. William Lever, one of Unilever's founding fathers, established as far back as 1885 the right way to approach business and our responsibilities. Lever's approach was to look to larger needs, lifting many out of poverty, giving access to health and hygiene, and looking to leave the world in a slightly better way than he had found it. Later, other leaders, like Robert Wood Johnson, continued to establish a better form of capitalism. Johnson created Johnson & Johnson's "Credo" to guide business priorities and place customers and larger needs first, and shareholders and profits as a fifth priority. Contrary to what some in the financial markets would have us believe, putting a larger purpose at the core of doing business is not at odds with corporate structures or legal requirements (see Chapter 12, this volume). Fair returns to shareholders are more than fine; they are desired. The companies with the most resources can do the most good. But those returns are an outcome, not a goal. There is more to business than just profit maximization—but the path of responsible business is a profitable one (see also Chapter 17, this volume).

We can go even further than the simple idea that it is profitable to do right. Unilever's business model is increasingly based, as I have argued, on a simple premise: business should serve the common good, not just take from communities and environments on which it relies. Increasingly, we will become a positive net contributor, where being less bad is not nearly good enough, and is an inferior way to do business. Purpose-driven business creates private value for companies, but it creates much more value for a combination of itself *and* society. We hope to go beyond even this shared value concept to shared values, where business understands that it does not stand apart from social or environmental challenges, but is an integral part of the fabric of society (see also Chapters 9 and 19, this volume).

We are in the most important time in human history—a seminal era where we will discover if we are able to come together to manage our shared challenges and build a prosperous world. The *Financial Times* summed up well the plight we face when it argued in a lead article: "A globalisation that enriches the richest and impoverishes the rest is not sustainable. The case for open, inclusive societies has to be remade" (Stephens, 2014). Business can and must take the lead in these efforts, but corporate leaders need to see their role differently. *They* have to remake the case for open, inclusive societies. In this volatile and transparent world, the organizations that work to solve the largest challenges in partnership with their peers, communities, employees, and customers will thrive. The responsible organizations will outcompete their more self-centered and short-term-focused peers, solving increasingly complex challenges for all—in essence, finding the ultimate purpose of business, filling a need and profiting because of it.

Those companies that fail to see that business has a much larger social purpose and value than making money will struggle to survive. Society will reject them. But in the right hands, the purpose of business can move beyond just private financial gain. We can be a real force for good, helping the world and its people prosper in every way possible.

ACKNOWLEDGMENTS

This chapter is a revised and extended version of my contribution entitled "Solving Problems that Matter" to the *Perspectives on the Long Term* volume, put together by the Focusing Capital on the Long Term initiative, founded by the Canada Pension Plan Investment Board and McKinsey & Company, which kindly waived their copyright.

REFERENCES

Adams, S. (2014). "Trust in Business Isn't Any Better but Trust in Government Gets Even Worse," *Forbes*, January 20. Available at: <http://www.forbes.com/sites/susanadams/2014/01/20/trust-in-business-isnt-any-better-but-trust-in-government-gets-even-worse/> (accessed January 29, 2015).

Barton, D. (2011). "Capitalism for the Long Term," *Harvard Business Review*, 89(3): 84–91.

Carrington, D. (2014). "Extreme Weather Becoming More Common, Study Says," *Guardian*, August 11. Available at: <http://www.theguardian.com/environment/2014/aug/11/extreme-weather-common-blocking-patterns> (accessed January 14, 2015).

Coalition for Inclusive Capitalism (2014). *Making Capitalism More Inclusive*. Conference on Inclusive Capitalism. Available at: <http://www.inc-cap.com/conferences/conference-2015/book/> (accessed January 5, 2015).

Friedman, T. L. (2009). "Trucks, Trains and Trees," *New York Times*, November 11. Available at: <http://www.nytimes.com/2009/11/11/opinion/11friedman.html?_r=0> (accessed February 6, 2015).

Gober, P. (2008). "Global Warming Aside, Fresh Water Dwindling," *Arizona Republic*, August 17. Available at: <http://archive.azcentral.com/arizonarepublic/viewpoints/articles/2008/08/17/20080817vip-gober0817.html> (accessed January 22, 2015).

Gowdy, J. (2014). "The Leaders and Laggards of Sustainability Goals," *J Gowdy Consulting: Profitable Sustainable Solutions*, December 19. Available at: <http://jgowdyconsulting.com/blog/view.php?blogID=36> (accessed January 6, 2015).

Harvey, F. (2011). "Extreme Weather Will Strike as Climate Change Takes Hold, IPCC Warns," *Guardian*, November 18. Available at: <http://www.theguardian.com/environment/2011/nov/18/extreme-weather-climate-change-ipcc> (accessed January 14, 2015).

Helbling, T. (2010). "What Are Externalities?" *Finance and Development*, 47(4): 48–9. Available at: <http://www.imf.org/external/pubs/ft/fandd/2010/12/basics.htm> (accessed April 28, 2015).

IPCC (2014). "Intergovernmental Panel on Climate Change AR5 Synthesis Report," Joint Establishment of the United Nations Environment Programme (UNEP) and the World Meteorological Organization (WMO). Available at: <http://www.ipcc.ch/report/ar5/syr/> (accessed January 5, 2015).

Kunzig, R. (2014). "A World with 11 Billion People? New Population Projections Shatter Earlier Estimates," *National Geographic*, September 18. Available at: <http://news.nationalgeographic.com/news/2014/09/140918-population-global-united-nations-2100-boom-africa/> (accessed January 5, 2015).

Nierenberg, D. and Small, S. (2014). "Could Milan Protocol Lead the World to Food Sustainability?" *Christian Science Monitor*, June 5. Available at: <http://www.csmonitor.com/layout/set/print/Business/The-Bite/2014/0605/Could-Milan-Protocol-lead-the-world-to-food-sustainability> (accessed January 29, 2015).

Our Planet (2014). "Step Change in Ambition," United Nations Environment Programme. Available at: <http://www.ourplanet.com/ourplanet.html> (accessed January 28, 2015).

Oxfam (2016). "An Economy for the 1%: How Privilege and Power in the Economy Drive Extreme Inequality and How This Can Be Stopped." Available at: <http://policy-practice.oxfam.org.uk/publications/an-economy-for-the-1-how-privilege-and-power-in-the-economy-drive-extreme-inequ-592643>.

Puzzanghera, J. (2014). "Wealth of 85 People Equals that of Billions of Poor, Charity Says," *Seattle Times*, January 20. Available at: <http://seattletimes.com/html/nationworld/2022716321_wealthinequalityxml.html> (accessed January 14, 2015).

Stephens, P. (2014). "Scotland Independence Vote Exposes the Established Order," *Financial Times*, September 18. Available at: <http://www.ft.com/cms/s/2/66eea470-3e76-11e4-b7fc-00144feabdc0.html#axzz3YiFH0KE1> (accessed April 29, 2015).

Risky Business (2014). *Risky Business: The Economic Risks of Climate Change to the United States*, June. Available at: <http://riskybusiness.org/site/assets/uploads/2015/09/RiskyBusiness_Report_WEB_09_08_14.pdf> (accessed April 28, 2014).

UN (2014). "One Year On: An Open Letter from Former Members of the UN Secretary-General's High-Level Panel of Eminent Persons on the Post-2015 Agenda," *United Nations*. Available at: <http://www.un.org/sg/management/hlppost2015.shtml> (accessed September 22, 2014).

UNEP (2014). "World's Leading Institutional Investors Managing $24 Trillion Call for Carbon Pricing, Ambitious Global Climate Deal," *United Nations Environment Programme News Centre*, September 18. Available at: <http://www.unep.org/newscentre/Default.aspx?DocumentID=2796&ArticleID=10984> (accessed January 5, 2015).

UNICEF (2014). *Committing to Child Survival: A Promise Renewed*. United Nations Children's Fund. Available at: <https://www.unicef.at/fileadmin/media/Infos_und_Medien/Aktuelle_Studien_und_Berichte/A_Promise_Renewed_2014/APR_2014_13Sep_eversion.pdf> (accessed January 30, 2015).

Water.org (2015). *Billions Daily Affected by Water Crisis*. Available at: <http://water.org/water-crisis/one-billion-affected/> (accessed January 22, 2015).

Winston, A. S. (2014). *The Big Pivot: Radically Practical Strategies for a Hotter, Scarcer, and More Open World*. Boston, MA: Harvard Business Press.

World Bank (2014). "73 Countries and Over 1,000 Businesses Speak Out in Support of a Price on Carbon," *World Bank Group*, September 22. Available at: <http://www.worldbank.org/en/news/feature/2014/09/22/governments-businesses-support-carbon-pricing> (accessed January 13, 2015).

3

Business and Society

Reshaping Global Systems

Kathleen McLaughlin and Doug McMillon

INTRODUCTION

Over the past decades, there have been intense discussions about capitalism, centered on defining both what a business is and what its obligations are toward customers, shareholders, employees, suppliers, and society at large (e.g., Barton, 2011; Porter and Kramer, 2011). Recent discussions are inspiring a new narrative of capitalism, one that acknowledges care for a broad set of stakeholders—including care for the environmental and social systems that businesses require to function—as essential to sustained value creation (see Chapters 9 and 10, this volume).

This chapter is structured as follows. First, we set out an aspiration and rationale for how business can serve society: (a) creating value not only for shareholders or customers, but for stakeholders and society more broadly; and (b) contributing to changing and strengthening the environmental, social, and market systems upon which businesses and all of society rely. We then discuss how this can be done, drawing on the example of our own company to highlight broad principles, including: (i) prioritizing issues related to the company mission; (ii) drawing on the company's particular capabilities; (iii) aiming for a triple bottom line; (iv) reshaping the system for lasting societal improvement; (v) engaging others in transforming systems; and (vi) embedding triple-bottom-line values in the business. This is followed by a brief summary.

PREMISE: BUSINESS EXISTS TO SERVE SOCIETY

The obligations of business to society have been defined in different ways at different points in time and place (see Chapters 1, 9, and 21, this volume).

Some hold that businesses in a capitalist system should prioritize shareholders, and that the primary purpose of a corporation should be to maximize shareholder value, with a profits-first focus (Martin, 2010). Others, including many retailers such as Walmart founder Sam Walton, have prioritized the customer and associates (employees), with the view that the resulting loyalty and engagement will translate into success for other stakeholders (see also Chapter 4, this volume).

Over the past 20 years, the discussion on capitalism has broadened to consider the importance of multiple stakeholders, and to recognize that in the long run, the interests of stakeholders converge. The expansion of movements such as shared value, double bottom line, triple bottom line, etc. underscores the connection between business success and social progress. What's more, companies are beginning to recognize an opportunity and even an obligation to use their scale and expertise to reshape global systems in ways that address the complex problems facing society (see also Chapters 2 and 9, this volume).

Adding Value for Society

When it comes to serving society, a company's first task is to ensure that its core business is fundamentally value creating for a broad range of stakeholders, i.e., customers, employees, suppliers, communities, etc., while still delivering a return to shareholders. Value provided by the company could include, for example, offering compelling goods and services to customers and communities, providing employment and advancement opportunities, helping drive economic growth and develop supplier businesses, sourcing responsibly, contributing taxes back to the community, helping to mitigate externalities, and pursuing a range of initiatives that create value not only for the business and its immediate stakeholders, but society more broadly— such as disaster relief, energy efficiency, financial inclusion, and health and wellness programs.

In the future, the success of a company will depend not only on its business model, but also on its relationship with society and the environment. Many companies have begun to incorporate the triple-bottom-line framework to evaluate their performance along the interrelated dimensions of profits, people, and the planet (e.g. Slaper and Hall, 2011). Stakeholders increasingly expect companies to provide a net positive return for them and society more broadly, to maintain a social license to operate (Eccles et al., 2012). This means not only running a good business, but also attempting to mitigate possible negative externalities through responsible operating practices. It also means looking for opportunities to deliver shared value: social and environmental benefits through the very initiatives that benefit the business.

Of course, companies must still deliver strong shareholder returns. Research provides convincing evidence that initiatives aimed at sustainability do pay off for the business. For example, companies that manage their environmental and social performance have superior financial performance by attracting more loyal customers and keeping more committed employees (see Chapter 17, this volume). Yet financial short termism still drives day-to-day decision-making for much of the corporate world. When driven by profit maximization, creating value for stakeholders becomes a by-product or a means to an end. Launching social initiatives only tenuously linked to the core business, instead of seeking ways to drive shared value, limits impact on social, environmental, and economic outcomes. If, as recent studies have shown, communication of these activities among external or even internal stakeholders is ineffective, such corporate social responsibility initiatives will not deliver strategic benefits for the company (Du et al., 2010).

As societal expectations of responsible environmental and social practices continue to increase, the performance advantage of companies adopting them into their core business will increase too, as stated by Paul Druckman, CEO of the International Integrated Reporting Council (quoted by Adams, 2014: 415):

> The company of tomorrow will operate in a different capital market imperative where rewards are in terms of a responsible business which creates value for itself and for its stakeholders in the long term. These rewards feature in the share price of a company that has this responsible approach as the "catch 22" cycle has been turned on its head, with sustainable business and a sustainable planet/society being intrinsically connected.

Businesses that anticipate and manage economic, environmental, and social trends are more likely to create a competitive advantage and long-term stakeholder value (Dow Jones, 2014).

Going Beyond the Core to Change the System

A healthy, high-performing company can and must go further. The idea of "capitalism for the long term" (Barton, 2011; Barton and Wiseman, 2014) challenges companies to actively reshape the systems in which they operate. Those systems include, as examples, the complex of logistical and shipping services that move goods around the globe, the agricultural systems that produce raw commodities and finished product, and the array of energy suppliers that fuel worldwide operations. They suggest companies jettison a short-term orientation—revamping structures, roles, and incentives to focus the whole organization on the long term. Long-term capitalism takes a deeper view of the role of business in society, recognizing that, in the long run, the interests of stakeholders converge with the interests of the broader community (see also Chapter 10, this volume).

This view recognizes that the world has fundamentally changed. Rapid population growth, new technologies, and globalization have led to unprecedented complexity and severity of global social and environmental issues. Furthermore, increased interdependence means the actions of any one company may reverberate throughout the various systems in which it operates. This in turn can have indirect second- and third-order effects on an industry and value chain. Finally, we are also in a new era of transparency, in which everyone can see what everyone else is doing (see also Chapter 13, this volume). Customers and consumers are becoming more alert about the social responsibility of corporations, and while global brands tend to be the first to take action, the pressure for more sustainable operations and production is "trickling up" the value chain (Hack and Berg, 2014). These forces have increased the opportunities—and the responsibilities—of business.

What long-term capitalism suggests is that companies should take concerted action to ensure constant improvements to the systems upon which they rely. A large range of stakeholders must engage and collaborate on solutions; no one actor can resolve these challenges single-handedly. Governments and civil society are increasingly calling business to the table, as global corporations have a civic duty to contribute to sustaining the world's well-being in cooperation with others. Business must engage with regulators, both must engage with communities, non-government organizations (NGOs) must engage with all of these parties, and everybody must be prepared to collaborate—and, if necessary, compromise—in order to find workable solutions (Adams, 2014; see also Chapter 9, this volume).

This approach is fundamentally in the interests of society and businesses, which rely on the same environmental and social systems to thrive. If the discussion over the past 20 years has been on the need for business to serve stakeholders beyond just the customer and the shareholder, then in the next 20 years it will revolve around the need for companies to improve the networks and systems they depend on. Leading businesses need to actively use their scale and their particular assets to accelerate progress on tough social and environmental issues. As Adams (2014: 423) puts it,

> The company of the future, as part of an increasingly globalized and complex world, will be a connected and dynamic part of the fabric of society. Not only will the boundaries around its constituent departments/divisions/functions be increasingly blurred as companies recognize the need to take a multi-functional

and multi-disciplinary approach to solving complex and interconnected problems, but also the boundaries around the organization will be increasingly fuzzy as companies recognize that their success depends on their taking responsibility for the environment, employees, suppliers, customers, and other stakeholders.

To discuss how companies can develop and define their unique contribution to making society stronger and attempt to improve the systems of which they are an integral part, let us look at Walmart and the food system.

THE WALMART EXAMPLE

At Walmart, six principles help us prioritize and pursue efforts to create value for our business and society. To draw out insights that we hope will be useful to others, we share some examples from our work in the food system.

Prioritize Issues that Are Relevant to the Company Mission

Like most companies, we look for issues where our business interests and the interests of society converge. For example, as the world's largest grocer, we believe the sustainability of the world's food supply is one area in which we can make a significant contribution. The United Nations projects that the food supply must increase by roughly 70 percent to feed the estimated 9 billion people who will inhabit the planet by 2050 (FAO, 2012). We will need to meet that challenge in a way that is sustainable for the environment and equitable for consumers and farmers, who make up two-thirds of the population in some emerging markets. Our goal is to make the food system safer, more transparent, healthier, and more accessible—and to lower the "true cost" of food for the environment and the people along the supply chain.

Draw on the Company's Particular Capabilities

Companies can have greater impact on complex societal problems by drawing on their particular business capabilities. In our own efforts, we try to add value in ways that are different from—but will ideally enrich—what others do. For example, to help address hunger in the United States, we make use of assets such as unsold food, refrigerated trucks, and logistics know-how. Since 2009, we have donated more than 3 billion pounds of food to food banks across the United States, including an increasing amount of fresh food nearing the end of its shelf life. In addition to capacity-building grants provided through the

Walmart Foundation, Walmart and the Walmart Foundation donated more than 225 trucks, some refrigerated, as well as time and expertise in logistics to help build a sustainable cold chain in the charitable sector.

Aim for a Triple Bottom Line

We design our business initiatives as much as possible to promote benefits for both Walmart and society. We set ambitious targets, and track and report our progress annually. For example, eleven years ago we set an aspirational goal to create zero waste across our operations, and today, we are diverting over 80 percent of materials previously considered waste in our US operations. Our food waste reduction program not only reduces the amount of food Walmart sends to landfills—thus lowering operating cost—it also helps improve nutrition among those most in need, and in essence increases available food supply. Our food waste reduction initiatives include not only our food donations, but also attention to food ordering, forecasting, and handling through distribution centers and stores. As Winkworth-Smith et al. (2014) have shown more generally, there is ample opportunity in developed countries to reduce uncertainties in forecasting demand and therefore overproduction, oversupply, and the resulting waste of key commodities.

As another example, in food sourcing we pursue initiatives that lower the environmental and financial cost of food production. One of these initiatives— row crop optimization—has the potential to reduce greenhouse gas emissions by 9 million metric tons across 23 million acres of land by 2020, by making more effective use of fertilizer and other inputs. We measure progress by asking suppliers to report greenhouse gas emissions, water, yields, and other critical factors per ton of food produced by category. Similar initiatives across our food and non-food supply chain have helped reduce greenhouse gas emissions by a reported 35 million metric tons since 2010.

Taken together, these initiatives work toward triple-bottom-line results: for people, an increased number of healthy meals into the charitable meal system, and lower operating costs for farmers; for the environment, less waste, lower greenhouse gas emissions, less land use, and less nutrient runoff into water- ways; and for business, lower landfill costs, lower utility bills, and stable commodity costs.

Reshape the System for Lasting Improvement

We have suggested that the complex social and environmental challenges facing society require wholesale rewiring of supply chains and other systems to resolve. Businesses—by harnessing their expertise, leveraging their scale, and appropriately partnering or collaborating with like-minded organizations—can significantly help with this task (see also Chapters 2, 4, 5, and 6, this volume).

The food system, as noted above, faces significant issues in the coming decades. Farmers and food manufacturers must produce enough food to feed a growing and more prosperous world population, while preserving natural resources for future generations (Foley, 2015). Smallholder farmers can be an important part of the solution. Walmart has been working with suppliers, development agencies, NGOs, and others to help improve their yields, adopt more environmentally sustainable practices, enhance the value-added of their crops, connect them to markets in ways that sustain or enhance their liveli-hoods, and engage and empower women farmers in food production.

Through the "direct farm initiative" in Central America, for instance, USAID and its implementing agencies have provided agricultural expertise and training, as well as financial capital to smallholder farmers, to prepare them for selling into the organized retail sector. Walmart complements USAID's efforts by providing specifications based on consumer preferences, guidance on timing for different crops and varieties, and regular purchase orders for off-take of farm production. The collective actions of Walmart, USAID, and others reshape and enhance the social, environmental, and business sustainability of the smallholder part of the food system. Small-holders benefit from competitive prices, reduced risk, a more stable income, and the skills to improve yields and profitability; local customers gain a wider variety of fruits and vegetables at the time of year when they want to buy; and the agriculture sector gains productivity while becoming more viable and also environmentally sustainable. Such initiatives are helping to reshape the agri-cultural system in a way that is more sustainable for the planet and beneficial for the people who work in it.

Engage Partners in New and Creative Ways

Because of the complexity of global supply chains and the interdependence and complementary capabilities of stakeholders, achieving lasting solutions to social and environmental challenges requires collaboration among leaders of the systems we seek to strengthen. The difficult challenges facing the world today are well beyond the scope of any single player to address. Solutions will depend on cooperation among leading organizations in all sectors, which must work together on issues of common concern, even if they might be in competition elsewhere.

The United Nations, the World Wildlife Fund (WWF), and the Carbon Disclosure Project, among others, have set guidelines to inform and accelerate the policies most urgently needed to support a stable global economy. To achieve the magnitude of change called for in food production and distribution, in the next ten years leaders of the food system must take concerted, coordinated action to reduce water usage and private-sector greenhouse gas emissions and to increase yield (Caring for Climate, 2013).

In recent years, there has been an explosion in the number of multi-stakeholder collaborations in the food system, some of which have served to demonstrate the importance of such alliances and endeavors: the Consumer Goods Forum, which aligns retailers and manufacturers in order to achieve global food commitments, such as sourcing 100 percent sustainable palm oil and soy; the World Economic Forum with its Grow Africa and related initiatives; USAID's Global Development Lab, which works to harness the power of the private sector and others in addressing development challenges; and the Clinton Global Initiative, with its innovative approach to sparking collaborative commitments from corporations. This is just to name a few.

Embed Triple-Bottom-Line Values in the Business

The commitment to address social and environmental issues should be a "whole company" undertaking, woven into day-to-day business activities—not just a matter of corporate philanthropy. Many companies, including Walmart, develop social and environmental priorities as part of annual business-planning efforts. We have made bold, public commitments to focus our efforts and force innovation. One example is our aim to help train 1 million farmers and farmworkers by the end of 2016, and another is our recently achieved goal to require 100 percent of the palm oil in our private brands to be sourced sustainably by the end of 2015.

Leaders in our company set the social and environmental agenda for respective parts of the operation. We set targets and cascade those down the line into the individual performance evaluations and business reviews of our team members. Overall, the capital-planning process explicitly addresses our social and environmental agenda. We have found that it's the passion of our associates at all levels that makes the biggest difference.

CONCLUDING REMARKS

In the long term, a company's business interests and the interests of society converge. Every healthy, high-performing company has an obligation to use its strengths to help society, and each can do so in ways that enhance the viability of the business, too. Social and environmental commitments must be woven into a business's day-to-day activities, and made a key priority by leadership. From how products are grown and made, to how they are transported and sold, companies can pursue innovative new methods and processes that provide lasting benefits to their stakeholders and to the communities in which they operate.

Companies, communities, individuals, and governments: we are all interdependent, and we can only tackle large challenges through collaboration. Large-scale change does not happen overnight, but the stakes are high and the potential benefits are immense.

ACKNOWLEDGMENTS

This chapter is a revised and extended version of our contribution entitled "Business and Society in the Coming Decades" to the *Perspectives on the Long Term* volume, put together by the Focusing Capital on the Long Term initiative, founded by the Canada Pension Plan Investment Board and McKinsey & Company, which kindly waived their copyright.

REFERENCES

Adams, C. A. (2014). "Sustainability and the Company of the Future," in "Reinventing the Company in the Digital Age." *BBVA OpenMind*: 411–30. Available at: <https://www.bbvaopenmind.com/wp-content/uploads/2015/04/BBVA-OpenMind-book-Reinventing-the-Company-in-the-Digital-Age-business-innovation.pdf>.

Barton, D. (2011). "Capitalism for the Long Term," *Harvard Business Review*, 89(3): 84–91.

Barton, D. and Wiseman, M. (2014). "Focusing Capital on the Long Term," *Harvard Business Review*, 92(1/2): 44–51.

Caring for Climate (2013). *Guide for Responsible Corporate Engagement in Climate Policy*. A Caring for Climate report, by the UN Global Compact, the secretariat of the UN Framework Convention on Climate Change, the UN Environmental Programme, the World Resources Institute, CDP, WWF, Ceres, and the Climate Group, November. Available at: <http://www.unep.org/climatechange/Portals/5/documents/Guide-RespCorpEng.pdf> (accessed March 31, 2015).

Dow Jones (2014). "Corporate Sustainability," Dow Jones Sustainability Indices (in collaboration with RobecoSAM). Available at: <http://www.sustainability-indices.com/sustainability-assessment/corporate-sustainability.jsp> (accessed January 27, 2015).

Du, S., Bhattacharya, C. B., and Sen, S. (2010). "Maximizing Business Returns to Corporate Social Responsibility (CSR): The Role of CSR Communication," *International Journal of Management Reviews*, January 15. Available at: <http://

onlinelibrary.wiley.com/doi/10.1111/j.1468-2370.2009.00276.x/full> (accessed February 20, 2015).

Eccles, R., Ioannou, I., and Serafeim, G. (2012). "Is Sustainability Now the Key to Corporate Success?" *Guardian*, January 6. Available at: <http://www.theguardian.com/sustainable-business/sustainability-key-corporate-success> (accessed February 18, 2015).

FAO (2012). *How to Feed the World in 2050*. Food and Agriculture Organization of the United Nations. Available at: <http://www.fao.org/fileadmin/templates/wsfs/docs/expert_paper/How_to_Feed_the_World_in_2050.pdf> (accessed February 20, 2015).

Foley, J. (2015). "A Five-Step Plan to Feed the World," *National Geographic*. Available at: <http://www.nationalgeographic.com/foodfeatures/feeding-9-billion/> (accessed March 3, 2015).

Hack, S. and Berg, C. (2014). "The Potential of IT for Corporate Sustainability," *Sustainability*, 6(7), July. Available at: <http://www.mdpi.com/2071-1050/6/7/4163/htm> (accessed February 20, 2015).

Martin, R. (2010). "The Age of Customer Capitalism," *Harvard Business Review*, January. Available at: <https://hbr.org/2010/01/the-age-of-customer-capitalism/ar/1> (accessed January 14, 2015).

Porter, M. E. and Kramer, M. R. (2011). "Creating Shared Value," *Harvard Business Review*, 89(1/2): 62–77.

Slaper, T. F. and Hall, T. J. (2011). "The Triple Bottom Line: What Is It and How Does It Work?" *Indiana Business Review*, Spring. Available at: <http://www.ibrc.indiana.edu/ibr/2011/spring/pdfs/article2.pdf> (accessed February 18, 2015).

Winkworth-Smith, C. G., Morgan, W., and Foster, T. J. (2014). "The Impact of Reducing Food Loss in the Global Cold Chain," University of Nottingham. Preliminary Report, September. Available at: <http://naturalleader.com/wp-content/themes/natlead/images/UoN%20Food%20Loss%20Preliminary%20Report.pdf> (accessed March 3, 2015).

4

Family Firms and "Patient Capital"

Thinking in Decades, Not Quarters

Galen G. Weston

INTRODUCTION

Family firms have played an important role in economies of all varieties, past and present. Many of the largest and longest-lived businesses around the world were founded and continue to be managed by families. We can think here of India's Tata group founded in 1868 and still a global leader, Samsung and the chaebols of South Korea, or Walmart, where the Walton family remains the majority shareholder and the founder's son, Rob Walton, recently passed the baton to his own son-in-law. Statistics on this topic bear interesting insights. Family firms are the most prevalent corporate structure across the globe (La Porta et al., 1999). McKinsey & Company found that they represent one-third of the S&P 500 and 40 percent of the 250 largest companies in France and Germany (Casper et al., 2010). Here in Canada, publicly traded family firms outperformed the benchmark TSX index by 25 percent between 1998 and 2013 (Spizzirri and Fullbrook, 2013).

Across eras and geographies, family firms are prevalent, influential, and successful. In this respect, some suggest their stories are also understudied. Some of Canada's leading companies are owned and managed by generations of families: one of the nation's largest financial services firm, Power Financial Corporation; one of its best-known food companies, McCain Foods; and a world-class media company, Thomson Reuters; to name only a few. Our own company, George Weston Limited, offers one example, as an organization whose holdings include Loblaw Companies Limited and Weston Foods. It is more than 130 years old and among Canada's largest companies on various measures. As executive chairman, my father represents the third generation of family leadership. As deputy chairman, I am the fourth.

According to the Family Business Institute, research suggests our company had just a one-in-ten chance of making it to my father's generation with family ownership intact (Fernández-Aráoz et al., 2015). This reminds us that most family firms do not survive. Often, I am sure, because they are not more like widely held or non-family-owned companies, which, for the purpose of simplicity, I call "public companies" in this chapter—recognizing that our own company is in fact publicly traded. This chapter offers my observations on successful family firms, and the suggestion that those that do survive and thrive likely hold similar characteristics—grouped nicely under the notion of "patient capital." I would argue that these traits are common among highly successful companies, family owned or otherwise, but that they are greatly enabled by family control. This chapter also portrays some of the fault lines in family firms—complacency, internal strife, intergenerational succession—and how they can be navigated. The end result holds lessons for family firms, non-family firms, and policymakers interested in the traits that make some of history's most successful companies work.

FOUR TRAITS OF "PATIENT CAPITAL" IN FAMILY FIRMS

Among other measures, the success of companies can be charted on the basis of value creation over time. In the case of family firms that time is often defined as decades and generations, rather than the quarter-by-quarter growth of more meteoric success stories that may also create value, but which lack longevity. Similarly, for my family, retention of control is another important measure. If you support this view of longevity and control as complementary to value creation in measuring success, there is no question that family firms reap the benefits of "patient capital"—a concept which has been well defined by various scholars. Sirmon and Hitt (2003: 343), for example, call it "financial capital that is invested without the threat of liquidation for long periods." James (2006) highlights a "non-economic reason to exist" in the ability of family firms to overcome upheaval and outlast instability. And Landes (2006) charts an attitude he calls "stewardship" in the effort to prolong multi-generational inheritance in 13 family firms he studied.

These definitions ring true in my experience, family, and company. While it may sound unimaginative, when I think of family business I have a difficult time separating the two concepts—family and business. With George Weston Limited they are one. In personal terms, you are born into the business, you fulfill different levels of executive stewardship, and you have an enduring responsibility that makes retirement an unfamiliar concept. You own the past, present, and future all at once. In business terms, you have a time horizon that is unavailable or irrelevant to most executives.

The average CEO who owns less than 1 percent of their company's stock lasts five and a half years. In terms that short, patience is anathema. In contrast, executives who own at least 1 percent lead for an average tenure of 13.4 years—more than twice that of others (Coates and Kraakman, 2010). In terms that long, patience is a necessity and a precondition. Let's assume tenure equates to both a commitment by the leader and to the leader. Then imagine the multiplying sense of commitment as 1 percent ownership becomes 51 percent or more. That is the degree of real, implied, and emotional commitment family firm leaders feel. Continuity, patience, and the luxury of a long view are fundamental to the success of family firms. By creating value over decades and generations, rather than quarters and years, successful family firms outperform those seeking short-term shareholder returns. This manifests itself in four characteristics: (i) a predisposition for capital preservation and risk management over time; (ii) a reliance on company values and related people strategies; (iii) an ability to buck conventional thinking; and (iv) an appreciation for long-term social, demographic, and environmental trends. We can examine each of these in turn.

A Predisposition for Capital Preservation and Risk Management over Time

Successful family firms are predisposed to understanding the tradeoff between the short-term acceleration and the long-term accumulation of value. The short-term perspective of some public companies may favor immediately gratifying gambles. The legacy perspective of family firms often favors caution, capital preservation, and risk management. The result? The US Small Business Administration has found that family businesses have a 6.7 percent greater return on assets than non-family firms (Anderson and Reeb, 2003).

Returning to the notion of a family executive who owns the past, present, and future, it is easy to imagine how that might factor into business decision-making. In a negative sense, it could incite paralysis—a fear of risk, creativity, or innovative new sources of value. More positively, it favors businesses with stable returns that outpace the cost of capital, and which have the flexibility to course correct when needed. Interestingly, in the current era, there has been a trend toward free cash flow among public companies. For family firms seeking longevity, this is no trend—it is fundamental. Metaphorically, in baseball terms my family would rather hit a safe single than swing for the fence and risk striking out. Therefore, our balance sheet is pragmatic and efficient. We will not invest more than we can afford to lose. But that does not mean we will not invest. As an example, in 2014, Loblaw Companies Limited, where I am the second generation to serve as chairman, completed the largest acquisition in Canadian retail history, a $12-billion purchase of the nation's leading pharmacy, Shoppers Drug Mart. Painstakingly constructed, the deal took half a decade to complete and was widely greeted as a strategic investment, not a gamble.

In contrast, when we announced plans for the global expansion of Joe Fresh, an apparel brand originally conceived as our own private label, some believed we had made too big a bet. I disagree. The business generates domestic sales that cover development costs, the profit and loss impact of international expansion is negligible, and its capital demands do not materially stress the broader company. At the same time, global expansion offers purchasing power today and promise tomorrow. In sum, the cost, risk, and consequences of being wrong are low, the potential reward is high. This justification might not satisfy those who question why a Canadian grocer like Loblaw owns an international apparel venture. But—beyond the justification of low risk outlined above—this cynicism also misses a broader point.

Once just a grocer, our company now operates food, pharmacy, financial services, real estate, and, yes, global apparel businesses. Over time, we have invested to buffer against the risks in our heritage business, such as the inflationary pressure of processed grocery products. We have created a portfolio where no single piece demands undue financial resources and each contributes, often in a different, complementary, or hedged fashion. It is worth noting that, while not always the case, many of the world's largest and most enduring family firms are highly diversified. The Tata Group is perhaps the best example with operations that have spread to encompass airlines, engineering, electricity generation, financial services, steel, beverages, telecom, hospitality, retail, IT, consumer goods, automotive, construction, and chemicals (see also Chapter 6, this volume).

Loblaw's cautious acquisition, calculated global expansion, and strategic diversification are just three examples of the contribution that capital preservation and risk management make to patient capital. The lesson for any company is that a patient posture does not require inaction, it requires *strategic* action. And while every company will claim they are strategic, not all can claim they have the *patience* of a family firm. Those that do often have highly engaged, highly influential, high-impact leaders.

Where I propose patience is a virtue for family firms, it also has an edge. Long horizons are a great excuse for inaction or poor decisions. "Oh well, we are losing money now, but that's because we're investing for the next generation," offers considerable cover at the dinner table. One protection against this sort of wavering is a strong independent board and a public float. Our own public disclosure and directors instill both transparency and discipline. Not just around the boardroom table, but throughout an organization, the presence and input of strong people beyond the bloodline is essential in family firms—not unlike the value of differing opinions in any management team—and underpins the important role of company values.

A Reliance on Company Values and Related People Strategies

Hands-on family leadership has taken many forms over the last 134 years at George Weston Limited, and has been omnipresent at Loblaw since my father was first appointed CEO in 1972. Since then not a single year has passed without a family member at the helm. We subscribe to a concept that Brown Forman, maker of spirits such as Jack Daniels, calls "planned nepotism" (Bellow, 2003: 489). We do not seek professionals to run our family business; we use our business to develop professionals within our family. In our history, we have also struck the tricky balance between understanding the business is family run and understanding it cannot be run by family alone. In this respect, there may be an even greater need in companies like ours to foster people, culture, and talent—though most modern, successful companies also make this a priority.

Like any family values, ours have taken shape over generations. In truth, there is little difference between values passed from the rocking chair on a porch and those passed from the seat in a boardroom. I think of my grandfather's commitment to consistent fairness and the notion that if you always do right you might not win every time, but you will win over time. This was equally present during my father's time and now in my own. Like any company, our values flow from many influences. We come from a strong Methodist background and, while we are not motivated by religion, the culture of hard work as an end not a means is present to this day. This has traveled generations without eroding, to the point where I cannot envision a life where I was not working hard, despite having no financial necessity to do so. The same is true of my sister and cousins, just as it was with my father and his family. Through consistency over generations, our commitment to hard work has become a company value—though each of us has applied those convictions in a way that fits our personality and our times.

These beliefs have become so entrenched in our day to day that when asked, 81 percent of our colleagues articulate an understanding of these shared values and how they shape our business. We are not alone in this regard. Work by McKinsey & Company has shown that family firms generally outrank others on organizational-health metrics such as worker motivation and culture (Björnberg et al., 2015). Every business has values. Whether well managed or poorly managed, culture grows around them. In a family firm, this phenomenon is amplified. Our company's culture is in part a product of our family—the things I learned in the boardroom, but also through anecdotes, conversations overheard, and as my dad pushed me in a shopping cart through stores as a child. It is also a product of our colleagues—the smart, ambitious, thoughtful, caring people who have worked here over generations. Our ambition is to value their contributions, as much or more than we might those of our own family, since we entrust them with advancing the family business. Those who have the greatest impact and careers with us do not need to have a family relation—but they need to understand and attach themselves to our values.

If successful family firms are notably more committed to highly defined values, what positive characteristics are implied? For one, in a decreasingly loyal world, family firms value loyalty perhaps more than the rest. To that end, many explanations are available. Key among them are the personal financial and reputational stakes that family businesses bear. In an era of fleeting customer and employee loyalty, people around the world actually trust family businesses more than others (Hall and Astrachan, 2015). To risk trust or loyalty is to literally risk the fortunes of the family. In our company, trust and loyalty manifest in many ways. Sometimes in manners that seem inconsistent. For instance, although we have no tolerance for consistent underperformance, we are renowned for our loyalty to long-term colleagues who have made substantial contributions during their tenure. Again, this is founded on the belief that an organization demonstrates its values when it honors past contributions as a career comes to an end. Companies that take this approach make a symbol of individuals who have worked hard, done right, and advanced the vision and ambitions of the business.

A culture that reveres long-serving employees can also become a liability. This tendency must be balanced with a performance culture and a healthy inflow of new and innovative contributors. As people enter or mature into the business, career development is a catalyst for performance and trust. A long view of organizational health suggests successful family firms must get young people, move them into senior roles quickly, and appreciate their fresh perspectives, particularly if they align with established values. Very quickly, renewal and loyalty begin to grow in stride—from within. By relying most on your own people, you create a stronger culture. As the ranks of loyal contributors swell, their commitment to business performance and culture takes on a generational tone. The value of this sort of self-perpetuating cycle is one any company could create, but which is even more critical to the success of family firms. On many levels, people strategies such as culture, loyalty, trust, and a commitment to long-term development create the momentum that propels successful family firms. Over the long term, they allow them to hold a consistent tone, while still tuning themselves to the needs of the day.

An Ability to Buck Conventional Thinking

Like virtually anything in life, business principles shift in eras. With few exceptions, wise strategy one year can be poor the next. When you are on the clock—as most short-tenured CEOs are—conventional thinking is a sound approach. Move the business forward. Achieve short-term goals. Match prior performance. Deliver immediate gains. In contrast, family firms can make transformative decisions with a more balanced concern for their short-term impact, focusing instead on their long-term relevance. The diverging paths of our family's businesses in the UK and Canada provide a good illustration. In the 1970s the two businesses were near identical conglomerates, with operations touching the full life cycle of confectionary and baked goods, from ingredients and packaging, to grocery store shelves. My uncle took over the UK business, following a strategy that ultimately divested the retail business and increased investment in ingredients—oils, flours, sugars, and the like. My father took over the Canadian business, following a strategy that ultimately focused on baked goods and the retail channels through which they are sold. Half a century later, the UK and Canadian businesses still reflect those decisions. In a different sense, they reflect the personalities of my uncle and father. Both made bold decisions based on personal belief and preference, understanding they were in it for the long run, and supported by our family structure.

This ability—and willingness—to make such transformative, sometimes tough decisions matters even more when the competitive and market context is difficult. Take the start of my father's tenure, which marked a challenging period for the Canadian business. His ability to weather those challenges and bring the business back to profitability hinged on making unconventional decisions, the first of which was a dramatic rationalization of the Loblaw store network. My father told a journalist at the time, "As a 200-store chain, we didn't look very good. As a 100-store chain, we looked very good indeed" (Dow, 1973). He would remake the company many times over many decades. Family control always afforded him the time for creative destruction and renaissance. It also allowed him to hand control to me during a time of turmoil and inevitable change. Similarly, in my tenure, we repositioned Loblaw once early on and then a second time more recently. I have been able to make sweeping changes to our organization, invest in our customer while taking a considerable write-down, execute a $12-billion acquisition, and much more, all in slightly longer than the average tenure of most CEOs. Few public company leaders could have done this, in part because few public company boards would have supported it.

In a more subtle sense, successful family ownership as I have defined it allows—or perhaps demands—significant attention to strategic planning. We scrutinize our business model every five years and truth-test our strategy annually to either confirm it or initiate change. Then, we can set and pursue our direction with focus and conviction. One family firm, Carlson, has done just that over the last 78 years. First starting as a supermarket trading stamp company in 1938 and subsequently shifting its focus into hospitality through the acquisition of its first Radisson hotel in 1962. Each decade that followed saw a strategic shift, first into food service through TGI Fridays in 1975, then into business travel services through a combination with Accor Travel Group in 1994. Most recently, Carlson's 2014 decision to sell its stake in TGI Fridays and acquire full ownership of Carlson Wagonlit Travel underlines that such strategic discipline is as much about deciding which businesses to exit, as it is which to build.

Turning back to Loblaw, we can consider our acquisition of Shoppers Drug Mart for an illustration of the different options available to the family firm and the public company. Shoppers Drug Mart is a leading pharmacy retailer with a track record of growth. When that trajectory ran its course, the company had years of debate on whether to acquire or be acquired. With few tried-and-true options at their disposal, momentum took over and the status quo prevailed. At the same time, our family firm was actively seeking an acquisition that would establish a growth platform for the next decade. Several regional grocers fit the traditional profile of an attractive target, but Shoppers Drug Mart stood out as a uniquely strategic asset in a less familiar, but complementary space. We did the requisite due diligence to satisfy our board and subsequently pursued the unprecedented path of a national grocer buying a national pharmacy.

Beyond the numbers, much of our conviction about Shoppers Drug Mart was and remains its fit with our company purpose—"Live Life Well"—and our family's belief that our combined companies can make Canadian lives better through nutrition and wellness. In short, the numbers and business rationale were sound, but patient capital allowed a $12-billion acquisition that was largely based on the family's values and vision for the future.

An Appreciation of Long-Term Social, Demographic, and Environmental Trends

Combining many of the themes above—a generational horizon for business, values, and people—successful family firms are particularly attuned to long-term trends. In some respects, this might suggest a humanist or environmentalist take on patient capital, but from a capitalist perspective this trend watching ensures that a business either profits from or perseveres through the developments that make the world a better or worse place. I should acknowledge, practically, that because we believe our family and company reputations move in lockstep, we also believe our business activities should land on the right side whenever catalyzing issues are on the horizon.

Identifying long-term trends can be a challenge for any company. In family firms it often becomes a personal pursuit. We pay a great deal of attention to news, books, opinion, and the expertise of those around us, and we match it against our own ideals and interests. Once opinions are established internally, we look outside to test if they are as accurate and as important as we suspect. Outside expertise is a great source of counsel and clarity and we have sought it enthusiastically as various issues have crossed the path of our business. As a grocer, we have seen growing concern around nutrition, food security, animal welfare, seafood sustainability, bee health, and more. In each case we have enlisted the help of Canadian and international academic experts.

Decades ago my father sought such outside expertise to help establish Canada's first eco-brand—our PC G.R.E.E.N. label. This was an uncertain choice that proved prescient over time. We have tried to replicate that process and pattern again and again. While many of our ventures have proven well intentioned, well informed, and well received by the public, there is no guarantee.

Years ago I developed an opinion about the need for action on two fronts: seafood sustainability and nutritional awareness.

This first came to light because, as I looked at the data, I could not shake the staggering fact that three-quarters of the world's fisheries—the leading source of protein for 2 billion people globally—are in some state of depletion or exploitation (FAO, 2010). I was surprised this was not yet bigger news and imagined the mayhem that would ensue in Canada if 75 percent of productive farmland were destroyed.

When we applied the lens of our family business, we came to quick conclusions. If we run out of fish, stocking our fish counters will be challenged. If we run into regulatory intervention, the freedom of our business will be challenged. And, if our customers react to these circumstances, our sales will be challenged. So, we got ahead of the issue, certain it would escalate quickly. We approached Dr Jeffrey Hutchings, professor of marine science at Dalhousie University on the coast of the Atlantic Ocean. He helped us understand the data, shaped our perspective, and set us on a pragmatic course—identifying species we should or should not have on our shelves, and helping us establish our definition of sustainable seafood. Further, he helped us partner with the World Wildlife Fund and Marine Stewardship Council in their global efforts on sustainable seafood. With programs in place and progress underway, we sat back and waited for our efforts to catch the imagination and attention of consumers. We are still waiting. To this day, it appears sustainable seafood does not resonate with them.

In contrast, the position we have taken on nutrition has struck a much stronger chord with our customers. As with the previous example, our interest turned to intent by seeking out the counsel of experts in the field. In this case, they were professional dietitians and "Guiding Stars." Although obvious upon reflection, bringing dietitians into our stores alongside the food they were recommending was a leap of faith. Since then, not only has it opened the door to helping those with specific dietary requirements, it has engaged all of our customers in a dialogue about the link between health and the food we eat. Our commitment to Guiding Stars followed a similar pattern. By providing customers with a simple nutritional rating for almost all the products they buy, at the point at which they buy them, we bet on the opportunity to break down barriers around nutritional information. Since its launch in 2012, the strong response to that program has encouraged us to invest in further innovation, linking it to our digital loyalty platform. The result is that 6 million Canadian households now have access to real-time, personalized nutritional scorecards online. Together, dietitians and Guiding Stars have engaged consumers in a conversation about wellness that is core to our values as a company, and which we believe will be a source of sustained competitive advantage.

As the pace of change accelerates, one risk for a family firm is the tendency to be overzealous or indiscriminate in demonstrating its values. Companies that jump into action each time an issue is raised dilute their energies and attention, and may obscure meaningful commitments with those that carry less weight and consequence. Volume is no substitute for substance. Priorities should be aligned to a business's values and future. Take Mars, the confectionery giant, which relies heavily on cocoa from more than 5 million small farmers across West Africa, Southeast Asia, and the Americas. These farmers continually struggle with unproductive, aging cocoa trees they cannot afford to replace. The result is declining yields. Through its Vision for Change program, Mars has committed to training 150,000 farmers in the Côte d'Ivoire on planting materials, fertilizers, and good agricultural practices. Within five years, the plan will triple farmer yields and, by extension, their incomes and sustainability.

Through each of these examples, we can see that rallying around substantial, relevant trends is the foundation for value creation over the long term. This focus is not unique to family firms, but is often at odds with the short-term objectives that burden public company executives who might only be inclined to act when facing imminent consequences.

A NOTE OF CAUTION: AVOIDING COMMON PITFALLS

For family firms, patient capital, and the four related characteristics I have presented here are no panacea. They do not replace solid and consistent business management. Nor do they automatically bridge the many challenges common to family firms. Early in this chapter, I listed three out of dozens of potential risks: complacency, internal strife, and intergenerational succession. In the wrong combination or degree, otherwise positive traits—like a long view of investments and trends, or a preoccupation with values and legacy—can actually create complacency and inaction. Our family has buffered against that risk with a commitment to articulating clear five-year strategies, stress-tested annually. Similarly, we have held ourselves to account with a public float and independent board. And, less tangibly but equally importantly, we have fostered the family tradition of hard work, hired leaders who enhance our values, and made it a defining feature of our company for over a century.

The sister risks of internal strife and intergenerational succession are near inevitable in any family firm. Ours is no exception. However, at times when I have seen these risks managed well, one or more of the following conditions have contributed to the solution:

(i) *Empowered leaders*—consider the family's allowance of my father and uncle to make coinciding but notably different choices, or our board's recent support for the unprecedented acquisition of Shoppers Drug Mart.

(ii) *Consistent family control*—consider our choice to use the business to professionalize our family as leaders, or the assumption that family members will be life-long contributors, never becoming mere observers (or critics) and remaining intimately involved.

(iii) *The influence of non-family advisors and leaders*—consider those who have helped the company advance, always with an appreciation for the risk and benefit of family influence.

CONCLUSION: PATIENT CAPITAL
BEYOND FAMILY FIRMS

This chapter is intended to promote patient capital—specifically as illustrated by the four common traits in successful family businesses—as a worthy consideration for family firms, non-family firms, and policymakers alike. For non-family firms, I earlier offered the perhaps unhelpful view that the four positive traits of patient capital might rest beyond their grasp. Let me challenge my own assertion and say that the four traits promoted in this chapter are available to any business.

A long view of capital and risk, a reliance on values, bucking conventional thinking, and attention to trends are not difficult in and of themselves. What is difficult is the commitment required to make them truly central to an organization's strategy and operations. Finding a public company leader willing to risk such a commitment—while facing the short tenure and expectation of immediacy most CEOs face—may be even more difficult. For any public company leadership looking to mimic family firm management, simply combining and applying the three definitions of patient capital I cited at the outset might be a start. They were "financial capital that is invested without the threat of liquidation for long periods," a "non-economic reason to exist," and, simply "stewardship." In a family firm, these conditions may exist almost in spite of the leader, in a public company they cannot exist without a uniquely strong one.

Finally, for policymakers and economy builders, the case is clear. In a world of industry consolidation and globalization, the long-term orientation and thoughtful risk management of successful family firms will become table stakes for all companies. At the same time, their ability to buck conventional thinking will distinguish those that can keep pace with the acceleration of change that, although perhaps born in Silicon Valley, is now commonplace across all industry landscapes. As change becomes constant, so too will the importance of steadfast values and culture that can guide an organization towards growth that bridges from quarters to years, and from years to decades. This combination of characteristics lies at the core of successful family firms' stubborn outperformance of stock markets across the globe, and their ability to focus on the long-term social, demographic, and environmental trends that address some of the world's biggest challenges. For those who agree with this point of view, two logical conclusions emerge: (i) the need to enable family firms to thrive; and, (ii) the opportunity to encourage all firms—family managed or otherwise—to adopt the traits I have outlined in this chapter as their own.

ACKNOWLEDGMENTS

I would like to express my appreciation for the assistance of Matthias Kipping, Gordon Currie, Kevin Groh, and Andrew Graham, all of whose input helped shape this chapter.

REFERENCES

Anderson, R. C. and Reeb, D. M. (2003). "Founding-Family Ownership and Firm Performance: Evidence from the S&P 500," *Journal of Finance*, 58(3): 1301–28.
Bellow, A. (2003). *In Praise of Nepotism: A Natural History*. New York: Doubleday.
Björnberg, Å., Elstrodt, H., and Pandit, V. (2015). "Joining the Family Business: An Emerging Opportunity for Investors," *McKinsey on Investing*, 2, Summer. Available

at: <http://www.mckinsey.com/insights/financial_services/joining_the_family_busi ness_an_emerging_opportunity_for_investors>.

Casper, C., Dias, A. K., and Elstrodt, H.-P. (2010). "The Five Attributes of Enduring Family Business," *McKinsey Quarterly*, January. Available at: <http://www.mckinsey. com/insights/organization/the_five_attributes_of_enduring_family_businesses>.

Coates, J. C. and Kraakman, R. (2010). "CEO Tenure, Performance and Turnover in S&P 500 Companies," ECGI, Finance Working Paper No. 191/2007; Harvard Law and Economics Discussion Paper No. 595. Available at: <http://ssrn.com/abstract= 925532>.

Dow, A. (1973). "The Summit Meeting that Changed the Course for Giant Loblaw," *Toronto Star*, January 25.

FAO (2010). *The State of World Fisheries and Aquaculture*. Rome: Food and Agriculture Organization of the United Nations.

Fernández-Aráoz, C., Iqbal, S., and Ritter, J. (2015). "Leadership Lessons from Great Family Businesses," *Harvard Business Review*, 93(4): 82–8.

Hall, C. and Astrachan, J. (2015). "Study: Customers Really Do Trust Family Businesses More," *Harvard Business Review*, April 27. Available at: <https://hbr.org/ 2015/04/study-customers-really-do-trust-family-businesses-more>.

James, H. (2006). *Family Capitalism: Wendels, Haniels, Falcks, and the Continental European Model*. Cambridge, MA: Belknap Press of Harvard University Press.

La Porta, R., Lopez-de-Silanes, F., and Shleifer, A. (1999). "Corporate Ownership around the World," *Journal of Finance*, 54(2): 471–517.

Landes, D. (2006). *Dynasties: Fortunes and Misfortunes of the World's Great Family Businesses*. New York: Viking.

Sirmon, D. G. and Hitt, M. A. (2003). "Managing Resources: Linking Unique Resources, Management, and Wealth Creation in Family Firms," *Entrepreneurship Theory and Practice*, 27(4): 339–58.

Spizzirri, A. and Fullbrook, M. (2013). "The Impact of Family Control on the Share Price Performance of Large Canadian Publicly Listed Firms (1998–2013)," University of Toronto, Rotman School of Management, Clarkson Centre for Board Effectiveness. Available at: <http://www.rotman.utoronto.ca/-/media/Files/Programs-and-Areas/ CCBE/CCBE%20Family%20Firm%20Performance%20Study%20June%202013.pdf>.

5

Cooperatives

Stakeholder-Oriented by Design, Long-Term Focused by Necessity

Monique Leroux

INTRODUCTION

In the months that followed the economic meltdown of 2008, governments around the world began bailing out private sector financial institutions with trillions of dollars in funding. But there was one type of financial institution that largely withstood the tremors that rocked the entire industry: the *cooperative*. A study conducted in 2009 for the International Labour Organization found that financial cooperatives required little or no government support and had strong balance sheets following the crisis. According to the report, because the "customer-owned cooperative banking system ... is more risk-averse and less driven by the need to make profits for investors and bonuses for managers, it was able to avoid the kind of financial losses experienced by many private, investor-owned banks" (Birchall and Ketilson, 2009: 3). The report went on to note that (2009: 9):

> it is interesting to see just how strongly cooperative banks, savings and credit cooperatives and credit unions are performing during the current banking crisis, and how little help they have needed from governments, in contrast to their investor-owned competitors who have had to be bailed out with staggeringly large amounts of public funding.

Moreover, the World Council of Credit Unions reported that there was not a single instance of a credit union anywhere in the world that received government recapitalization as a result of the financial crisis (Crear, 2009). Of note, however, is the fact that a number of credit unions and financial cooperatives which had demutualized and become publicly traded banks just a decade earlier collapsed during the crisis. The most well known of these demutualized financial institutions was Northern Rock in the UK, originally founded as a "building society" or financial cooperative in 1850. The failed bank was subsequently nationalized. Some have attributed Northern Rock's demise to "the adoption of unsustainable lending practices" and the use of financial instruments that it could never have obtained—or even desired—when it was previously a financial cooperative (Klimecki and Wilmot, 2009).

But not only did cooperatives escape much of the financial carnage that tore through the industry; many of them continued to grow in terms of revenues and employment in the years that followed. In the United Kingdom, for example, the overall economy shrunk by nearly 2 percent from 2008 to 2012, whereas the cooperative economy grew by almost 20 percent (Co-operatives UK, 2013). And, as an additional example, my own organization Desjardins Group, the fifth largest financial cooperative in the world and the sixth largest bank in Canada, saw revenues grow in each of the years following the economic crisis (see also Kanter and Malone, 2013). So, what is it about cooperatives that enable them to often perform better during economic downturns than private and publicly traded companies? What makes cooperatives so resilient?

This chapter argues that what makes cooperatives so resilient in crises and so sustainable overall can be found in the very DNA of the cooperative enterprise: first and foremost, the democratic governance by its member-owners, which ensures a balanced and broadly based stakeholder focus and in turn leads to a long-term approach to conducting business, since members are not interested in maximizing short-term profitability on a quarterly basis. The remainder of the chapter first provides an overview of the history and characteristics of cooperatives, and then explore the cooperative model and its advantages in some more detail, highlighting its benefits for both stakeholders and society at large, before examining some of the drawbacks or limitations of this type of enterprise, particularly from the viewpoint of managers. The chapter concludes by discussing how cooperatives might—at least partially—serve as a role model of sorts for 21st-century businesses looking to create long-term, sustainable value.

COOPERATIVES: HISTORY AND CHARACTERISTICS

According to the International Co-operative Alliance (ICA), a non-profit association representing more than 280 member organizations in over 90 countries, a cooperative is "[a]n autonomous association of persons united voluntarily to meet their common economic, social, and cultural needs and aspirations through a jointly-owned and democratically-controlled enterprise" (ICA, 2015a: definition). Two of the key defining features of all cooperatives are shared ownership and democratic control. Unlike publicly traded companies, which are shareholder owned, cooperatives are owned by their members, which can be customers or employees, and these members have a democratic say in how the organization is managed and a vote in determining the organization's key strategic decisions.

The ICA further characterizes the cooperative model as "a commercially efficient and effective way of doing business that accounts for a wider range of human need, time horizons and values in decision-making" (ICA, 2015b). Alban D'Amours, Desjardins Group chair, president, and CEO from 2000 to 2008, expands upon this definition by highlighting another essential attribute that differentiates cooperatives from most other businesses—namely that they represent "an ownership model whose business philosophy is service, not profit" (cited by Leroux, 2014). This underlying commitment to service is why cooperatives are often described as people-based enterprises rather than profit-based enterprises.

Cooperatives come in all shapes and sizes. As businesses that are owned by the members they serve, they exist in sectors ranging from agriculture and banking to retail and insurance, and vary in size from small daycare centers to multinational financial organizations. Cooperative enterprises in the world employ 250 million people and have 1 billion members. With US$2.2 trillion in revenue, the top 300 cooperatives are equal to the world's seventh largest economy (World Co-Operative Monitor, 2014). Some of the world's largest and most successful cooperatives include State Farm Group, an insurance and financial services provider and Fortune 500 company; Kaiser Permanente, a California-based health-care consortium; and the Co-operative Group, a UK-based retail conglomerate with businesses ranging from grocery stores and travel agencies to electrical products.

Many of the world's largest cooperatives are in the insurance or financial services sector, including Desjardins Group, with more than 7 million members and clients and over $250 billion in assets, and Rabobank Group, the largest financial cooperative in the Netherlands. Both Desjardins and Rabobank were founded on some of the same guiding principles first established by Friedrich Wilhelm Raiffeisen, as were Groupe Crédit Mutuel and Groupe Crédit Agricole in France, two of the largest cooperatives in the world. Considered by many as the father of the modern-day cooperative movement, Raiffeisen created the first credit union in 1862 and inspired the establishment of cooperative banks and credit unions around the world (ICA, 2015c).

The core values at the heart of Raiffeisen's philosophy included self-help, self-governance, and sustainability, with a common goal of "permanent economic improvement." Interestingly, Raiffeisen's desire to attain economic improvement came with the following caveat: "Fast results do not always serve this goal." As a symbol for his new venture, Raiffeisen chose "The Gable Cross"—two horses' heads crossed in the shape of the letter "X." This symbol was frequently found during that time on people's homes as a talisman to ward off danger. For Raiffeisen, it became a symbol of how the cooperative could protect its members' assets from economic volatility (RZB, 2015). Raiffeisen's views heavily influenced Alphonse Desjardins, who established the first credit union in Canada, in Lévis, Quebec in 1900, originally called *caisses populaires* and at the origin of today's Desjardins Group. He also created the first credit union in the United States, thereby earning him widespread recognition as the father of the North American credit union movement (Bérubé and Lamarre, 2012: 64).

Equally influential in the early history of the cooperative movement was the groundbreaking work of the Rochdale Society of Equitable Pioneers, who established a consumer cooperative in England in 1844. The most enduring legacy of the so-called Rochdale Pioneers was the creation of a set of principles that still stand to this day as the defining characteristics of cooperatives. These principles include democratic member control and economic participation by all member-owners (ICA, 2015d).

Cooperatives have traditionally been clustered primarily in sectors that produce products and provide services that people need or use in their day-to-day lives: the food they eat, the lumber to build their homes, the banking and insurance transactions that help them pay bills, protect their property, and grow their personal savings. As a result, cooperatives tend to be rooted in the "real economy," the economy that is most tangible and closest to people. One could say cooperatives are, at their core, a grassroots way of doing business.

Cooperatives straddle the public and private sectors, possessing attributes of both non-profit and for-profit organizations. They operate within the market economy, selling the same products and services as for-profit companies, and compete directly with those same for-profit companies. Although they are not primarily profit driven, they nevertheless focus on innovation, efficiency, productivity, and customer service to the same extent as businesses operating in the private sector. And despite the widespread perception that cooperatives are a low-growth type of enterprise due to their inherent aversion to risk, some studies have shown that in fact their rates of growth are similar to publicly traded companies (Bérubé et al., 2012). At the same time, cooperatives also fulfill some of the same social needs as NGOs or public sector companies. If cooperatives had to fall within a particular part or segment of the economy, it would probably be the domain of the so-called "for-benefit" or "Fourth Sector" organizations—enterprises that simultaneously pursue both social and economic objectives on behalf of their stakeholders (Fourth Sector Network, 2008).

Many of the largest and most successful cooperatives have stood the test of time, growing and prospering over numerous decades. With 1 billion members worldwide, they are a massive but often overlooked part of the global economy. Given their longevity and track record in job creation, it is surprising that the cooperative model has not been more widely adopted. Part of the reason for this is that they have flown under the radar for many years, operating quietly yet very effectively on the fringes of the mainstream business world. Since cooperatives are not publicly traded, they are not as closely followed and written about by the financial media, are largely ignored by business academia, and are rarely studied in business schools.

In an effort to raise the profile of cooperatives, the United Nations designated the year 2012 as the International Year of Cooperatives. That same year, Desjardins cohosted an International Summit of Cooperatives together with St Mary's University and the ICA. Close to 3,000 participants from more than 90 countries attended the event, which featured panel discussions from cooperative leaders and the latest research on the cooperative sector. The International Summit gave cooperatives from around the world the chance to learn best practices from one another, to explore strategic alliances, and to showcase the enormous value they provide in terms of wealth creation, economic ownership, and employment. Following the summit, the ICA published a blueprint designed to make cooperatives the fastest-growing business model in the world by 2020 and a global leader in economic, social, and environmental sustainability (ICA, 2013).

THE COOPERATIVE MODEL AND ITS ADVANTAGES

Democratic Governance

At its core, the cooperative model is democratic by nature. Cooperatives arose from the need of individuals to work together by jointly owning and managing the enterprise, and they have largely remained true to their democratic roots. One of the main guiding principles of a cooperative, as outlined by the ICA, is the principle of democratic member control (ICA, 2015a: principles):

> Co-operatives are democratic organisations controlled by their members, who actively participate in setting their policies and making decisions. Men and women serving as elected representatives are accountable to the membership. In primary co-operatives members have equal voting rights (one member, one vote) and co-operatives at other levels are also organised in a democratic manner.

How cooperative democracy actually works can be illustrated by the example of the Desjardins Group, where all members participate in decision-making in accordance with a "one member one vote" policy. The group has millions of members linked to more than 300 *caisses* or credit unions located in the provinces of Quebec and Ontario, with more than 20 subsidiaries. At each *caisse* there is a board of directors comprised of between 15 to 25 directors in total who are elected as officers of the *caisse* and who represent the

members. In total, Desjardins has approximately 5,000 elected officers, representing hundreds of different communities, and these officers elect other
members to represent them at the regional level. The president of each region
sits on the overall board of directors of the group. The board is completely
independent and reflects a wide range of communities and stakeholder interests. The chair of the board, president, and CEO is elected by the members at
the regional level.

Because of this democratic approach to managing the enterprise, cooperatives are less likely to be led by the vision or interests of *one* executive or a
narrow stakeholder group. Since cooperatives are democratically controlled by
their member-owners, decision-making instead tends to be broad-based,
representing the diversity of stakeholders within the enterprise and balancing
the needs of all stakeholders. Put differently, a broad stakeholder orientation
and a more balanced business approach of a cooperative are built right into the
governance of the organization.

Serving Stakeholders

Outlining his vision for a "Capitalism for the Long Term," the global
managing director of McKinsey & Company, Dominic Barton, urged publicly
traded companies to shift from managing primarily for shareholders to managing for all stakeholders, arguing that this strategy is the best way to create
value. According to Barton (2011), "[e]xecutives must infuse their organizations
with the perspective that serving the interests of all major stakeholders—
employees, suppliers, customers, creditors, communities, the environment—is
not at odds with the goal of maximizing corporate value; on the contrary, it is
essential to achieving that goal" (see also Chapters 10 and 17, this volume).

Stakeholders, from member-owners to employees and suppliers, are an intrin-
sic part of the cooperative business model. In many cases, the various stakeholders are often one and the same person—member, owner, employee, and
resident of the community. As a result, there is a natural alignment of interests
between the different stakeholder groups. This stakeholder approach to doing
business has been one of the chief features of cooperatives since their formation.
In fact, one could argue that serving the needs of stakeholders is the raison d'être
of a cooperative. They are, by their very structure and design, stakeholder-
oriented. One of the main reasons for this is that they are based on associations
of people, rather than capital. Simply stated, they put the needs of their people,
i.e., their members, before profits, and regard capital as a tool to meet those needs.

Consider one of the key publicly stated values of Desjardins Group: "Money
at the service of human development: At Desjardins, we think money constitutes a lever for the autonomy and development of people and communities.
Our members' and clients' interests are what drive our actions." Similar

expressions regarding the values, mission, and mandate of the organization exist at most cooperatives around the world. Land O'Lakes, Inc., a leading US food producer and one of the largest producer cooperatives in America, states on its website: "We believe the customer is fundamental to our success—working together to meet their needs is the basis for all that we do." Northwestern Mutual Group, a US financial services mutual with more than $25 billion in revenues, describes its values this way: "At Northwestern Mutual, it's our mission to do what's right, put people first, provide financial strength and take a long-term view."

Studies have shown that one area where cooperatives appear to outperform their private sector competition is growth in market share, and one major reason for this may be their closeness to their members/customers and the deeper, more nuanced understanding they have of their customers' needs as a result of this proximity (Bérubé et al., 2012). By placing the interests of their member-customers ahead of short-term profits, cooperatives are better able to secure long-term customer loyalty and attract new members. In addition, because of their insight and knowledge about their customers' needs, cooperatives are well positioned to deliver a richer, more satisfying customer experience (Bérubé et al., 2012).

One of the key stakeholder groups for any cooperative is the community in which it operates. Cooperatives of all stripes tend to be closely tied to the community (see also Chapter 6, this volume). Part of the reason for this is that historically cooperatives were enterprises that were formed to address some sort of specific social or economic necessity within a specific community. Many of them were founded during times of crisis and were created to fill a gap in the local economy that could not be adequately filled by the public, private, and non-profit sectors. Cooperatives are most effective—and perhaps most necessary—during "periods of unmet needs" (Bérubé and Lamarre, 2012: 61). Indeed, some of the biggest areas of growth for cooperatives going forward will be in areas such as health care, retirement housing, and education—areas where the public sector is increasingly scaling back its involvement and funding. These areas represent the "holes in the economy" that cooperatives typically fill (Bérubé and Lamarre, 2012: 63).

Having a strong community orientation and treating the community as a valued stakeholder can also fundamentally alter the way an organization conducts business. For example, a financial cooperative is less likely to approve or underwrite a development project that could potentially damage the natural environment in the community. And when it comes to financing a business, cooperatives are less likely to cut the financial lifeline for a money-losing business than a commercial bank. On the contrary, they will be more inclined to try to help turn around the failing business, due in part to the fact that the member-owners of the cooperative all have a financial stake in the success of the business.

Taking the Longer View

In his aforementioned article Barton (2011) urged business leaders to "break free from the tyranny" of short-term decision-making and to transition from "quarterly capitalism" to a longer-term capitalism—one characterized by investing, planning, and building for the next quarter century rather than the next fiscal quarter. Cooperatives, by their very structure and make-up, have always been free from the "tyranny of short-termism" and "mania over quarterly earnings" described by Barton. Since cooperatives are sheltered from the unrelenting pressure that public companies face to maximize profits and drive up share price, they can more easily adopt a longer-term perspective and deploy longer-term strategies. This inherent long-term orientation is actually one of the salient competitive advantages enjoyed by cooperatives. Unlike publicly held corporations, which are traded on the stock market, cooperatives are not owned or controlled by shareholders. This gives cooperatives breathing room and a longer-term horizon for making decisions—a luxury not possible for most publicly traded companies fixated on day-to-day stock price fluctuations, analyst ratings, and quarterly earnings as well as the constant threat of a hostile takeover.

A number of leading management experts increasingly argue that adopting a long-term perspective is a defining feature of *any* successful, long-lasting company. In the article "How Great Companies Think Differently," Harvard business professor Rosabeth Moss Kanter asserts that great companies—those that endure for generations and consistently perform at a high level—embrace a long-term focus (Kanter, 2011). Because cooperatives are not shackled to the short-term demands of stock performance or quarterly results, they have more time to focus on other business imperatives from seeking new and innovative ways to create value for their customers and clients to implementing long-term growth strategies. And while public companies strive to maximize return on equity in the short term, cooperatives seek instead to minimize volatility by managing capital on a long-term basis. This fundamental difference in operating philosophy means that cooperatives like Desjardins typically value long-term financial stability over short-term higher profits. Part of the reason for this goes beyond philosophy and is rooted in financial pragmatism. For example, cooperatives strive for greater stability in managing their capital because they cannot access capital as easily as public companies, which are able to issue common stock.

The innate financial conservatism of cooperatives manifests itself in other ways. They favor a management philosophy that rejects growth at any cost in favor of more balanced, sustainable growth. They also do not regard profit as an end in itself, but rather as a tool to support growth, innovation, or enhanced customer service. The challenge for cooperatives, however, is to avoid using this built-in long-term orientation as an excuse for not taking short-term action or hard decisions that are necessary for the organization.

What is an advantage could turn into a disadvantage—an inclination to put off short-term required actions that jeopardize the organization's long-term viability. And while longevity is not by itself evidence that cooperatives are committed to a longer-term view in business, it is striking to note how many of the world's leading cooperatives have histories that date back nearly a century or more.

Examples of this include Desjardins Group in Canada, the Rabobank Group in the Netherlands, and US financial cooperatives like Farmers Insurance Group, Northwestern Mutual Group, and Nationwide Mutual Insurance Company. Longevity among cooperatives is commonplace in other sectors as well, and includes companies such as Ace Hardware Corp., a leading US retail hardware cooperative founded in 1921 with more than 4,000 stores and $3 billion in annual sales; Ocean Spray, an agricultural cooperative founded in 1930 whose beverage products are sold worldwide; and Danish Crown, a European livestock cooperative founded in 1887 that is today the world's largest exporter of pork. But despite an impressive track record of sustainability and resiliency across industries and across countries, cooperatives—no matter how large or successful or well established—still remain vulnerable to the same global competition and macro-economic trends that affect all businesses, as the multi-industry Spanish worker cooperative Mondragón Corporation experienced in 2013 when one of its original business units, the large appliance manufacturer Fagor, went bankrupt.

THE BENEFITS AND CHALLENGES OF COOPERATIVES

Based on these inherent advantages, cooperatives offer a number of socioeconomic benefits to society. For one, they provide an alternative economic model *within* capitalism to publicly traded companies. Thus, cooperatives are still driven to deliver strong financial results and be competitive. Without that, they simply would not be viable and would be of little benefit to their members, their communities, and society as a whole. But, financial results are not the only metric used by cooperatives to measure success. The cooperative business model proves that an organization can be economically successful while also being socially responsible. The economic impact of cooperatives is even more pronounced in the developing world, where they deliver badly needed products and services in vital areas such as health, agriculture, and finance, and create income for member-owners, which reduces poverty. The modern-day cooperative movement, represented by the International Co-operative Alliance and other organizations, is stepping up its efforts to educate governments, regulatory authorities, and universities about the merits of this business model. They are becoming more active in fostering the values and business philosophies that make them unique, both individually and collectively.

Although the structure and guiding principles of cooperatives give these organizations a number of competitive advantages, they also present them with some major challenges. Perhaps the most significant of these is decision-making. Generally, in a public company the key stakeholder is the shareholder, and the overriding objective is to maximize shareholder equity and provide a return to investors (cf. Chapter 12, this volume). But in a cooperative, there are multiple objectives and numerous stakeholders. And because cooperatives are more democratic in make-up and more consensus-driven, decisions can often take a lot longer and require a greater deal of discussion. And unlike a private or publicly traded company, where most major decisions are made by relatively few high-level managers, cooperatives require consensus from their member-owners before taking action. In moments when immediate action is required, this can place cooperatives at a disadvantage vis-à-vis other types of private sector companies, in which top-down decisions are made rapidly.

Since cooperatives do not issue shares, they are free from the short-term, return-on-equity pressures that public companies face. And yet the inability to issue stock can be a disadvantage at times. For example, following the 2008 financial crisis, governments around the world have imposed much more stringent rules and regulations governing financial institutions. They are now being asked to significantly increase their capitalization to mitigate risk. But these regulations did not take into account the conservative nature and strong liquidity of most financial cooperatives. Unlike publicly traded banks, financial cooperatives cannot access equity markets to increase capital, forcing them to find other methods or to become even more rigorous in the way they manage their financial assets.

Other challenges that cooperatives face in addition to accessing financial capital include the constant need to remain close to their members, operational scale in a rapidly globalizing world, and finding innovative approaches to competition, including greater cooperation between cooperatives themselves.

THE COOPERATIVE ENTERPRISE: A BUSINESS MODEL FOR THE 21ST CENTURY?

In the wake of calls to reform capitalism by various business leaders and thinkers, many corporations are looking for ways to align their business strategies with the interests of their stakeholders to create greater long-term value and sustainability. Even companies still very much bound to maximizing profits in the short term are exploring ways in which they can produce social and economic value and are reshaping their business strategies along these lines. Moreover, this approach is gaining currency through the concept of "creating shared value" based on the idea that the competitiveness of a company and the well-being of their communities are inextricably linked, and that by addressing social needs, corporations can create a competitive advantage (Porter and Kramer, 2011; cf. Chapter 11, this volume).

We are today witnessing an explosion of new types of enterprises, social and for-benefit, all driven by the common goal of blending social purpose with economic goals (see also Chapters 9 and 11, this volume). For these enterprises, social objectives are not seen as separate from business objectives, and they take as their mantra the slogan "doing well *and* doing good." These enterprises share some of the same attributes and principles as cooperatives, which provide a powerful, real-world example of how successful business strategies can be aligned with longer-term societal benefit, creating greater sustainability in the process. Cooperatives also play an important role in creating a more pluralist economy—one that encompasses a vibrant private sector, a public sector, a not-for-profit sector, as well as a stable and growing cooperative sector. They provide greater economic choice, greater competition, and enhanced service in fields such as food, health care, insurance, and energy. They have also sheltered jobs during times of financial crisis, provided stable employment, and are deeply rooted in the communities where their employees live.

In conclusion, the view of the cooperative as an antiquated relic from an earlier era is fading. The economic recession has re-affirmed the inherent value of cooperatives and their many virtues—not the least of which are economic stability, durability, and a balanced approach to conducting business for the long term. During the demutualization wave that swept the UK during the 1990s, one that saw many cooperatives become publicly traded companies, the cooperatives were likened to steam trains in an electric train age (Birchall and Ketilson, 2009: 5). In the months following the economic meltdown, however, it was the tried-and-tested cooperatives that were still standing, whereas many of the former cooperatives and mutual building societies that had converted to public companies, including Northern Rock, were wiped out—and so too were the savings of tens of thousands of former members.

In much the same way that biodiversity in nature provides a more balanced, resilient, and adaptable ecosystem, the same can be said to be true of the economy. The cooperative business model exists alongside public sector organizations and not-for-profits on one end, and privately held companies, family enterprises, and publicly traded corporations on the other. A vibrant cooperative sector not only provides enhanced consumer choice and greater business competition; it also helps lessen the economic shocks that occur as a result of market crashes and economic recession.

REFERENCES

Barton, D. (2011). "Capitalism for the Long Term," *Harvard Business Review*, 89(3): 84–91.

Bérubé, V. and Lamarre, E. (2012). "Another Way to Do Business: An Interview with the President and CEO of Desjardins Group," in M. T. Borruso (ed.), *McKinsey on Cooperatives*. New York: McKinsey & Company, pp. 60–7. Available at: <http://www.mckinsey.com/client_service/strategy/latest_thinking/mckinsey_on_cooperatives>.

Bérubé, V., Grant, A., and Mansour, T. (2012). "How Cooperatives Grow," in M. T. Borruso (ed.), *McKinsey on Cooperatives*. New York: McKinsey & Company, pp. 4–11. Available at: <http://www.mckinsey.com/client_service/strategy/latest_thinking/mckinsey_on_cooperatives>.

Birchall, J. and Ketilson, L. H. (2009). *Resilience of the Cooperative Business Model in Times of Crisis*. Geneva: International Labor Office. Available at: <http://www.ilo.org/empent/Publications/WCMS_108416/lang—en/index.htm>.

Co-operatives UK (2013). "Homegrown: The UK Co-operative Economy 2013." Available at: <http://ica.coop/sites/default/files/media_items/homegrown_co-op_economy_2013_final_0.pdf>.

Crear, S. (2009). "Cooperative Banks, Credit Unions and the Financial Crisis." Prepared for the United Nations Expert Group Meeting on Cooperatives, New York, April 28–30, World Council of Credit Unions. Available at: <http://www.un.org/esa/socdev/egms/docs/2009/cooperatives/Crear.pdf>.

Fourth Sector Network (2008). "The Emerging Fourth Sector." Available at: <http://www.fourthsector.net/learn/fourth-sector> (accessed December 11, 2015).

ICA (2013). "Blueprint for a Co-operative Decade," International Co-operative Alliance, February. Available at: <http://ica.coop/en/media/library/member-publication/blueprint-co-operative-decade-february-2013> (accessed March 28, 2015).

ICA (2015a). "Cooperative Identity, Values and Principles," International Co-operative Alliance. Available at: <http://ica.coop/en/whats-co-op/co-operative-identity-values-principles> (accessed March 28, 2015).

ICA (2015b). "The Need for Change," International Co-operative Alliance. Available at: <http://ica.coop/en/blueprint-co-op-decade/need-change> (accessed March 28, 2015).

ICA (2015c). "Friedrich Wilhelm Raiffeisen," International Co-operative Alliance. Available at: <http://ica.coop/en/history-co-op-movement/friedrich-wilhelm-raiffeisen> (accessed March 28, 2015).

ICA (2015d). "The History of the Co-operative Movement," International Co-operative Alliance. Available at: <http://ica.coop/en/history-co-operative-movement> (accessed March 28, 2015).

Kanter, R. M. (2011). "How Great Companies Think Differently," *Harvard Business Review*, 89(11): 66–78.

Kanter, R. M. and Malone, A.-L. J. (2013). "Monique Leroux: Leading Change at Desjardins," Harvard Business School Case 313–17, February (revised April 2013).

Klimecki, R. and Wilmot, H. (2009). "From Demutualization to Meltdown: A Tale of Two Wannabe Banks," *Critical Perspectives on International Business*, 5: 120–40.

Leroux, M. F. (2014). *Conversations on Cooperation*. Lévis: Federation des Caisses Desjardins.

Porter, M. E. and Kramer, M. R. (2011). "Creating Shared Value," *Harvard Business Review*, 89(2): 62–77.

RZB (2015). "Raiffeisen: An Idea Becomes a Success," Raiffeisen Zentralbank Österreich AG. Available at: <http://www.rzb.at/eBusiness/01_template1/832624473864488257-832624426888283369_832626739996609179-832626739996609179-NA-2-EN.html> (accessed March 28, 2015).

World Co-operative Monitor (2014). *Exploring the Co-operative Economy: Report 2014*. Available at: <http://ica.coop/sites/default/files/WCM2014.pdf>.

6

Corporate Community Involvement in the 21st Century

Ratan N. Tata, with Dirk Matten

In a free enterprise, the community is not just another stakeholder in our businesses, but is in fact the very purpose of its existence.

Jamsetji N. Tata, Founder, Tata Group

INTRODUCTION

Corporate community involvement (CCI) is a phenomenon that has been a feature of many companies since the Industrial Revolution. CCI refers to activities by business firms targeted at the improvement of their direct communities—in many cases largely synonymous with their employees. Companies and/or their owner-managers took care of, among others, infrastructure, education, health care, access to affordable housing, and everyday consumption—an approach today commonly referred to as paternalism.

This chapter will discuss CCI and its relevance for forms of capitalism in the contemporary business environment. In doing so we will also refer to the specific angle of the largest Indian business group, Tata. We are aware that the CCI of Tata and its group companies is on a scale which to comprehensively describe would clearly transcend the scope of this chapter. For more details we refer the reader to the comprehensive material published on various websites of the Tata Group (see <http://www.tata.com>, and in particular the various sections at <http://www.tata.com/sustainability/sub_index/Tata-Sustainability-Group>) as well as to a growing number of studies and articles published in the academic literature on the topic (e.g., Elankumaran et al., 2005; Haugh and Talwar, 2010; Shah, 2014; Sundar, 2000; Surie and Ashley, 2008; Worden, 2003).

The focus of this chapter is to highlight—from the perspective of senior leadership of the Tata Group—the basic elements of Tata's CCI approach and contextualize it in the broader context of this volume on alternative approaches to contemporary capitalism. In what follows we first contextualize CCI in an historical perspective and then move to discussing the core strategic questions. These include the definition of "community," the motives and drivers of CCI, and the role of corporate purpose and ownership for community engagement. We also briefly discuss the relevance of geographical context, and position the importance of CCI for the wider debate on re-imagining capitalism.

A BRIEF HISTORY OF CORPORATE COMMUNITY INVOLVEMENT

Looking back at the first shareholder-owned companies—the railroad companies set up in North America in the 19th century—the discussion around a separate role for "communities" would not have resonated at the time. After all, these companies had their "communities" at the core of their purpose: to provide safe, efficient, and affordable transportation in a continent that was as of then underserved by this service. Of course, these corporations had shareholders—after all, capital was an important resource for their pursuit—and to reward them adequately was an important condition of their operation. But serving the cities, towns, and states—in short, the communities of these corporations—was their main purpose.

In other parts of the world, most notably in Europe, entrepreneurs during the Industrial Revolution discovered fairly early on that employees in fact were their first and foremost community that warranted specific engagement. This approach, often dubbed "paternalism," was concerned with the well-being and health of their employees and their families. For the early Cadburys, Rowntrees, Thyssens, or Krupps, the community was their workers, often literally and physically placed as a community in company-provided housing next to the factory gates (Cannon, 2012).

Over the course of the 20th century the focus of community engagement shifted increasingly towards the direct neighborhood of a company, its town or city, or even country. Community engagement of large American and European firms then appeared prominently in the form of philanthropy and voluntary donations in the area of health care, education, the arts, or other social services. Certainly in North America, many companies, when using the more contemporary language of "corporate social responsibility" (CSR), still refer to the way they engage in philanthropic activities (Porter and Kramer, 2011). Finally, in the second half of the 20th century it was particularly the environmental movement that highlighted the physical, ecological environment, and the people that depended on it, as a common aspect of what constitutes a corporation's community.

In the case of the Tata Group we observe a somewhat different trajectory. Jamsetji Tata's main impulse for founding the company in the second half of the 19th century, and setting community engagement as its core goal, was to create a company that served India as a country and provided a basis for self-reliance against the British colonial rule (Worden, 2003). Certainly, in Jamsetji Tata's time it was obvious that he was driven by a great urge of national development and the purpose was, in most cases, to create industries that the British said could not be created in India. It was a question of what an Indian company could achieve and of the role of business in building India up as an industrial nation. It is probably fair to say that he did something on the scale of being equal to anything that was being done elsewhere in the world at the time. His ambition for his company was to not be a second-class operation and he was indeed successful in becoming world class at that time, be it in textiles or energy. Furthermore, Jamsetji Tata was driven by creating value for the users of the products—the Indian consumer. It was his view that he valued his country more than anything else and that whatever was best for the country he would try to achieve, using scale and technology that were state of the art at that time.

This aspect of Tata being part of a wider project of "nation building," as former Tata Sons director Krishna Kumar still puts it, remains a core motivation for community engagement by the Tata Group. This notion, however, is today less contextualized in anti-colonial sentiments but rather relates to the opportunities a business group such as Tata sees in contributing to the social and economic development of India. What is also worth noting is that, for Tata, engagement with the community was always, and still is, looking at a host of stakeholders without necessarily prioritizing employees over customers, or employees over such parts of the local community that do not enjoy a direct relationship with the organization.

COMMUNITY ENGAGEMENT IN THE 21ST CENTURY

Defining the "Community" for Today's Multinationals

While, in a historical perspective, the definition of what exactly constitutes the "community" of a corporation appears to have been rather straightforward, this proves to be by no means an easy task for contemporary corporations. After all, a company today depends and touches upon such a broad array of stakeholders that often clearly transcend physical communities. This leads to the more general question as to what differentiates the "community" of a corporation from its other stakeholders, such as creditors, investors, suppliers, or governments.

When we talk about "community" we face a group of stakeholders who at least partially lack a direct economic link with the corporation. That is most clear with the physical community around a factory or plant: these people, if they are not employees or customers of the company, have no direct leverage to engage with the company and the degree to which they are treated well depends largely on the company's discretion. In some cases, this may also include customers, which for instance in a situation of (natural) monopolies, such as railway operators or utility companies, have limited economic leverage over the company and largely depend on its discretion with regard to quality and price of the service. Or, to refer to another of our historical examples, it could include employees, which, in the absence of strong regulation, like during the Industrial Revolution in Europe, depend very much on the discretion of the company with regard to working and living conditions. If we approach the idea of communities as stakeholders from this angle there is arguably a rather broad range of groups who would qualify. This becomes particularly complex for multinational companies and a lot has been written about which communities are worthy of a corporation's engagement (Jones et al., 2007).

From the perspective of the Tata Group there are different definitions of communities. There are what one could refer to as the "elite communities," i.e., the well-endowed communities in India which are able to look after themselves. But then there are the less fortunate communities that are in various stages of economic development. The worst case are those in the rural or the semi-urban/semi-rural areas where there is either abject poverty or disadvantage, disproportionate bias against education, or a general lack of acceptance by wider society. It is that segment of the community which the Tata Group thinks deserves attention from industry but is often ignored. It is also that segment of the community that the Tata Group for a hundred years or more has considered embracing around its plants, i.e., not just confined to their workers, but going beyond to include the often rural communities that adjoin the operations of the Tata Group— often pragmatically defined by a radius of 30 to 50 miles. Here, the company has traditionally provided health services, some form of skills enhancement education, sometimes under trees in the rural areas, but nevertheless some education. The company has also endeavored to try and connect these communities to future employment by teaching, for instance, the women in the rural areas to stitch uniforms or to produce lunch boxes, which the Tata company then would use in its plants. The inevitable aspiration for this segment of the community is to just give them jobs but there are of course limits as a company is always trying to produce more with fewer people. But what the Tata Group is trying to do is to make this segment of the community more self-reliant and eventually more prosperous.

Of course the question of which communities to serve remains complex, in particular for a Tata Group that now has become a multinational enterprise. In the case of its many manufacturing operations, defining the community might still be rather straightforward. But for a company with a global array of multiple stakeholders the question of which groups to consider their community will continue to be challenging, in particular when the issues are global ones, such as protection of the ecosystem, climate change, or biodiversity (see also Chapters 2 and 3, this volume).

Motives and Drivers of Corporate Community Involvement

So far, we have argued that CCI is largely dependent on the discretion of the company. So an important area of understanding CCI is the question of what motivates and drives companies to engage with their communities. We can identify three basic drivers of CCI, which we would characterize as pragmatic, strategic, and normative.

First, for many companies CCI is just a *pragmatic way of securing their wider license to operate* in a certain town or country (Smith, 2003). In order to attract well-qualified and motivated employees, there has to be a good school, decent hospitals, and a safe environment. In many developing country contexts, for instance, mining companies engage in this type of CCI as it is a vital condition for them to operate (Kemp and Owen, 2013; see also Chapter 19, this volume). In some cases we can even speak of company towns where a large company in fact runs and supports an entire town as its basis for successful economic performance (Muthuri et al., 2012).

Second, more recently and certainly with a focus on North America, we have seen a debate emerging that sees CCI, in particular philanthropic activities, as something the firm can use *strategically to enhance its competitiveness* (Porter and Kramer, 2002). For instance, Apple or Microsoft for a long time provided computers to schools and libraries. While this was a valuable enhancement of the education levels in those communities, it also created the skills necessary to turn all those students and library users into future consumers of their products.

Third, *normative arguments* start from the assumption that companies have some moral duty to engage with their communities—regardless of the fact that it might just make their operations possible, let alone open more strategic opportunities for them. In its most basic form such engagement is often dubbed as "giving back" to the community and reflects a basic idea of fairness and justice. This argument has been a longstanding motivation for companies and their owners to engage in philanthropy (Carroll, 1991). It gained some more prominence in recent years when President Obama coined his famous "you did not build that" argument during a campaign speech (White House, 2012):

> There are a lot of wealthy, successful Americans who agree with me—because they want to give something back. They know…if you've been successful, you didn't get there on your own…If you were successful, somebody along the line gave you some help. There was a great teacher somewhere in your life. Somebody helped to create this unbelievable American system that we have that allowed you to thrive. Somebody invested in roads and bridges. If you've got a business—you didn't build that. Somebody else made that happen.

The basic idea here is that companies implicitly use many resources from their surrounding communities, such as infrastructure or educational institutions, without directly paying for them. In a basic understanding of justice and fairness then community involvement is about "giving back" some of those resources.

Another, slightly more substantial justification of CCI is based on an ethics of duty, as espoused by the enlightenment philosopher Immanuel Kant. At the core of this argument is that companies have to treat workers, neighbors, and other stakeholders not just as a means to their instrumental ends, but as human beings with some inherent dignity and interests of their own. This approach often overlaps with "the golden rule," and thus can be found in many companies where the owners or the management are motivated by religious thought. For instance some of the early philanthropists, such as the Cadburys or Rowntrees in the UK, are said to be strongly motivated by their Christian Quaker religion (Smith et al., 1990; see also Chapter 4, this volume).

For Tata management, a first motivation to engage in CCI is based on the fairness and justice argument. It has always been their conviction that one cannot have enormous prosperity within the walls of the company while tolerating destitution and poverty around the factory premises. If a company is fortunate enough to create prosperity for its employees it is important to avoid a line of cleavage between employees and the people that they go home to and live with every day. As a company, one would like to be seen to be more benevolent with that community. This may not always include direct transfer payments. But a company can be assisting in providing better schools, or better community facilities, and thus sharing its prosperity to some extent with the community.

The second driver is the simple fact that Tata as a company lives off the communities that it provides products for or that it serves. Those are customers of the aspiring middle class with some basic levels of prosperity. Therefore Tata's community orientation is to design products for that community, in particular the less advantaged. Of course, the Tata Group is aware that this is not easy and that, in general, many companies rarely look at the bottom of the pyramid because that is lower in margins and profit. It is here where, arguably, the Tata Group differs most from other companies, which predominantly look at shareholder value as the criteria of their success in the market place (see also Chapter 12, this volume). While the Tata Group as a business of course pursues a profit motive, the company's leadership has always been convinced that enhancing shareholder value takes place not just by giving out dividends or maximizing profits, but by creating social harmony and a sense of social well-being (see also Chapter 10, this volume).

The cost of doing that has always been framed within this broader context in the Tata Group. The underlying contrast became quite palpable in the 1990s when India started to allow foreign investment in the Indian stock exchange, and when the Tata Group started to have investment or private equity firms invest in their companies. Often, the first thing these investors asked was: "Why are you spending all this money on rural welfare, after all it's our money? At the end of the day, as your potential investor, these are funds which ultimately belong to us and which you cannot just give away to the community." This line of thinking was rather strongly against that of the Tata Group for generations. Tata leadership never thought of community involvement in terms of "giving something away." On the contrary, these community investments were perceived as investments into goodwill, into harmony with workers and staff. Of course it is hard to make a business case for each and every one of these investments but arguably the fact that the Tata Group over the years has hardly had any labor strife, for example, is considered a tangible benefit, even though these benefits are hard to quantify in terms of opportunity costs.

To summarize, the Tata Group's rationale for CCI is to engage in a cascading mix of motivations rather than embarking on just one of these drivers. At the top of what the company does with regard to communities we see a clear commitment to a moral stance. This relates back to the founding days, which were very much rooted in a perceived *moral duty* to contribute to the flourishing of the Indian nation. However, there is also a *pragmatic insight* that inequality of wealth within the company, including its employees, versus the rest of local residents is unsustainable and ultimately inhibits the economic success of the company. Finally, as we will discuss in the next subsection, there are also *strategic motives* at the core of CCI at Tata. They inform an acute awareness that once a company embarks on this trajectory a complementary relation between the profit motive of a private company and its community involvement is driving CCI, most notably the question as to where exactly to locate the core attention of CCI projects.

In this context it is worth mentioning that the founder of the group, Jamsetji Tata, being a Zoroastrian priest, has led some commentators to speculate about the religious foundations of Tata's specific community orientation (Worden, 2003). However, the current senior management of the Tata

Group would argue that religious motivations are more or less irrelevant. Today, the company's overall motivation for CCI then is a mix of pragmatic, moral, and, to some extent, strategic motivations.

Corporate Purpose and the Business Case for CCI

In the context of this volume on alternative approaches to capitalism, it seems important to contextualize Tata's approach to CCI. After all, when we look at standard textbook treatments of CCI the strategic arguments abound (e.g. Crane et al., 2013). CCI is warranted, in this view, if it contributes either to secure—even augment—revenues, lower costs, or mitigate risks for the company.

This dominance of strategic thinking though is predicated on one crucial assumption: that the core purpose of the firm is (short-term) profit maximization (cf. Chapter 12, this volume). CCI from this perspective is only warranted if contributing to the public good at the same time feeds into the corporate bottom line. What companies should pursue is "shared value," meaning that only such projects should be pursued which simultaneously contribute both to the public good and the company's bottom line (Porter and Kramer, 2011). Ultimately, this predicament points back to the fundamental question of the purpose of the firm, which of course is predominantly shaped by the ownership of the corporation (see also Chapters 4, 5, and 9, this volume).

It is here where Tata is arguably the most peculiarly different from many Western companies: the ownership structure and the commitment to values actually define the purpose of business as being intimately linked with service to the community. Those are very unique differentiators for Tata locally and globally. The fact that at the level of the holding company Tata is principally held by charities makes a big difference in the way the company defines its responsibility to the community. It is worth noting that these holding units are charities in the true sense of the word, rather than tax-saving endowments that are created by a family to, for instance, avoid inheritance tax. They are clearly intended from the get-go to be committed towards giving wealth away to support charitable causes in society, largely centered around education, health, and now increasingly other spaces as well. So, ownership has been a differentiator and so has the philosophy of the leadership of the group, which roots the role of business in the community.

Core Approaches to CCI

There are a number of ways companies are able to approach CCI. One can differentiate five major ways that companies can do this: (i) charitable giving,

(ii) employee volunteering, (iii) cross-sector partnerships with civil society groups/non-government organizations (NGOs), (iv) developing products and services for disadvantaged communities, and (v) engaging in public policy. We will discuss each of these in turn in some detail.

First of all, *charitable giving and sponsorship*—often referred to as philanthropy—is one of the oldest approaches to CCI but still enjoys large popularity for many companies. Increasingly, in tune with a strategic approach to CCI, this approach is linked to marketing strategies through cause-related marketing. Donations are increasingly expected to provide tangible benefits to the firm in terms of increased sales, brand recognition, or brand identification among consumers. The Tata Group engages in many philanthropic activities and projects along these lines, as will be discussed further down in more detail.

Second, *employee volunteering* has gained increasing momentum, especially when linked to human resource development strategies. Increasingly, employees are extolled to go beyond simply donating their time and effort to local community projects, and are encouraged to select projects that will enhance their transferable skills and competences in ways that are of benefit to themselves and their employers. At the Tata Group, volunteering plays a big role in many aspects of community involvement. One example worth mentioning in this context is the Tata Relief Committee. Anybody in the company can be involved in disaster relief, and when the tsunami hit in 2005, the Tata Group gave employees leave to go and work in those troubled areas if they wanted to. Back then, Tata built 700 homes, and provided relief to the widows and families of the fishermen that died. This relief also included the orphaned children by creating schools for them, or even facilitating foster parents for them. The volunteer program was executed by Tata employees that went to these areas and lived in difficult conditions just because—as the word implies—this was what they voluntarily wanted to do. In terms of funding these efforts, the Tata Group matched 100 percent of all donations in terms of time and foregone wages by their employees. At the same time the Tata Group was careful to not use its brand in the relief efforts, being only too aware that people knew that at a time of need, it was the company that stood by them. Since as a business group we touch the lives of people in so many areas, the Tata leadership is convinced that these activities should not just be driven by a short-term business case, let alone by the shareholder value this might ultimately create. It all has to do with the purpose of the firm to make a difference in the communities it serves.

Third, and more broadly, *partnerships* can help companies deliver on community projects with groups that share the same concerns for certain needs of the community. This may also help build reputation and legitimacy with the public, as well as specific competence in managing social issues. Working with NGOs is widely touted to be a win-win strategy for businesses facing a trust deficit in the community and charities facing a skills or resource deficit. It only takes a quick glance at the website and the annual reports of the Tata Group to see the manifold and dense network of civil society organizations the company is partnering with in their CCI.

Fourth, often discussed under the label of "base of the pyramid" strategies, companies have started to think about *serving disadvantaged communities* through their core operations (see also Chapter 2, this volume). The core insight that informs this approach is that many constituencies in the developing world are excluded from the consumption of goods and services because of lower disposable incomes and different product delivery conditions in those contexts (Kolk et al., 2014). The Tata Group has thought in many of its operations about serving communities better and reaching out to improve the lives of the poorer and more disadvantaged segments of society. The most celebrated example is perhaps the Tata Nano automobile, which was designed with the intention of improving individual mobility for customers who would be unable to afford even the cheapest cars produced by mainstream car manufacturers at the time.

Fifth, a fairly recent debate has come up about the role of companies in community initiatives and their *relations to government institutions*. This is a debate that is by no means uncontroversial and has initially been one of the main criticisms of CSR and CCI. Most notably, back in the 1970s Milton Friedman (1970) argued that social initiatives for the public good should not be left to the discretion of managers, but fall into the responsibility of (democratic) governments. Today, however, companies often face rather different constraints. Governments might not be able to solve public health, education, or infrastructure challenges on their own. This may be due to lack of resources, corruption, or due to the fact that some issues are clearly beyond the reach of a single government (see also Chapter 9, this volume). What we see emerging then is that companies often engage in a rather complex way with government authorities, which Valente and Crane (2010) have summarized through distinct approaches, characterizing them as "supplement" or "substitute," when companies provide, respectively, public services partially alongside governments or wholesale in the absence of government action, and "support" or "stimulate," when companies sustain or encourage and enable government capacity to provide public goods.

The Tata companies, over time, have been in different roles as their operations progressed. Tata Steel at times ran schools and there are hospitals operated by the Tata organization. However, in many cases, if public institutions are able to provide a basic infrastructure, the company steps more into a supporting and stimulating role. From the perspective of senior management though, the relationship to governments over time has not always been without tension. Certainly in the post-war period in India until the 1990s, during the so-called "License Raj," companies had to get permission from the government to expand their business (Dwivedi, 1989; Tripathi and Jumani,

2007). This certainly was a period of serious challenges to the underlying ethical values of the company because obtaining a permit often included various forms of corruption. So, for years the Tata Group was not able to expand its textile business into synthetics, which was a rapidly growing domestic market at the time. Under J. R. D. Tata's chairmanship (1938–91), the group actually suffered quite significantly from its fierce denial to engage in corruption with government bodies. This delayed entry into manufacturing passenger cars, for instance. It also led to the loss of its airline, banks, and insurance companies due to nationalization. This was the price the Tata Group paid for not letting go of its values. J. R. D. Tata would have seen his life's work and achievement ruined if his company had submitted itself to any form of corruption. He was prepared to pay whatever price there was to live by the value system that he believed the company stood for.

Differences between Developing and Developed Countries

As a group that, over the last two decades, quickly moved from a predominantly Indian company to a globally active multinational enterprise, there has always been the question of how far the approach to CCI should be different in India, as opposed to Europe, for instance. When Tata acquired the British-Dutch steel manufacturer Corus, the company had to lay off staff because the European economy at the time embarked on a downturn. The Tata Group approached the different governments in the European locations of Corus and—as Tata believed the downturn was not going to be permanent—suggested keeping employees on the payroll instead of putting them out of work and disadvantaging their communities. Tata offered to pay half their wages, with the respective government paying the other half, for two years. The idea was similar to how the company would have approached this issue in India: to enable the employees' children to continue to go to school or to enable workers to look for another job in the interim. Interestingly, among the governments Tata talked to at the time only the Dutch government took up the offer. The experience of the Tata Group going global, then, is that the basic expectations of communities are not that vastly different from India. However, the way CCI is practiced and the environment existing in other countries are different and in some ways, given the group's legacy and networks in India, the opportunities are still more conducive in the group's home country.

Expanding globally, management at Tata got the sense that there is need in developed economies to deal more humanely with manpower than they have been doing traditionally. For example, when that same downturn took place at Jaguar, the normal thing would have been to reduce working hours at the plants down to three days a week, or to lay off employees temporarily. What senior management at Tata decided though was to put more funds into new projects so that when Jaguar would come out of the downturn the company would be set up much more competitively with many more innovations. The Tata Group bought Jaguar for $1.6 billion net and, according to estimates by senior management, during the downturn has invested some $2 billion more in new product development and other innovations. So, while Jaguar may have slowed down production, it increased the amount of internal work and this paid off. Of course Tata management is aware that it cannot afford to take this approach all the time, because manpower is expensive. In that sense then the company also learned that the strife for the underlying benefits to employers in Europe is different from what they encounter in India. As the ongoing discussions about the future of the group's British steel manufacturing operations show, Tata is clearly facing new challenges to its overall approach to addressing community needs.

CONCLUSION: CCI AND THE RE-IMAGINING OF CAPITALISM

This chapter has examined the role and importance of a company's community and, particularly, how the Tata Group has approached this constituency over the years. Given the theme of this book, it appears obvious that some of the principles that have governed CCI in the Tata Group may inform the debate on imagining alternative versions of successful business in a context of free markets and private property.

One of the main facilitators of CCI in the Tata Group is the broad *purpose* of the company which has been not only historically at the root of the company's foundation but has been maintained until today. With the explicit purpose of serving its community, be it customers, employees, or the wider surrounding constituency, including the entire Indian nation, Tata starkly differs from most large multinationals of similar size and standing. And while profitability has always been an important imperative for running the company successfully for more than a century, the interests of shareholders have always been just one important goal for a company that sees itself in the service of all stakeholders—to use the language of Freeman, Parmar, and Martin (Chapter 10, this volume). This is certainly a complex task but it also proves shareholder value proponents such as Michael Jensen (2010) wrong, who contend that managers can only successfully run a company when they pursue a single financial goal (see also Chapter 12, this volume). Serving the community with a profitable business is admittedly a complex task, and the structure of multilayered management committees and task forces is witness to this. But the Tata example shows that it is certainly possible to be a successful capitalist player while serving communities in need of new products, education, health care, or other social wants.

The difference in purpose, however, is also closely linked to a rather complex and different *ownership* model. While initially family owned, Tata today is 66 percent owned by the Tata family-established foundations whose purpose is to serve the community with the profits generated by the group. It is therefore no surprise that the strong values regarding service to the community are relatively easier to implement if the majority of shares are owned by a group of individuals who prize such a broader purpose to begin with. It is obvious that the community commitment of a company that is, for instance, owned by dispersed shareholders with exclusively financial interests is much harder to establish and puts management in a constant legitimacy pressure to justify CCI as a means to enhance value for these shareholders. While the Tata approach is not necessarily a panacea for addressing all the contemporary critics of capitalism, the example of the Tata Group raises the necessity to rethink forms, motives, and governance mechanisms for alternative types of ownership of private corporations (see also Chapters 4 and 5, this volume).

A third aspect that jumps out is that the leadership of the Tata Group had, and still has, a sincere commitment to *values and integrity*. Community involvement at Tata is clearly rooted in these values. Of course much has been written about how to achieve a culture of integrity in an organization (e.g. Brown, 2005; Paine, 1994). Looking at the Tata Group over the generations two things stand out. First, the personal values and a strong commitment to integrity within the leadership of a company is essential for sustained service to the community (Solomon, 1999). And while this seems to be slightly easier in a family-controlled organization the second aspect is nonetheless equally crucial: over the many decades of its existence the commitment of the Tata leadership has created what one could refer to as an "administrative heritage" (Bartlett and Ghoshal, 1988) so that today a commitment to these values is relatively firmly embedded in the personal attitudes of current leaders as well as in the organizational structure of the group. This of course has implications for a number of issues in the debate about reforming contemporary forms of capitalism—and its detrimental side effects as elucidated in the financial crisis of 2008. Not only is a credible commitment and conviction about basic ethical values a necessary condition for an economic system that serves communities better, but it also raises questions as to whether such changes can be achieved in the short term and by legal reforms alone (for the latter see Chapter 16, this volume).

Ultimately, it is worth highlighting that the example of the Tata Group shows the pivotal role of the underlying values that drive CCI. Admittedly, certainly in the historical perspective, some of these, and in particular those at the core of Jamsetji Tata's strategic view when founding the group, are rather idiosyncratic and shaped by the specific circumstances of time and geographic place. Others, in particular the desire to address economic inequality in society, appear to be as timely today as they were in the 19th century. Indeed, the problem of income or economic inequality is not just a topic for so-called developing or emerging economies; on the contrary, certainly post-2008, the debate about the unsustainability of income inequality is as urgent—if not more relevant—in the developed economies of the global North (Piketty, 2013).

As the contributions in this volume highlight, the private business firm as the key institution of wealth creation and accumulation plays a pivotal role in this debate. Corporations have encountered dramatic erosions of trust, since they are perceived as the most powerful drivers of such economic inequalities. CCI is one of the most urgent areas by which corporation can potentially address this imbalance. The example of the Tata Group shows that this pertains, first and foremost, to the way a corporation creates value in the way it manages relations to customers, employees, neighbors, or other interest groups of the company; but the example of the Tata Group may also inform an ongoing debate of re-imagining the role of business in society in the way the created value is distributed and shared with constituencies beyond just the owners or shareholders of private corporations.

ACKNOWLEDGMENTS

We gratefully acknowledge the support from a number of Tata executives in putting the chapter together, in particular Dr Mukund Rajan, Member, Group Executive Counsel, Brand Custodian, and Chief Ethics Officer, Tata Sons Limited, and Krishna Kumar, until 2013 Member, Group Corporate Centre, Tata Sons Limited and Chairman of various companies of Tata Sons Limited.

REFERENCES

Bartlett, C. A. and Ghoshal, S. (1988). "Organizing for Worldwide Effectiveness: The Transnational Solution," in P. J. Buckley and P. N. Ghauri (eds), *The Internationalization of the Firm: A Reader*, Vol. 2. London: Routledge, pp. 295–311.

Brown, M. T. (2005). *Corporate Integrity: Rethinking Organizational Ethics and Leadership*. Cambridge: Cambridge University Press.

Cannon, T. (2012). *Corporate Responsibility: Governance, Compliance and Ethics in a Sustainable Environment*, 2nd ed. London: Pearson Education.

Carroll, A. B. (1991). "The Pyramid of Corporate Social Responsibility: Toward the Moral Management of Organizational Stakeholders," *Business Horizons*, July–August: 39–48.

Crane, A., Matten, D., and Spence, L. (2013). *Corporate Social Responsibility: Readings and Cases in Global Context*, 2nd ed. London: Routledge.

Dwivedi, O. (1989). "Editor's Introduction: Administrative Heritage, Morality and Challenges in the Sub-Continent since the British Raj," *Public Administration and Development*, 9(3): 245–52.

Elankumaran, S., Seal, R., and Hashmi, A. (2005). "Transcending Transformation: Enlightening Endeavours at Tata Steel," *Journal of Business Ethics*, 59(1): 109–19.

Friedman, M. (1970). "The Social Responsibility of Business Is to Increase Its Profits," *New York Times Magazine*, September 13: 70–1, 122–6.

Haugh, H. M. and Talwar, A. (2010). "How Do Corporations Embed Sustainability across the Organization?" *Academy of Management Learning and Education*, 9(3): 384–96.

Jensen, M. C. (2010). "Value Maximization, Stakeholder Theory, and the Corporate Objective Function," *Journal of Applied Corporate Finance*, 22(1): 32–42.

Jones, I., Pollitt, M. G., and Bek, D. (2007). *Multinationals in Their Communities: A Social Capital Approach to Corporate Citizenship Projects*. Basingstoke: Palgrave Macmillan.

Kemp, D. and Owen, J. R. (2013). "Community Relations and Mining: Core to Business but Not 'Core Business,'" *Resources Policy*, 38(4): 523–31.

Kolk, A., Rivera-Santos, M., and Rufín, C. (2014). "Reviewing a Decade of Research on the 'Base/Bottom of the Pyramid' (BOP) concept," *Business and Society*, 53(3): 338–77.

Muthuri, J. N., Moon, J., and Idemudia, U. (2012). "Corporate Innovation and Sustainable Community Development in Developing Countries," *Business and Society*, 51(3): 355–81.

Paine, L. S. (1994). "Managing for Organizational Integrity," *Harvard Business Review*, 72(2): 106–17.

Piketty, T. (2013). *Le capital au XXIe siècle*. Paris: Seuil.

Porter, M. E. and Kramer, M. R. (2002). "The Competitive Advantage of Corporate Philanthropy," *Harvard Business Review*, 80(12): 56–69.

Porter, M. E. and Kramer, M. R. (2011). "Creating Shared Value," *Harvard Business Review*, 89(2): 62–77.

Shah, S. (2014). "Corporate Social Responsibility: A Way of Life at the Tata Group," *Journal of Human Values*, 20(1): 59–74.

Smith, C., Child, J., and Rowlinson, M. (1990). *Reshaping Work: The Cadbury Experience*. Cambridge: Cambridge University Press.

Smith, N. C. (2003). "Corporate Social Responsibility: Whether or How?" *California Management Review*, 45(4): 52–76.

Solomon, R. C. (1999). *A Better Way to Think about Business: How Personal Integrity Leads to Corporate Success*. New York: Oxford University Press.

Sundar, P. (2000). *Beyond Business: From Merchant Charity to Corporate Citizenship, Indian Business Philanthropy through the Ages*. New Delhi: Tata McGraw-Hill.

Surie, G. and Ashley, A. (2008). "Integrating Pragmatism and Ethics in Entrepreneurial Leadership for Sustainable Value Creation," *Journal of Business Ethics*, 81(1): 235–46.

Tripathi, D. and Jumani, J. (2007). *The Concise Oxford History of Indian Business*. New Delhi: Oxford University Press.

Valente, M. and Crane, A. (2010). "Public Responsibility and Private Enterprise in Developing Countries," *California Management Review*, 52(3): 52–78.

White House (2012). "Remarks by the President at a Campaign Event in Roanoke, Virginia," July. Available at: <https://www.whitehouse.gov/the-press-office/2012/07/13/remarks-president-campaign-event-roanoke-virginia>.

Worden, S. (2003). "The Role of Religious and Nationalist Ethics in Strategic Leadership: The Case of JN Tata," *Journal of Business Ethics*, 47(2): 147–64.

7

The Gifts of Breadth

Insights from Leaders with Non-Linear Careers

Nick Lovegrove and Matthew Thomas

Our age reveres the specialist, but humans are natural polymaths, at our best, when we turn our minds to many things.

British poet, writer, and explorer Robert Twigger

INTRODUCTION: THE ERA OF SPECIALISTS

As consumers and citizens, we tend to place ourselves in the hands of technical experts. We all want to hear that our pilot has flown thousands of hours, our surgeon has performed hundreds of similar operations, and our architect has designed lots of beautiful buildings. In his best-selling book *Outliers* Malcolm Gladwell popularized the "10,000 hour rule," which sees obsessive, linear focus as a means to realizing your potential. He illustrated "the idea that excellence at performing a complex task requires a minimum level of practice surfaces again and again in studies of expertise," citing examples of world-class experts such as chess phenomenon Bobby Fischer and master pianist Wolfgang Amadeus Mozart (Gladwell, 2008).

This all makes perfect sense when we are talking about specialist roles like a pilot, surgeon, chess player, and pianist. But, in recent years, our obsession with depth has gone well beyond that. It has become the central premise for how we organize our society and the most significant sectors within it—governments, businesses, and non-profit organizations. We label and celebrate the best in each sector as a "policy wonk," "business tycoon," or "miracle worker," respectively—implicitly eschewing recognition of broad, non-linear experiences. The terms "polymath" and "Renaissance man" or "Renaissance woman"—references from the 15th century to people whose expertise spans a significant number of different subject areas—are vestiges of a bygone age. As we have entered the 21st century, we have been led to believe that the route to professional excellence and success, and thus to personal fulfillment and happiness, is through deep specialization and focused preparation.

This route now starts at school. Thus, in the US, there are a number of recently established high schools that focus intensively on "STEM" education—science, technology, engineering, and math. In the UK, students aged 15 are recommended to choose just three or four subjects to study at A-level prior to university—a decision that will direct the course of their future studies and career options. We see a similar trend in the narrowing of post-secondary education, with the percentage of humanities majors in US universities now hovering around 7 percent (half the already modest 14 percent share in 1970) and the number of liberal arts colleges on the decline—to 130 colleges today from 212 colleges in 1990—a 39 percent drop (Brooks, 2013). We are increasingly viewing educational attainment as a vocational training exercise, which reduces a population's dynamism and ability to innovate (Phelps, 2013). This kind of pressure carries over from school right into the job market. One student pursuing a dual-graduate degree in business and public policy told us he "can't get a job in the public or private sector" because employers question his motive for pursuing the "other sector's" degree. As a result, many of us have adjusted our resumes to appear as specialists in our professional careers.

Our research, however, suggests that there is much to say in favor of breadth instead of excessive specialization. Based on interviews with leaders who have rejected the pressure to specialize in one area, and instead have gone on to lead institutions in multiple sectors and address some of the world's most complex challenges, this chapter argues that people who deliberately seek out a diversity of broad, non-linear experiences throughout their careers might be better suited to solve the most complex challenges facing their personal lives, their organizations, and society as a whole.

In what follows we first examine the consequences of too much depth, especially with respect to the 2008 financial crisis. We then illustrate how the highest priority challenges facing society are wide-ranging and multi-faceted, and assert that leaders who are equally broad—individually having a wide array of experiences across multiple sectors, disciplines, cultures, functions, and issues—are better suited to address these kinds of complex challenges. We then explain in some more detail our research methodology, which primarily involved interviewing over 150 broad leaders based in the United States, Canada, and Hong Kong to identify their repertoire of skills, tools, and mindsets. This research revealed six important traits of leaders who have successfully "gone broad"—intellectual thread, transferable skills, integrated networks, contextual intelligence, balanced motivations, and prepared mind—each of which we discuss and illustrate with select examples. We close the chapter by providing guidance to individuals on developing the six distinguishing traits of broad leadership, and a call to action for leaders in business, government, non-profits, and higher education to embed non-linear career development within their people development and engagement policies.

DEPTH AND ITS CONSEQUENCES

The result of the pressure to specialize in education and work is clear: future leaders are incentivized to focus their development in niche areas, and established leaders most often have only their own sectors to draw meaningful insight from—at great cost to all. The near collapse of the world's financial system in 2008 and 2009 is a profound example of a system designed, operated, and nearly destroyed by the provision of almost unfettered authority to deep specialists. They typically spoke in an industry-specific language that few could understand, using words and especially acronyms known only to each other. Year after year, they applied their expertise and technology to develop more and more sophisticated, complex, and opaque financial products. The gap between what they did and what the rest of us understood inexorably widened.

As the financial crisis unfolded, however, it became painfully apparent that these deep specialists lacked the breadth of experience and perspective to address crucial blind spots in the financial system—like what would happen when lots of people have taken out mortgages they cannot afford; when you package these mortgages in derivatives that nobody understands; and when financial contagion spreads to countries that are already massively exposed by their own financial profligacy and ill discipline. Making those kinds of broad judgments was not their job. However, the critical issue is that there were too few people within the financial system with the breadth of experience and perspective to understand the interlocking roles that homebuyers, selling agents, investment banks, financial literacy educators, credit unions, credit agencies, pension funds, legislators, regulators, central banks, and other actors play in the mortgage system—globally, nationally, and locally. There was nobody with the breadth of intellectual disciplines to assess the economics, mathematics, finance, history, sociology, and psychology of borrowing and asset bubbles.

The 2008–9 financial crisis was not the first time our faith in deep specialists having the right answers proved flawed. Beginning in the 1980s, University of Pennsylvania professor Philip Tetlock sought to analyze the accuracy of forecasts by both experts in their fields, and non-experts (Tetlock, 2005). For his study, he picked an area that, similar to the financial markets, was rife with uncertainty: geopolitical outcomes. Tetlock tracked 80,000+ predictions made by 284 professional forecasters in various complex political scenarios both within and outside of their areas of expertise, and found that non-experts were actually the most accurate at making predictions. Based on this research he found that

> what experts think matters far less than how they think. If we want realistic odds on what will happen next, we are better off turning to those who "know many little things": individuals who draw from an eclectic array of traditions and accept ambiguity and contradiction as inevitable features of life—than those who "know one big thing": people who toil devotedly within one tradition, and reach for formulaic solutions to ill-defined problems.

In today's world nothing is simple, linear, and one-dimensional, however clear-cut experts can make issues appear. Instead, the highest priority "wicked problems" facing leaders and society today are wide-ranging, multi-faceted, and complex, with various stakeholders who hold contrasting views on cause and effect, and even greater disagreements about alternative solutions. The list of issues is as long as it is profound: health-care quality and affordability, access to education, food security and safety, energy security, climate change, and sustainable economic growth and employment. Addressing these challenges requires meaningful collaboration and collective action because no single individual, organization, or sector has the ability to resolve these issues in isolation.

Deep-seated and overly confident experts display traits detrimental to the process of making accurate predictions: they underestimate the complexity of the world, are less open to different opinions after their own mind is made up, dislike questions that could be answered in several ways, make decisions quickly and confidently, are less able to understand how the opposing side's viewpoint could be right, and prefer to interact with people whose opinions are not very different to their own (Tetlock, 2005). In a more recent study, he and other colleagues found that expertise is not all bad all the time, however. Good predictors often have a relevant level of "domain knowledge"—diverse pockets of applicable content knowledge (Mellers et al., 2015). Having both breadth and depth allows leaders to avoid the common pitfalls associated with just depth.

RESEARCHING BROAD LEADERS

The first question to ask is why an individual needs to appreciate and understand all these areas—is that not what having a diverse team is for? While collective diversity—drawing together many people with different backgrounds, experience, and skills—is better than no diversity, what we are talking about is different. Broad leaders have what we call inner breadth. Psychological and organizational research show that people with this kind of inner breadth can be more effective than non-diverse leaders in various critical ways. They are generative of new ideas and inventions (Boh et al., 2014); central in key decision-making (Bunderson, 2003); connected to a larger and diverse network (Cannella et al., 2008); able to overcome communication barriers within a team setting (Bunderson and Sutcliffe, 2002); better and faster learners (Dries et al., 2012); and, for those seeking upward movement, likely to be promoted (Campion et al., 1994). It follows then that individuals (and organizations) who reject the supposed primacy of specialism, and instead embrace breadth, will be best equipped to more effectively tackle the complex and pressing challenges facing them.

For our study we defined "non-linear" or "broad," at the outset, as being based on sectors, i.e., leaders who are able and experienced in the business, non-profit, and government sectors. Based on this definition, we identified 150 broad leaders to interview, who had worked as senior executives or representatives in their organizations (so as to ensure our subjects had amassed enough breadth to reflect on their experiences); and had worked full or part time in each of the business, government, and non-profit (including university) sectors. The typical subject would have worked full time in and transitioned often between two sectors (usually business and government) and worked part time in the third sector (usually non-profit). Of the 150 leaders we interviewed, 60 were based in the United States, 70 in Canada, and 15 in Hong Kong and 5 in other countries (Singapore, Russia, and the United Kingdom). They include leaders such as Jarrett Barrios, CEO of the American Red Cross, Los Angeles; Doug Black, Senator of Canada; Carol Browner, Senior Counselor at Albright Stonebridge Group; Bernard Chan, President of Asia Financial Holdings; Naheed Nenshi, Mayor of the City of Calgary; Jeff Seabright, Chief Sustainability Officer of Unilever; Stacey Stewart, US President of the United Way; Michael Wilson, Chairman of Barclays Canada; and Rosanna Wong, Executive Director of the Hong Kong Youth Federation.

To identify their repertoire of skills, tools, and mindsets, we conducted 60- to 90-minute interviews (on average) in a semi-structured format using a pre-defined list of questions. We asked them to: (1) narrate their overall education and career experiences with special attention paid to when and why they made transitions; (2) explain what unique skills and resources they accumulated in each context and transferred to new contexts; (3) identify examples of impact attributable to their broad experiences and resources; (4) reflect on lessons they have learned while building a non-linear career and advice they would give to someone pursuing one; and (5) examine the relevance of broad experience in the context of current and future challenges faced by organizations and society. Interviews were recorded and transcribed.

Insights were derived through a combination of reading transcripts, detailed interview coding/analysis, and research team discussions/problem solving.

On a more general level, our research has revealed that in addition to sector breadth, many of the leaders interviewed displayed one or several additional dimensions of breadth: (i) intellectual breadth, i.e., an understanding of multiple fields of knowledge such as arts, sciences, engineering, business, and law; (ii) cultural breadth, i.e., a nuanced understanding of how different geographies and cultures impact the issue at hand; (iii) functional breadth, i.e., a knowledge of how different functions can inform and work together, such as finance, human resources, and operations; and (iv) industry breadth, i.e., an appreciation of the interactions between different industries, such as the food, water, and energy nexus.

More specifically, our research, combined with our own personal experiences as broad leaders spanning multiple generations, as well as insights of psychological and organizational research, allowed us to identify six important traits of leaders who have successfully "gone broad." You might call them the Broad Leader's DNA—a common set of attributes that, together, create a compelling language and value proposition for how diverse experiences combine to form a leadership strength, not deficit. For each of these six distinguishing traits of broad leaders we then examined (i) its benefits and relevancy, (ii) the experiences that support its development, and (iii) its associated challenges and risks.

To validate our initial findings we conducted a review of the popular literature as well as the relevant academic literature, with the latter turning out to be rather tangential—most probably because the notion of building cross-sector careers has been relatively unexplored by academics. On the whole, we found sufficient support for our findings and refined/nuanced them when discovering additional and alternative evidence. In the following, we will present the six traits identified and illustrate them with select examples from our broad leaders.

THE SIX DISTINGUISHING TRAITS OF BROAD LEADERS

Intellectual Thread

This means the individual has subject-matter expertise on a particular issue informed by perspectives and knowledge across the dimensions of breadth. Having breadth is only as good as your ability to apply the resulting insights and skills in impactful ways—which can be particularly acute when oriented around a particular issue of focus. In a sense, this is where depth meets breadth, in that you need to go deep on something in order to leverage your breadth most effectively. The most effective broad leader, therefore, is not one who is a "jack-of-all-trades, master of none," but rather one that is a "jack-of-all-trades, master of one" (or some)! They develop a "T"-shaped profile—knowing a little about a lot of things (the horizontal bar), and a lot about one thing (the vertical "I"). That one particular thing is what we call the broad leader's "intellectual thread," which they develop by studying and acting on a particular issue or theme over time from multiple perspectives, building subject-matter expertise in the process. Developing and applying an intellectual thread gives broad leaders the capacity to "get on the balcony" to see the bigger picture and transcend some of the constraints that narrow leaders face when dealing with complex issues (Heifetz and Laurie, 1997).

Carol Browner, a broad leader and pioneer of the environmental movement for nearly 30 years, has environmental sustainability as her intellectual thread. She developed her expertise while serving in the grassroots lobbying group Citizen Action, as then-senator Al Gore's legislative director, as the head of Florida's Department of Environmental Regulation, as the administrator of the Environmental Protection Agency under President Clinton, as a partner in the Albright Stonebridge consultancy, and finally as President Obama's assistant for energy and climate change policy. "I have this interesting experience of having advocated for legislation as a non-profit leader, having developed legislation as a congressional staffer, having implemented those same laws while in the executive branch of government, and now having advised business on how the laws impact their strategies. Experiencing each side has given me a deep and holistic understanding of how each sector approaches the challenges they face," Carol told us.

In her most recent posting with the Obama Administration, Carol applied her intellectual thread in 2009 to bring together three government entities—the state of California, the Environmental Protection Agency, and the US Department of Transportation, ten automobile companies, including Ford, Chrysler, and General Motors, and several non-profit actors, including the United Auto Workers and leaders in the environmental community, to agree on a new national policy for fuel efficiency standards and greenhouse gas emissions for all new cars and trucks sold in the United States.

Carol reflects that, by virtue of her intellectual thread, she knew exactly what the private sector automobile companies could live with and without—and created a policy that worked for both the private and public sectors: "A clear and uniform national policy is not only good news for consumers who will save money at the pump, but this policy is also good news for the auto industry which will no longer be subject to a costly patchwork of differing rules and regulations." The Obama Administration estimated the resulting standards will save 1.8 billion barrels of oil over the life of the program and eliminate approximately 900 million metric tons in greenhouse gas emissions (Environmental Protection Agency, 2009).

Many people will not know their intellectual thread yet—and that can be a good enough reason to stick with what they know and keep doing what they are currently doing. But we think the opposite is true—when you do not know what you want, go broad and increase your chances of discovering the area you want to focus on in life.

Transferable Skills

This refers to the individual learning skills and capabilities that are unique to each dimension of breadth, and applying those that are transferable across contexts. The concept of president of the United States as "CEO" attracted significant attention in the 2012 presidential election campaign as a key feature of Mitt Romney's candidacy. Given his unquestionable success in business as CEO of private equity firm Bain Capital, the Republican nominee suggested that he could apply his management skills to "fix" the US government.

This general line of reasoning is not new; both government and non-profit organizations are often under pressure to run more like a business—efficient, strategic, performance-driven, you name it. That concept, however, risks missing the richness of broad leadership. Successful leaders do not simply apply models blindly from one context to another; rather, they accrue building blocks from each sector and experience, drawing upon them equally in order to build a successful, non-linear career and have impact. As a consequence, business has just as much to learn from the government and non-profit sectors as the other way around. This sentiment is reflected with the inclusion of "transferable skills" as a trait of successful broad leaders.

The broad leaders we have interviewed have found that mixing naturally developed and best-in-class skills from business, government, and non-profits yields an impressive and unique array of skills. As far as sectors go, business executives excel at allocating scarce resources to quickly capture attractive market opportunities. Non-profit leaders typically focus their more limited resources on advocating for marginalized persons, and devise creative ways to further the environmental and social good. Government officials bring competing interests together to create legal, policy, and incentive frameworks for the benefit of the general public. Similarly, the mindset and skills that studying many disciplines, such as the social sciences, creative arts, economics, and law impart can be remarkably inventive when transferred into new arenas—such as the flourishing application of design thinking to business issues like improving store layouts, operational processes, and customer service.

Hong Kong-based Dr Rosanna Wong is another great example of a broad leader who has acquired a variety of transferrable skills while working in the non-profit sector as Executive Director of the Hong Kong Federation of Youth Groups; serving on Hong Kong's Legislative and Executive Councils (part-time political roles); acting as a board member and advisor to HSBC, CK Hutchison Holdings Limited, Hutchison Telecom, and Mars; and earning graduate degrees in sociology, social policy and planning, and the arts. Rosanna brings a very unique perspective to her colleagues as the only non-business member of her corporate boards:

> I try to focus on long-term sustainability, culture and values—such as honesty and integrity. I feel my role is to be a reminder that money is not just spent on corporate responsibility, but also investments in helping nurture the right behaviors to create a people-centric culture. Perhaps this is because of my training as a sociologist, which helps me to look at how people mix together. I believe that how people work together is important to ensure higher efficiency delivery. In the end, it's all about people.

And the transfer certainly goes both ways:

> People in the business sector have a different perspective and I learned a lot from them about how to run a better, more effective and efficient NGO. I now look not only at risk management, but also at strategic and financial planning, as well as performance scores to make sure that our clients and those that we serve get the best out of us.

The government sector has a lot of relevant skills as well, as Coca-Cola found when it hired Jeff Seabright in the early 2000s. The company hired him to resolve its emerging water security crises in India, Mexico, and Thailand where its bottling plants were being forced to shut down due to excessive water consumption and poor environmental practices. Although Jeff had briefly worked as vice president for policy planning at Texaco, he was a relative newcomer to the private sector, having had extensive political and diplomatic experience with the Foreign Service, the US Senate, USAID, and President Clinton's White House Task Force on Climate Change.

To make a concrete business case for water conservation, Jeff drew upon analytical methodologies from his environmental work in the government and non-profit sectors and commissioned a geographic information system map. It showed that 39 percent of Coca-Cola's plants were located in the world's most water-stressed areas—precisely the places where the company expected the bulk of future growth and margins. This was the first time that the company's senior leaders had seen such a thorough and disciplined piece of work on the natural resources consumed by their business. It persuaded them to give Jeff a budget for several water-sustainability initiatives resulting in Coca-Cola reducing the amount of water required to produce their products by a third, and meeting their 2020 target for 100 percent water replenishment by 2015—5 years ahead of schedule.

Developing transferable skills requires you to first account for the core skills you currently have, and identify ways to adapt (and not blindly adopt) them to new environments. It is one of the most effective ways to show immediate value in new environments.

Integrated Network

This refers to individuals leveraging diverse networks to advance their career and knowledge base, build top leadership teams, and convene decision makers for impact. When we asked our interview subjects, "How did you end up crossing so many boundaries in your career—and what triggered your interest?" our respondents most commonly told us that a mentor, colleague, or friend pulled them into their newest position. Networks can be essential for any career; however, it is hard enough moving around in your own sector, discipline, or country—imagine how much harder it is when you want to significantly cross domains. Because hiring managers so rarely look outside their established sources of talent, having a diverse integrated network is even more vital to building a non-linear career—and experiencing its benefits.

Broad leaders depend on their integrated network to do more than just advance their careers, however; they help broad leaders expand their knowledge and diversify their perspectives, helping them take more creative approaches to life and work. By drawing from insights of their peers in other domains of work, broad leaders are able to gather information and tactics to problem solving that are typically inaccessible to their more specialized colleagues. At their most impactful level, the networks of broad leaders can also be employed to address and resolve tricky and complex issues facing society.

In 2010, IBM was having difficulty hiring qualified candidates for open positions despite high rates of unemployment and millions of people out of work across the US. Stan Litow, IBM's Vice President of Corporate Citizenship and Corporate Affairs, recognized the skills mismatch in the labor market for information technology companies and drew from his network to craft an innovative solution. Stan worked across sectors to create the Pathways in Technology Early College High School (P-TECH), a network of grades 9–14 schools with a rigorous academic program designed to equip students with both a high school diploma and an associate's degree in college along with the skills needed to compete for high-growth technology jobs (see also Chapter 20, this volume). He leveraged his broad expertise and contacts, coupled with his networks that included Chancellor Joel Klein at the New York City Department of Education, and Chancellor Matt Goldstein at City University of New York. Stan told us:

> I had a longstanding personal relationship with the City University of New York chancellor. IBM'S former CEO Sam Palmisano had a similar relationship with former New York City Mayor, Michael Bloomberg. Both were essential in getting us over difficult challenges. And because I had previously been deputy chancellor of the City of New York Department of Education, I had deep content knowledge and credibility with Chancellor Joel Klein and both educators and political leaders, and knew the school system and its structure first hand.

The expertise, funding, prestige, and other resources of Stan's network provided legitimacy for the project during its initial phases. The collaboration resulted in the establishment and implementation of P-TECH, now serving over 500 students in its fifth year of operations. Over half of P-TECH's students have exceeded New York state high school graduation requirements in three years or less. The program's results are so compelling that President Obama, after a visit to P-TECH with IBM CEO Ginni Rometty, featured P-TECH in the 2013 State of the Union address and announced a $100 million grant program to foster high school redesign along the lines of P-TECH. Later that year, New York Governor Andrew Cuomo announced 16 winners of a statewide competition to implement the P-TECH model. By the fall of 2016, there will be 60 P-TECH schools in six states, with 200 different industry partners, offering a range of technical degrees in areas like advanced manufacturing and health information technology.

Few of us have networks like Stan, but we all can develop an integrated network with sincere effort and time. To ensure you are building the right kind of network, focus on diversity and filling gaps across sectors, intellectual disciplines, cultures, functions, and industries.

Contextual Intelligence

This refers to the leader's understanding of the fundamental (and nuanced) similarities and differences between varying sector contexts, and their ability to fluently exercise empathy and leadership throughout. In his book *The Powers to Lead* Joseph Nye explores why some leaders succeed in one context and fail in another, noting that "many leaders have a fixed repertoire of skills, which limits and conditions their responses to new situations" (Nye, 2008). We have found that broad leaders meanwhile are adept at avoiding this limitation: they are able to adapt and adjust to changing circumstances and scenarios, and especially capable of adjusting their leadership style to the motivations, culture and language, performance measures, and decision-making processes of their organizational and cultural context. We call this ability "contextual intelligence."

This trait becomes particularly relevant when addressing complex cross-sector and cross-disciplinary challenges. It helps to intuitively appreciate the deep-rooted perspective of each partner at the table, and know what to say and do to maintain the collaboration's level of performance—not to mention your own performance, too. Underlying contextual intelligence is a seasoned emotional intelligence—the capacity for self-awareness, social-awareness, and, most fundamentally, empathy (Goleman, 2006). Some of these attributes are learned organically—pursuing broad roles and activities will naturally help you to refine the elements of your emotional intelligence, while others require deliberate attention to personal development. It is no wonder why so many professional vocations—lawyers, consultants, journalists, advisors, and bankers—feature often among the resumes of broad leaders. These jobs require an ability to operate effectively in different sectors, industries, geographies, and on multiple issues. Broad leaders need to demonstrate contextual intelligence in each new scenario, and especially during times of crisis when cross-sector collaboration is often necessary to resolve the problem.

When Coca-Cola was going through its water security crisis in 2001, Jeff elected to frame the issue not as an environmental risk, but rather as strategic, financial, and operational risks. He highlighted how the company's highest growth and margin plants were also located in the most water insecure areas, and therefore at risk of interrupted production. Furthermore, Jeff knew that Coca-Cola's success derived greatly from its marketing and brand value, and therefore used language that highlighted the emerging reputational risk of its water crisis in India.

> Turning it from a technical, environmental challenge into a marketing and reputational issue helped to show the issue's importance. I distilled my findings into a short, bumper sticker-type pitch, which used compelling graphics and company-friendly language that centered upon the risk to our brand if we did not deal with the challenge immediately.

In implementing his change and cross-sector partnership agenda, he also grounded communication in the incentives that each sector responded to (Coca-Cola's bottom-line requirements, the non-profits' sustainability mission, the needs of USAID's constituents), leveraged knowledge of USAID's bureaucracy to determine which specific departments to partner with, and on-boarded partners based on what benefits each organization could bring to the effort. The World Wildlife Fund, for example, had watershed expertise that Coca-Cola needed.

Jeff used his contextual intelligence by asking himself: Do I understand their needs and priorities? How am I being heard by my audience? Am I framing my point of view in terms and language that will resonate with them? On the face of it, this seems a fairly clear and straightforward method to influencing. Yet, it is notable how many new joiners fail to follow this kind of a structured approach to their new environment, often because they let biases—such as "business is fast-moving, cut-throat, and all about making money"; or "government is slow-moving, bureaucratic and lazy"; or "non-profits are idealistic, under-resourced and impractical"—get in the way. Overcoming such biases may be hard, but it is essential to building a non-linear career.

Balanced Motivations

This refers to individuals having to balance and reconcile several competing motivations, such as creating wealth, doing good, driving change, having influence, and improving themselves by crossing boundaries and ensuring they are creating public value. Broad leaders rely on their core values and deep motivations to guide their path to personal and professional breadth. They each carry with them strong "career anchors"—a term popularized by MIT's Edgar Schein to describe core motivations and values that guide career choices. Like many of us, however, broad leaders are motivated by many different things at once. Typically, they maintain a desire to create wealth for themselves and society; serve the needs of the vulnerable and the environment; seek power to have significant impact on key decisions; improve their skills, leadership, and personal lives; and drive change and advance progress. Not every motivation can or will be primary; in fact, some secondary motivations—the "means"—serve to enable a primary motivation—the "end." One broad leader told us she seeks power in order to drive change, and drives change in order to create wealth, while others had their own unique order to how their motivations interact and support one another.

The challenge is that few roles or organizations will satisfy all of these varied motivations simultaneously—especially given each sector operates with a different purpose and set of motivations. Wealth creation, for example, is strongly associated with work in the private sector, and even with certain industries within the business world. Others—like having the power to influence and lead large-scale change—are most associated with government. The non-profit sector, meanwhile, is typically most associated with helping vulnerable populations and/or protecting the environment.

As a consequence, broad leaders struggle to pursue all of these motives simultaneously; they necessarily have to make tradeoffs between them at any given time. Furthermore, sometimes several motivations are in direct conflict with each other, creating ethical and moral dilemmas in the process. That is where the most underlying motivation of broad leaders kicks in: their desire to create "public value," as noted by Joseph Nye. He explained to us in an interview: "It can happen in whatever sector they are working in. They carry that sense between the sectors." The desire and resolve of broad leaders to satisfy their varied motivations and create public value over time defines the fifth trait: balanced motivations.

Michael Wilson is someone who has developed and acted on his balanced motivations, and has made several significant career changes in order to do so. Hailing from Canada, he has focused on economic growth and competitiveness throughout his career, serving as chairman of both UBS and Barclays Capital's Canadian operations, and minister of finance and Canadian ambassador to the United States. Michael's catalysts for taking a non-linear career path were personal, especially when it came to involvement in the non-profit sector. Michael lost two high school friends to cancer in his early 20s—leading him to canvass in Toronto for the Cancer Society and take on increasing roles of responsibility as they required. More tragic still, he lost his eldest son to depression and suicide almost 20 years ago—leading Michael to devote much of his time to chairing mental health research, treatment, and fundraising initiatives in Canada:

> Even before our son died, I felt this area needed more attention. There are still challenges of stigma, and there are funding challenges. When you look at the burden of illness in a country, you automatically think of cancer and heart disease, but rarely of mental illness. There's a very high incidence of it—higher than people realize—and there's an ongoing cost to families and community.

Achieving all the aspirations within professional and personal well-being also requires broad leaders to develop clear personal priorities and a strong moral compass for when ethical or moral dilemmas arise—like Jeff Seabright faced while evaluating an offer to join oil company Texaco's global public policy team from the White House on the Task Force for Climate Change. Jeff was intrigued, but taking the job seemed implausible at first. On top of his lack of private sector experience, Jeff had come to think of the oil majors like Texaco as the "bad guys, the climate change deniers." Texaco after all was a member of the Global Climate Coalition (GCC), a lobbying group opposed to government regulation on climate change issues. So Jeff set a condition to Texaco's chairman Peter Bijur—he would join them if the company left the GCC, which would make it the first major US oil company to do so. When Peter agreed, Jeff felt compelled to accept his offer—having been convinced that he could do more to further his environmental concerns by joining the company than by remaining in government. "I took a lot of crap from my NGO friends for 'selling out,'" he recalls, "but within the first two weeks I was working on putting millions of dollars into efficient infrastructure to address energy challenges—and having much more impact. Did I really sell out, or was I moving up?"

So how do you deal with the choices available to you over the course of your path to breadth? The answer is that you find a way to understand, evaluate, and reconcile your own motives—to develop a "motivation map." In constructing this map, you will put comparative weights on the various motivations you have—determining which matters most to you and charting a course that reflects this weighting. Developing and navigating this motivation map will be the work of a lifetime, however, for the simple reason that your motivations will change as your circumstances change.

Prepared Mind

This means the individual exhibits a willingness to follow her curiosity and take the "road less traveled," welcoming the accompanying financial and career risks along the way. In all our interviews, we asked the question: "Did you set out to be a broad leader, or did it just happen?" In almost every case, the answer was "it just happened." After a while, we grew suspicious that so many non-linear careers had been based exclusively on serendipity. But then we were reminded by Bob Hormats—an accomplished leader in both business and government and the current vice chairman of Kissinger Associates—of Louis Pasteur's famous saying, "In the fields of observation, chance favors only the prepared mind." Bob explained that "Even though you don't know what's going to happen, you should be prepared to take advantage of any opportunity that might occur." It is then we realized what so many broad leaders have in common—a "prepared mind."

It describes broad leaders' curious—almost instinctual—ability to take advantage of opportunities from across the dimensions of breadth. It is by no means a structured and deterministic life plan, but rather a deep intellectual curiosity that leads you to undiscovered territory, a certain readiness to seek (and take) the road less travelled in life and career, and the mental fortitude for the inevitable career risks that ensue. Broad leaders reject the premise that breadth is "too hard" in the first place, believing instead they cannot afford not to take on the challenges and risks that come with tying together multiple areas of interest—even without clear foresight into how it will all successfully fuse over time. This is not to say that building a broad life and non-linear career does not require any thought and direction setting, however. Amongst other things, it requires some personal financial planning so that you are almost certainly able to say "yes" no matter which unique opportunities arise.

"Chance favors only the prepared mind." Think of that in the context of the story that Steve Jobs told in his 2005 Stanford University commencement address. He recounted how, at the age of 17, he dropped out of Reed College after 6 months, but stayed around as a drop-in for another 18 months before he "really quit." He added: "The minute I dropped out I could stop taking the required classes that didn't interest me, and begin dropping in on the ones that looked interesting…And much of what I stumbled into by following my curiosity and intuition turned out to be priceless later on." One of those classes was in calligraphy.

> Reed College at the time offered perhaps the best calligraphy instruction in the country. Throughout the campus, every poster, every label on every drawer, was beautifully hand calligraphed…I decided to take a calligraphy class to learn how to do this. I learned about sans serif typefaces, about the varying amount of space between different letter combinations. It was beautiful, historical, artistically subtle in a way that science can't capture, and I found it fascinating.

He did not think that any of this would have practical application, until ten years later, when he was designing the first Macintosh computer. "We designed it all into the Mac. It was the first computer with beautiful typography." He reflected: "If I had never dropped in on that calligraphy class, the

Mac would never have had multiple typefaces or proportionally spaced fonts. And since Windows just copied the Mac, it's likely that no personal computer would have them." Jobs never used the phrase "prepared mind" in this or any other address. But it was implied in what he said next: "You can't connect the dots looking forward; you can only connect them going backwards. So you have to trust that the dots will somehow connect in your future." That mindset, in many ways, is what prepared mind is all about.

Take the case of Jarrett Barrios as well, who started his career as a corporate services lawyer, became the first Latino and openly gay man elected to the Massachusetts State Legislature, served as president of the Blue Cross and Blue Shield of Massachusetts Foundation and the Gay and Lesbian Alliance against Defamation (GLAAD), and is now CEO of the American Red Cross Los Angeles Region. Jarrett was forced to "shamefully defend himself for not choosing a major in college." He instead chose to study a mix of anthropology, economics, and jurisprudence. Shortly thereafter, his post-secondary experience was supplemented by legal studies from a school that, notably, did not rank as highly as others he had been accepted into—but that had a reputation for taking a particularly multi-disciplinary approach to the pedagogy of law. His path upon graduation, into a corporate law firm, appeared unusual to his peers who similarly sought to participate in public life at a senior level in the future. While his classmates entered the public service directly, Jarrett's path appeared to be the slower route.

> My colleagues were 'ahead' of me in their pursuit of a senior governmental position for a few years after graduation. But 10 years later, when I was an elected representative and they were still making their way up the ladder in the public service, they looked up and said 'what did he know that I didn't?'

Having a prepared mind is a critical aspect to going broad—indeed, it is the one and only trait that gives you the confidence to take such unconventional risks in the first place. If it does not come naturally, it can be developed through forceful thinking and taking "small steps" as you traverse the dimensions of breadth. Critically, a prepared mind is not a one-time thing—it is a personal and professional journey. Few of us retain the exact same interests and objectives throughout our lives—we evolve. The question is, will they evolve to broaden or deepen our options, to encompass a wider or narrower range of interests and opportunities?

CLOSING THOUGHTS

It is inspiring to meet exceptional people who are building brilliant careers dedicated to addressing some of society's most pressing problems. But the leaders you have read about here are the exception to the rule. Society reveres specialists—figures of authority and expertise. But single-sector specialism has its drawbacks and should not be the path for future aspiring leaders. Instead, we need more future leaders to be broad—good at many things, and able to engage and collaborate with diverse stakeholders by drawing from multiple sectors, intellectual disciplines, cultures, functions, and industries.

Many readers may find that the individuals above are intimidating— perhaps impossible—persons to emulate. You may shudder that, in today's world, it is not that easy to be broad and effective. But going broad effectively is not as difficult and far away as you might think if you hone and apply the six traits of broad leaders. They are all within your reach and build upon innate characteristics with which you were born, such as being curious about new experiences, i.e., have a *prepared mind*, and then doing what feels right based on *balanced motivations*. And they probably reflect your better instincts too— such as applying *transferable skills* you are good at, calling a smarter friend from your *integrated network* to ask them about something you need help with, using your *contextual intelligence* to make an authentic connection with a new colleague, and learning more about a subject you care about because of your *intellectual thread*. If you embrace these traits and make them your defining qualities, you will be broad—and that will not just make society a better place to live in—you will be a more innovative leader, too.

Our call to action does not begin and end with individuals alone. Institutions across sectors have a large role to play in enabling this ecosystem of frictionless participation—in particular by valuing leaders with non-linear profiles and the six distinguishing traits appropriately, e.g., higher compensation, increased visibility, faster track to senior management, etc., and centering their talent management policies on seeking breadth, not just depth, of experience in key hires at the top, middle, and entry levels. Academic institutions—in which we place our trust to appropriately educate our future leaders—must also rethink their philosophy and approach to educating. University provosts, deans, and professors should ask themselves: What is the true purpose of education and are we preparing our students to lead in complex, cross-sector environments?

REFERENCES

Boh, W. F., Evaristo, R., and Ouderkirk, A. (2014). "Balancing Breadth and Depth of Expertise for Innovation: A 3M Story," *Research Policy*, 43(2): 349–66.

Brooks, D. (2013). "The Humanist Vocation," *New York Times*, June 20. Available at: <http://www.nytimes.com/2013/06/21/opinion/brooks-the-humanist-vocation.html?smid=tw-share&_r=0>.

Bunderson, S. (2003). "Team Member Functional Background and Involvement in Management Teams: Direct Effects and the Moderating Role of Power Centralization," *Academy of Management Journal*, 46(6): 458–74.

Bunderson, S. and Sutcliffe, K. (2002). "Comparing Alternative Conceptions of Functional Diversity in Management Teams: Process and Performance Effects," *Academy of Management Journal*, 45(5): 875–93.

Campion, M. A., Cheraskin, L., and Stevens, M. J. (1994). "Career-Related Antecedents and Outcomes of Job Rotation," *Academy of Management Journal*, 37(6): 1518–42.

Cannella, A. A., Jr., Park, J.-H., and Lee, H.-U. (2008). "Top Management Team Functional Background Diversity and Firm Performance: Examining the Roles of Team Member Colocation and Environmental Uncertainty," *Academy of Management Journal*, 51(4): 768–84.

Dries, N., Vantilborgh, T., and Pepermans, R. (2012). "The Role of Learning Agility and Career Variety in the Identification and Development of High Potential Employees," *Personnel Review*, 41(3): 340–58.

Environmental Protection Agency (2009). *Press Release: President Obama Announces National Fuel Efficiency Policy*, White House. Available at: <https://www.whitehouse. gov/the-press-office/president-obama- announces-national-fuel-efficiency-policy>.

Gladwell, M. (2008). *Outliers*. London: Penguin Books.

Goleman, D. (2006). *Emotional Intelligence*. New York: Bantam.

Heifetz, R. L. and Laurie, D. L. (1997). "The Work of Leadership," *Harvard Business Review*, 75(1): 124–34.

Mellers, B., Stone, E., Atanasov, P. et al. (2015). "The Psychology of Intelligence Analysis: Drivers of Prediction Accuracy in World Politics," *Journal of Experimental Psychology: Applied*, 21(1): 1–14.

Nye, J. (2008). *The Powers to Lead*. Oxford: Oxford University Press.

Phelps, E. (2013). *Mass Flourishing*. Princeton, NJ: Princeton University Press.

Tetlock, P. E. (2005). *Expert Political Judgment: How Good Is It? How Can We Know?* Princeton, NJ: Princeton University Press.

Part II

Engaging: Broader Views for a Better Capitalism

8

Understanding and Misunderstanding the Triumph of Capitalism

John Kay

INTRODUCTION

The triumph of the market system over the planned economy was probably the defining economic event of our lifetime, its symbol the collapse of the Berlin Wall in 1989. In the advanced economies of the West, increased government intervention in the economy, more or less unchecked through the 20th century, was halted in 1980 by the ideologically conservative governments of Reagan and Thatcher, with policy innovations that were widely, if often reluctantly, imitated elsewhere. Asia, China, and India followed some of their smaller neighbors into the market economy and the global trading system. These developments provoked the hubris famously framed as *The End of History* by Francis Fukuyama (1989; 1992), who argued that a combination of liberal democracy and lightly regulated capitalism was now an inevitable form of political and economic organization. If one country was the standard bearer for that new vision of the 21st century, it was the United States. If one industry was the standard bearer for that new view, it was the financial services industry.

Today, that assertion lacks conviction. If there were defining events in that revisionism, analogous to the breaching of the Berlin Wall, they would be—for politics—the collapse of the Twin Towers and its bungled consequences, and for economics the bankruptcy of Lehman seven years later. There is, evidently, no end of history—as, indeed, Fukuyama today readily acknowledged (2006). But the critique of the market economy that has followed the global financial crisis is, as it has been since the end of socialism, largely incoherent—an incoherence nicely captured in the demonstrator's slogan "capitalism should be replaced by something nicer" (Wolff, 2003). But the conventional defense of the market economy is not necessarily more coherent. Supporters often do no more than point to the wealth of countries that have adopted it—and to their own personal wealth. That is not necessarily a bad argument, but it looks tarnished today. When the people who are the largest beneficiaries of the market system have done such substantial damage to the prosperity of other people, such an argument becomes more difficult to sustain.

There are three elements to the triumph of the market economy. The first I will describe under the heading of "prices as signals": the price mechanism is generally a better guide to resource allocation than central planning. The second element is "markets as a process of discovery": a chaotic process of experimentation is the means through which a market economy adapts to change. The third heading is "diffusion of political and economic power." The economic point here is that prosperity and growth require an entrepreneurial energy that should be focused on the creation of wealth, rather than the appropriation of the wealth of other people.

In what we teach, in what we say, in our economic research, and most importantly in the policies we adopt, we put too much emphasis on the first of these elements—prices as signals to guide resource allocation—at the expense of the, possibly more important, second and third elements—markets as process of discovery, markets as mechanism for the diffusion of political and economic power. The result is that both supporters and critics of the market economy have often confused policies that are pro-business with policies that are pro-market. That confusion has both undermined the social and political legitimacy of the market economy, and led to serious policy errors that follow from a mistaken, or at least incomplete, understanding of how a market economy works. I will illustrate that proposition by reference to three areas of policy—financial services, inevitably, digital media, and competition policy. These sectors are only a topical selection from what could be a much longer list.

There is one central theme that runs through all three strands in the success of the market economy, a theme which I have called disciplined pluralism (Kay, 2003). When prices act as signals decentralized enterprises and decentralized information are brought together to create a coherent result. Markets as a process of discovery are based on freedom to experiment, combined with discipline: unsuccessful experiment is acknowledged and terminated. Markets as a means of decentralizing power represents the area where politics and economics meet. If the essence of markets is their pluralist character, then there is an inevitable association between the successful market economy and other components of an open society—freedom of expression, and democratic institutions. While it is evident that authoritarian regimes have operated market economies, at least for a bit, the combination is probably not sustainable in the long run. There is an important corollary: political freedom is jeopardized by excessive concentrations of economic power. Even if Fukuyama was wrong in his assertion of inevitability, the identification of an elective affinity between liberal democracy and lightly regulated capitalism was entirely appropriate.

PRICES AS SIGNALS

The model of "prices as signals" describes how self-interested agents—individuals or firms—might, through independent decisions, make consistent and efficient choices about how to organize production and distribution, and the allocation of capital, labor, and other resources. In a loose formulation, this idea has been around since the beginnings of economics. Many people interpret Adam Smith's famous remark about "the invisible hand," and his observation that it was not the benevolence of the baker, but his self-love, that furnished our table in this way (Smith, 1976). In an astonishing demonstration of the power of spontaneous order, decentralized markets manage the process of coordinating complex production systems better than centralized direction.

Although it appears to be an empirical fact that markets achieve this, economists did not offer a comprehensive explanation of why until the 1950s. That explanation proved both that a competitive equilibrium might exist and that, if it did exist, it could be efficient. That general equilibrium model based on the behavior of rational agents (concisely, "the model") proved highly influential, both in shaping the research agenda of the economic profession and in providing an intellectual basis for economic policy among people who may know nothing of the underlying arguments. The implication is that profitable transactions are socially beneficial: indeed that their social benefit is demonstrated by their profitability. A corollary is the "market failure doctrine," which is a central influence today on the making of economic policy: intervention in markets is justifiable only in the light of a narrowly defined list of market failures, which is generated by deviations between the world and the assumptions of the model—externalities, insufficient competition, information asymmetry (see, e.g., Balls et al., 2004 and the critique by Kay, 2007).

The model also provides a rationale for a certain kind of market fundamentalism. Not only is interference with market forces usually inappropriate, but market outcomes are efficient, even morally justifiable, simply by virtue of being market outcomes. Not only are markets good, but more markets are better than fewer markets. The emergence of new markets for financial products, for example, is presumptively beneficial. Among economists, the popularity of this approach is in part the result of physics envy: the model provides a universal explanation of economic affairs which resembles in many ways the equilibrium models that have proved so powerful in the natural sciences. Rigor has become the measure of the quality of a theoretical economic argument, where rigor means logical consistency, which readily finds mathematical expression.

Outside the academy, the simple message that government should go away and leave business alone has wide appeal to business people; and the simple message that greed can serve a constructive social role also has wide appeal to greedy people. The claim that profitability demonstrates, and may even be the measure of, public benefit relieves people of any worries they might have harbored about the utility of their personally rewarding activities. These simple messages, however, are extremely resistible to intellectuals who are indifferent to, or ignorant of, the theoretical arguments. They are also resistible to the population at large, which is not involved in the management of business, benefits only indirectly from the activities of business, and is not necessarily enamored of greed. The political world today is one in which both parties and voters in Europe acknowledge the empirical success of the market, but dislike almost every aspect of it. "The market" and "market forces" are the source of our prosperity, but are also terms of abuse. We have succeeded in providing a description of how markets work that is at once repulsive and substantially false.

The model probably contributes something to our understanding of how markets work. But that contribution is largely misunderstood and greatly overemphasized. One problem is that there is no real acknowledgment of uncertainty in the model, or, to be more precise, uncertainty is acknowledged only in essentially formal ways. This omission is of fundamental importance when the model is used to describe financial markets, in which trading in risk is the essence of the transaction. In such markets, the means of incorporating uncertainty into the model requires, in effect, that there is some true underlying value of an asset, which is independent of beliefs about that value, and that market transactions involve a process of convergence towards the true value. Experience has demonstrated clearly that this claim is a hopelessly inadequate account of the actual operation of financial markets.

A larger problem is that the model fails to recognize the extent to which a functioning market economy is embedded in the society of which it forms part. Property rights are not a fact, but a social construction, and there are many alternative ways in which these rights could be defined (Ostrom, 1990; Kay, 2003: 60). In a modern economy characterized by complex products, sellers generally know more about what they are selling than buyers about what they are buying. Trust relationships and supplier reputation are the market's mechanisms for handling this problem.

These observations are not theoretical quibbles: they are problems at the center of recent events. There were always two broad accounts of the reasons for the explosion of trade in complex structured products in the financial sector. In one, these developments represented a more sophisticated form of risk sharing and risk transfer, an exemplification of the benefit of the creation of new markets. In another, the trade was mainly driven by information asymmetry: the products were bought by people who overestimated their value (see the discussion between Rajan, Kohn, and Summers at the now notorious 2005 Jackson Hole symposium (Summers, 2005)).

The consequences of these explanations are very different. When structured products bring about more efficient risk allocation, the private profitability is mirrored by public benefits in the form of lower costs of risk. When products are bought by people who do not understand them, private profitability overall is illusory and disappears when asset prices ultimately revert to the underlying value of the asset. In retrospect, it is evident that this latter explanation is closer to the truth. Trade was driven by differences of information and interpretation, and the profits from it evaporated when these errors were revealed. The world is uncertain: not just risky, but uncertain, in the sense used by Keynes (1921) and Knight (1921). Not only do we not know which future outcomes will happen; we are also unable to fully specify what these possible outcomes will be. If we could predict or anticipate the invention of the wheel, we would have already invented it. Market economies do not predict the future, they explore it. That is a fundamental—perhaps the most fundamental—difference between a planned and a market economy.

MARKETS AS A PROCESS OF DISCOVERY

Hayek (1945), following von Mises (1927), continues to be the most eloquent expositor of the concept of the market as a process of discovery. His argument was a priori, but vindicated by the failures of the eastern bloc in the post-war era. These planned economies failed in the development, not just of consumer products but also of business methods. Their technological development was disappointing in almost all not related to military hardware. Centralized systems experiment too little. They find reasons why new proposals will fail—and mostly they are right in finding reasons why they will fail because most experiments do fail. Market economies thrive on a continued supply of unreasonable optimism. And when, occasionally, the experiments of entrepreneurs succeed, they are quickly imitated. It is a sad fact of the market economy that even for innovations that are commercially successful, few are commercially successful for the innovator.

If market economies are better than planned societies at the origination and diffusion of new ideas, they are also better at disposing of failed ideas. Honest feedback is not welcome in large bureaucracies. In authoritarian regimes, such feedback can be fatal to the person who delivers it. In less draconian contexts, unwanted messages can be fatal to careers. And when I talk about large bureaucracies here, I am talking just as much about large private bureaucracies as large public ones. Disruptive innovations most often come to market through new entrants—from Google, to EasyJet, to Amazon. Incumbents have good reason to be suspicious of novelty and protective of their established markets and activities. The health of the market economy depends, therefore, on constant replenishment of the business sector by new entrants. If, as planner or sponsoring department, you had been planning the future of aviation in the 1970s, would you have asked Herb Kelleher, the founder and former CEO of Southwest Airlines? If, as planner or sponsoring department, you had been planning the future of the computer industry in the 1980s, would you have asked Bill Gates and Paul Allen? If, as planner or sponsoring department, you had been planning the future of retailing in the new century, would you have asked Jeff Bezos? Of course not: whether you were the politburo or cabinet secretary you would have asked men in suits like yourself.

Watching the impact of electronics and the internet on children and grandchildren, makers of business and public policy have at least understood these issues. Committees of the middle-aged tweet about technology like embarrassing adults trying to have fun at the teenagers' disco. But, like those adults at the party, we are not really serious. Whether planners or governments of a market economy, we see industries through the eyes of established firms in the industry. And in doing so, miss the pluralism that is the market economy's central dynamic. That leads directly to the third group of reasons for the superior performance of market economies.

DIFFUSION OF POLITICAL AND ECONOMIC POWER

If I were to offer a one-sentence description of why some countries are poor and others rich, it would be that the politics and economics of poor countries are dominated by rent seeking and the politics and economics of rich countries are not. Rent seeking is the process by which the ambitious find it more rewarding to batten on the wealth created by other people than to create it themselves (Tullock, 1967; Kay, 2003: 287–300). Rent seeking takes, and has taken, many forms—castles on the Rhine, the Wars of the Roses; 10 percent on arms sales, or 7 percent on new issues: awarding yourself control over former state assets, stealing the revenues from your country's resource deposits, seeking protection from foreign competition, blocking market access by new entrants; winning sinecures or overpaid positions by ingratiating yourself with public servants or corporate employees. The mechanisms of rent seeking range from the application of armed force to victory in democratic election; the methods pursued range from lobbying on Capitol Hill and in the restaurants of Brussels, through access to the King or the Chief Executive.

But while rent seeking is ineradicable, we can have more of it, or less. Politics everywhere used to be dominated by rent seeking; factions would battle for control of the state and when they won such control would use it to steal as much as they could get their hands on. In much of the world, it is like that still. *It's Our Turn to Eat* is the stomach-churning title of one fascinating recent book about the corrupt—and moderately democratic—politics of modern Kenya (Wrong, 2009). We have come to recognize the resource curse—wealth from national resources does more harm than good in many countries because of the rent seeking it attracts—and foreign aid may have some of the same characteristics.

The ability of a political/economic system to resist rent seeking depends, in substantial part, on the degree of economic decentralization. If there are concentrations of economic power, individuals will try to get their hands on the rents these concentrations of power attract whether they are found in the public sector, in private businesses, or in groups of private business. The wider the extent of the opportunities this creates, the greater the tendency for individuals to gain wealth and influence for themselves by attaching themselves to power rather than exploiting their own individual talents and by developing distinctive capabilities in their own economic activities.

There is a strong tendency for private concentration of economic power to be self-reinforcing. This problem was widely recognized in America's "gilded age" at the end of the 19th century (Tarbell, 1904; Josephson 1934). The well-founded fear was that the new mega-rich—the Rockefellers, the Carnegies, the Vanderbilts—would use their wealth to enhance their political influence and hence enhance their economic power further, subverting both the market economy and the democratic process. These concerns were the origin of anti-trust legislation, a point often forgotten today, when the conduct of anti-trust policy is largely based on complex and speculative cost-benefit analyses of consumer welfare. The process that concerned Americans then is the problem we see in Russia—and elsewhere in the world—today.

The ability of a market economy to restrict rent seeking, its capacity to channel the desire for acquisition into channels that create wealth rather than extract it, depends on measures both to prevent the concentration of economic power and to limit the terms of access to such concentration. These are constraints on the economic power of the state: constraint on the concentration of economic power in large businesses, constant vigilance at the boundaries between the state and business, and a mixture of external supervision and internal restraint which prevents individuals who pull levers of economic power from using these levers to direct rents to themselves. Because the last decades have confused a pro-business stance with a pro-market stance, we have emphasized some of these conditions at the expense of others. Western—and especially Anglo-Saxon—societies have constrained the economic role of the state. These measures have reduced the scope of one focus of rent seeking—that by organized groups of public employees. But a substantial element of such rent seeking remains in areas that are inescapably within the public sector. And the explosive growth of corporate lobbying has become a major—and in the US an increasingly dominant—influence facilitating rent seeking. The expression of opinions people have been paid to hold is not free speech, but its negation. Corruption is a slippery slope, long and gentle.

There was a recent time, however, when similar restraint applied in large business: when people knew, as people in finance ministries and international economic organizations do know but people in the Kenyan treasury and private banks apparently do not, that a lot of money may pass through your hands without any of it being yours. The senior managers of corporations before the 1980s did not pay themselves large salaries because they did not think it appropriate to do so. They would have been insulted by the idea of a bonus or success fee in much the same way as a doctor or teacher would still be insulted by a bonus or a success fee. They saw their jobs as a responsibility rather than a reward. These conventions are gone, and the diversion of a substantial part of the rents earned by large corporations into the hands of senior managers is now a serious issue. This is, however, a side show. The larger issue is the concentration of power of large business, or groups of large businesses, and the use of the leverage that power gives to strengthen established positions and enhance the economic and political power further. I'll focus on two industries, which have traditionally been key to the interface between business and politics: financial services and media. The issue, which is common to both, is the malign consequence of viewing the industry through the eyes of established firms.

The problems of the financial services sector are too familiar to require much elaboration. The governments of the world have pumped unbelievably large amounts of money into the system: directly through recapitalization and purchase or underwriting of so-called toxic assets; more substantially, if indirectly, through wide-ranging implicit and explicit guarantees of liabilities. Even if these explicit guarantees expire, a "too big to fail" doctrine has been established, which means that implicit guarantees persist indefinitely. The criteria needed to qualify for these guarantees are, essentially, that the firm is large, well established, and unsuccessful commercially. It is difficult to think of a policy more directly contradictory to the dynamic of the market economy. Behind that public support for large banks lies the central fact of modern political life—that the financial services industry, and particularly its investment banking arm, has become the most powerful political force in the United States and Western Europe. The reasons are clear enough: the rents available in the financial sector have attracted much of the ablest talent in the two continents and created a generation of financiers who are both smart and wealthy.

Digitization is transforming all media industries (see also Chapter 13, this volume). The change was most immediate in music. You read regularly that the music industry is under pressure. The music industry is thriving. The demand for live performances is growing rapidly. As with so many leisure activities, people will pay much more for concerts than had traditionally been imagined. Recorded music can be distributed much more cheaply and at higher quality than before. Overall expenditure on music has been increasing, and so has the share of revenue going to artists. New technology is not a problem for the music industry, but an opportunity. New technology is a problem, however, for some established firms in the music industry. Music publishers attempted to use legal restrictions to prevent internet distribution, to preserve their established business model, and failed. Piracy took off, not as an alternative to legal downloading, but as an alternative to no downloading at all. The result of this resistance to inevitable change was that these businesses marginalized themselves. They ceded market dominance to, bizarrely, Apple (see, for an account, Witt, 2015).

We can already observe a similar problem in books. The idea of a universal digital library may be the most exciting development in books since printing. The issue is presented as a problem for authors. It is not. Not only will authors have expanded opportunities to make their work available, but the prospect of a digital library potentially solves the problem that has dogged authors and limited their economic opportunities for centuries: the absence of any direct contact between author and reader. The problem is, as it is in music, what is the role for existing publishers in the new era? Their ability to insist that policymakers must find one may delay the application of new technologies for decades.

No one knows what the shape of a world of digital media will be. Determining its future is a matter of perpetual small-scale experiments, mostly unsuccessful, and we will all be surprised to discover which developments turn out to be seminal. It is almost axiomatic that committees of wise people from the industry, and consultations dominated by vested interests and their acolytes, will not include those who are likely to be the important players. There will be no Steve Jobs, Jeff Bezos, or Herb Kelleher. Government should not attempt to shape the industry, but give maximum opportunity for the industry to shape itself. There are clear common elements in what is happening, and what should be happening, in both financial services and media. There is a need for policy, but a market policy, not an industry policy; policy aimed at supporting the market, not supporting the industry; policy towards breaking up the industry, not promoting concentration; policy towards facilitating entry, not conferring artificial advantages on established firms; and policy towards removing distortions of competition, not creating them.

THE WAY FORWARD

A policy for markets is, above all, a policy for competition. But competition policy has gone seriously wrong in the last two decades, and economists bear a large share of responsibility. The case for the market economy has three pillars—the role of prices as signals, the role of markets as a process of discovery, and the need to restrict the rent seeking which arises from the concentration of economic power. The recent development of competition policy has focused almost entirely on the first of these; and on the economic analysis, which is derived from what I described as "the model." The apparent, but I fear largely spurious, precision that this approach seems to offer has led to a naïve exaggeration of what economics can achieve; in particular, to a belief that it is possible to make case-by-case assessments of the costs and benefits of alternative market structures.

This task cannot be done, and the consequence of attempting to do it is a competition policy that, although quite intrusive, is also protracted and ineffectual. Competition cases today are arcane exercises in which experts exchange conflicting and inconclusive theoretical assertions and counter-assertions, often for years. Businesses can pay lawyers and economists sums, which, although absolutely large, are small in relation to overall turnover, to undertake this work. What these exercises miss, almost completely, is the wider dimensions of the power of markets. By focusing on the first pillar—prices as signals—policy underestimates the strength of markets as a process of discovery, and the vital political and economic role of markets in restraining concentrations of economic power. Markets are not well-oiled physical machines; they are a constantly changing, adaptive biological system. Pluralism is their motive force, their essence chaotic, their development inherently uncertain. If we could predict the evolution of markets, we would not need markets in the first place.

REFERENCES

Balls, E., O'Donnell, G., and Grice, J. (2004). *Microeconomic Reform in Britain*, with foreword by Gordon Brown. London: Palgrave Macmillan for HM Treasury.

Fukuyama, F. (1989). "The End of History," *National Interest*, 16, Summer: 3–18.

Fukuyama, F. (1992). *The End of History and The Last Man*. New York: Free Press.

Fukuyama, F. (2006). "After Neoconservatism," *New York Times*, February 19.

Hayek, F. A. (1945). "The Use of Knowledge in Society," *American Economic Review*, 35(4): 519–30.

Josephson, M. (1934). *The Robber Barons: The Great American Capitalists, 1861–1901*. New York: Harcourt, Brace, and Co.

Kay, J. (2003). *The Truth about Markets: Why Some Nations Are Rich but Most Remain Poor*. London: Penguin.

Kay, J. (2007). "The Failure of Market Failure," *Prospect*, August 1.

Keynes, J. M. (1921). *A Treatise on Probability*. London: Macmillan.

Knight, F. H. (1921). *Risk, Uncertainty and Profit*. Boston, MA: Houghton Mifflin.

Kohn, D. L. (2005). "Commentary: Has Financial Development Made the World Riskier?" *Proceedings*, Federal Reserve Bank of Kansas City, August: 371–9.

Ostrom, E. (1990). *Governing the Commons: The Evolution of Institutions for Collective Action*. New York: Cambridge University Press.

Rajan, R. G. (2005). "Has Financial Development Made the World Riskier?" *Proceedings*, Federal Reserve Bank of Kansas City, August: 313–69.

Smith, A. (1976). *An Inquiry into the Nature and Causes of the Wealth of Nations*, edited by R. H. Campbell and A. S. Skinner. Oxford: Oxford University Press.

Summers, L. H. (2005). "General Discussion: Has Financial Development Made the World Riskier?" *Proceedings*, Federal Reserve Bank of Kansas City, August: 387–97.

Tarbell, I. M. (1904). *The History of the Standard Oil Company*. New York: McClure, Phillips, and Co.

Tullock, G. (1967). "The Welfare Costs of Tariffs, Monopolies, and Theft," *Western Economic Journal*, 5 (3): 224–32.

Von Mises, L. (1927). *Liberalismus*. Jena: Gustav Fischer.

Witt, S. (2015). *How Music Got Free*. London: Bodley Head.

Wolff, J. (2003). *Why Read Marx Today?* Oxford: Oxford University Press.

Wrong, M. (2009). *It's Our Turn to Eat*. London: Fourth Estate.

9

Engagement Required

The Changing Role of the Corporation in Society

Andrew Crane and Dirk Matten

INTRODUCTION

The idea that corporations are simply economic actors with a purely economic function in society is becoming increasingly untenable. The power, scope, and influence of the modern corporation are such that today it is a key actor in social change and political deliberation and debate. When we consider the greatest challenges currently facing mankind, from poverty to climate change, it is now inconceivable that we can ignore the actions and agendas of companies. In this chapter we will address this changing and expanding role of the corporation, examining in particular the idea that corporations increasingly play a major social and political role in addition to their economic one. In doing so, we significantly advance the debate beyond simply "corporate social responsibility," which after all is chiefly designed to contribute to the economic performance of the firm (McWilliams and Siegel, 2001; Smith, 2003) and thus does not typically question in any meaningful way the more fundamental role of the corporation that we are concerned with.

The debate about the social and political role and power of the corporation is hardly a new one (e.g., Akard, 1992; Nader and Green, 1973; Useem, 1984), but since the turn of the century it has taken on a new urgency in the light of an increasingly conspicuous role played by the corporation beyond its economic function (e.g., Klein, 2007; Korten, 2001). Most recently, the corporate role in climate change (Klein, 2014), income inequality (Piketty, 2014), and the decline in democratic institutions (Reich, 2010) has been publicly discussed, often raising—short of condemning the entire system—the demand for an alternative approach to capitalism.

In this chapter we first analyze key drivers and pressures on the corporate world that have led to this changing and expanded role. We then move on to analyzing four specific areas of change—the involvement of corporations in protecting human rights, providing public goods, engaging in public policy, and furthering international development. We then propose that such shifts require us to move beyond simple business case thinking and instead engage in a serious reconsideration of the nature of three elements: corporate purpose, performance, and partnerships. Ultimately, we argue, the corporation of today will need to engage in more fundamental, systemic change, in order to create our desired societies of tomorrow. It is this, we contend, that should form the basis for a re-imagining of capitalism.

DRIVERS OF A MORE EXPOSED SOCIAL AND POLITICAL ROLE OF THE CORPORATION

In the way that they have been set up as shareholder-owned, manager-governed entities, corporations have a predominantly economic purpose. They are in many respects an ingenious coordination mechanism for natural, human, and financial capital, which, when skillfully combined, create value in a way humans could not achieve individually. However, the very success of the corporation as an economic institution has put it in a societal space far beyond this initial economic purpose (Ciepley, 2013; Scherer and Palazzo, 2011). Today they have new roles and responsibilities that are as much social and political as they are economic. Of course some of these aspects, particularly with regard to multinational corporations (MNCs) and their relative power over nation-state governments, have been debated for more than 40 years now (Vernon, 1991). However, such a political—or one might even say quasi-governmental—role (Matten and Crane, 2005) has only emerged as a widespread phenomenon, and indeed concern, in recent years. So what has been driving these changes?

A first group of drivers for an enlarged role for the corporation is clearly *political*, if not ideological, in nature. Since the 1970s we have seen the rise and proliferation of more libertarian economic policies in many countries. Often linked to economists of the Chicago School or politicians such as Augusto Pinochet, Ronald Reagan, or Margaret Thatcher, many countries have liberalized labor markets, privatized large parts of government-owned businesses and public service providers, and generally lowered trade barriers and encouraged the creation of transnational economic and political spaces, such as the European Union, North American Free Trade Agreement, or Association of South East Asian Nations. The fall of the Iron Curtain at the end of the 1980s exacerbated this trend towards an economic system where (more or less) free markets and private property are now the governing principles of most economies globally, often referred to as the "Washington Consensus" (Serra and Stiglitz, 2008).

Liberalization has thus created a space where national governments have gradually ceded more influence and governing space to private actors, most notably companies and civil society groups—whose ascent in importance parallels our account of a rising social and political role of corporations.

These political changes have paralleled a number of crucial *economic* shifts. The rise of international trade regimes, the emergence of global markets for capital, commodities, and labor, as well as the global spread of supply chains and production networks has created huge economic opportunities for corporations. Simultaneously, we have also seen a remarkable rise in size and economic influence of corporations. It is hence often by default that companies today attract social expectation because—be it General Motors as an employer in the US, or Walmart in China—they are considered as the actors whose economic power, resources, and capabilities are much more likely to address specific social demands than governments (Crane et al., 2008; Wilks, 2013).

Finally, corporations have assumed a much more exposed role in society because of *technological* progress. Over the last decades we have seen unprecedented innovation in telecommunication and transport technology globally. On the one hand this has made corporations much more visible in their dealings across the world than they once were, and it has enabled critics to coalesce much more easily to draw attention to the role of corporations in social and environmental problems. On the other hand, most of these new technologies, due to the political shifts mentioned above, are now managed, run, and governed by private corporations. Similarly, new technologies, such as the internet or biotechnology, have for much of the 20th century put corporations in a space where many public interest issues are enacted and contested in spaces predominantly governed by private companies. When privacy of personal information is discussed, whether in the US, Germany, or China—it is Facebook, Google, or Apple as private companies that are often in the limelight (Martin, 2015).

CORPORATIONS AS SOCIAL AND POLITICAL ACTORS

As a result of these changes, the social and political role of the corporation has both changed and enlarged. Four key areas illustrate these changes most profoundly: human rights, public goods, public policy, and development.

Human Rights

Human rights can be defined as "basic, inalienable entitlements that are inherent to all human beings, without exception" (United Nations, 1948).

Over the last few decades, increasing numbers of multinational companies (MNCs) have extended their supply chains and the markets they serve across the globe and are often perceived—in the absence of effective governments— to be the most powerful and competent actors to address basic human rights within their sphere of influence (Clapham, 2006; Hsieh, 2009). With most of these MNCs headquartered in industrialized countries, there have been major tensions between the values and standards expected in their home countries and those practiced by the companies or their partners on the ground in host countries in the developing world (Donaldson, 1996). One of the most striking aspects of this tension has been the call for companies to respect core human rights wherever they operate, even though their scope of operations may include jurisdictions where the protection of human rights is highly challenging. Consider, for example, the problems faced by Google in protecting the human rights of its users in China (Naughton, 2006), or the challenges Barrick Gold had to confront at their Pogera mine in Papua New Guinea in the wake of a spate of incidents of mine workers sexually assaulting local women residents (Knuckey, 2013). As a result, the role of corporations in assuming responsibility for human rights has today become a staple topic within most company policies on sustainability or corporate social responsibility (CSR). Another major development in this respect has been the emergence of the United Nations Guiding Principles on Business and Human Rights (Ruggie, 2014).

Considering that until relatively recently human rights were regarded as solely a consideration for governments, there is clear evidence that the general trend is towards more active business engagement. Increasingly this has necessitated not just respecting human rights, but also becoming involved in establishing appropriate systems of protection and remediation of human rights (Hsieh, 2009; Kobrin, 2009). Google, for example, has been involved in setting up the Global Network Initiative, "a collaborative approach to protect and advance freedom of expression and privacy in the ICT sector" (Global Network Initiative, 2015) and Barrick has responded to its problems in Pogera by developing and funding a non-judicial remedy framework in the region.

Public Goods

If we look at the provision of so-called "public goods"—such as public transport, water, electricity, health care, and education—we can again see that private corporations have taken on an expanded role in recent decades. Initially, the provision of public goods by government was considered to be part of responsible government catering to basic civic entitlements (Marshall, 1965). However, fundamental ideological shifts in public policy as outlined earlier have seriously questioned government involvement in the provision of public goods. Deutsche Bahn, British Telecom, or EDF today are all private companies. Electricity, telecommunication, or public transport can all be produced by private companies, however, how these companies provide and charge for their services often faces higher expectations from the public since such public goods are still considered basic civic entitlements rather than just consumer goods.

Public Policy

A typical strategy course in most MBA programs today will introduce public policy as an external parameter which smart companies should either seek to avoid, e.g., by finding favorable tax regimes, or exploit by adapting their operations to benefit from certain regulatory contexts. This instrumental approach has been discussed extensively in the literature on corporate political activity (Hillman et al., 2004). This perspective, however, proves to be too simplistic if we think of the role of business in public policy at the outset of the 21st century. To begin with, it is now fairly openly discussed that the degree of lobbying, revolving doors between business and governments, and other ways of shaping public policy has risen to an unprecedented level in many democracies: the total spending on lobbying in the US was $3.3bn in 2015, with some 12,000 lobbyists working in Washington (Collins, 2015). Although the US is often said to lead this trend, lobbying in Europe seems to have recently overtaken that in the US in some respects, with 30,000 lobbyists in Brussels allegedly shaping 75 percent of European Union legislation in some form (Traynor, 2014). While economic interests may drive such practices, they have a profound effect on the democratic process that simply cannot be discounted with the claim that it is "just business" after all.

The changing role of the corporation in public policy is not just explained by increasing levels of influence on politicians, but also by the involvement of corporations in entirely new forms of public policy. Whether it is child labor, environmental performance, or anti-corruption, private corporations and business associations are increasingly participating in regulating their own practices (Leipziger, 2010). That is, over the past two decades corporations have started engaging in the development, implementation, and enforcement of new standards designed to prevent irresponsible practice. The resulting voluntary standards are proliferating across different industries and countries, with the intention to tackle all kinds of social and environmental issues (Abbott and Snidal, 2009). Of course, they are different and noticeably "softer" than traditional governmental imperative regulation. This means that their relative success or failure in measurably preventing irresponsible practices remains a subject of considerable controversy (Banerjee, 2010; Vogel, 2010). However, what is significant is that they show how corporations have become much more engaged in self-regulation and other essentially political behavior as a way of addressing their social responsibilities beyond the economic. So while economic incentives may still be part of these initiatives, e.g., by introducing an eco-label that can be used to attract consumers, and governments may still be involved in setting up many such agreements, engagement in public policy and regulation—rather than its avoidance—is very much a part of the modern MNC's strategic portfolio beyond its immediate, short-term pursuit of financial returns.

Development

Finally, the area of development—in the sense of supporting the social and economic progress of countries with low standards of living—is another field that has seen corporations take a more active role in recent years (see also Chapter 6, this volume). Again, this has often been driven by the economic pursuits of corporations, but has taken them deeper into social and political territory. Consider when a number of corporations founded the Global Business Coalition on HIV/Aids (today GBCHealth) in 2001 to address the HIV/Aids pandemic. Many of these corporations were exposed to the economic impacts of HIV/Aids through their employees in developing countries, but looked to tackle the disease more systematically. Similarly, when Coca-Cola became involved in community water conservation in developing countries their "water stewardship" was initially spurred by the need to secure their own supplies and bolster their reputation. However, down the line their involvement has seen them engaged in broader areas of development. Examples abound: be it fair-trade sourcing, bolstering local entrepreneurship, or other forms of poverty alleviation—corporations have become major players in delivering many of the development goals that governments and aid organizations have tried for decades to deliver through other means (see also Chapters 2, 3, and 4, this volume).

The involvement of MNCs in "Bottom of the Pyramid" strategies has perhaps been the most visible manifestation of this shift (Karnani, 2007; Kolk et al., 2014; Prahalad, 2005). Companies have discovered that even the poorest communities can be active producers and consumers of their products, often in a form adapted to the needs, specific geographic, and climatic circumstances, and—most importantly—different economic situations of such communities. As a prominent example, consider the telecommunications industry, which has achieved wide degrees of access to mobile communication and internet services in many developing countries—with remarkable knock-on effects on health, access to medication, and economic opportunities for hitherto isolated communities (Vodafone, 2005). A similarly pivotal role has been played by the financial sector in developing micro-finance models that have opened up economic opportunities to many previously excluded communities in the developing world (Cull et al., 2009).

While these developments are by no means uncontroversial and far from being a panacea, our general point here is to outline the new and expanded social and political roles that corporations have assumed over the last decades—with consequences that will be examined in the next section.

IMPLICATIONS: TOWARDS A NEW FORM
OF ENGAGEMENT

So what are the implications of these broad shifts in society? Corporations have long been involved in social issues but the changes outlined here, as well as those outlined throughout much of the rest of this book, suggest something quite transformational is afoot that will require fresh thinking. Existing models of corporate social responsibility probably will not suffice (see also Chapter 10, this volume). Rather, we argue, corporations need to change in core strategic areas that are building blocks of a more long-term, socially sustainable, and responsible model of capitalism.

One popular answer is to re-assert the importance of aligning responsible business with companies' financial performance. The surge in attention to "shared value," for example, is heavily driven by the promise of aligning social betterment with economic value creation (Porter and Kramer, 2011). This type of thinking is often considered essential for getting the buy-in of executives, and indeed it is hard to conceive of an effective approach that does not consider firm success as one of its prerequisites (see also Chapter 17, this volume). But at the same time, we also have to recognize that thinking *only* in terms of the business case is not going to be sufficient when the stakes are human rights, public goods, public policy, and development (see also Chapter 11, this volume). Should a firm act to avoid using slave labor even if it is not good for business? Can companies turn off clean drinking water to poor communities that have no other reasonable access even if it can get a better return serving their more well-heeled neighbors?

The point is there are limits to the business case for social responsibility when we are talking about deeper social and political responsibilities. These are not just generous donations to help out but essential investments into the very fabric of society. Such investments cannot be made without any consideration of firm self-interest but they also have to be able to accommodate a broader sense of public service. We think that this is best captured in terms of the three Ps: purpose, performance, and partnerships. These three Ps, we suggest, are the essential elements in re-imagining the role of the corporation in any revised conception of a more responsible, long-term capitalism. Our framework is provided in Figure 9.1 and discussed in more detail below.

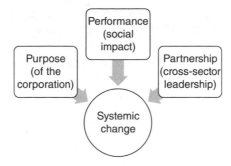

Figure 9.1. Three Ps framework for systemic change

Purpose

The discussion on corporate purpose has largely centered on the debate between those advocating a shareholder view of the firm and those promoting a more stakeholder-oriented perspective. Those subscribing to the former argue that corporations exist to maximize value for shareholders—and that this is the *only* true way of effectively evaluating executives (e.g., Jensen, 2001; Sundaram and Inkpen, 2004). Those arguing for the latter suggest that the purpose of the corporation is "creating value for stakeholders," including—but not necessarily prioritizing—shareholders (e.g., Freeman et al., 2004, 2007). In a sense, both views agree that the original point of creating the corporate form was to achieve a more efficient means of creating value in society. Where they differ is in what exactly that value is—i.e., just shareholder value, economic value more broadly, or societal value—and who that value is created for—shareholders or stakeholders.

The recognition of a broader social and political role for the corporation immediately requires us to consider this debate about corporate purpose (see also Chapter 2, this volume). If one believes that the purpose of corporations is to maximize shareholder value then we must see any enlarged role through this lens. So, for instance, if we are concerned about corporations switching off drinking water to communities in need, we need to find a way to either align these broader responsibilities with shareholder value maximization, e.g., by introducing incentives to encourage wider access, or we need to turn to regulation to force compliance with society's expectations. If we view corporate purpose more in terms of a stakeholder perspective, we need to consider what kinds of "stakes" are going to come into play. It is one thing to say that companies should keep their customers and employees happy but an enlarged social and political role requires deeper consideration of the rights and obligations corporations owe different constituencies in society. Many would argue that a broadened role therefore necessitates a redefinition of corporate purpose (Basu, 1999). Of course, there is much rhetoric expounded on the importance of defining *the* purpose of a corporation, but the reality is that companies can have a variety of purposes, and indeed the larger and more complex the corporation, the more likely it is to have multiple purposes.

One increasingly influential way of thinking about purpose in this way is to conceive of certain types of companies as social purpose companies—namely hybrid organizations that aim to combine social goals with financial sustainability (Haigh et al., 2015). As such, social purpose companies specifically identify their purpose as the advancement of social or environmental goals, much as a non-profit would, but typically seek to achieve these goals through commercial or market-based tools, as a company would. While many such hybrid organizations are boutique green companies or social enterprises, there are also a number of more well-known companies stating their purpose in such ways. Consider Patagonia, the US-based outdoor clothing company, which states its purpose to "build the best product, cause no unnecessary harm, use business to inspire and implement solutions to the environmental crisis" (Patagonia, 2015). Unilever also has an explicit hybrid purpose to "make sustainable living commonplace" while doubling the size of its business (Chapter 2, this volume).

Pursuing an explicit social purpose and combining multiple logics within one organization can create significant internal conflict and tension. These include challenges of aligning divergent goals and metrics, tension among employees with different value systems, and the need to balance short-term and long-term time horizons (Smith et al., 2013). Hybrid organizations can also struggle with mission drift (when commercial priorities shift attention away from the original social purpose) and challenges in discharging accountability to multiple stakeholders with different expectations and demands (Ebrahim et al., 2014). Consider SKS, the largest micro-finance company in India, with a mission to help the poor improve their lives. After the company successfully went public in 2010, its social mission came under severe threat when it became mired in controversy regarding its role in a spate of suicides in rural Andhra Pradesh due to forceful collection of loans and public shaming of clients. Police jailed dozens of SKS employees, including on charges of abetment to suicide—essentially driving people to kill themselves, a crime under Indian law (Associated Press, 2012).

An important development therefore has been new ways of creating more or less official categories for social purpose companies either through legislation or certification (Rawhouser et al., 2015). Benefit corporations, for example, are a new class of corporation in the US that are required to take into account their stakeholders and are accountable for pursuing a social purpose. Specifically, they are required by law to pursue a general public benefit—and may pursue a specific public benefit—in addition to profit; measure such benefit against an independent and transparent third-party standard; and produce an annual benefit report. By 2015, this new legal form had been passed in 27 US states since being launched in 2010. Well-known examples include Seventh Generation and Method, the home-cleaning products companies, as well as Patagonia, mentioned above. Not all attempts to redefine corporate purpose require a legal change. However, such legislation does have the effect of protecting corporate leaders from having to face legal challenges to abandon or reduce their social obligations in order to maximize benefits for shareholders.

Performance

Another critical area to consider in the context of new roles and responsibilities for corporations, and our second P, is performance. By this we mean the need for greater attention to be paid to: (i) the *level of performance* or impact the corporation has on society; and (ii) the *ways in which corporations account* for these impacts to the public and other stakeholders. The issue of corporate performance has traditionally been considered purely in relation to financial performance or other types of economic performance such as market share. As more attention has shifted to social and environmental issues, companies have invested considerable efforts in also assessing and communicating their performance on non-financial issues. This has been reflected in a growing number of companies issuing sustainability reports, and the gradual development of common standards such as the Global Reporting Initiative (see Chapter 15, this volume). One recent survey suggested that 93 percent of the largest 250 companies worldwide now issue corporate responsibility reports (KPMG, 2013).

The bigger question here though is whether—from the point of view of an expanded social and political role for the corporation—the measures used by companies or researchers are actually the most salient. That is, although there have been significant advances in determining the materiality of issues for reporting, many of the metrics used still focus primarily on inputs, or at best outputs, rather than actual outcomes for, or impacts on, relevant stakeholders. As Salazar et al. (2012) contend, "firm-level measures of [corporate social performance] tend to focus on inputs, such as the value of corporate contributions or number of volunteer hours donated, rather than the impacts of the firm's CSR activities on the intended beneficiaries (e.g., lives saved, improvements in health, incomes raised, increased happiness, etc.)." However, as Epstein and Yuthas (2014) argue,

> we know that measuring outputs is not the same as measuring success on the goal of increasing social impacts. The goals should not typically be about measuring numbers of children in school (outputs) but rather how many are better educated and better able to achieve a set of life goals possibly including employability

(impacts). This should not be about collecting more data but rather about collecting and properly analyzing the data that matters and is more relevant to the project's or organization's objectives.

The point is, it is still next to impossible to gauge what the real impact of a company is on society, or to the constituencies that are impacted by it. This is especially true for the impacts of the company as a whole, but even project-based assessments of CSR initiatives are rare and often poorly conceived (Salazar et al., 2012). Indeed, there is little evidence to date that increased levels of assessment and reporting have led to any meaningful impact on the perceived legitimacy of corporations. At present, companies are far more likely to consult stakeholders in an opportunistic manner in order to build consensus for what they are already doing rather than genuinely engaging stakeholders in a two-way conversation that involves them in meaningful decision-making about what constitutes performance and how it should be assessed (Manetti, 2011). As O'Dwyer and Owen (2005: 208) note, "many academic researchers have been critical of key features of emerging practice [of sustainability reporting], given its tendencies towards managerialism at the expense of accountability and transparency to stakeholder groups." Analyses even of leading social reports suggest that while improvements are evident, significant deficiencies in many core quality indicators persist (Manetti, 2011; Owen and O'Dwyer, 2008).

It is clear that, to date, despite decades of attention to corporate responsibility and sustainability reporting, companies have still not yet made much headway in assessing their real impacts on society. Of course, such assessments are extremely challenging. However, there have been a number of notable pilot projects that suggest some possible ways forward. Consider Puma's environmental profit and loss account that provided for the first time a full assessment of the costs of a company's impacts on nature. Puma's account placed a monetary value on all of its environmental impacts from the production of its raw materials right through to the point of sale. In 2010, Puma estimated their net environmental impact to be valued at some €145m. New methodologies for assessing social impact from an investment perspective are also emerging, driven by the "impact investing" movement (Bugg-Levine and Emerson, 2011). These can range from "reduction in average incarceration time," or "increase in percentage of employment" in the case of the New York State Social Impact Bond which targets ex-offenders, up to "increase in average household income" of farmers in East Africa in the case of the One Acre Fund, which aims to improve livelihoods in rural Africa (Social Impact Investment Task Force, 2014). If we are to take the changing social and political role of the corporation seriously, these performance measures will have to become more refined and widely adopted.

Partnerships

Finally, we come to our third P—partnerships. Collaboration among organizations from different sectors of society to tackle social problems has been widely hailed as a critical tool for addressing an array of serious challenges facing society. Having first emerged in the guise of public–private partnerships in the 1980s (Wettenhall, 2003), cross-sector partnerships have since become both more encompassing in terms of sectors and issues involved, and more expansive in terms of their global reach (Crane and Seitanidi, 2014). For example, the World Wildlife Fund-Coca-Cola partnership aimed at conserving the world's freshwater resources includes projects to enhance the resilience of 11 major freshwater basins across three continents, as well as targeting improvements in water efficiency, carbon footprint, packaging waste, and sustainable sourcing across the beverage company's global value chain (WWF, 2015). Or consider the Extractive Industry Transparency Initiative, a multi-stakeholder coalition of governments, companies, investors, and civil society organizations that is active in 48 countries. The initiative requires signatory countries to "disclose information on tax payments, licenses, contracts, production, and other key elements around resource extraction" with a view to "promoting open and accountable management of natural resources" across the globe (EITI, 2015; see also Chapter 19, this volume).

Thus, partnerships today are used to tackle everything from climate change to health and poverty to corruption. One recent survey reported that 90 percent of business managers thought that businesses needed to collaborate to address the sustainability challenges they face (Kiron et al., 2015). However, as the same report noted, "despite nearly unanimous consensus on the importance of sustainability collaborations, practice lags behind belief…less than 30 percent of all surveyed managers say their companies are engaged in successful sustainability partnerships" (p. 5). Partnerships are a key part of the response to the changing role of the corporation. There are three main reasons for this.

First, many of the issues that corporations now have to deal with, like human rights, public goods, public policy, and development are ones where they do not have all the answers. Much of the expertise in devising and implementing solutions to these problems is held in the public and civil sectors, and so business needs to engage in partnerships in order to develop effective strategies. Consider the case of development. Non-profit organizations have decades of experience in development programs. Even if corporations decide that delivery should shift to market mechanisms, they still need to understand the complexity of international development contexts in ways that only seasoned operatives from other sectors can bring (McKague et al., 2015). A recent example is Nestlé's "Cocoa Plan," an initiative to address rampant child labor and human trafficking in cocoa production in the Ivory Coast. The company has started to engage comprehensively in addressing education and other social conditions of their workers by partnering with, among others, the Fair Labor Foundation and the Fairtrade Foundation (Nestlé, 2015).

Second, even if corporations did know what to do in tackling social problems, they could not necessarily implement their proposed solutions without the participation of government and/or civil society. This is because many of the solutions to such problems require the involvement of non-market actors, whether in convening, delivering, assessing, or enforcing social programs. Consider the case of human rights. Although corporations have increasingly started to take their human rights responsibilities seriously, governments still have the ultimate responsibility to protect their citizens' rights while non-government organizations (NGOs) have taken on the critical role of policing whether corporations meet their human rights obligations. Hence, human rights can be considered part of the "global public domain" where multiple actors are active (Whelan et al., 2009). Corporate initiatives that do not also consider government and NGO roles and responsibilities are unlikely to meet with much success. Similarly, corporate involvement in public policy, e.g., through voluntary self-regulation, has often relied on governments to convene relevant actors together and on NGOs to act as credible assessors and enforcers of new standards for companies (Abbott and Snidal, 2013; Beer et al., 2012). Consider the "Accord on Fire and Building Safety in Bangladesh" that was set up by 200 companies, NGOs, and trade unions in the aftermath of the Rana Plaza factory collapse in 2013 but which is chaired by the intergovernmental International Labour Organization (Labowitz and Baumann-Pauly, 2014).

Third, corporations typically lack the legitimacy to tackle such problems alone—that is the public does not sufficiently trust the private sector to act in its interests when developing solutions to public welfare problems. International public opinion polls consistently show that NGOs are much more trusted by the public than either corporations or governments to do what is right (Edelman, 2015). NGOs typically adopt the position of representing the public interest and so it is their perceived moral legitimacy in the eyes of the public that is often needed in developing solutions aimed at addressing social and political deficits (Baur and Palazzo, 2011). For example, when Apple faced criticism about the labor conditions in their Chinese suppliers in 2013, the company engaged the Fair Labor Association to comprehensively and continuously audit their suppliers. Rather than setting up an in-house task force or hiring a consulting firm, they sought to enhance the legitimacy and credibility of their efforts through the external validation of an NGO (Fair Labor Association, 2012).

Partnerships are clearly not a panacea to solving complex global problems (Kolk, 2014). Successful cross-sector partnerships are difficult to get right and require time, commitment, and considerable resources in order to create positive alignment and genuine impact. The task for corporations, therefore, is to provide cross-sector leadership to ensure that partnerships not only become more commonplace, but more critically, that they reap positive impacts with respect to the social and environmental problems they aim to tackle. There are already many examples of companies taking a leadership role in developing effective cross-sector partnerships. Unilever, for example, was instrumental in establishing the Marine Stewardship Council, which provides standards and certification for sustainably managed fisheries (Chapter 2, this volume; see also Chapter 4, this volume). Walmart took a lead in developing the Sustainability Consortium in order to develop tools to quantify and communicate the relative sustainability of products (Chapter 3, this volume). But in general, business has tended to take a secondary role, with governments and NGOs often playing the main role in convening multi-stakeholder initiatives.

As these partnerships become more ubiquitous, more strategic, and more about deeper change in the systems in which corporations are embedded, corporate leaders will have to recognize that partnerships are essentially a changing mode of social and political action. More and deeper partnerships means yet more engagement in the social and political, challenging business leaders to develop a whole new set of competencies as "tri-sector athletes" (Barton, 2011; see also Chapter 7, this volume). A particular way in which companies have attempted to change the mindsets and capabilities of employees and engage more directly with civil society are volunteering programs. Many corporations now send their employees on company time to work for NGOs and community organizations not just as a CSR contribution by the company but also as a way to enable their employees to better understand and interact with partners in civil society. A well-discussed example is Pfizer's Global Health Fellow program which sends employees to do health-related work with NGOs and charities in Africa for long periods of time (Vian et al., 2007).

CONCLUSION: SYSTEMIC CHANGE AND RE-IMAGINING CAPITALISM

So where does this leave us? We have little doubt that the corporation will continue to play an enlarged role in our societies going forward. The question then becomes how do we best tame it to enable us to still reap the specific economic benefits that come from a consolidated, hierarchical form of economic organization—such as efficiency and coordination—while also ensuring that it lives up to its newly exposed role appropriately. A move towards a redefined corporate purpose, a rethink in how corporate performance is conceived and assessed, and a shift towards cross-sector leadership are not minor adjustments in our conception of the corporation and its role in society. In particular, changes in the corporate purpose—in some cases accompanied by corresponding legal changes in the corporate charter—will have significant implications for how corporations are governed and how concomitant norms of public accountability and transparency of companies will be reshaped. Taken seriously, these constitute a systemic change in the nature of the corporate form. But in our view it is this kind of systemic change that is necessary to take account of the changing social and political role of the corporation today.

And what, then, of capitalism, or more pointedly, re-imagining capitalism? The idea that corporations are not simply economic actors certainly might be seen to threaten some conventional ideas of capitalism. But it is important to remember that capitalism is not just an economic system but is also variously defined as a "social system" or "an economic and political system" that emphasizes private ownership of the means of production, a market economy, and the use of wage labor. Social and political questions have always been part of the debate about how capitalism should and does work. So the kind of systemic change we have pointed to here does not seek to fundamentally threaten any of the core elements of capitalism but it does suggest some movement in the type of capitalism we might aspire to. Systems of capitalism vary considerably across the world, and these national systems themselves have undergone continual change over time (see also Chapters 1 and 21, this volume).

The suggested "3P model" in this chapter certainly asks questions about the degree to which the rights of shareholders should also be mirrored with certain duties of ownership (see also Chapters 12 and 16, this volume). Similarly, a broader concept of corporate performance might not only extend market thinking into new social spaces but might eventually also limit the degree of how "free" we allow certain other markets to be, most notably those for labor and capital. Finally, an extended engagement with partnership might not only replace market structures in some stakeholder relations, but also transform labor relations in what is already now referred to in some countries as a "social partnership" (Iankova and Turner, 2004). In our view, any shift to a more responsible form of capitalism will by necessity involve some major changes in how we conceive of the corporation as not just an engine of economic value creation but also as a key social and political actor.

REFERENCES

Abbott, K. W. and Snidal, D. (2009). "The Governance Triangle: Regulatory Standards Institutions and the Shadow of the State," in W. Mattli and N. Woods (eds), *The Politics of Global Regulation.* Princeton, NJ: Princeton University Press, pp. 44–88.

Abbott, K. W. and Snidal, D. (2013). "Taking Responsive Regulation Transnational: Strategies for International Organizations," *Regulation and Governance*, 7(1): 94–112.

Akard, P. J. (1992). "Corporate Mobilization and Political Power: The Transformation of US Economic Policy in the 1970s," *American Sociological Review*, 57(5): 597–615.

Associated Press (2012). "SKS under Spotlight in Suicides," *Wall Street Journal*, February 24. Available at: <http://online.wsj.com/news/articles/SB10001424052970203918304577242602296683134>.

Banerjee, S. B. (2010). "Governing the Global Corporation: A Critical Perspective," *Business Ethics Quarterly*, 20(2): 265–74.

Barton, D. (2011). "Capitalism for the Long Term," *Harvard Business Review*, 89(3): 84–91.

Basu, S. (1999). *Corporate Purpose: Why It Matters more than Strategy.* New York: Routledge.

Baur, D. and Palazzo, G. (2011). "The Moral Legitimacy of NGOs as Partners of Corporations," *Business Ethics Quarterly*, 21(4): 579–604.

Beer, C. T., Bartley, T., and Roberts, W. T. (2012). "NGOs: Between Advocacy, Service Provision, and Regulation," in D. Levi-Faur (ed.), *The Oxford Handbook of Governance.* Oxford: Oxford University Press, pp. 325–38.

Bugg-Levine, A. and Emerson, J. (2011). "Impact Investing: Transforming How We Make Money while Making a Difference," *Innovations*, 6(3): 9–18.

Ciepley, D. (2013). "Beyond Public and Private: Toward a Political Theory of the Corporation," *American Political Science Review*, 107(1): 139–58.

Clapham, A. (2006). *Human Rights Obligations of Non-State Actors.* Oxford: Oxford University Press.

Collins, M. (2015). "Buying Government with Lobbying Money," *Forbes*, March 28. Available at: <http://www.forbes.com/sites/mikecollins/2015/03/28/buying-government-with-lobbying-money-2/#f355dbf45879>.

Crane, A. and Seitanidi, M. M. (2014). "Social Partnerships and Responsible Business: What, Why, and How?" in M. M. Seitanidi and A. Crane (eds), *Social Partnerships and Responsible Business: A Research Handbook.* London: Routledge, pp. 1–12.

Crane, A., Matten, D., and Moon, J. (2008). *Corporations and Citizenship.* Cambridge: Cambridge University Press.

Cull, R., Demirgüç-Kunt, A., and Morduch, J. (2009). "Microfinance Meets the Market," *Journal of Economic Perspectives*, 23(1): 167–92.

Donaldson, T. (1996). "Values in Tension: Ethics away from Home," *Harvard Business Review*, September–October: 48–62.

Ebrahim, A., Battilana, J., and Mair, J. (2014). "The Governance of Social Enterprises: Mission Drift and Accountability Challenges in Hybrid Organizations," *Research in Organizational Behavior*, 34: 81–100.

Edelman (2015). *2015 Edelman Trust Barometer.* Available at: <http://www.edelman.com/2015-edelman-trust-barometer/>.

EITI (2015). *What is the EITI?* Available at: <https://eiti.org/eiti>.

Epstein, M. J. and Yuthas, K. (2014). *Measuring and Improving Social Impacts: A Guide for Nonprofits, Companies, and Impact Investors.* San Francisco, CA: Berrett-Koehler Publishers.

Fair Labor Association (2012). *Assessments of Apple Supplier Factories.* Available at: <http://www.fairlabor.org/2013-apple-quanta-shanghai-changshu>.

Freeman, R. E., Wicks, A. C., and Parmar, B. (2004). "Stakeholder Theory and 'the Corporate Objective Revisited,'" *Organization Science*, 15(3): 364–9.

Freeman, R. E., Harrison, J. S., and Wicks, A. C. (2007). *Managing for Stakeholders: Survival, Reputation, and Success.* New Haven, NJ: Yale University Press.

Global Network Initiative (2015). Available at: <https://www.globalnetworkinitiative. org>.

Haigh, N., Walker, J., Bacq, S., and Kickul, J. (2015). "Hybrid Organizations: Origins, Strategies, Impacts, and Implications," *California Management Review*, 57(3): 5–12.

Hillman, A. J., Keim, G. D., and Schuler, D. (2004). "Corporate Political Activity: A Review and Research Agenda," *Journal of Management*, 30(6): 837–57.

Hsieh, N. (2009). "Does Global Business Have a Responsibility to Promote Just Institutions?" *Business Ethics Quarterly*, 19(2): 251–73.

Iankova, E. and Turner, L. (2004). "Building the New Europe: Western and Eastern Roads to Social Partnership," *Industrial Relations Journal*, 35(1): 76–92.

Jensen, M. C. (2001). "Value Maximization, Stakeholder Theory, and the Corporate Objective Function," *Journal of Applied Corporate Finance*, 14(3): 8–21.

Karnani, A. (2007). "The Misfortune at the Bottom of the Pyramid," *Greener Management International*, 51: 99–110.

Kiron, D., Kruschwitz, N., Haanaes, K., and Reeves, M. (2015). "Joining Forces: Collaboration and Leadership for Sustainability," *MIT Sloan Management Review*, January 12. Available at: <http://sloanreview.mit.edu/projects/joining-forces/>.

Klein, N. (2007). *The Shock Doctrine: The Rise of Disaster Capitalism.* Toronto: Alfred A. Knopf Canada.

Klein, N. (2014). *This Changes Everything: Capitalism vs. the Climate.* New York: Simon and Schuster.

Knuckey, S. (2013). "On Australia's Doorstep: Gold, Rape, and Injustice," *Medical Journal of Australia*, 199(3), July 22: 1.

Kobrin, S. J. (2009). "Private Political Authority and Public Responsibility: Transnational Politics, Transnational Firms and Human Rights," *Business Ethics Quarterly*, 19(3): 349–74.

Kolk, A. (2014). "Partnerships as a Panacea for Addressing Global Problems? On Rationale, Context, Actors, Impact and Limitations," in M. M. Seitanidi and A. Crane (eds), *Social Partnerships and Responsible Business: A Research Handbook.* London: Routledge, pp. 15–43.

Kolk, A., Rivera-Santos, M., and Rufin, C. R. (2014). "Reviewing a Decade of Research on the 'Base/Bottom of the Pyramid' (BOP) Concept," *Business and Society*, 53(3): 338–77.

Korten, D. C. (2001). *When Corporations Rule the World*, 2nd ed. Bloomfield, CT: Kumarian Press.

KPMG. (2013). *International Survey of Corporate Responsibility Reporting.* Amsterdam: KPMG.

Labowitz, S. and Baumann-Pauly, D. (2014). "Business as Usual Is Not an Option: Supply Chains Sourcing after Rana Plaza," Stern Center for Business and Human Rights. Available at: <http://stern.nyu.edu/sites/default/files/assets/documents/con_047408.pdf>.

Leipziger, D. (2010). *The Corporate Responsibility Code Book,* 2nd ed. Sheffield: Greenleaf.

McKague, K., Wheeler, D., and Karnani, A. (2015). "An Integrated Approach to Poverty Alleviation: Roles of the Private Sector, Government and Civil Society," in V. Bitzer, R. Hamann, M. Hall, and E. W. Griffin-El (eds), *The Business of Social and Environmental Innovation.* Heidelberg: Springer, pp. 129–45.

McWilliams, A. and Siegel, D. (2001). "Corporate Social Responsibility: A Theory of the Firm Perspective," *Academy of Management Review,* 26(1): 117–27.

Manetti, G. (2011). "The Quality of Stakeholder Engagement in Sustainability Reporting: Empirical Evidence and Critical Points," *Corporate Social Responsibility and Environmental Management,* 18(2): 110–22.

Marshall, T. H. (1965). *Class, Citizenship and Social Development.* New York: Anchor Books.

Martin, K. E. (2015). "Ethical Issues in the Big Data Industry," *MIS Quarterly Executive,* 14(2): 67–85.

Matten, D. and Crane, A. (2005). "Corporate Citizenship: Towards an Extended Theoretical Conceptualization," *Academy of Management Review,* 30(1): 166–79.

Nader, R. and Green, M. J. (1973). *Corporate Power in America.* New York: Grossman Publishers.

Naughton, J. (2006). "Google's Founding Principles Fall at Great Firewall of China," *Observer,* January 29.

Nestlé (2015). *Nestlé Cocoa Plan.* Available at: <http://www.nestlecocoaplan.com>.

O'Dwyer, B. and Owen, D. L. (2005). "Assurance Statement Practice in Environmental, Social and Sustainability Reporting: A Critical Evaluation," *British Accounting Review,* 37(2): 205–29.

Owen, D. L. and O'Dwyer, B. (2008). "Corporate Social Responsibility: The Reporting and Assurance Dimension," in A. Crane, D. Matten, A. McWilliams, J. Moon, and D. Siegel (eds), *The Oxford Handbook of Corporate Social Responsibility.* Oxford: Oxford University Press, pp. 384–409.

Patagonia (2015). *Our Reason of Being.* Available at: <http://www.patagonia.com/ca/patagonia.go?assetid=2047>.

Piketty, T. (2014). *Capital in the 21st Century.* Cambridge, MA: Harvard University Press.

Porter, M. E. and Kramer, M. R. (2011). "Creating Shared Value," *Harvard Business Review,* 89(2): 62–77.

Prahalad, C. K. (2005). *The Fortune at the Bottom of the Pyramid.* Upper Saddle River, NJ: Wharton School Publishing.

Rawhouser, H., Cummings, M. E., and Crane, A. (2015). "Benefit Corporation Legislation and the Emergence of a Social Hybrid Category," *California Management Review,* 57(3): 13–35.

Reich, R. B. (2010). *Aftershock: The Next Economy and America's Future*. New York: Alfred A. Knopf.

Ruggie, J. G. (2014). "Global Governance and 'New Governance Theory': Lessons from Business and Human Rights," *Global Governance*, 20(1): 5–17.

Salazar, J., Husted, B. W., and Biehl, M. (2012). "Thoughts on the Evaluation of Corporate Social Performance through Projects," *Journal of Business Ethics*, 105(2): 175–86.

Scherer, A. G. and Palazzo, G. (2011). "The New Political Role of Business in a Globalized World: A Review of a New Perspective on CSR and Its Implications for the Firm, Governance, and Democracy," *Journal of Management Studies*, 48(4): 899–931.

Serra, N. and Stiglitz, J. E. (2008). *The Washington Consensus Reconsidered: Towards a New Global Governance*. Oxford: Oxford University Press.

Smith, N. C. (2003). "Corporate Social Responsibility: Whether or How?" *California Management Review*, 45(4): 52–76.

Smith, W. K., Gonin, M., and Besharov, M. L. (2013). "Managing Social-Business Tensions: A Review and Research Agenda for Social Enterprise," *Business Ethics Quarterly*, 23(3): 407–42.

Social Impact Investment Task Force (2014). *Measuring Impact*. Available at: <http://www.thegiin.org/binary-data/IMWG_Whitepaper.pdf>.

Sundaram, A. K. and Inkpen, A. C. (2004). "The Corporate Objective Revisited," *Organization Science*, 15(3): 350–63.

Traynor, I. (2014). "30,000 Lobbyists and Counting: Is Brussels under Corporate Sway?" *Guardian*, May 8.

United Nations (1948). *The Universal Declaration of Human Rights*. New York: United Nations. Available at: <http://www.un.org/Overview/rights.html>.

Useem, M. (1984). *The Inner Circle: Large Corporations and the Rise of Business Political Activity in the US and UK*. Oxford: Oxford University Press.

Vernon, R. (1991). "Sovereignty at Bay: Twenty Years After," *Millennium: Journal of International Studies*, 20(2): 191–5.

Vian, T., McCoy, K., Richards, S. C., Connelly, P., and Feeley, F. (2007). "Corporate Social Responsibility in Global Health: The Pfizer Global Health Fellows International Volunteering Program," *Human Resource Planning*, 30(1): 30–5.

Vodafone (2005). *Africa: The Impact of Mobile Phones*, Vodafone Policy Paper Series, No. 3. Available at: <http://www.vodafone.com/content/dam/vodafone/about/public_policy/policy_papers/public_policy_series_2.pdf>.

Vogel, D. (2010). "The Private Regulation of Global Corporate Conduct: Achievements and Limitations," *Business and Society*, 49(1): 68–87.

Wettenhall, R. (2003). "The Rhetoric and Reality of Public-Private Partnerships," *Public Organization Review*, 3(1): 77–107.

Whelan, G., Moon, J., and Orlitzky, M. (2009). "Human Rights, Transnational Corporations and Embedded Liberalism: What Chance Consensus?" *Journal of Business Ethics*, 87(2): 367–83.

Wilks, S. (2013). *The Political Power of the Business Corporation*. Cheltenham: Edward Elgar.

WWF (2015). "Renewing Our Partnership. Expanding Our Impact." Available at: <http://www.worldwildlife.org/partnerships/coca-cola>.

10

Responsible Capitalism

Business for the 21st Century

R. Edward Freeman, Bidhan L. Parmar, and Kirsten E. Martin

INTRODUCTION

The last ten years have seen clarion calls for the reform of capitalism, as evidenced by the chapters in the present volume. However, most calls fall well short of what is needed, and represent only partial success. The main reason for a lack of thoroughgoing reform is the standard story of business and capitalism that is deeply embedded in our culture in the West and, indeed, has taken hold around the world. This main narrative about the nature of business and capitalism focuses on the pursuit of profits and "the physics of money" (Freeman et al., 2010) as the main characters in the story. Human actors are depicted as self-interested economic beings who are in constant competition with each other, either individually or within their business organizations. Most attempts at reform retain this standard narrative.

True reform of the idea of capitalism must address this underlying narrative and propose a different story, and that is our task here. In these few pages we can only briefly sketch the story; however, the good news is that this new narrative of business is being realized every day by a collection of companies that span the spectrum from start-ups to multinationals (see, for example, Sisodia et al., 2014; Mackey and Sisodia, 2014). Indeed, we shall argue that once we understand this new narrative we can become more aware of how its main tenets have always been present, if underemphasized, in great businesses and business leadership.

We proceed as follows. In the next section we sketch the tenets of the old narrative more precisely, and we highlight some of the partial suggestions for reform. Then we turn to a set of principles developed by a group of scholars over the last 40 years in what has come to be called "stakeholder theory," and suggest that these stakeholder principles are more useful in understanding how businesses need to operate in the 21st century. Finally we summarize with some principles of what we call "Responsible Capitalism."

SOME PARTIAL SOLUTIONS

The standard understanding of business by many is mainly from an economic point of view. In this view there are buyers and sellers, each looking to attain what the other offers at the lowest possible price. Economic theory is a set of propositions about the conditions under which this is possible and is one of the main vocabularies through which we understand business. The most common understanding goes something like this: business is about maximizing the returns—measured in profits, or stock price, or some such financial measure—to the owners of capital, i.e., shareholders, banks, bondholders, etc. By seeking to maximize the interests of these owners, society is better off, at least according to certain strands of the theory (Friedman, 1970; Jensen and Meckling, 1976). In addition, in order to maximize their investment, owners of capital must adequately control the activities of the business. In short, we can see business people on this view as solely concerned with profits and money. Further, in the language of economics human beings are typically depicted as only caring about—and maximizing—their own self-interest, where as in reality people may also be other regarding. The drive to compete and win is the ultimate energizing force of business, and the realization of that drive makes society better off.

There is much that is wrong with this characterization of business and capitalism, not the least of which that it is something of a "straw man" argument—easily blown over, as well as a characterization of actual practice. However, the picture does resonate with the popular conception that business is primarily about profits, money, and self-interest. We shall leave a more nuanced parsing of this view for another occasion or other scholars (see Chapter 8, this volume). Suffice it here to say that there have been calls for reform, especially given the global financial crisis (GFC) that has been laid directly on the doorstep of this view of capitalism.

For starters, some have argued, since Marx, that the primary deficiency of capitalism is that it pits "capital" against "labor" (Jameson, 1991). In such a battle, capital is bound to win, unless labor can organize, call strikes, etc. In modern terms, some theorists have called for more participation in the management of the business by its employees, not just its executives. Companies such as Toyota, who have empowered assembly line employees to be responsible for product and manufacturing quality, have indeed outperformed their more classical capitalist rivals such as General Motors. Many have argued that pitting capital versus labor is a false dichotomy (Follett, 2011). It is surely in the interests of owners, managers, and employees to cooperate together to create value. However, the old story of business says that this value is always claimed by the owners of capital at the expense of labor. This assumption prevents more thoroughgoing reform.

Second, some have argued that we need to take more account of the role of government. According to the standard narrative (Freeman et al., 2010), the appropriate role of government is to regulate the otherwise unbridled search for profits by businesses; without regulators, business would be allowed to create havoc for society. This role of government is often attributed to Keynes and his followers. Government action is as necessary as is the tending of a gardener to a garden, according to their metaphor (Keynes, 2006). Without government there would be chaos and disorder. Whether the modern-day monetarists such as Friedman agree or disagree with Keynes makes no difference. The idea of government as a necessary actor to ameliorate the fluctuations of the market and the behavior of business is the same.

Surely, the GFC taught us that business does not exist in a vacuum. Rather, we should see it as an institution that is embedded in other societal institutions, with government being one of these. There have been a number of calls for regulation, since the GFC, as well as real regulatory reform, such as Dodd-Frank in the United States, and a number of regulations on executive pay in other parts of the world. Again, the problem is that the basic assumptions about business remain the same. Dodd-Frank assumes that businesses and banks remain best described as driven by profit, and that there should be side constraints imposed on this "natural" drive. Reform is again piecemeal and partial.

Finally, there are a number of reforms that are aimed at improving "corporate governance" by paying more attention variously to the interests of shareholders, executives, and employees in the basic structures of boards of directors and the day-to-day management of the business. All of these reforms are well meaning yet they stop short of questioning the basic assumptions of business (Bebchuk, 2006). It is to those basic assumptions that we now turn.

STAKEHOLDER THEORY AND THE BASICS OF BUSINESS

What makes any business successful and sustainable over time? The answer from a practical point of view is that it continuously creates value for its customers, suppliers, employees, communities (and civil society), and its financiers. If it loses the support of any one of these groups, then it is vulnerable to failure. If it ignores any one of these groups over time in a free society, that group uses the political process to enforce its claims. Business is a voluntary activity, for the most part. And, those who engage with a business do so voluntarily, since they usually have some amount of choice about whether to do so. Of course, the existence of choice depends on the underlying structure of society, but as in the case of neoclassical economics, we want to assume that some form of property rights or some other basic moral regime can be appealed to in order to give business some legitimacy—issues that are complex and beyond the scope of this chapter.

So, any business must create some value for its customers with products and services that make their lives better off, so that customers are willing to pay for them. Any business must work with suppliers, as their customers, for the same reasons. Businesses must create value for employees so that they are willing to learn how to operate various aspects of the business. And, research is clear that the more employees are engaged in the business, the more successful the business (Edmans et al., 2014). It is a bit more controversial that business must create value for communities, but nonetheless it is true. Communities have often spoken out via the regulatory process or the courts and prevented a particular business from operating within its boundaries. More often communities have sought restitution when a business has damaged a community. And, of course, any business must have the support of its financiers, a point acknowledged by the old narrative.

However, we need to go further. The interests of each of these stakeholders do not exist in isolation. How engaged our employees are surely affects our ability to innovate and produce quality products for our customers, and there are similarities among all stakeholders. There is now a burgeoning and substantial literature on how stakeholder interests affect all areas of business (see Freeman et al., 2010; and Parmar et al., 2010 for the arguments and references). Indeed, all real businesses continually try and satisfy stakeholders. The introduction of this simple and practical idea of "creating value for stakeholders" turns the old narrative on its head (see also Chapter 12, this volume). In fact, we can suggest a number of different assumptions that form this new narrative of business, which are summarized in Table 10.1. Please note that we are not trying to be complete and mutually exclusive here, but merely aim to illustrate the kind of ideas that are necessary to really reform our old idea of business and capitalism.

Let us discuss each of these in turn:

The Unit of Analysis Assumption

A useful unit of analysis of business is the set of stakeholder relationships rather than discrete economic transactions. Most businesses consist of the voluntary cooperation of at least customers, suppliers, employees, communities (including civil society), and financiers. This cooperation includes the ability to make agreements that extend over time periods based on fairness and trust, rather than merely transaction by transaction. Value gets created for each stakeholder because each can freely agree to cooperate with the others.

Table 10.1. Changing the assumptions of the business narrative

New assumption		Replaces old assumption	Implications
The unit of analysis assumption	Businesses consist of the voluntary cooperation of at least customers, suppliers, employees, communities (including civil society), and financiers.	Business is conducted transaction by transaction.	If capitalism is to flourish it will be because individuals and groups of individuals can work together to create value for each other. Collaboration only works when there is freedom of association and choice.
The interdependence of stakeholders assumption	There is a jointness to stakeholder interests. Each stakeholder contributes to the value that is created for the others.	Executives have to make tradeoffs where the value created for one shareholder reduces the value created for stakeholders.	Business is fundamentally a cooperative enterprise built to create value, trade, and make ourselves, and others, better off.
The complexity of human motivation assumption	We are pro-social, language-using collaborators. And, most of the time we aspire to be a part of something that is larger than our own individual self-interest.	We are primarily self-interested and opportunistic.	Most of us, most of the time, want to and actually do take responsibility for the effects of our actions on others.

Most people keep most of their agreements most of the time (see below for its underlying moral framework). By looking at a large group of stakeholder relationships, rather than a single transaction, scholars and practitioners can better understand the effects of managerial decisions on a broader system of relationships. This is important because it allows us to create ways to make decisions that benefit the ecosystem of stakeholder relationships, rather than trying to maximize a particular variable within a transaction and then causing value-destroying consequences in other areas.

The Interdependence of Stakeholders Assumption

There is a "jointness" to stakeholder interests. For instance, employee well-being is connected to customer well-being, etc. Each stakeholder contributes to the value that is created for the others. Value is created within the context of others. And, rarely is this process reducible to mere contracts. The task of the executive is to continuously work to get stakeholder interests going in the same direction. This works best when executives see the interdependence among stakeholders. It works least well when executives have to make tradeoffs where the value created for one stakeholder reduces the value created for others. This interdependence requires a set of skills and ideas that use executive imagination. And, this is best exercised in full engagement with the stakeholders themselves. Stakeholder engagement is sometimes thought to entail corporate social responsibility. Nothing could be further from our idea here. Stakeholder engagement is about how a particular firm's business model creates value.

The Complexity of Human Motivation Assumption

Capitalism works because human beings are complex creatures. We are at once self-interested and other regarding. We are capable of both selfish and selfless acts. We are pro-social, language-using collaborators. And, most of the time, we aspire to be a part of something that is larger than our own individual self-interest. Most of us, most of the time, want to and actually do take responsibility for the effects of our actions on others. The complexity of human behavior is writ large in our culture, our art, music, and literature. As we learn more about human behavior from its scientific and literary study we find less application of the simplifying motivational structures of traditional economic theory.

The three basic assumptions together with the implicit moral framework here form a different basis for understanding business. The implicit moral framework is not some idealistic fantasy, but one based in both science and cultural theory. Human history is partially a history of us cooperating together to achieve lifting billions out of poverty, and making a better life for ourselves, our families, and our communities. Such a project flounders if the participants have no need to be responsible to those whom they affect with their actions. Indeed, the stakeholder idea is simply based on the idea that we need to be responsible for the effects of our actions on others. Such a basic principle is a part of every ethical system, religious belief, and guide to human interaction that has ever been invented or discovered. Of course, there are some who take advantage, but the idea that the main way we create value for each other depends on our willingness to "get away with whatever we can" is an idea that has long outlived any usefulness it may have had. Such an idea of "cowboy capitalism" should be put aside and made optional at best.

Any reasonable reform of capitalism and business must be put on a firm ethical foundation so that "business ethics" ceases to be a joke or an oxymoron. We argue that we do not need a very high edifice here, but rather a garden-variety common-sense view, that we teach all of our children simply to be responsible for the effects of our actions on others. Note that this assumption of responsibility applies to stakeholders in a business as well as to employees and executives. In the current parlance, many assume that it is only companies who need to be responsible (Goodstein and Wicks, 2007), but this assumption is as faulty as its opposite.

RESPONSIBLE CAPITALISM

The previous section suggests that we have come to see business differently. Business is fundamentally a cooperative enterprise built to create value, trade, and make ourselves and others better off. Since it is fully embedded in societal institutions we can also sketch the moral ideals on which it is based. So let us briefly sketch a set of criteria for proposals of reform of capitalism and business from our earlier discussion:

Responsibility Criterion

Any reform of capitalism must address the question of who is responsible for the effects of business activity on particular stakeholders and on society. We believe that the answer to this question is best given as "a business and its stakeholders," but we recognize that there may be alternatives. Also, "responsibility" is a devilishly tricky philosophical notion. Often responsibility is a joint endeavor, and it can be opaque due to difficult causal mechanisms, or ignorance of those mechanisms. These difficulties just add urgency to the requirement to understand responsibility in more nuanced ways, and to use all of the disciplines at our disposal to do so.

Voluntary Collaboration

If capitalism is to flourish it will be because individuals and groups of individuals can work together to create value for each other. Collaboration only works when there is freedom of association and choice. Forced labor, or forced cooperation, or forced consumption, or forced investment, carry negative consequences. However, it is not often so clear what is voluntary and what is not. The very low percentage of people who are actively engaged in their work is in part a function of very low perceived freedom to act and to do what is best for their organizations. In the thriving businesses of the 21st century, employees must have the ability to work with others to create value, and they must have the time and resources to push value creation in new and innovative directions.

Competition as Emergent Property

Businesses, and business schools, are often obsessed with the idea that business is fundamentally a competitive activity. We believe that such an assumption simply misses the main engine of capitalism. Capitalism works because we cooperate together to create value that can then be traded to make everyone better off. Competition is important in that a free society encourages voluntary agreement. And, if we can figure out a better way to do something, then we can satisfy a network of stakeholders better than they are currently being satisfied. Venkataraman (2002) has suggested that the entrepreneurial process leads to such equilibration as the result of a competitive economy. However, it may well be just a mistake to attribute the system-wide property of competitiveness to individual actors in the system.

Continuous Creation

Schumpeter (2013) famously wrote about the idea of creative destruction. Every company would eventually be replaced and destroyed by those who came after. However, this idea simply ignores the genius of the corporate form. Companies may well have a kind of limited immortality. In the 21st century companies don't stand still. They look for the next disruptive innovation, and some even look to disrupt themselves. Very large companies don't immediately go out of business when a better mousetrap gets to the market. They adapt. The adaptiveness of the corporate form is its innovativeness. It has good and bad qualities, but it lends some stability to a fast-changing world.

Government as Facilitator of Value-Creation Criterion

In calls for reform of capitalism, there are many proposals for the further regulation of business, usually from the left, and suggestions for "smart regulation," often from the right. Surely government has a role to play as referee, especially given the scope of the old narrative of capitalism. However, it stands to reason that if the main engine of business is collaboration to create value for stakeholders, one obvious question would be how government and other civil society organizations can facilitate the creation of value by businesses. We see a great deal of progress in this area as more companies are collaborating with non-government organizations (NGOs) on issues that range from industry working conditions to specific geographical and ecological issues. Companies such as Whole Foods Market routinely collaborate with animal welfare organizations to develop more awareness about conditions under which food is produced. McDonald's collaborates with environmental organizations on some issues of ecological significance. And, we have begun to see the emergence of public-private partnerships, usually involving private companies, NGOs, and governments cooperating together to solve problems that no single one of these organizations could easily solve (see also Chapter 9, this volume).

We believe that in addition to its traditional role of referee and redistributor of value, government can play an important role as facilitator of value creation. There are a number of roles here, such as (1) coordinating, communicating, and validating information; (2) smart policies that encourage voluntary agreements to create value; (3) assisting education around business and entrepreneurship; (4) providing infrastructure to make business start-up and growth easier; (5) facilitating business growth and trade at an international level. Practical policies include the support of business incubators, changes in tax laws and regulatory regimes, the establishment of free and fair trade, encouraging companies to think broadly about stakeholder value, and making examples and role models out of the companies that do it right.

SUMMARY

We believe that we are at an inflection point in the history of capitalism. It is time to think broadly and creatively about the very best in capitalism, and how to avoid its historical weaknesses. In this chapter we have outlined that many of the weaknesses of capitalism come from inaccurate and unhelpful assumptions about the nature of business including its purpose and level of interdependence, as well as assumptions about the complexity of human beings. Without addressing these fundamental assumptions, calls for reforming capitalism— whether from business leaders or policymakers—will have limited impact. We have suggested that the scholars and executives, who have been working on stakeholder theory and its practice have given us ways to talk differently about these assumptions that unleash our potential to work together, increase responsibility, and make each other better off. These narratives must become more widespread and engrained in practice. Much work remains to be done in both developing theory and practice to continue this progress.

ACKNOWLEDGMENTS

This essay is based on a number of earlier attempts to define stakeholder capitalism (see especially Freeman et al., 2006, 2007, 2010). We are grateful to co-authors, editors, and publishers of the earlier attempts for permission to continue to develop the ideas here.

144 Freeman, Parmar, and Martin

REFERENCES

Bebchuk, L. (2006). *Pay without Performance*. Cambridge, MA: Harvard University Press.

Edmans, A., Li, L., and Zhang, C. (2014). "Employee Satisfaction, Labor Market Flexibility, and Stock Returns around the World," *National Bureau of Economic Research*, w20300.

Follett, M. P. (2011). "Business as an Integrative Unity," in M. E Godwyn and J. H. Gittell (eds), *Sociology of Organizations: Structures and Relationships*. Thousand Oaks, CA: Sage, pp. 7–13.

Freeman, R. E., Martin, K., and Parmar, B. (2006). "Ethics and Capitalism," in M. Epstein and K. Hanson (eds), *The Accountable Corporation*, Vol. 2: *Business Ethics*. Westport, CT: Praeger, pp. 193–208.

Freeman, R. E., Martin, K., and Parmar, B. (2007). "Stakeholder Capitalism," *Journal of Business Ethics*, 74(4): 303–14.

Freeman, R. E., Harrison, J., Wicks, A., Parmar, B., and de Colle, S. (2010). *Stakeholder Theory: The State of the Art*. Cambridge: Cambridge University Press.

Friedman, M. (1970). "The Social Responsibility of Business Is to Increase Its Profits," *New York Times Magazine*, 13: 32–3.

Goodstein, J. D. and Wicks, A. C. (2007). "Corporate and Stakeholder Responsibility: Making Business Ethics a Two-Way Conversation," *Business Ethics Quarterly*, 17(3): 375–98.

Jameson, F. (1991). *Postmodernism, or, the Cultural Logic of Late Capitalism*. Durham, NC: Duke University Press.

Jensen, M. C. and Meckling, W. H. (1976). "Theory of the Firm: Managerial Behavior, Agency Costs and Ownership Structure," *Journal of Financial Economics*, 3(4): 305–60.

Keynes, J. M. (2006). *General Theory of Employment, Interest and Money*. New Delhi: Atlantic Publishers and Distributors.

Mackey J. and Sisodia, R. (2014). *Conscious Capitalism*. Cambridge, MA: Harvard University Press.

Parmar, B. L., Freeman, R. E., Harrison, J. S., Wicks, A. C., Purnell, L., and De Colle, S. (2010). "Stakeholder Theory: The State of the Art," *Academy of Management Annals*, 4(1): 403–45.

Schumpeter, J. A. (2013). *Capitalism, Socialism and Democracy*. New York: Routledge.

Sisodia R., Wolfe, D., and Sheth, J. (2014). *Firms of Endearment*, 2nd ed. Upper Saddle River, NJ: Pearson Press.

Venkataraman, S. (2002). "Stakeholder Value Equilibration and the Entrepreneurial Process," in R. E. Freeman and S. Venkataraman (eds), *Ethics and Entrepreneurship*. Charlottesville, VA: Philosophy Documentation Center, pp. 45–57.

11

Being Good and Doing Well

Not as Easy as You Think

Bryan W. Husted

INTRODUCTION

It is a cliché that firms can do well by being good. In fact, this saying is at the heart of re-imagining capitalism by suggesting that win-win opportunities abound for both business and society. Although this saying is sometimes true, it is not always so. It illustrates an obsession on the part of many scholars and practitioners to study and demonstrate the "business case" for corporate social responsibility (CSR), exemplified most recently by Porter and Kramer's (2011) concept of shared value. However, the business case for CSR does not occur spontaneously or naturally. Nor is it necessarily the most likely relationship between being good and doing well. Indeed, managers often have to face difficult tradeoffs as they try to be good and do well. Failure to discriminate the conditions under which these two possibilities are compatible will likely create an overly optimistic approach to CSR and stakeholder management that is doomed to disappoint.

As I will show, there are at least three sets of conditions that determine whether firms can do well financially by being good in terms of reducing negative social and environmental impacts and increasing positive impacts. First, there are moral conditions. There may be situations where no moral option exists. In other words, the business activity or specific decision is not compatible with an ethical course of action—something that takes into account the "common good," however that is defined. Second, there are technical conditions that determine whether it is feasible to do well by being good. Much social innovation explores the limits within which the appropriate means can be developed to satisfy these two goals. Some solutions are not feasible. Finally, there are also institutional conditions that permit being good and doing well. For example, where a "tragedy of the commons" situation exists

(Hardin, 1968), there may be no option whereby a single firm can actually be good alone; solutions must be approached collectively. By exploring the conditions in which being good and doing well are compatible, managers can make better decisions to guide their firms in ways that meet both goals.

In the rest of this chapter, I describe the conditions under which being good and doing well may be compatible. Then, assuming that these conditions are met, I outline the steps firms need to take in order to be good and do well. I end by exploring the limits of the business case and developing the implications for practice.

A SIMPLE MODEL

What does it mean to be good? In the context of doing well by being good, being good means simply to act ethically. A utilitarian approach would suggest that being good has to do with individual utility and social welfare, where social welfare is simply the sum of the individual utilities in a society. For Bentham (2000), utility was the happiness of the individual. For the Kantian deontologist, being good requires obeying the categorical imperative—treating all persons as ends, not means, and acting upon those decisions that can serve as universal rules for all (Kant, 1993). In the business world, doing good is often thought of concretely in terms of CSR, which typically involves "further [ing] some social good, beyond the interests of the firm and that which is required by law" (McWilliams and Siegel, 2001: 117). What is doing well? Doing well for a firm means to be profitable, at least in the long term. Although Amazon was successful at delaying profits for its investors, somehow firms have to create value, cash flow, or net income in order to be financially sustainable in the long run (Ruddick, 2014).

So a lot of literature has focused on the question of the relationship between ethical conduct or CSR and firm profitability—doing well by being good (Margolis and Walsh, 2001; Orlitzky et al., 2003). This literature is sometimes called "the business case" as it argues that being ethical or socially responsible makes business sense—it is profitable. In my approach, I argue that being good and doing well are independent and unrelated constructs. Essentially, there should be no correlation between one and the other. Nevertheless, I will argue that there may be some very specific conditions under which a correlation will emerge. Table 11.1 provides a convenient way of examining how doing well relates to being good.

Table 11.1 displays two dimensions: being good and doing well. Quite simply, it suggests that firms either do well or they do not and that they do good or they do not. Each cell describes the conditions that characterize these situations. So there are conditions when doing well by being good is possible; this is cell 1—the business case. However, there are many other situations

Table 11.1. Being good and doing well

		Doing well	
		Yes	No
Being good	Yes	1. Integrative, win-win solutions. In the language of Jensen, this is the area where there are monotonic transformations of doing well and doing good.	3. This is also a trade-off. Although moral and institutional conditions may exist, the technical conditions do not exist.
	No	2. Either the moral, technical, or institutional conditions do not exist for pursuing business solutions to social problems. As a result, there is a situation of trade-off.	4. Not interesting. Generally speaking, it would be irrational for anyone to pursue this quadrant.

where such an outcome is impossible. This framework allows us to explore the moral, technical, and institutional conditions under which being good and doing well do correlate. This framework does not seek to be exhaustive, but rather to encompass some of the relevant conditions that affect how firms may be good and/or do well.

If we look at the remaining cells, cell 4 is easy to discard. Here the firm is not doing well, nor is it being good. Clearly no firm wants to be situated in this cell. Cells 2 and 3 are the tricky ones, and indeed suggest that there are important trade-offs for firms. The business case implies that trade-offs are rare and can usually be transformed into a win-win solution. I will argue that such solutions may sometimes be possible, but that often the moral, institutional, and technical conditions may not permit the transformation of an ethical problem into a win-win solution.

The trade-off in cell 2 occurs because the moral, technical, or institutional conditions do not exist for being good. In other words, there simply is either no moral circumstance under which a business solution might be pursued, or there is no technical solution available, or the institutional framework makes the ideal win-win solution impossible. As a result, there is a situation of trade-off. In the case of cell 3, there is also a trade-off, but of a different kind. Here a moral solution may exist, but there is no circumstance under which a profitable business model can arise to be good. There are no financially attractive options available to the firm. As a result, not-for-profit organizations or government organizations may need to fill the need to do good in this case. Although moral conditions may exist, either the technical conditions or institutional conditions do not exist. Institutional conditions may include the absence of intellectual property protection, which could allow a firm to profit from the implementation of a possible solution. In the following section, we examine in greater detail the moral, technical, and institutional conditions that influence the possibility of being good and doing well.

CONDITIONS AND OUTCOMES

Moral Conditions

Is there a moral space within which firms can maximize profits? Sometimes no such space exists. The moral conditions of a problem define whether a given solution is moral. So the central question is to determine whether a solution or decision is moral or not. However, as mentioned in the brief reference to utilitarianism and deontology above, there are considerable differences in the concept of what is moral. For example, Hardin (1988: 3) writes that "the moral impulse of utilitarianism is to define the right as good consequences and to motivate people to achieve these." On the other hand, according to Hosmer (1987: 3), ethical issues "represent a conflict between an organization's economic performance (measured by revenues, costs, and profits) and its social performance (stated in terms of obligations to persons both within and outside the organization)." So, on the one hand, morality has to do with good consequences and, on the other, it has to do with duties and obligations. This crude distinction between utilitarianism and deontology does not take into account the many other approaches to understanding what is moral, such as virtue ethics or discourse ethics, but represents the two most widely used approaches and a reasonable place to start.

Regardless of the approach one takes to ethics, my point is that there are circumstances where producing good consequences for oneself and others or fulfilling obligations and duties is simply not possible. Not all problems have a win-win solution. Sometimes there are trade-offs. At best, the problem of the business firm is one of constrained optimization, where firms maximize profits within moral limits of either good consequences or duties. Unfortunately, the solution for such a problem can often be the null set. Certainly there are many circumstances where economic performance can be reconciled with social performance. Such is the inspiration of Porter and Kramer's (2011) notion of shared value as well as Husted and Allen's (2011) development of corporate social strategy. Milton Friedman (1970) argued that if in fact there are win-win opportunities, there was no sense in speaking of corporate social responsibility, because it was the economically appropriate thing to do. Nevertheless, finding and developing these win-win opportunities often requires a kind of social innovation that respects the constraints set by both objectives.

Even so, there are cases where it is impossible both to do well financially and be good morally. Let us examine two such cases. First, there may be internal contradictions in terms of being good. Social performance has often been understood as stakeholder performance (Clarkson, 1995). The fundamental problem is that doing well by some stakeholders may mean hurting the interests of other stakeholders. It is almost impossible to align the interests of all stakeholders. Take, for example, the case of a wage increase for employees. If no increase in technical efficiency accompanies the wage increase, then that increase can only come at the expense of stakeholders or customers. Someone will be hurt. Here a utilitarian approach may provide a solution by focusing on the greatest good for the greatest number of stakeholders. However, there may be conflicts between the duties owed to different stakeholders, so that a viable, moral solution is not available. Second, deontologists argue that one must do good for its own sake and not to improve firm financial performance (Bowie, 2002). As a result, positive financial performance would have to be the happy, but unplanned-for result of being good. There may be situations where a sincere intent is a requirement for doing the right thing. However, the business case is mostly about doing the right thing because it will benefit the business, not because something is the right thing to do. If such is the case, then the business case is not moral by definition.

Technical Conditions

By technical, I mean the relationship of the means to the ends. The ends are being good and doing well. Two kinds of technical conditions come into play. The first set of conditions relates to the existence of a technical solution. In other words, there must exist means that lead to the ends of being good and doing well. The second set relates to the effective discovery and implementation of technical solutions. This first set may be related to the state of the science in a particular area. The second is tied to human factors that affect the implementation of technical solutions. Let us examine each one of these conditions in greater detail.

First, in order for private firms to be good and do well, technical solutions to social and environmental problems must exist. Many emerging approaches to social issues management, such as social strategy, social innovation, and social entrepreneurship are meant to harness business methods in order to solve social problems. These solutions may not always exist. For example, suppose a pharmaceutical company sets out to find a cure for stomach cancer as a matter of the social responsibility it feels toward its sufferers. As of the writing of this chapter, the five-year survival rate of stomach cancer is less than 10 percent. There may be a technical solution that will arise in the future, but at least for now a technical solution does not exist. The result is that some firms may pursue these solutions, but their achievement is risky. In the case of river blindness, Merck did find a technical solution, but it was not an economically viable one for the benefited population. Merck's river blindness initiative never made money for the company (Sturchio, 2001). There was no business case. For Merck, it was simply the right thing to do. Possibly Merck gained from good publicity, but it is doubtful that the good publicity compensated the millions of dollars that went into research and development. Fortunately, for humankind, even though there was no viable market for Mectizan, Merck gave it away.

If we conceive of a firm's CSR strategy as a portfolio of social action projects (Husted and Allen, 2011), the technical problem becomes more readily apparent. At the project level, research indicates that many well-intentioned projects do not necessarily produce real social benefits (Salazar et al., 2012). To speak of a corporation's social performance (impact) is almost nonsensical without speaking of the social impact of its specific projects and activities. A firm may gain a reputation or be evaluated for an overall social perform-ance, but until that social performance is tied to the positive and negative impacts of specific projects and activities, the firm has little ability to strategize and improve its performance. Unfortunately, many projects may have no social or environmental impact.

The technical conditions partly depend on a lack of appropriate measure-ment (Peloza, 2009). With good measurement, it is easier to track progress toward solutions. For example, CSR financial performance research needs to be conducted at the project level in order to see whether specific CSR initia-tives actually produce economic benefits (Salazar et al., 2012). A lot of firms are undertaking environmental certification, but does it actually increase the consumer's willingness to pay a price premium (Husted et al., 2014)? Only measurement at the level of the specific program or project will reveal such a relationship. Examining firm-level correlations between its portfolio of social initiatives and financial performance are of almost no use to managers in making decisions about specific projects (Peloza, 2009). So, the specific means of achieving the end of being good and doing well needs to be measured at the appropriate level, i.e., the project level.

In a related vein, research into certified social/environmental programs indicates that the well-known ISO 14001 certification for environmental management systems (EMS) has no positive impact in reducing emissions among Mexican firms (Henriques et al., 2013; but see Dasgupta et al., 2000, for contrary findings). The problem is that not all social initiatives actually improve social impact. The presence of an EMS certified by ISO 14001 may be a good thing, but such a certified system, in and of itself, does not necessarily lead to actual reductions in environmental emissions. Apparently, the design of the program is crucial (Henriques et al., 2013). Firms that seek certifications directly tied to emissions reductions, rather than the implemen-tation of EMS, may see important reductions in emissions.

Second, technical solutions may not always be implemented effectively (Christmann and Taylor, 2006). CSR is plagued with accusations of symbolic implementation, sometimes referred to as "greenwashing" (Entine, 1994). Often adequate means may exist, but there is no intent in implementing them substantively. Although intent is not a sufficient condition for effective implementation, it is a necessary condition. Firms must implement environmental management systems with the intent of reducing impacts. If implementation is motivated by pressure from stakeholders, they will fail to implement them substantively (Aravind and Christmann, 2010). Similarly, take the case of Patrimonio Hoy, a project specifically designed by Mexican cement company Cemex to assist low-income beneficiaries in constructing sound housing and creating social benefits. Although the project did in some sense help to generate positive economic benefits for the firm, the project failed to really make a difference for the intended beneficiaries (Salazar et al., 2012). Implementation may also be clouded by a lack of consensus or clarity about what the firm should achieve. In the case of Patrimonio Hoy, there was a lack of clarity among managers regarding the objectives sought, which in turn led to problems with measurement, impeding implementation (Salazar et al., 2013). Once consensus around clear objectives exists, it may be possible to recognize areas of opportunity where firms can make progress with respect to social problems and implement solutions substantively.

Institutional Conditions

The institutional context affects the ability of firms to be good and do well in four ways. First, strong, effective institutions may be absolutely necessary to overcome social and environmental resource conditions (common-pool resources) that make it impossible for firms to be good and do well. Second, corruption may undermine the ability of even well-designed institutions to function properly. The third is related to the tragedy of the commons and presents what could be called a "competition conundrum," which suggests a situation where doing well requires undermining the basis for competition. Finally, there exist a number of different institutional CSR settings through national regulatory systems and regional organizational fields that can enable or hinder being good in ways that firms may also do well.

First, common-pool resources make it impossible for firms to compete and engage in socially responsible activity in the absence of strong institutions. Common-pool resources are rival goods in that the use of the resource prevents others from using it, e.g., fish stocks. It is possible to exclude potential beneficiaries from using the resource, but only with great difficulty. Without effective coordination among competitors for common-pool resources, the overuse of those resources by firms seeking to do well is inherently in conflict with firms, which seek to be good by exercising voluntary restraint. This situation is the well-known "tragedy of the commons." The tragedy of the commons usually refers to overharvesting of an environmental/social common-pool resource (Hardin, 1968). The tragedy of the commons suggests that sometimes my doing well may prevent us all from doing well as a system.

There are numerous examples of the commons in business. Fishing, tele-marketing, and even debt provide examples of situations where a little may be fine for the overall system, but as such activities increase beyond a usually unknown tipping point, the natural (fish population) or social resource (sup-ply of trust) may collapse. A specific firm may prosper, but the whole system degenerates (Hardin, 1968). In such situations, "responsibility is the product of definite social arrangements" (Charles Frankel, as cited in Hardin, 1968). So, in the case of fishing, does a private sector solution (social arrangement) to overfishing exist? Well, an individual firm may fish less, but it does not solve the problem of overfishing. All fishing companies have to participate in the solution. If a single firm refrains from overfishing, it is punished by doing less well than other firms that continue to overfish. By its nature, the tragedy of the commons requires a collective solution. It is almost impossible for a single firm to restrict its activity voluntarily, if other firms do not. A similar situation occurs with climate change, where the atmosphere serves as an inexpensive dumping ground for the greenhouse gases generated by industrial processes.

Nobel prize-winning economist Elinor Ostrom talks about the kinds of rules to maintain a common-pool resource. She develops specific design principles for institutions that can help govern the commons (Ostrom, 1990). She states that clear boundaries need to be defined in order to effectively exclude unentitled third parties and coordinate the use of the resource by entitled parties. She also argues that rules need to be adjusted for local circumstances, entitled parties should be involved in the decision-making process, and effective and independent monitoring must be available. Pro-gressive punishment needs to penalize unentitled appropriators who break local rules and conflict-resolution mechanisms must be easily accessible. Finally, higher-level authorities need to accept the right of the community to establish its own rules. Failure to design institutions according to these principles will lead to the inability of sustaining common-pool resources in the long run. Given Ostrom's approach, the responsibility of the firm is to ensure that effective rules are in place and to follow them. Once effective rules are in place, then firms may be ethical and competitive at the same time.

A second institutional deficiency that prevents firms from being good and doing well is corruption. Corruption undermines the ability of rules to func-tion effectively. For example, if the institutional context is such that obtaining a procurement contract requires paying a bribe, it may be that the only ethical option is to forego the contract. However, that ethical option invariably means that the firm will do less well than those firms that engage in corrupt activities in that context. Corruption alters the competitive playing field in such a way that it becomes nearly impossible to be good and do well.

Third, the competition conundrum also describes institutional conditions that impede being good and doing well. The competition conundrum refers to a situation where the resolution of an environmental or social problem requires that the innovative action of an exemplary firm be replicated on a broad scale. However, replication goes against the idea of competitive advantage. Instead of protecting the intellectual property associated with a given social initiative, intellectual property needs to be shared if it is to have an impact (Christensen et al., 2006). By sharing social innovation, the firm undermines the very thing that allows it to be competitive. Sometimes, but not always, first-mover advantages may exist. By being first, a firm is further along the learning curve, which permits reductions in costs that are not available to followers. However, where learning curves are not important, and intellectual property needs to be shared in order for a solution to be effective, the possibility of being good and doing well is significantly reduced. For example, Solar Cookers International (SCI) shares solar cooking technology in remote regions of Africa in order to provide emission-free cooking. Such cooking technology will only have an impact to the extent that its use is widely diffused. In the case of solar cookers, SCI scales up the use of its technology via partnerships with other non-government organizations and local governments. This model would not work in a competitive market.

Finally, differences in national CSR regimes as well as in the legitimacy of CSR engagement in a region affect the ability of firms to do well by being good. In terms of national regimes, Matten and Moon (2008) distinguish between implicit versus explicit CSR. Implicit CSR is a national system of public policy that seeks to level the playing field so that competition is not affected by the varying costs of providing public goods. However, some nations either choose not to implement this kind of system or else implement it only to a limited extent. In this latter case, institutional voids may exist. Under such circumstances, firms have the opportunity to implement explicit CSR, where the provision of public goods is undertaken in part by private firms. Firms can compete on the basis of CSR, and thus do well by being good. Where CSR is implicit—say in the case of universal health care—firms cannot compete by offering health care. If institutions do not cover basic needs for education, health, security, then firms can provide those public goods and compete. For example, before Obamacare many US automobile firms relocated from Michigan to Ontario in order to take advantage of the province's universal health care for workers. Locating in Ontario was cheaper than providing expensive health benefits for employees in Michigan. This case illustrates how the institutional context can either foster or hinder the incentive for firms to engage in certain arenas of CSR activity.

CSR clusters or regions, such as Minneapolis, St. Paul, provide a benchmark for the CSR standards to which nearby firms should comply (Galaskiewicz, 1997; Husted et al., 2012). Where CSR is more explicit and institutional arrangements are weaker, the presence of nearby neighbors who also engage in CSR tends to strengthen the CSR engagement of the local firm. These CSR clusters provide institutional support, foster innovation, and stimulate the organization of non-profit companies. Knowledge spillovers and imitation occur within these regions. The presence of CSR clusters can facilitate CSR by reducing the costs associated with engaging in it. Within these clusters, investors are especially important. Generally speaking investors favor local firms. If a CSR cluster exists, then local investors likely see CSR as legitimate. Such clusters enable CSR firms to engage and experiment in ways that will in fact be rewarded by investors and consumers, thus being good and doing well.

In each case, either due to the competitive context (tragedy of the commons, corruption, competition conundrum) or due to the institutional context (governance regimes, CSR clusters), there may or may not exist institutional conditions that foster being good and doing well. Together with the moral conditions and technical conditions, this section describes how the possibilities for operating in quadrant 1 are actually more limited than usually acknowledged in many rosy depictions of win-win opportunities for firms that desire to be socially responsible.

WHAT NEXT?

Together these moral, technical, and institutional conditions define a space where firms can engage in strategy and innovation that permit being good and doing well. Here doing well and being good are morally compatible, technical solutions are feasible, and no institutional impediment exists. In such spaces, according to the basic Porterian approach, firms can either compete based on (1) reducing costs, say through eco-efficiency; (2) creating a differentiation by which customers are willing to pay more, or at least willing to break ties in favor of the socially or environmentally responsible product (Orsato, 2006); or (3) interacting strategically with government policy (Reinhardt, 1999). Let's briefly review each strategic option.

First, costs can be reduced through a number of mechanisms. For example, increased employee loyalty inspired by working for a company where CSR is important can decrease costs associated with turnover, especially hiring and training. Investors may be willing to accept a lower cost of capital for firms with higher CSR because they are perceived as less risky. Firms may find opportunities of lower costs through eco-efficiency programs or recycling. Second, differentiation is possible where (a) customers are willing to pay a price premium for products with social or environmental attributes; (b) they have access to credible information about the quality of these products or services, and (c) such products and services with environmental and social attributes are difficult to imitate (Reinhardt, 1998). Finally, firms can lobby governments to strengthen regulation in order to take advantage of the lower costs they enjoy with respect to competitors due to being further ahead on the learning curve. For instance, Honda actively lobbied the US Congress for stricter requirements under the Corporate Average Fuel Economy program, because of their technological advantages in manufacturing highly efficient automobile engines (Shaffer, 1992).

If firms can operate in the space that allows them to be good and do well, then they need to formulate the firm's social strategy plan (Husted and Allen, 2011). The actual process follows the strategic planning process for ordinary kinds of strategy. Like other cases of strategy formulation, the strategist has to take into account the competitive environment, and firm resources and capabilities, including the firm's identity and culture. Frequently, the firm will need to acquire additional resources and capabilities. In any case, it will need to develop a plan, implement it, and measure its progress. Probably the biggest difference between traditional business strategy and social strategy is the need to identify a social issue opportunity. It involves identifying a social need that the firm can fulfill in a way that benefits both the firm and society. Given the moral, technical, and institutional conditions that such an opportunity must fulfill, such opportunities may be rarer than previously thought. Rather, managers will need to make trade-offs as they face genuine ethical dilemmas.

CONCLUSION

In this chapter, I have sought to define the conditions under which being good and doing well are compatible. I described the moral, technical, and institutional conditions that define the space in which firms operate so that they may be good and do well. Once these conditions are met, then firms are free to compete responsibly; however, often these conditions are not fulfilled. Certainly there may exist low-hanging fruit where win-win options exist, but the real challenges for the firm occur after this low-hanging fruit is harvested. The challenges are twofold.

The first challenge is innovation. Where the technical or institutional conditions do not quite exist, firms may need to engage in social innovation in order to develop the technical solutions or fill the institutional voids (Mair et al., 2012). So, for example, in the case of common-pool resources, firms will need to engage in institutional entrepreneurship to ensure that appropriate rules, either based on grassroots, bottom-up initiatives or on top-down, government initiatives, are in place. However, even after buttressing the technical and institutional requirements, the moral conditions may not be met.

So, the second challenge is that the firm may simply have to face a trade-off front on. That is, the firm has to accept the trade-off and choose between being good and doing well. Sometimes this trade-off will not be black and white, but involve shades of gray as managers make decisions at the margin and ask: How much profit is the company willing to forgo in order to fulfill a little bit more its moral obligations? Still, at some point, firms will have to determine the non-negotiable values that will guide them as they compete. Yes, a business case does exist, but it cannot always save managers from the hard work of making ethical decisions.

ACKNOWLEDGMENTS

The author thanks co-editor Matthias Kipping for his insightful comments, which helped to strengthen this chapter.

REFERENCES

Aravind, D. and Christmann, P. (2010). "Decoupling of Standard Implementation from Certification," *Business Ethics Quarterly*, 21(1): 73–102.

Bentham, J. (2000 [1781]). *An Introduction to the Principles of Morals and Legislation*. Kitchener, ON: Batoche.

Bowie, N. (2002). "A Kantian Approach to Business Ethics," in T. Donaldson, P. J. Werhane, and M. Cording (eds), *Ethical Issues in Business: A Philosophical Approach*, 7th ed. Upper Saddle River, NJ: Prentice Hall.

Christensen, C. M., Baumann, H., Ruggles, R., and Sadtler, R. (2006). "Disruptive Innovation for Social Change," *Harvard Business Review*, December: 94–101.

Christmann, P. and Taylor, G. (2006). "Firm Self-Regulation through International Certifiable Standards: Determinants of Symbolic versus Substantive Implementation," *Journal of International Business Studies*, 37: 863–78.

Clarkson, M. E. (1995). "A Stakeholder Framework for Analyzing and Evaluating Corporate Social Performance," *Academy of Management Review*, 20(1): 92–117.

Dasgupta, S., Hettige, H., and Wheeler, D. (2000). "What Improves Environmental Compliance? Evidence from Mexican Industry," *Journal of Environmental Economics and Management*, 39(1): 39–88.

Entine, J. (1994). "Shattered Image," *Business Ethics: The Magazine of Corporate Responsibility*, 8(5): 23–8.

Friedman, M. (1970). "The Social Responsibility of Business Is to Increase Its Profits," *New York Times Magazine*, September 3.

Galaskiewicz, J. (1997). "An Urban Grants Economy Revisited: Corporate Charitable Contributions in the Twin Cities, 1979–1981, 1987–89," *Administrative Science Quarterly*, 42(3): 445–71.

Hardin, G. (1968). "The Tragedy of the Commons," *Science*, 162(3859): 1243–8.

Hardin, R. (1988). *Morality within the Limits of Reason.* Chicago, IL: University of Chicago Press.

Henriques, I., Husted, B. W., and Montiel, I. (2013). "Spillover Effects of Voluntary Environmental Programs on Greenhouse Gas Emissions: Lessons for Mexico," *Journal of Policy Analysis and Management,* 32(2): 296–322.

Hosmer, L.T. (1987). *The Ethics of Management.* New York: Irwin.

Husted, B. W. and Allen, D. B. (2011). *Corporate Social Strategy: Stakeholder Engagement and Competitive Advantage.* Cambridge: Cambridge University Press.

Husted, B. W., Jamali, D., and Saffar, W. (2012). "Location, Clusters, and CSR Engagement: The Role of Information Asymmetry and Knowledge Spillovers," *Proceedings of the Seventy-Second Annual Meeting of the Academy of Management (Best Papers)* (CD), 2012: 1–6, doi: 10.5465/AMBPP.2012.72, ISSN 1543-8643.

Husted, B. W., Russo, M. V., Meza, C. E. B., and Tilleman, S. G. (2014). "An Exploratory Study of Environmental Attitudes and the Willingness to Pay for Environmental Certification in Mexico," *Journal of Business Research,* 67(5): 891–9.

Kant, I. (1993). *Grounding for the Metaphysics of Morals.* Indianapolis, IN: Hackett Publishing.

McWilliams, A. and Siegel, D. (2001). "Corporate Social Responsibility: A Theory of the Firm Perspective," *Academy of Management Review,* 26(1): 117–27.

Mair, J., Martí, I., and Ventresca, M. J. (2012). "Building Inclusive Markets in Rural Bangladesh: How Intermediaries Work Institutional Voids," *Academy of Management Journal,* 55(4): 819–50.

Margolis, J. D. and Walsh, J. P. (2001). *People and Profits? The Search for a Link between a Company's Social and Financial Performance.* New York: Lawrence Erlbaum Associates.

Matten, D. and Moon, J. (2008). "'Implicit' and 'Explicit' CSR: A Conceptual Framework for a Comparative Understanding of Corporate Social Responsibility," *Academy of Management Review,* 33(2): 404–24.

Orlitzky, M., Schmidt, F. L., and Rynes, S. L. (2003). "Corporate Social and Financial Performance: A Meta-Analysis," *Organization Studies,* 24(3): 403–41.

Orsato, R. (2006). "Competitive Environmental Strategies: When Does It Pay to Be Green?" *California Management Review,* 48(2): 127–43.

Ostrom, E. (1990). *Governing the Commons: The Evolution of Institutions for Collective Action.* Cambridge: Cambridge University Press.

Peloza, J. (2009). "The Challenge of Measuring Financial Impacts from Investments in Corporate Social Performance," *Journal of Management,* 35(6): 1518–41.

Porter, M. E. and Kramer, M. R. (2011). "Creating Shared Value," *Harvard Business Review,* 89(1/2): 62–77.

Reinhardt, F. (1998). "Environmental Product Differentiation: Implications for Corporate Strategy," *California Management Review,* 40(4): 43–73.

Reinhardt, F. (1999). "Market Failure and the Environmental Policies of Firms: Economic Rationales for 'beyond Compliance' Behavior," *Journal of Industrial Ecology,* 3(1): 9–21.

Ruddick, G. (2014). "Will Amazon Ever Be Profitable?" *Telegraph,* July 25. Available at: <http://www.telegraph.co.uk/finance/newsbysector/retailandconsumer/10990659/Will-Amazon-ever-be-profitable.html> (accessed March 3, 2015).

Salazar, J., Husted, B. W., and Biehl, M. (2012). "Thoughts on the Evaluation of Corporate Social Performance through Projects," *Journal of Business Ethics*, 105(2): 175–86.

Shaffer, B. (1992). "Regulation, Competition, and Strategy: The Case of Automobile Fuel Economy Standards, 1974–1991," in J. Post (ed.), *Research in Corporate Social Performance and Policy*, Greenwich, CT: JAI Press, pp. 191–218.

Sturchio, J. L. (2001). "The Case of Ivermectin: Lessons and Implications for Improving Access to Care and Treatment in Developing Countries," *Community Eye Health Journal*, 14(38): 22–3.

12

"Maximizing Shareholder Value" Is an Unnecessary and Unworkable Corporate Objective

Lynn Stout

INTRODUCTION

What is the purpose of a corporation? Many academics and activist investors would say the answer is obvious: corporations exist to maximize their shareholders' wealth. Indeed the notion has become something of a modern corporate mantra. It should be noted that, in the broad sweep of business history, this is a relatively recent development. From the 1930s through the 1980s—the so-called managerialist era—corporate managers and the American public alike believed business companies should not only provide good returns to shareholders but also create secure, well-paying jobs for employees, offer quality goods and services to customers, and serve the nation (Davis, 2013). Today, however, conventional wisdom holds that corporate managers have only one legitimate objective: "maximize shareholder value."

This view, while still widely held, increasingly is being challenged on a number of grounds (Stout, 2012a; see also Chapters 8 and 10, this volume). Shareholder value thinking is criticized for encouraging socially irresponsible corporate behavior (Elhauge, 2005). It is thought to drive companies to sacrifice the interests of important stakeholders, like employees and customers (Blair and Stout, 1999; Denning, 2011; Porter and Kramer, 2011). It is feared to encourage managers to adopt short-sighted business strategies, like leveraging and cutting payroll and research and development, that discourage innovation and erode long-term performance (Aspen Institute, 2009; Lazonick, 2014; Montier, 2014). But the notion that managers ought to maximize shareholder value is vulnerable to a deeper and more devastating critique, a critique that goes beyond the possibility of negative effects. In brief, despite its superficial appeal, the idea that a corporation can or should "maximize shareholder value" turns out to lack any solid intellectual foundation.

This chapter takes a closer look at the idea of maximizing shareholder value as a corporate objective by unpacking each of the three concepts involved: maximizing, shareholder, and value. It concludes that each concept is highly problematic. For example, while the idea of maximizing something is straightforward and easy to understand, it is far less clear *why* maximizing a single variable should be desirable. The normative case for maximization as a corporate desideratum turns out to be extraordinarily weak. Meanwhile, the idea of "the shareholder" is, as a positive matter, highly questionable. "Shareholders" are implicitly presumed to be homogenous entities with common interests. Yet no such homogenous entities exist: in reality, shares of companies are held, directly or indirectly, by human beings with diverse and often conflicting interests. Treating them as if they were homogenous raises serious problems. Finally, perhaps the most intellectually empty element in the "maximize shareholder value" mantra may be the idea of value itself. Unless we define shareholder value in terms of observable short-term metrics like today's stock price, the "value" of a share in a company necessarily depends on expectations about uncertain future events. This makes shareholder value in turn uncertain, subjective, and perhaps ultimately useless as a concept for judging corporate performance.

Closer inspection reveals that the idea of "maximizing shareholder value" lacks intellectual rigor. Describing shareholder value as the ultimate corporate objective provides an illusion of precision and objectivity that lacks any foundation in logic or reality. Worse, it distorts corporate behavior in ways that end up harming not only shareholders themselves, but society as a whole.

WHY MUST CORPORATIONS MAXIMIZE ANYTHING?

Let us start by examining one of the most interesting things about the notion of maximizing shareholder value—it presumes that corporations necessarily must maximize something in the first place. Rarely is this presumption subject to careful examination or explanation. A notable exception can be found in an article by influential economist Michael Jensen (2010) entitled "Value Maximization, Stakeholders Theory, and the Corporate Objective Function." In this article, Jensen argued that it was a "necessity for any organization to have a single valued objective as a precursor to purposeful or rational behavior" (p. 34). This was true, according to Jensen, because "it is logically impossible to maximize in more than one dimension at the same time…[T]elling a manager to maximize current profits, market share, future growth profits, and anything else one pleases will leave that manager with no way to make a reasoned decision. In effect it leaves the manager with no objective" (p. 34).

Jensen's claim that it is impossible to maximize in more than one dimension is uncontroversial. But his statement that one needs to maximize a single objective as a precursor to purposeful or rational behavior is a naked assertion unsupported by logic or evidence (Stout, 2012b). Contrary to Jensen's assertion, people purposefully and rationally pursue projects with more than one objective every day. Consider how you decided what to have for lunch yesterday. Does rationality demand that you focus only on the pleasure of good taste while ignoring calories (in which case you may still be eating)? Or that you concern yourself only with nutrition, confining your diet to tofu and kale? Or that you minimize calories, in which case you are in for a long fast? And if a person can rationally have more than one objective in choosing what to eat for lunch, why can a corporation not have more than one objective in operating a business? As another example, students in undergraduate corporate finance classes are typically taught that corporations must focus solely on maximizing shareholder value. They are simultaneously taught—in the very same classes!—that investors should have at least two objectives: increasing returns and decreasing risk. This makes the claim that a single objective function is a "necessity" to rationally operate a large corporation—a far more complex task than picking an investment portfolio—seem even odder (see also Chapter 9, this volume).

In fact, the idea that organizations can and should pursue multiple objectives has a long and respectable—if sometimes forgotten—lineage in economic theory. In 1978, Herbert Simon won the Nobel Prize in economics for his work showing how in an uncertain world, rational decision making in business organizations not only permitted but required managers to "satisfice" multiple objectives ("subgoals") rather than maximizing only one (Simon, 1978). Only by meeting each of these subgoals in at least an adequate fashion—for example, focusing on attaining "positive profits rather than maximum profits" (p. 502)—could the organization ensure its survival. Simon's work has a broader parallel in the analytical method called systems analysis, an approach to understanding and modeling complex systems often used in computer science, engineering, biology, ecology, and evolutionary science (Meadows, 2008). In each of these fields, it is common to observe complex phenomena—machines, organisms, ecosystems—that must remain within certain parameters to survive and function. For example, a machine, organism, or ecosystem must remain within a certain temperature range, becoming neither too hot or too cold; it must take in a certain amount of energy, but not too much; it must be subject to a certain degree of stress (for example, the standard force of gravity) but not too much stress (multiple g forces). Only by staying within several parameters can the machine, organism, or ecosystem continue to function.

Like a machine, organism, or ecosystem, a business corporation is a complex system that cannot survive unless it stays within certain parameters. To continue to exist, a business corporation must make adequate profits, but it must also invest in research and development, employee loyalty, customer satisfaction, and maintaining good relations with regulators and the general public. Simon's insight was that in a world of uncertainty, it can be better to focus on satisfying each of these essential subgoals, than to try to maximize a single variable such as share price.

Of course, the systems approach presumes subgoals matter because they are necessary to achieve a higher goal: for the system to continue to exist and to function. This seems a sensible higher goal for many and perhaps most business corporations. One of the most unique and interesting characteristics of the corporate form is that corporations are legal entities that can exist in perpetuity. The characteristic of perpetual life makes the corporation uniquely suited to pursuing large-scale, long-term projects under conditions of uncertainty— projects that can span not only years or decades, but human generations (Schwartz, 2012; Stout, 2015). As we shall see later, the idea of a measurable "value" becomes almost meaningless in the context of such long-term, uncertain projects. Thus system survival becomes a more concrete, pragmatic, and measurable corporate objective than maximizing shareholder value. This may be why case law formulations of the fundamental legal doctrine known as the business judgment rule typically state that corporate directors must act, not to maximize something, but "in the honest belief that the action was taken in the interest of the company" (*Cede and Co.* v. *Technicolor, Inc.*, 634 A.2d 345, 360 (Del. 1993)).

It is important to acknowledge that not all corporations will, or should, survive in perpetuity. But this is not a problem that needs to be addressed through human intervention: as a general rule, market forces kill off dysfunctional companies (see Chapter 8, this volume). A satisficing approach to the corporate objective is thus consistent with a thriving corporate sector.

At this point, those who defend shareholder value maximization as the sole corporate objective typically turn to another argument: that unless we have a single metric to gauge corporate performance, corporate executives and boards of directors will run amok, serving their own interests and inflicting out-of-control "agency costs" in the process. As noted corporate law scholar Mark Roe has put it, these experts fear that without shareholder value maximization as a unifying goal, managers are left with "so much discretion that [they] could easily pursue their own agenda, one that might maximize neither shareholder, employee, consumer, nor national wealth, but only their own" (Roe, 2001: 2065).

The agency-cost argument is probably the most frequently offered justification for embracing shareholder wealth maximization as the corporate goal. For example, corporate law professor Stephen Bainbridge recently asserted in a *New York Times* opinion piece that "if directors were allowed to deviate from shareholder wealth maximization, they would inevitably turn to indeterminate balancing standards, which provide no accountability" (Bainbridge, 2015). This unsupported assumption, which is typical in the academic literature, shows a curious intellectual blindness. Suppose that rather than asking corporate managers to maximize a single variable like share price, we asked them to satisfy several corporate objectives: earn at least a certain amount of profits, while also keeping employee turnover beneath some level, while also meeting or exceeding minimum benchmarks for revenue growth. It is true that, once each of these subgoals has been met, managers enjoy a degree of discretion over whether and how any corporate surplus is used. But this is hardly the equivalent of "no accountability." Should they fail to meet any of the required subgoals, the managers' heads are on the metaphorical block. And if they do meet the subgoals, the company survives and thrives. In the process, it generates useful products for consumers, salaries for employees, taxes for governments, and decent—if not "maximized"—investment returns for shareholders. This would seem a pretty happy state of affairs.

In other words, there are many ways to constrain—if not eliminate—agency costs, to hold managers accountable, and to ensure successful companies, that do not require embracing a single metric. Which raises the questions: Why is this obvious possibility so often overlooked? Why do so many corporate governance experts, especially in academia, unthinkingly assume maximization of a single variable is a necessity? Why do they assume that minimizing agency costs is a more important problem than ensuring that corporations survive and contribute to society? Herbert Simon suggested the answer may be the academic desire to make corporate governance "computationally tractable" (1978: 499). If we gauge corporate performance by a single, quantifiable metric—especially something easy to observe, like share price—it becomes far easier to reduce corporate performance to an elegant mathematical equation. It becomes far easier to draw conclusions about what is "good corporate governance" from readily available public information analyzed in the comfort of one's own office. And it becomes far easier to hold oneself out as an expert who can offer silver-bullet solutions to every corporate problem, without bothering to take account of the messy complexities, uncertainties, and idiosyncrasies of individual organizations.

Thus the siren song of mathematical tractability tempts academics and corporate governance experts into assuming that maximizing a single objective, rather than satisfying many, should be the corporate goal. In the process, they sacrifice usefulness and accuracy on the altar of simplicity, mathematical ease, and the opportunity for unjustified claims of expertise.

THE FICTIONAL "SHAREHOLDER"

As we have seen, the normative case for maximizing rather than satisficing as a corporate objective is, to put it mildly, highly questionable. Even more fundamental problems appear when we look more closely at a second element of shareholder value maximization thinking: its conception of the shareholder.

The phrase "shareholder value" implicitly treats shareholders as a homogeneous mass with common interests. The shareholder becomes a Platonic ideal, a faceless entity with only one concern: maximizing value, whatever that may be. (We turn to the awkward question of what value means in the next section.) This Platonic shareholder, however, does not exist. In the real world, shares of corporations are held by individuals, either directly or indirectly through institutional investors like mutual funds and pension funds. As a result, there can be no single shareholder value because *different shareholders have different interests.*

To see how shareholders' interests differ, let us start by comparing the interests of shareholders planning to sell in the near future, with those of longer-term investors planning to hold for years or decades. During the heyday of the efficient market hypothesis—an economic theory once believed to predict stock prices always accurately reflected fundamental value—some experts argued that short-term and long-term investors had identical interests, because an efficient stock market would punish management strategies that harmed future performance (Easterbrook and Fischel, 1981). Today, finance economists have a far more modest view of market efficiency, and acknowledge prices often bear only a loose relationship to value (Stout, 2003; see also Chapter 8, this volume). This means it is possible to temporarily raise a company's share price while harming its long-term prospects (Aspen Institute, 2009; Stout, 2012a). Perhaps the most obvious example is an accounting fraud of the Enron sort. But corporate short termism can manifest itself in more subtle ways, for example in cutting payroll and research and development to increase accounting profits, or in borrowing to fund big dividend or share repurchase programs.

This puts the interests of short-term traders and long-term investors at odds. The long-term investor wants the company to invest in its future. The short-term trader, on the other hand, wants managers to do whatever will raise the share price long enough for them to sell. And there are many short-term traders in today's market. In 1960, when fixed brokerage commissions made stock trading relatively costly, shares on the New York Stock Exchange changed hands on average once every eight years. Today the average holding period for shares in US companies is only about four months (Stout, 2012a: 66). Modern shareholders do not so much own stocks, as rent them (Bogle, 2005).

A related, if intellectually distinguishable, source of conflict between shareholders arises from the fact that companies can benefit when important stakeholder groups believe the company will treat them more fairly than the law requires. For example, when they trust a corporation to look after their interests, employees and customers become more willing to make "firm-specific" investments, e.g., acquiring expertise unique to doing a particular job or using a particular product. In the parlance of economics, loyal stakeholders contribute to profitable "team production" (Blair and Stout, 1999). At the same time, after stakeholders have put their faith in the firm, shareholders might profit from exploiting this trust and loyalty. For example, the company might stop supporting an existing product to force its customers to purchase an otherwise unnecessary upgrade, or pressure its long-term employees into accepting reduced benefits by threatening job cuts.

Of course, when companies routinely behave this way, they lose the trust of employees and customers, who become reluctant to make future firm-specific investments. Ex ante, shareholders do better when companies treat stakeholders fairly (Wharton School, 2012). Nevertheless, the ex-post temptation remains to abandon fairness, and opportunistically exploit stakeholder loyalty. This creates an interesting conflict between shareholders' ex-ante interests, and shareholders' ex-post interests; a conflict between shareholders' past selves and future selves, if you will. Before stakeholders make any firm-specific investments, shareholders want the firm to treat stakeholders fairly. After stakeholders have become vulnerable, profit-minded shareholders want the company to exploit that vulnerability. Which approach truly serves "shareholder value"?

Yet a third source of conflict between shareholders arises from the reality that shareholders are human beings who have other interests at stake (Hawley and Williams, 2000). The Platonic shareholder of conventional wisdom cares only about the stock price of a single company. But real shareholders typically have diversified equity portfolios, as well as investment interests in corporate bonds, government bonds, and real estate. They often have jobs they rely on for income. Moreover, real shareholders are not only investors and employees, but also consumers who buy goods and services, citizens who pay taxes, and organisms that must breathe air and drink water.

As a result real shareholders care not only how much money the companies they invest in make, but also *how* those companies make money. The diversified shareholder who owns stock in a mining company and a lakeside resort hotel does not want the mining company profiting from practices that poison the hotel's lake. The employee who invests in a retirement savings fund does not want the fund pressuring companies in its investment portfolio to cut payroll if this means eliminating the employee's own position. Shareholders who value a healthy environment do not want the companies they invest in to save money by eliminating pollution controls. And shareholders who are also consumers benefit when their companies create and sell lightweight computer tablets and self-driving cars. In other words, many costs and benefits that would be externalities from the perspective of a Platonic shareholder are internalized for real shareholders.

Of course, not all the external costs and benefits from corporate activity are likely to be internalized. Investors in the developed world may reasonably believe they won't personally suffer if companies they invest in pollute or abuse employees on the other side of the globe. And investors alive today may not personally benefit from corporate research to cure cancer and extend the human lifespan.

But this does not mean investors are indifferent to such corporate externalities. The idea of shareholder value maximization treats shareholders as purely selfish actors who care only about their own wealth, and not about ethics or others' welfare. Extensive empirical evidence proves, however, that most people are in fact "prosocial," meaning they are willing to make at least some sacrifice to follow ethical rules and to help, or at least avoid harming, others (Stout, 2011). The small percentage of the population not willing to do this are labeled psychopaths. Concrete evidence of shareholder prosociality can be seen in the growing popularity of socially responsible investing strategies that consider social costs and benefits in addition to financial returns. For these prosocial shareholders, "shareholder value" includes the value of knowing the companies whose shares they hold are making profits in ethical, socially beneficial ways. Thus prosocial shareholders may have different ideas of value than asocial shareholders do.

When we consider all these differences between and among real shareholders, it becomes obvious that shareholders are not a monolithic group, and their interests often conflict. How should that conflict be managed? Using a "satisficing" approach, corporate directors and executives might manage intershareholder conflict by seeking to do an adequate but not perfect job of satisfying many different shareholder groups' interests. For example, they might try to ensure the company remains profitable and pays some dividends for short-term, asocial shareholders, while simultaneously trying to operate in an environmentally sustainable fashion and re-investing some profits in research and development that serves prosocial, longer-term investors. In contrast, asking managers to maximize one variable forces them to make a choice, and focus only on the interests of some subset of shareholders, rather than the diverse interests of the shareholder body.

Here is where one of the most destructive consequences of shareholder value thinking is made apparent. As the next section discusses, because the concept of value turns out to be uncertain and subjective, lawmakers, academics, and business people as a practical matter are often forced to focus instead on more immediate and objective metrics, like share price. Yet when they do this, they are implicitly privileging the interests of only a small subset of shareholders: the subset of shareholders who are most shortsighted, untrustworthy, blithely unconcerned about "external costs" they end up bearing themselves, and utterly indifferent to the truly external costs borne by others. In other words, they are implicitly treating shareholders as if they were impatient, opportunistic, self-destructive, conscienceless psychopaths. The result is a single metric—but hardly a desirable one (Stout, 2012a).

"VALUE" IS A MEANINGLESS ABSTRACTION—AND PRETENDING IT'S NOT IS DANGEROUS

Closer inspection thus reveals the first two elements of "maximizing shareholder value" as a corporate objective to be deeply problematic. Nothing in law or logic demands that corporations maximize a single variable, especially when we recognize that the homogenous shareholder is a fiction and that real shareholders' interests are diverse. These difficulties pale, however, in comparison to the difficulties created when we tell corporate directors and executives to focus on "value."

What, exactly, is the value of a shareholder's shares? The only time the answer to this question is clear is when the shareholder is in the process of becoming an ex shareholder; that is, when the shareholder sells his or her shares. At that brief moment in time, the value of the selling shareholders' interest is perfectly captured by the price of the shares. The selling shareholder has no stake in what the corporation does in the future. At any other time, however, the value of the shareholder's interest depends very much on what the corporation will do in the future. This includes not only its future profits and future share price but possibly (as just discussed) also expectations about the future external costs and benefits it may generate. And when value depends on what will happen in the future, value becomes uncertain.

Understanding uncertainty is central to understanding why value becomes an indeterminate concept once we leave behind the safe, tidy metric of today's share price (Stout, 1990; Radcliffe, 2015). Laypersons often use the words "risk" and "uncertainty" as synonyms. Since the days of Frank Knight, however, economists have viewed risk and uncertainty as quite different concepts (Knight, 1921). Risk refers to variation in future outcomes where both the possible outcomes, and the probabilities of the possible outcomes, are fully known; a coin toss is risky but not uncertain because, while we do not know if the coin will come up heads or tails, we know heads and tails are the only possible outcomes, and we know each is 50 percent likely. Uncertainty is a more ornery beast. Uncertainty describes situations where either the possible future outcomes, or the probabilities of the possible future outcomes, or both, are unknown. Whether China will become the world's dominant power, whether the human population will be decimated by epidemic disease, and whether we will be using sustainable energy sources 30 years from now are all uncertain. Similarly, whether Apple can design a breakthrough product without Steve Jobs at the helm, or whether Google's Calico project will succeed in extending the human lifespan, are uncertain. Corporations' futures are rife with uncertainty—not merely risk.

Because risk is mathematically tractable and uncertainty is not, modern finance theory tends to ignore uncertainty. The ability to predict all possible outcomes is assumed, and probabilities are assigned by extrapolating from the past or even by simple speculation. The dangers of this professional disinterest in uncertainty were the subject of Nasim Taleb's runaway bestseller *The Black Swan* (Taleb, 2010). Yet in real life, dealing with uncertainty is unavoidable, even in a risk-oriented business like a casino. In illustration of this point, Taleb recounts the story of a casino whose biggest losses stemmed not from some lucky high roller—casinos have no problem calculating and protecting themselves from the predictable risks of big wins—but from a popular performing tiger's unexpected attack on one of its human trainers (p. 30).

Uncertainty is a crucial concept in understanding the limits of valuation. This is because uncertainty about the future allows disagreement. Where one investor thinks Apple will thrive without Steve Jobs, another predicts the firm is destined for decline; where one analyst expects Google's Calico to produce results, another predicts the project will be a bust. Which is right? Which has the better view of Apple's or Google's true value? Uncertainty and disagreement make the business of valuing any ongoing business notoriously subjective, as witness the hundreds of pages of finance texts devoted to different valuation techniques and the thriving market for investment bankers' "fair value" opinions. There are a variety of ways to approach the valuation problem—one can focus on book value, discounted cash flow, EBIT, EBITDA, earnings multiples, etc.—and each requires the person doing the valuing to make a number of assumptions. Will earnings increase, decrease, or remain steady in the future? What discount rate applies? Not surprisingly, professional evaluators often refuse to settle on a single number, instead committing themselves only to a range of possible "fair" values. Even so, different evaluators frequently disagree in their opinions—a contest between valuation experts is a standard feature of corporate litigation.

The subjectivity inherent in attaching any number other than today's market price to a shareholder's interest in a company defeats the claim that asking managers to focus on "shareholder value" somehow adds simplicity, objectivity, or rigor to the messy business of gauging whether corporate directors and executives are doing a good job. Far from providing a solid basis for holding managers accountable, describing the corporate objective in terms of value invites subjectivity, disagreement, and manipulation. The CEO's claim that her chosen strategy will maximize shareholder value "in the long run" and the activist fund manager's claim that he can "unlock shareholder value" are equally unfalsifiable—and equally useless—to the shareholder who plans to hold his or her shares. When, if ever, does the "long run" arrive? Put bluntly, shareholder value is a meaningless metric that cannot measure performance. Business professor Dana Radcliffe recounts the story of a friend who asked his accountant what maximize shareholder value meant and was told "anything you want it to mean" (Radcliffe, 2015).

Indeed, embracing value as the corporate objective is worse than useless—it is downright dangerous. This is because emphasizing the supposed goal of shareholder value invites corporate directors, executives, and investors to pursue strategies that cause corporations to perform more poorly not only for society but also for shareholders themselves. The danger comes from the irresistible temptation to treat "value," which is uncertain, subjective, and open to disagreement, as synonymous with "today's share price," which is known, objective, and universally agreed upon (Stout, 2005). The tendency for value to be unthinkingly equated with share price can be seen in the common academic habit of measuring corporate performance using "Tobin's Q," i.e., the ratio between share price and book value. It can be seen in executive compensation packages that supposedly tie pay to performance by emphasizing stock options or restricted stock. It can be seen in the behavior of the pension funds charged with the long-term goal of supporting their beneficiaries' retirements that measure progress toward that goal in terms of annual or even quarterly changes in the prices of the stocks in their portfolios.

The common conflation of value and stock price leads to a number of dysfunctional corporate behaviors. One is corporate short termism—which, as noted in the previous section, serves short-term speculators at the expense of longer-term investors. For example, in the quest to unlock value, managers may try to raise reported earnings by cutting expenses like payroll, marketing, or research and development. This produces an immediate increase in accounting "profits" that can raise share price, but also leaves the company in a weaker long-term position (Aspen Institute, 2009). A second common form of dysfunctional corporate behavior driven by shareholder value thinking is using share repurchase programs to manipulate stock price. Share repurchases can raise price, because in a world of uncertainty, investors disagree in their subjective estimates of a stock's value. Given likely market imperfections, this investor disagreement results in a downward-sloping demand curve for the stock (Miller, 1977; Stout, 1990). Downward-sloping demand means that if a company increases the supply of stock available on the market by issuing new shares, it has to lower the price to induce marginal investors to buy; conversely, restricting the supply of stock available to investors through corporate buyback programs drives price upwards. Unfortunately, when corporate managers focus their attention on such "financial engineering," they are distracted from the more difficult business of operating the company effectively. And when they borrow to fund repurchases, they increase firm risk and the likelihood of failure (Lazonick, 2014).

Another problem created by treating share price as synonymous with value is that this encourages wasteful corporate mergers and acquisitions. In the typical corporate acquisition, the bidder pays a premium over the market price for target's stock. This makes it look on first inspection as if the sale created "value." Empirical studies have found, however, that on average the bidder does not run the acquired company more efficiently or profitably, and the increase in the target's stock price is offset by a decline in the bidder's

(Moeller et al., 2005). This phenomenon can be explained as a result of the "winner curse" that causes winning bidders to overpay in auctions (Roll, 1986; Thaler, 1988). The practical result is that corporate mergers and acquisitions typically enrich activist investors and CEOs whose wealth is concentrated in the target's stock, but fail to benefit either diversified investors who own stock in both target and bidder, or society as a whole.

Yet another source of dysfunction arises when executive pay is determined by stock price performance. As Roger Martin has pointed out, if a talented and dedicated management team is already running a firm quite well, the price of the company's stock may already be quite high—management might plausibly claim the price is already maximized. In such a case, it will be near impossible for the management to raise the price further. If executive pay is tied to share price increases, the executive team must first give the market room to run by *decreasing* the price, effectively resetting the baseline against which performance is measured. The result is that focusing on increasing shareholder value can create perverse incentives for executives to periodically try to reduce share price, so they can subsequently enjoy share price increases (Martin, 2011).

Finally, one of the most destructive consequences of the modern fixation on maximizing shareholder value may be the way it discourages corporations from pursuing basic research—sometimes called pure research or discovery research—without a clear commercial goal. This downside to embracing shareholder value as an objective is easy for many experts to overlook, because of the training they receive in introductory economics and finance classes. These classes typically encourage students to think of economic efficiency in terms of incremental improvements made by re-allocating existing resources until we find the mix that puts us on the "efficiency frontier" (Markowitz, 1952). Economists who specialize in economic growth, however, argue that the vast majority of economic growth comes not from re-allocating existing resources, but from technological innovations that create new resources or discover new ways to use existing resources (Mowery and Rosenberg, 1989). The idea of "exogenous" growth was the basis for economist Robert Solow's 1987 Nobel Prize (Solow, 1987).

But if innovation is the key to growth, where does innovation come from? It comes from discovery—discovery that is by definition unknowable and unpredictable. After all, if something is known and predicted, it has already been discovered. The unpredictable, unknowable nature of discovery puts innovation and maximizing shareholder value immediately at odds with each other. Even the most perfectly efficient stock market cannot incorporate information into prices if the information in question does not yet exist. As a result, we cannot expect the stock market to reward companies that invest in pure research with no predictable commercial application. To the stock market, this sort of investment in discovery looks like a waste—even if it is exactly the sort of investment most likely to lead to the kinds of dramatic technological breakthroughs, like the light bulb or the transistor, that ultimately create the most future "shareholder value." Given the importance of innovation to economic growth, the possibility that an obsession with shareholder value maximization may be discouraging corporations from investing in pure research is something that should concern us all.

When this possibility is combined with the other corporate dysfunctions we encounter when shareholder value thinking shifts managers' focus to share price—dysfunctions like short termism, a shift from real engineering to "financial engineering," endless mergers and acquisitions, and the possibility of perverse incentives to drive share price down in order to be able to increase it later on—it becomes clear that embracing shareholder value maximization as the corporate objective is not only an irrational and intellectually empty idea, but a destructive one.

CONCLUSION

Modern corporations can be extraordinarily complex institutions. They can have millions of customers, shareholders, and employees. Some earn revenues greater than the gross domestic products of many nation-states. They provide benefits to—and impose costs on—a wide variety of groups: investors, employees, customers, taxing governments, members of the local community, people half a world away. They operate around the globe. As entities gifted with perpetual life, they can also operate across human generations.

Complexity is psychologically challenging. Some individuals even find it frightening. How much simpler it would be—how reassuring!—if we could find a single, quantifiable, easily observed criterion for measuring corporate performance. Then we would know, easily and immediately, which firms to invest in and which to avoid; which companies were run well and which were run poorly; which executives deserve a raise and which deserve the boot.

The desire to avoid complexity goes a long way towards explaining why the idea of maximizing shareholder value has been so eagerly embraced by so many. Unfortunately, closer inspection reveals that this approach offers only an illusion of precision and certainty, a mirage that disappears when we draw nearer and examine it more carefully. "Maximize shareholder value," it turns out, is an unnecessary, unworkable, and destructive corporate goal.

REFERENCES

Aspen Institute (2009). *Overcoming Short-Termism: A Call for a More Responsible Approach to Investment and Business Management.* New York: Aspen Institute.

Available at: <https://www.aspeninstitute.org/sites/default/files/content/docs/pubs/overcome_short_state0909_0.pdf>.

Bainbridge, S. (2015). "A Duty to Shareholder Value," *New York Times*, April 16. Available at: <http://www.nytimes.com/roomfordebate/2015/04/16/what-are-corporations-obligations-to-shareholders/a-duty-to-shareholder-value>.

Blair, M. and Stout, L. A. (1999). "A Team Production Theory of Corporate Law," *Virginia Law Review*, 85(2): 247–328.

Bogle, J. C. (2005). *The Battle for the Soul of Capitalism*. New Haven, CT: Yale University Press.

Cede and Co. v. Technicolor, Inc., 634 A.2d 345 (Del. 1993).

Davis, G. F. (2013). "After the Corporation," *Politics and Society*, 41(2): 283–308.

Denning, S. (2011). "The Dumbest Idea in the World: Maximizing Shareholder Value," *Forbes*, November 28. Available at: <http://www.forbes.com/sites/stevedenning/2011/11/28/maximizing-shareholder-value-the-dumbest-idea-in-the-world/>.

Easterbrook, F. H. and Fischel, D. R. (1981). "The Proper Role of a Target's Management in Responding to a Tender Offer," *Harvard Law Review*, 94(6): 1161–204.

Elhauge, E. (2005). "Sacrificing Corporate Profits in the Public Interest," *New York University Law Review*, 80(3): 733–869.

Hawley, J. P. and Williams, A. T. (2000). *The Rise of Fiduciary Capitalism: How Institutional Investors Can Make Corporate America More Democratic*. Philadelphia, PA: University of Philadelphia Press.

Jensen, M. C. (2010). "Value Maximization, Stakeholders Theory, and the Corporate Objective Function," *Journal of Applied Corporate Finance*, 22(1): 32–42.

Knight, F. H. (1921). *Risk, Uncertainty, and Profit*. Boston, MA: Houghton Mifflin Co.

Lazonick, W. (2014). "Profits without Prosperity," *Harvard Business Review*, 92(9): 46–55.

Markowitz, H. (1952). "Portfolio Selection," *Journal of Finance*, 7(1): 77–91.

Martin, R. L. (2011). *Fixing the Game: Bubbles, Crashes, and What Capitalism Can Learn from the NFL*. Boston, MA: Harvard Business Review Press.

Meadows, D. H. (2008). *Thinking in Systems: A Primer*. White River Junction, VT: Chelsea Green.

Miller, E. M. (1977). "Risk, Uncertainty, and Divergence of Opinion," *Journal of Finance*, 32(4): 1151–68.

Moeller, S. B., Schlingemann, F., and Stulz, R. M. (2005). "Wealth Destruction on a Massive Scale? A Study of Acquiring-Firm Returns in the Recent Merger Wave," *Journal of Finance*, 60(2): 757–82.

Montier, J. (2014). "Shareholder Value Maximization: The World's Dumbest Idea?" Video, 44:31, CFA Institute. October 17. Available at: <http://livestream.com/livecfa/EIC-Montier>.

Mowery, D. C. and Rosenberg, N. (1989). *Technology and the Pursuit of Economic Growth*. New York: Cambridge University Press.

Porter, M. E. and Kramer, M. R. (2011). "Creating Shared Value," *Harvard Business Review*, 89(1/2): 62–77.

Radcliffe, D. (2015). "Maximizing Shareholder Value: Why the Baseless Dogma Persists" (unpublished manuscript).

Roe, M. J. (2001). "The Shareholder Wealth Maximization Norm and Industrial Organization," *University of Pennsylvania Law Review*, 149(6): 2063–81.

Roll, R. (1986). "The Hubris Hypothesis of Corporate Takeovers," *Journal of Business*, 59(2): 197–216.

Schwartz, A. A. (2012). "The Perpetual Corporation," *George Washington Law Review*, 80(3): 764–830.

Simon, H. A. (1978). "Rational Decision-Making in Business Organizations," *American Economic Review*, 69(4): 493–513.

Solow, R. M. (1987). *Prize Lecture: Growth Theory and After*. Nobel Media. Available at: <http://www.nobelprize.org/nobel_prizes/economic-sciences/laureates/1987/solow-lecture.html>.

Stout, L. A. (1990). "Are Takeover Premiums Really Premiums? Market Price, Fair Value, and Corporate Law," *Yale Law Journal*, 99(6): 1235–96.

Stout, L. A. (2003). "The Mechanisms of Market Inefficiency: An Introduction to the New Finance," *Journal of Corporation Law*, 28(4): 635–69.

Stout, L. A. (2005). "Share Price as a Poor Criterion for Good Corporate Law," *Berkeley Business Law Journal*, 3(1): 43–57.

Stout, L. A. (2011). *Cultivating Conscience: How Good Laws Make Good People*. Princeton, NJ: Princeton University Press.

Stout, L. A. (2012a). *The Shareholder Value Myth: How Putting Shareholders First Harms Investors, Corporations, and the Public*. San Francisco, CA: Berrett-Koehler.

Stout, L. A. (2012b). "Why Do Corporations Need A Single Purpose?" *Harvard Business Review*, May 29. Available at: <https://hbr.org/2012/05/why-do-corporations-need-a-sin>.

Stout, L. A. (2015). "The Corporation as Time Machine: Intergenerational Equity, Intergenerational Efficiency, and the Corporate Form," *Seattle University Law Review*, 38(2): 685–723.

Taleb, N. N. (2010). *The Black Swan: The Impact of the Highly Improbable*, 2nd ed. New York: Random House.

Thaler, R. H. (1988). "Anomalies," *Journal of Economic Perspectives*, 2(1): 191–202.

Wharton School (2012). *Declining Employee Loyalty: A Casualty of the New Workplace*. Philadelphia, PA: Wharton School, University of Pennsylvania. Available at: <http://knowledge.wharton.upenn.edu/article/declining-employee-loyalty-a-casualty-of-the-new-workplace/>.

13

Narrowcasting

How Media and Political Disruption Changed the Economic Debate

John Stackhouse

INTRODUCTION

Just before noon on September 17, 2011, a few hundred demonstrators gathered around the Charging Bull statue at New York's Bowling Green Park. They were only two blocks from Wall Street, the heart of global capitalism. The crowd had responded to an appeal by *Adbusters*, a Canadian activist magazine, to form a protest against American-style market economics, and to do so peacefully. Dubbed "Occupy Wall Street," the group didn't storm the barricades, or even throw a rock. Instead, they listened to a marching band and held yoga and tai chi classes in the park, before moving to One Chase Manhattan Plaza where, just before the stock market closed for the day, they set up a "people's assembly" to challenge the financial establishment.

Nearly everything about the day was symbolic. Almost three years earlier to the day, on September 15, 2008, a financially shocked world turned its eyes to this corner of Manhattan as Lehman Brothers collapsed, threatening to take with it the global economy. Since then, Wall Street had rebounded, partly on the back of government money. The emotional and physical ashes of the adjacent World Trade Center, destroyed by terrorists a decade earlier, were also disappearing. And yet, Americans remained anxious about an economy that was not producing enough quality jobs or opportunities, and angry about the latest round of Wall Street bonus payments. On the streets around the people's assembly, and across the country, the resonance of hope and resilience continued to collide with that of fear and failure—a disconnect that the organizers of Occupy wanted to capture in order to prove, at least in their view, that America was again undermining itself. As unemployment, government debt, and income stagnation prevailed, they argued, something had to be done about the broader economic system. "We thought, why isn't there a backlash here?" one of the principals of the Occupy movement, Kalle Lasn, the editor-in-chief of *Adbusters*, told CNN Money. "We need to shake up the corporate-driven capitalist system we're in. To do that, we needed something radical" (Pepitone, 2011).

Occupy Wall Street went on to become a cultural icon and one of the most prominent social media memes of 2011. It had drawn inspiration from the Arab Spring, the collage of people's movements across the Middle East and North Africa that had been bubbling since 2010, culminating in the resignation in early 2011 of Egyptian president Hosni Mubarak. But unlike the protests in Cairo's Tahrir Square or Istanbul's Gezi Park, hundreds of thousands of people did not respond to #Occupy's rallying cry. At best, over the next two months, no more than a few hundred people gathered in the camp around Wall Street, while their desire for "something radical" met with ridicule. The *New York Times* did not cover the self-styled movement until the end of its first week, and even then its dismissiveness oozed from the headline, "Wall Street Occupiers, Protesting till Whenever" (Klienfield and Buckley, 2011). Many American media commentators showed contempt for the demonstrators, describing them as entitled, middle-class youth and pointing to their preference for things like Levi jeans, Starbuck's coffee, and iPhones as evidence of consumer hypocrisy. From the day the protests launched, politicians on both the left and right looked at it with equal askance. Few wanted to become the movement's target, fearing they would be labeled Wall Street apologists. Just as few endorsed its manifesto, fearing they would be labeled radical sympathizers.

And so, the movement designed to create an Arab Spring for America faded instead into the gray chill of autumn. On November 15, local authorities forced the Occupy camp to shut down, and the movement fizzled, leaving the world with a catchy name but little change to public discourse. Of course, the financial sector was not unscathed by a general public distaste for its role in the financial crisis. An array of regulations, more active oversight, and tighter capital controls continued to be thrust on Wall Street and its global counterparts. But for those who hoped for an informed debate about the system, rather than more policing of it, disappointment loomed. In Europe, post-crisis politics continued to be dominated by fiscal issues, primarily about fiscal deficits, stimulus, austerity, and the state's role in the economy. But more fundamental changes to the rules of capitalism, or reflection on its spirit and intent, were not to be.

This chapter shows how public discourse about the global economy has been curtailed by the disruption of journalism and politics over the last quarter-century, largely through the proliferation of digital media. The transition of news to internet-based, and more recently mobile-based, platforms has shortened news cycles and atomized audiences, and thus reduced the scope for serious debate among disparate groups of citizens. The narrowing of political debate has been accentuated by a secular decline in voter partici-pation and the pronounced influence of campaign financing and third-party engagement in public policy, particularly in the United States, which has narrowed the space for alternative points of view. The chapter examines the reasons behind Occupy Wall Street's limited impact, and explore the twin declines in participatory democracy and media engagement, the rise and limitations of social media, and the consequences to public debate, as seen through coverage of the 2008 financial crisis. It concludes with a review of alternative models for digital media and political dialogue, exploring whether they can re-energize public participation and again widen the range of policy options given serious public consideration.

WHY "#OCCUPYWALLSTREET" FAILED

#OccupyWallStreet was supposed to be a game changer in how economic policy was discussed in the West. It was not just people power, an age-old form of protest. It was meant to be a hub for global conversation, using social media to fly over the gates erected by commercial and even state-owned media. Traditionally, this was the sort of protest that media gatekeepers might view as fringe and not worthy of coverage. After all, innumerable protests, big and small, occur every day; only when they actually change something, the argu-ment goes, can they be considered news. Social media disrupted that theory, and restored the importance of volume to news. If something got retweeted enough, it became the virtual equivalent of the Million Man March, a dem-onstration of interest that caught the eyes of policymakers and interest groups, regardless of what traditional media said. That did not happen with #Occupy, where a surge of social media interest was ultimately disregarded by traditional media and government because the movement itself seemed to lack leadership or an agenda. It was seen largely as a protest.

What was lost along the way? In 2011, the economy was the single most important issue in most Western countries, and the role of finance in the economy was viewed skeptically across party lines. Why, then, were political parties not more vocal about fundamental changes to the economic system? And why did the mainstream media not give more airtime to fundamental questions? The director of University of British Columbia's journalism school, Alfred Hermida, boils it down to complexity: "When the media cover alter-native movements, they tend to focus on the clashes between protesters and police. Any political aims are buried by the accounts of violence," he writes in *Tell Everyone: Why We Share and Why It Matters* (Hermida, 2014). "Journal-ists are understandably perplexed at how to cover movements such as Gezi or

Occupy, which seemingly lack identifiable leaders or a set list of demands. Confrontation with the police makes for a much clearer narrative."

The same appeared to be true for Occupy, and the many protest movements it spawned. After an initial burst of confrontation or violence, media attention disappeared, and along with it any political concern. In early October 2011, according to an analysis by the Pew Research Center's Project for Excellence in Journalism (PEJ), the Occupy movement was mentioned in 10 percent of a sample of national news coverage (PEJ, 2011). That fell to about 5 percent during the first week of November and less than 1 percent in the second week, when the protestors were evicted. When reviewing the news reports, Alicia Shepard, a former ombudsman for National Public Radio, said most of the coverage "hasn't been about the issues, it's been about who's up and who's down" (quoted by Stelter, 2011). She compared it to the "horse race" style of coverage prevalent in political campaigns, and even then, interest waned quickly.

A half-decade later, much more is at play than "protest reporting." Behind short bursts of attention around events like Occupy Wall Street, the very technologies that enabled #Occupy have fragmented news consumers—and electorates—to such a degree that single, sustained discussions on serious issues are increasingly rare, even for well-resourced corporations, governments, and interest groups wanting to engage the public. The following section will examine some of the forces behind these shifts, and explore the consequences in more detail.

THE DRIVERS OF PUBLIC DISINTEREST

The fragmentation of Western society was well underway before the advent of digital technologies. The 20th century, particularly following the Second World War, was shaped by a decentralization of society, away from the institutions and forces—religion, media, labor, social strata—that bonded diverse groups of people around public issues. This fragmentation continued through the past two decades, even as the internet made people more connected than ever. Today, large segments of society organize themselves and their interests around smaller, virtual social circles that are disconnected from a global context.

The Decline of Democratic Participation

In the mid-20th century, the explosion of mass communications and mass transit combined to break down traditional communities and social networks. As individuals became untethered from political parties, churches, community associations, and traditional media habits—the evening newspaper, for instance—their ability to rally and sustain large groups around single issues or themes declined. This has been most visible in the secular decline in voter turnout. In Canada, a relatively stable and prosperous democracy, turnout remained remarkably consistent for a century after Confederation in 1867, hovering between 70 percent and 80 percent, with occasional dips into the high 60s. It began to turn in the early 1970s, and has stayed around 60 percent in four of the last five federal elections. Provincial elections have fared worse, dropping by about 20 percentage points in terms of turnout since the 1970s (Elections Canada, 2015). Technology appears to have played a role. Voter participation at the federal level reached record highs around the time of mass purchasing of color television, in the elections of 1958, 1962, and 1963, when turnout was over 79 percent. By contrast, the lowest turnout on record was around the ascent of smartphones, in 2008, when it was 58.8 percent (Elections Canada, 2015). The decline in voter participation is a clear pattern across affluent democracies. As a percentage of the voting age population in a cross-section of elections, the US in 2012 had a 53.6 percent turnout, Japan in 2014 saw 52 percent, Canada produced 54.2 percent, Italy 68.6 percent, and Germany 66 percent. France at 72.2 percent was highest among G8 countries, yet only 13th globally. Canada was 29th. Voter turnout in parliamentary elections between 2005 and 2015 was 61.9 percent in Canada, 68.6 percent in the Americas and 74.9 percent in Western Europe. An exception to the trend occurred in the October 2015 Canadian federal election, when voter turnout was 68.5 percent (CBC News, 2015).

The consequence has been obvious to both political parties and the media that cover them. As turnout fell, parties have learned to narrowcast their policies and pursue voter support with a blend of ideologies and transactional policies that appeal to small segments—niches—of the population. In the Canadian federal election in 2011, Stephen Harper's Conservatives won a parliamentary majority with 5.2 million votes out of 24.2 million eligible voters. Some 14.8 million votes were cast. Target politics—or base politics, as it is often called—is more acute in the United States. In the 2014 midterm elections, turnout of 36.4 percent was the lowest since 1942 (United States Election Project, 2014). In those elections, the Republicans were able to increase their hold on Congress by winning 60 percent of the white vote, while the Democrats won 89 percent of the black vote and 62 percent of the Latino vote (Pew Research Center, 2014).

The Decline of Traditional News Media

The narrowcasting of politics cannot be viewed in isolation from the narrowing of mass media over the last half-century. The power of the mainstream news business—the primary portal through which the public sees and understands economic policy, and indeed the evolving nature of the capitalist economy—has been dwindling since the 1950s, despite bursts of significance in every decade since. It is not simply an outcome of digital technology. Mass media was built on the backs of several technological revolutions: the telegraph, which made news current; radio, which brought live events into the home; television, which made news visual; and the microchip, which turned news into an interactive information business. The satellite and fiber optics accelerated these changes but also began to disintermediate and diminish traditional media by putting the creation and dissemination of news into the hands of individuals. Just as geographic mobility changed politics, electronic mobility changed media.

The first to be hit hard was the newspaper industry, which has been in steady decline since 1950, when at their height in the US newspapers published 350 copies for every 1,000 people. By 1990, it was 250. By 2010, it was 150 (Mitchell, 2015). Just as the mass reach of newspapers was lost to television and then the internet, their unique value to advertisers—cheap and targeted—was also trumped by digital. According to the 2015 *State of the News Media* report, ad revenue for newspapers is less than half of what it was a decade ago, and daily circulation is down 19 percent in the same period (Mitchell, 2015). For a glimpse of the economic carnage suffered by newspapers, consider classified advertising, once the highest margin line of business for newspapers. The *New York Times*' classified revenue fell from about $200 million a year to $10 million. In Britain, in just five years, classified ad spending in newspapers went from £2 billion a year to £1 billion. The direct loss of profit forced newspapers across the West to slash the size of their newsrooms. In the US alone, some 15,000 newsroom jobs were eliminated in the first decade of this century, forcing newspapers to be much more selective about what they covered (Jurkowitz, 2014).

The challenged state of media economics speaks to a much larger social force, which is the splintering of audiences, a force that began with digital and exploded with mobile. In the 15 years leading to 2012, the number of mobile phones grew 20-fold, to 6.2 billion. Audiences that were once beholden to a small number of publications and broadcasting outlets to understand the world around them suddenly had more choice than humans had ever known, and more than any human could comprehend: 634 million websites, a billion Facebook users and 3 billion hours a month of YouTube content (Pingdom. com, 2013). In Canada, a country of 35 million people, Facebook in 2014 said it had 20 million users—16 million who used the platform daily and visited, on average, 14 times a day. A threshold had been crossed, as Canadians spent as much time on Facebook—20 hours a month—as they once did with daily newspapers. Although newspaper journalism was one of the sources people read and shared on Facebook, the audience for any single discussion tended to be much smaller than it had been in the era of mass media (Usman, 2014).

The rise of social media led to a noted journalistic shift to populist fare—extreme weather videos, celebrity photo galleries, and "listicles," i.e., the telling of stories through lists—as traditional news organizations strove to maintain digital relevance and revenue. Equally important, the mobile revolution also led to a shift in current affairs, to a greater focus on local news, which in turn pulled people away from large societal issues. Local news is generally cheaper to produce, more compelling to mid-market audiences, and accessible to local advertisers. A significant study by the Pew Research Center, conducted during the summer of 2014 and published in 2015, looked at news habits in three distinct and disparate urban areas (Denver, Colorado; Macon, Georgia; and Sioux City, Iowa) and found a strong trend to local news (Mitchell et al., 2015). Nine in ten respondents said they followed local news, and about half said they did so very closely. Their preferred source of news also shifted from traditional media like newspapers to local TV and a growing number of source-generated news feeds, such as police forces, school boards, and local politicians.

News became briefer, too. The Pew study found 45 percent of news items in the Denver market were less than 30 seconds, and tended to be read by the anchor rather than a reporter: "Fewer than two in ten stories in each city were more than two minutes long" (Mitchell et al., 2015: 8). Perhaps a greater concern should be this: the study affirmed that newspapers are the only medium to focus on civic issues. It said 30 percent of *Denver Post* stories were on government, politics, economics, or education, while 11 percent of TV stories were devoted to those areas. And only newspapers did any significant amount of original reporting, although that, too, has been in decline.

The Decline of Public Trust

While the frenetic pace of our society has driven public attention away from long-term issues, the growing distrust of institutions has added to that distance. Even those in media and public policy who try to foster serious debate face an uphill climb for credulity. Skepticism of state, church, and media—three of the four estates—has grown steadily since the culture wars of the 1960s. The past decade has eroded trust more, fueled by the financial crisis, the Afghan and Iraq wars, exposés of sexual abuses in religious orders, and ethical breaches in large media organizations.

According to the *Edelman Trust Barometer*, which is produced by the US public relations firm Edelman (2015), business has regained much of the public trust it lost during the 2008 financial crisis, but government and media have not. Its 2014 trust rating put non-government organizations (NGOs) on the top of the heap, in terms of public confidence, with 64 percent of respondents to its survey saying they had total trust or a great deal of trust in NGOs. The figure had not changed from the previous year. Business was not far behind at 58 percent, and also stable, with trust in technology firms growing. By contrast, media had dropped five points in one year to 52 percent while government was down to 44 percent, a four-point decline in one year. The decline in trust in media was recorded in four out of every five countries Edelman surveyed, while business was consistently trusted more than government. This public cynicism fits with other research that shows two thirds of Americans believe their country is headed in the wrong direction, and only 20 percent trust Washington to do anything about it. Instead, they are turning to private networks—business associations, social movements, and NGOs—to try to tackle long-term and systemic challenges.

The decline of public financing for state media that began in the 1980s left a void in the early years of digital, as once-dominant state broadcasts—a common force in much of the world outside the United States—fell prey to general cuts to public spending. If those cuts were palatable politically, it was because the emerging internet ensured more access to media than the world had known. Suddenly, media—public or private—seemed less essential. Just as suddenly, the public had many other points of connectivity than traditional civic engagement. Today in Canada, only 30 percent of adults say they follow politics and public policy issues. In such an environment, as we have seen, politics has become local and transactional, leaving governments to focus more on service delivery and less on structure. Some view this in the broader context of "hunkering down"— of a globalized public that feels it has no control, indeed no say, in the bigger world around it, and is thus focused on its own needs, wants, ambitions, and fears. According to Canadian economist J. Peter Venton (Venton, 2015):

> Political parties compete to maximize their political power by chasing the 'centre.' But the centre is dominated by the affluent because they have high voter participation rates and because the remainder of the electorate have relatively low voter participation rates. The latter include most of the poor, the vulnerable and small 'l' liberals.

Toronto Star writer Susan Delacourt argues that citizens are not, for the most part, informed consumers (Delacourt, 2013):

> They tune in only to the politicians and governments who provide them with tangible improvements to their material world…In a nation of consumer-citizens, it's not the politician's job to change people's minds or prejudices, but to confirm them or play to them, to seal the deal of support.

Among the results, Delacourt writes, is that political parties become brands while policies become product launches. Social media was supposed to bend this arc, by engaging younger voters, informing politics, and energizing public debate, lifting it from the transactional to the transformational. And for a time it did—but only for a time.

The Shifting Sands of Social Media

Internet-based media became a significant political force in the late 1980s, as bloggers began to engage wider public audiences and the introduction of Really Simple Syndication feeds allowed readers to customize their own menus of news and ideas. In the middle of the 2000s, two other advances— 3G wireless technology and the iPhone—enabled the exponential growth of mobile media, and with it the social media channels that allowed real-time sharing and discussion of news among groups of citizens. The political ramifications grew apparent in the 2008 US presidential election campaign.

Barack Obama's run for the presidency that year was supposed to be a turning point in media, politics, and public policy. Just as John F. Kennedy in 1960 showed the strength of television to a political class still rooted in the Roosevelt radio era, Obama established the supremacy of social media in his first run for the White House. On Facebook, Obama had 2.4 million fans; his first rival John McCain, 620,000. On Twitter, Obama had 112,000 followers; McCain, 4,600. By 2012, Obama had 30.7 million Facebook followers; his second rival Mitt Romney, 8.8 million. The Twitter gap was 21 million to 1.3 million. The social surge was not lost on journalists, who saw the rise of democratic media as both a professional challenge and opportunity (Pilkington and Michel, 2012).

After several years of growing cynicism over the impact of government, from climate change to the Iraq War, social media seemed to be reconnecting Millennials, i.e., those born after 1980, with politics. A Pew Center-commissioned survey found one third of Millennials said they had engaged in the 2008 campaign, higher than either Baby Boomers, i.e., those born between 1945 and 1965, or Generation X, i.e., those born between 1965 and 1980 (Pew Research Center, 2008). That burst seems to have been short-lived, as Millennials began to disengage from the formal political process soon after the financial crisis. According to a survey commissioned by the Toronto-based organization Samara, which promotes democratic engagement, 91 percent of young people said they would not join a political party, 82 percent had not volunteered during a campaign, and, perhaps most remarkably, 70 percent said they did not post political content through social media. This is not simply a generational phenomenon. The Samara Citizens' Survey, which in December 2014 sampled 2,406 Canadians over the age of 18, found that only 31 percent felt politics affects them every day while 58 percent do not trust political parties. An astonishing 39 percent said they had not had a political conversation, online or offline, all year (Samara, 2015).

The trend of political disengagement is greatest among younger citizens. Yet, while major parties have focused on smaller and older niches of voters, the Millennial generation has channeled its interests and energies elsewhere. In 2014, the consulting firm Deloitte, which conducts a regular survey of media habits, detected for the first time that young adults were getting their news from social media as much as from television and more than from anywhere else. In its survey of 2,000 Americans, a quarter of a group it calls Trailing Millennials—aged 14–25—said they turned to social media first for news. Only 15 percent of old Millennials (26–31), 10 percent of Generation X (32–48), and 3 percent of Baby Boomers (49–67) gave the same response. About a quarter of older Millennials and Gen-Xers turned to online sites first (Deloitte, 2014). Political parties and news organizations can no longer treat young adults as a passive audience; they are equal shapers and distributors of content and ideas. That does not mean the social media generation is civically disengaged; they have just turned to more particular concerns and bespoke channels, many of them quite serious and certainly a challenge to traditional organizations wanting to control conversations—with the #BringBackOur-Girls Twitter campaign in protest of Boko Haram's kidnapping of hundreds of girls in Nigeria, and the Ice Bucket Challenge to support research into ALS (or Lou Gehrig's disease) as two recent examples.

CONSEQUENCES: THE FINANCIAL CRISIS OF 2008 AS A MISSED MOMENT

If ever there was a chance to break the shackles of debate, it came with the financial crisis of 2008. For the first time in at least a generation, the public was acutely aware of the limits of the economic system, and how indeed that system did not, in the eyes of many, enhance a common good. The US presidential campaign and the attendant media coverage nurtured a broader debate about capitalism. State ownership, relative tax burdens, Keynesian stimulants, trade policies, the very nature of risk and reward: everything seemed up for debate. But as soon as the economy went from crisis to mere challenge, the terms of debate changed once again.

In 2009, PEJ found media coverage of the evolving crisis to be narrow and largely determined by Washington action and New York reaction (PEJ, 2009a). The American middle was lost in between, and Main Street disengaged. The mainstream press focused on a relatively small number of major storylines, mostly generating from those two cities. Meanwhile, a companion analysis of a broader array of media using a new "meme tracker" technology developed at Cornell University found that phrases and ideas—the early parameters of debate—came mostly from government, particularly from the president and the chairman of the Federal Reserve (see PEJ, 2009a). In the heart of the crisis, three storylines accounted for 40 percent of economic coverage: help to revive the banking sector, the battle over the stimulus package, and the struggles of the US auto industry. Other topics—retail sales, food prices, the impact of the crisis on social security and Medicare, its effect on education and the implications for health care—combined to account for just over 2 percent of all the economic coverage.

If the range of issues was narrow, the dominant voices were even fewer. Another PEJ study on media coverage of the crisis found that nearly half of the stories studied were triggered by government officials and business leaders (PEJ, 2009b). The White House and federal agencies alone initiated nearly a third (32 percent) of economic stories studied through the first half-year of the Obama Administration. Business triggered another 21 percent. About a quarter of the stories (23 percent) was initiated by the press itself and did not rely on an external news trigger, and 17 percent of all stories were investigative or enterprise journalism. The study found that ordinary citizens and union workers combined to act as the catalyst for only 2 percent of the stories about the economy. Banking stories, in particular, were institutionally driven. On overall economic coverage from February 1 to July 3, 2009, the Obama Administration was the dominant newsmaker. Given public distrust of politicians and the media who cover them, this narrowing of news sources almost certainly had to lead to public disengagement—and thus a lost opportunity for a deeper structural debate.

A more reflective view in media coincided with the G20 leaders summits that, post-crisis, had assumed the pre-eminent voice on economic policy previously held by the narrower range of wealthy G7 countries plus Russia. It was meant to be the beginning of a broader, deeper, and more informed discussion of global economic policy—among governments as well as NGOs at the G20 summits and the worldwide media covering them. That hope didn't last long. The first G20 summit in this new format, in Toronto in 2010, saw media begin to focus on questions of economic structure, only to be distracted within hours of the summit's opening by street violence between police and protestors who, ironically, wanted to bring attention to systemic issues. Over the rest of the summit, both media coverage and political action turned to sabotage, police behavior, civil liberties, and the financial cost of such gatherings.

Through the early part of this decade, the anger around G20 summits and the hope of the Arab Spring combined to give rise to other popular movements that aimed to circumvent both mainstream media and official politics. The Occupy movement, as it took off in 2011, epitomized this approach. Was this yet one more attempt at a Third Way? Once again, media and political parties seemed to fall into line in terms of their positioning. Following Occupy, the Fraser Institute published in 2012 a study of coverage that indicated no great shift in media bias. As proxies, the study used the words "Occupy" and "corporate welfare" and "business subsidies" to see where coverage tacked: "The trend appears to be this: Media outlets usually considered more 'liberal' or 'left wing' or even anti-business—the CBC, *Toronto Star*, ABC News, MSNBC, the *New York Times* and National Public Radio (NPR)—don't often cover corporate welfare" (Milke, 2012). "Instead, it has been ostensible pro-business and 'right wing' media outlets such as the *National Post*, *Wall Street Journal* and Fox News that often report or comment on corporate welfare." During the time of Occupy, the study found that the *Wall Street Journal* mentioned corporate welfare about once for every 14 stories on Occupy. NPR had a ratio of 260 to 1. "In a full year of chatting, NPR never once mentioned 'corporate welfare' or 'business subsidies'" (Milke, 2012). In short, media played to their own niche audiences, enforcing biases rather than drawing in new readers, viewers, or users with more diverse perspectives.

The Fraser Institute perspective was quickly overshadowed by the publishing sensation of 2013, *Capital in the Twenty-First Century* by French economist Thomas Piketty (2014). Although the *Economist* said the book could change the way we think about two centuries of economic history, Piketty's work was quickly pilloried in the mainstream media over questions of methodology (Cassidy, 2014). Any discussion of the core issues was drowned out by media wanting to follow a right/wrong narrative and eschewed by politicians needing to cleave to the middle. Their rationale was understandable. Whether on the right or left, be they Rand Paul or Elizabeth Warren, politicians who have advocated more radical policies have tended not to win public support. Ed Miliband's Labour Party in 2015, Tim Hudak's Ontario Progressive Conservatives in 2014, Howard Dean's Democrats in 2004: those who pushed for structural reform to the economic system became easy targets for negative campaigning that focused on the costs of change. Such campaigns have been made all the more powerful by advocacy groups, ranging from labor unions to business organizations, that have a strong stake in the status quo.

Perhaps no issue has suffered so much from this rise of narrowcasting than the debate over climate change. Regardless of one's position, it is difficult to examine the political and media treatment of climate issues over the last quarter-century without a sense of disappointment. In a significant study the international journal *Geoforum* found a tendency among media to downplay the larger social, economic, or political contexts around climate change in favor of the human trials, tragedies, and occasional triumphs over nature (Boykoff and Boykoff, 2007): "Instead of concentrating on power, context, and process, the media tend to personalize social issues, focusing on the individual claim-makers who are locked in political battle." In order words, the macro has been forgone in favor of the micro. With notable exceptions like the *Guardian*, which has a staunchly anti-carbon editorial agenda, most major news organizations have tried to maintain a balanced approach, at the risk of giving voice to extreme views that tend to confuse or alienate the public. In its review of climate science coverage, the BBC Trust found in 2011, "Climate change 'deniers' continued to find a prominent place in reporting, despite occupying a marginal position in scientific debates" (BBC Trust, 2014). The report blamed an "over rigid" application of BBC editorial guidelines on impartiality in relation to science coverage, which fails to take into account the "non-contentious" nature of some stories. Subsequently, the BBC service appointed a science editor to bring more intellectual rigor to its choice and use of interview subjects.

The narrowing of political debate could lead to a cynical conclusion that political interests are now beholden to niche audiences and special interest groups that can use their own media channels to create and shape public interest and sway the outcome of plurality-driven votes. While such shifts should remain a concern, there is evidence that other forces are emerging to re-engage the public and challenge popular debate with new ideas and new narratives, using the tools of digital and mobile media that are more powerful than ever.

CONCLUSION: FROM DISRUPTION TO HOPE

The 2016 US presidential campaign posed a surprising challenge to many established policies—as well as to views about the relationship between media and political discourse. On the Republican Party side, Donald Trump generated support by attacking media and corporate interests, and claiming to be beholden to no interest group while espousing a populist view against many centrist policies, notably trade, taxation, and immigration. Bernie Sanders achieved impressive gains in the Democratic Party primaries by also claiming to be free of establishment interests and equally disavowing mainstream economic policies. Both insurgent candidates were able to reach mass audiences through social media, as well as through a disproportionate amount of mainstream media coverage drawn by their so-called radical (and colorful) views. In so doing, they moved out of the fringes and left some media wondering if they had in fact missed the signals from Occupy Wall Street.

With respect to the global economic system, alternative arguments have started to emerge from established organizations. The World Economic Forum has long advocated systemic reforms, from environmental regulation to financial sector governance (WEF, 2015). Bank of England governor Mark Carney moved the debate further with his 2014 speech, "Inclusive Capitalism," which argued that all societies aspire to a "trinity" of distributive justice, social equity, and intergenerational equity, not just on moral grounds but because of growing evidence that relative equality is good for growth (Carney, 2014).

In these new schools of economic thinking, the dominant forces of the past quarter-century—globalization and digitalization—have impaired the ability of governments to fulfill their social contract. In that void, a variety of businesses have tried to show greater leadership, adopting the triple bottom line: financial, social, and environmental (see also Chapters 2, 9, 15, and 21, this volume). Many institutional investors have pushed for change, as well, believing the consequences of inaction are too great to be left to a transactional arena of politics and media (see also Chapter 17, this volume). At a *Forbes* philanthropy session in New York in May 2015, the activist investor Bill Ackman urged for better measurements if the public wants business to pursue a more responsible corporate agenda. "If you measure it," he said, "business will respond" (Ackman, 2015).

So, too, will media and policymakers. News organizations tend to follow horse races, which produce a beginning and end, a victory and defeat, to be summarized as an event. Against this linear backdrop, a more context-driven approach to journalism is emerging, typically through new media ventures that are not beholden to a traditional model of selling newspapers or driving broadcast ratings. A notable example is the *Texas Tribune*, an online publication created in 2010 with financial support from Republicans and Democrats, corporations and foundations, wanting to enhance the discourse around Texas events and issues. Five years on, it boasts the largest newsroom in the United States devoted to state issues, and pursues issues such as a 15-part series on the shale boom. "It sounds very corny, but we always believed that there was a place where people of unlike minds could put down their weapons, get in a room and hash stuff out," its founding editor Evan Smith told the author (Stackhouse, 2015).

In a similar spirit of new media ventures, the Ford Foundation has backed the Poynter Institute's Sense-Making Project, to focus on the intersection between journalism and citizen engagement under a guiding question: "How will citizens make sense of the universe?" (Blais, 2014). The Ford Foundation has also supported the Center for News Literacy at the School of Journalism at the State University of New York in Stony Brook to educate current and future news consumers on how to judge the credibility and reliability of news. Such ventures are part of a boom in new media ventures in the US funded as either not-for-profits or venture capital plays, as investors stay away from traditional ad-based models. Even the *Guardian*, while growing its global audience, continues to lose tens of millions of dollars a year and, at current rates, risks depleting the trust fund on which it is based. The shift to newer forms of journalism, designed to serve and engage increasingly mobile audiences through newer platforms like Facebook and YouTube is still in its early stages. Political movements are likely to follow course, taking more cues from the digital narratives as well as the Obama campaigns to both engage audiences and hold on to them as they delve into the structural challenges of the global economy. Politicians and journalists alike must recognize that the best ideas for capitalism in the 21st century need to be surfaced, debated, and shared through 21st-century channels.

REFERENCES

Ackman, B. (2015). *The Fourth Annual Forbes 400 Summit on Philanthropy*. New York City, June 4.

BBC Trust (2014). "Trust Conclusions on the Executive Report on Science Impartiality Review Actions," July. Available at: <http://downloads.bbc.co.uk/bbctrust/assets/files/pdf/our_work/science_impartiality/trust_conclusions.pdf>.

Blais, J. (2014). *Sense Making Project*. St Petersburg, FL: Poynter.

Boykoff, M. and Boykoff, J. (2007). "Climate Change and Journalistic Norms: A Case Study of US Mass Media Coverage," *Geoforum*, January 5. Available at: <http://sciencepolicy.colorado.edu/admin/publication_files/2007.40.pdf>.

Carney, M. (2014). "Inclusive Capitalism: Creating a Sense of the Systemic," London, May 27. Available at: <http://www.bankofengland.co.uk/publications/Documents/speeches/2014/speech731.pdf>.

Cassidy, J. (2014). "Forces of Divergence: Is Surging Inequality Endemic to Capitalism?" *New Yorker*, March 31.

CBC News (2015). "Voter Turnout Spikes after a Long, Unpredictable Campaign." Available at: <http://www.cbc.ca/news/politics/canada-election-2015-voting-polls-turnout-1.3278838>.

Delacourt, S. (2013). *Shopping for Votes: How Politicians Choose Us and We Choose Them*. Madeira Park, BC: Douglas and McIntyre.

Deloitte (2014). "Digital Democracy Survey: A Look into the Minds of Media Consumers." Available at: <http://www2.deloitte.com/us/en/pages/technology-media-and-telecommunications/articles/digital-democracy-survey-generational-media-consumption-trends.html>.

Edelman (2015). *The 2015 Edelman Trust Barometer: Annual Global Study*. Available at: <http://www.edelman.com/insights/intellectual-property/2015-edelman-trust-barometer/>.

Elections Canada, Resource Centre (2015). "Estimation of Voter Turnout by Age Group and Gender at the 2011 Federal General Election." Available at: <http://www.elections.ca/content.aspx?document=index&dir=turn&lang=e&section=ele>.

Hermida, A. (2014). *Tell Everyone: Why We Share and Why It Matters*. Toronto: Doubleday.

Jurkowitz, M. (2014). "The Growth in Digital Reporting: What It Means for Journalism and News Consumers," *Pew Research Center: Journalism and Media*. Available at: <http://www.journalism.org/2014/03/26/the-growth-in-digital-reporting/>.

Klienfield, N. R. and Buckley, C. (2011). "Wall Street Occupiers, Protesting till Whenever," *New York Times*, September 30.

Milke, M. (2012). "How the Media Covered Occupy Wall Street—and Crony Capitalism," *Fraser Forum*, November/December. Fraser Institute.

Mitchell, A. (2015). "State of the News Media 2015," *Pew Research Center: Journalism and Media*. Available at: <http://www.journalism.org/2015/04/29/state-of-the-news-media-2015/>.

Mitchell, A., Holcomb, J., and Page, D. (2015). "Local News in a Digital Age," *Pew Research Center: Journalism and Media*. Available at: <http://www.journalism.org/2015/03/05/local-news-in-a-digital-age/>.

PEJ (2009a). "Covering the Great Recession: How the Media Have Depicted the Economic Crisis during Obama's Presidency," Project for Excellence in Journalism. Available at: <http://www.journalism.org/2009/10/05/covering-great-recession/>.

PEJ (2009b). "Who Drove the Economic News (and Who Didn't)?" Project for Excellence in Journalism. Available at: <http://www.journalism.org/2009/10/05/who-drove-economic-news-and-who-didnt/>.

PEJ (2011). "Biggest Week Yet for Occupy Wall Street Coverage," *PEJ News Coverage Index*, November 14–20, Project for Excellence in Journalism, Pew Research Center: Journalism and Media.

Pepitone, J. (2011). "Hundreds of Protestors Descend to 'Occupy Wall Street,'" *CNN Money*, September 17. Available at: <http://money.cnn.com/2011/09/17/technology/occupy_wall_street/>.

Pew Research Center (2008). "Young Voters in the 2008 Election." Available at: <http://www.pewresearch.org/2008/11/13/young-voters-in-the-2008-election/>.

Pew Research Center (2014). "Hispanic Voters in the 2014 Election," November 7. Available at: <pewhispanic.org/2014/11/07/hispanic-voters-in-the-2014-election/>.

Piketty, T. (2014). *Capital in the Twenty-First Century*. Cambridge, MA: Harvard University Press.

Pilkington, E. and Michel, A. (2012). "Obama, Facebook and the Power of Friendship: The 2012 Data Election," *Guardian*, February 17. Available at: <http://www.theguardian.com/world/2012/feb/17/obama-digital-data-machine-facebook-election>.

Pingdom.com (2013). "Internet 2012 in Numbers," *Tech Blog*, January 16.

Samara (2015). "Samara's Democracy 360: Talk. Act. Lead," September.

Stackhouse, J. (2015). Interview with Evan Smith.

Stelter, B. (2011). "Protest Puts Coverage in Spotlight," *New York Times*, November 20. Available at: <http://www.nytimes.com/2011/11/21/business/media/occupy-wall-street-puts-the-coverage-in-the-spotlight.html>.

United States Election Project (2014). Available at: <.http://www.electproject.org/2014>.

Usman (2014). "Facebook Says 20m Canadians Visit Site Monthly, Reveals Plans for More Apps," *iPhone in Canada*. Available at: <http://www.iphoneincanada.ca/news/20m-canadians-visit-facebook-per-month/>.

Venton, J. P. (2015). "Income Inequality," Fair Vote Canada Campaign. Available at: <http://campaign2015.fairvote.ca/income-inequality/>.

WEF (2015). *Our Global Challenges*. Geneva: World Economic Forum. Available at: <http://www.weforum.org/projects>.

Part III

Advancing: Suggestions for the Ways Forward

14

Imagining a Sustainable Financial System

Simon Zadek

INTRODUCTION

Imagine a financial system that serves the long-term needs of a healthy real economy, an economy that provides decent, productive, and rewarding livelihoods for all, and ensures that the natural environment remains intact and so able to support the needs of this and future generations. Imagine, furthermore, a financial system that is resilient and so able to serve its core purpose in the face of growing environmental and other sources of volatility. The purpose of this chapter is to explore what it might take to turn this vision into reality.

The chapter therefore examines efforts to shape financial and capital markets to both enhance environmental and social outcomes from lending and investment decisions, and to improve the resilience of the financial system to external social and environmental shocks. Such efforts have grown rapidly in recent years in both numbers and ambition, both at national and now also international levels. Although visibly accelerated through high-profile, systemic challenges such as climate change, drivers in practice have been more varied between countries and regions. The merits of such efforts ultimately depend on their impacts, and their comparative costs. Although in many instances efforts are at too early a stage to allow for definitive conclusions to be drawn, this chapter highlights convergent patterns and preliminary findings based on an intensive investigation of available evidence.

The chapter draws on ongoing investigation of the topic by the United Nations Environment Programme entitled the *Inquiry into the Design of a Sustainable Financial System* (henceforth, "the Inquiry"). The Inquiry involved casework across 13 countries, covering developed (i.e., France, the Netherlands, Switzerland, the UK, and the US), emerging (i.e., Brazil, China, India, and South Africa), and developing (i.e., Bangladesh, Colombia, Indonesia, and Kenya) examples. In addition, analysis was undertaken at subsector (e.g., institutional investors, insurance, equities), thematic (e.g., human rights), and technical (e.g., stress testing, Basle 3) levels. Altogether, 70 reports and working papers have been prepared reflecting the Inquiry's work, in collaboration with over 40 partners from 20 countries and including key international organizations and networks. The global report summarizing the work to date, *The Financial System We Need: Reshaping Finance for Sustainable Development* (UNEP, 2015), was released at the International Monetary Fund (IMF)/World Bank Annual Meetings in Peru in October 2015, and is available in seven languages. This body of knowledge can be accessed freely at <http://www.unepinquiry.org>.

The chapter is divided into four main sections. The next section establishes the problem in terms of the nexus between financing and real economy externalities, focusing particularly on the latter's environmental aspects. I then set out the reasons and merits for addressing the problem through interventions in the financial system (as opposed to, or alongside, the real economy). I then summarize the largely qualitative evidence regarding systemic interventions by rule makers in the financial system in pursuit of sustainable development outcomes. Finally, I draw some conclusions and point the way to both the potential of the field and the need for more research as more case material and comparative data become available.

FRAMING THE CHALLENGE: ENVIRONMENTAL DEGRADATION AND THE ROLE OF FINANCE

Extraordinary gains have been made in the last century. Worldwide, life expectancy has increased by 21 years since 1950, and poverty has fallen in the last half-century by more than at any time in human history. On the environmental side, the energy needed to produce a ton of steel has fallen by 30 percent in the last quarter-century, and the CO_2 emitted through the production of a kwh of electricity in Europe has fallen by 20 percent in the last 15 years (Zadek, 2012). At the same time, natural systems are severely degraded. Four out of nine "planetary boundaries" have been crossed: climate change, loss of biosphere integrity, land-system change, and altered biogeochemical cycles. Research suggests that measures of natural capital have declined in 116 out of 140 countries (UNEP, 2015), around one in eight people die from air pollution exposure—or 7 million people per year (WHO, 2014), greenhouse gas emissions add energy to the Earth's system at a rate equivalent to the detonation of four nuclear bombs every second (King et al., 2015), and almost 22 million people were displaced in at least 119 countries by natural disasters in 2013 (Norwegian Refugee Council, 2014), and 21 of the world's 37 largest aquifers have passed their sustainability tipping points (Alexander et al., 2015).

Such environmental data point to severe problems that are already, and will increasingly create human crises of both micro and macro dimensions. These problems, however, do not alone provide a root-cause perspective. Indeed, they are symptoms of deeper problems that lie in how humans are managing the interface between their approach to the economy and the wider ecology on which they depend. Root-cause analysis has almost no limit as it takes one into the realms not only of human invention but its very nature. Short termism, for example, is highlighted in this chapter as a problem in financial and capital markets, but can reasonably be argued to be a more pervasive problem across many aspects of human activity. For the purposes of this chapter, however, the analysis is limited to an exploration of aspects of economic endeavor and specifically the impact of the financial system on environmental outcomes.

Financing sustainable development will require the large-scale mobilization and redirection of investable funds. A range of estimates exists for different aspects of the financing challenge, notably access to energy, biodiversity, climate change, food security, water, and sanitation (ICESDF, 2015). In the most comprehensive assessment to date, the United Nations Conference on Trade and Development (UNCTAD) World Investment Report 2014 has estimated that US$5–7 trillion a year is needed to finance the Sustainable Development Goals. Developing countries will require some US$3.9 trillion per year; currently only US$1.4 trillion is being delivered, leaving a gap of US$2.5 trillion to be filled from private and public sources (UNCTAD, 2014). Public finance will only provide a small fraction of total financing needs (Greenhill et al., 2015). In China, for example, estimates by the People's Bank of China and the Development Research Centre of the State Council suggest total green finance needs up to about US$400 billion annually, of which no more than 15 percent will be met from public sources (PBoC/UNEP, 2015; DRC/IISD, 2015). The bulk of finance, in short, will need to come from financial and capital markets.

Tapping private capital to provide finance for investments that have public as well as private benefits has conventionally been understood as a matter for subsidizing incremental costs—essentially using public finance to pay for incremental costs of securing the targeted public goods. Certainly, such additional costs may be incurred in some areas of financing and so may legitimately attract public financial support. However, in other instances where there may be no additional or negative incremental costs, profitable opportunities may nevertheless be marginalized by policy and market failures in the financial system itself, which may lead for example to short-term investor horizons and the broader mispricing of financial risks. For so-called green investments this may be a particular challenge as many are characterized by high upfront costs and longer-term returns, which for some of the investments reflect the substituting of natural capital with technology (WEF, 2013). Financial and capital markets, furthermore, are intertwined with many existing public financial flows, established over decades and sometimes generations for diverse purposes. Such flows may well be effective in relation to their intended impacts, but overall will distort the market in unpredictable and in the main underexplored ways. Certainly, few are likely to be optimized to today's sustainable development imperatives, placing the matter of policy-inspired interventions firmly in the world of second-best choices (Yavrom and Bernatkova, forthcoming).

The twofold challenge is to determine what kind of financial system is needed to ensure the effective financing of the transition to sustainable development, and to determine furthermore the circumstances and manners in which interventions in the financial system are warranted in pursuit of such ends (UNEP, 2015; Zadek, 2013; Zadek et al., 2005).

FINANCIAL SYSTEM IMPACTS ON THE REAL ECONOMY

Conventional wisdom suggests that if the problem concerns real economy externalities, the solution is to intervene in the real economy. In many instances, this is exactly right. Addressing climate change does require that we price into markets for products and services the negative effects of greenhouse gas emissions. The IMF, for example, rightly points to the need to reduce energy subsidies estimated at US$5.3 trillion annually, or about 6.5 percent of global GDP, in addressing extensive negative environmental and public health effects (Coady et al., 2015).

Addressing sustainable development challenges, however, may also require action in the financial economy. Today, the financial system is emerging from its worst crisis in decades, originating in some of the world's most sophisticated financial markets. Policies, regulations, standards, and new institutions have been introduced to stabilize the system. Much has been achieved, but reform remains an unfinished agenda. In addition to remaining concerns of a more conventional nature, including governance, leverage, and the pervasive effects of the growing so-called shadow banking system (Wolf, 2014), are longer-term, more fundamental concerns summed up by John Lipsky, previously the IMF's first managing director: "Reforming the financial system remains unfinished business—we have stabilized the system, but have a long way to go in designing a financial system that meets the needs of sustainable development" (quoted by Thimann and Zadek, 2015).

Recent research by the Bank for International Settlements (BIS) and also the IMF has advanced our understanding of one aspect of this relationship through an in-depth quantitative analysis of the relationship between economic growth and financial system development (Cecchetti and Kharroubi, 2012).

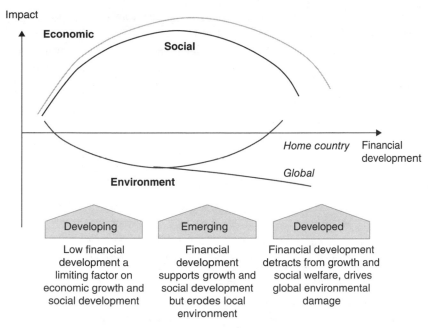

Figure 14.1. Business-as-usual hypothesis
Source: UNEP, 2015; reproduced with permission by the copyright holder (UNEP)

This work suggests a bell-shaped relationship, with the impact of the financial sector on its host, i.e., domestic, economy-wide productivity and growth first increasing and then falling as the financial sector continues to develop and grow relative to the size of that economy—with growth, size, largeness, and smallness referring to the size of the financial sector *relative* to the economy as a whole. A number of reasons are advanced for this observed relationship, including the drag of resources into, and higher rent taking by the financial system. Comparable hypotheses can be advanced as to the relationship between financial system development and the evolution of environmental and broader sustainable development outcomes. Two testable hypotheses are proposed here: one reflects the "business-as-usual" relationship between financial system and sustainable development (see Figure 14.1), and one views the relationship if there was progress towards a sustainable financial system (Figure 14.2) (UNEP, 2015).

For the business-as-usual hypothesis, presented in Figure 14.1, the essential argument is that negative environmental externalities grow rapidly as a result of financial systems development during the rapid economic growth phase of development, and then subsequently have a declining domestic effect and yet continuous growth for the global footprint of developed financial systems. The reason for the divergent domestic and global effects is that domestic environmental regulation is strengthened and enforced, whereas the same is not true

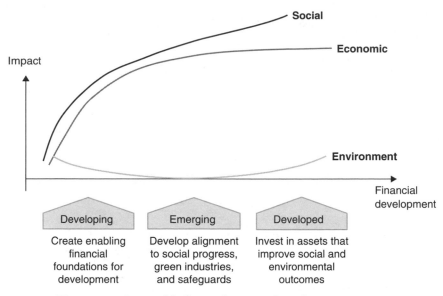

Figure 14.2. Sustainable financial system, desired

Source: UNEP, 2015; reproduced with permission by the copyright holder (UNEP)

internationally as the financial system increasingly outgrows the domestic real economy and seeks financing opportunities elsewhere.

The counter-factual, or desired, relationship hypothesized between the evolution of the financial system and sustainable development is presented in Figure 14.2. Initially, there is a similar starting point where an underdeveloped financial system has little effect on social, environmental, or economic outcomes. As the financial system begins to impact significantly on economic productivity and development, negative environmental externalities are minimized through effective safeguards and the economy, in part as a result, evolves with a lower natural resource intensive and pollution profile. At a more developed system level where global financing gains in importance, the environmental footprint continues to improve, in part because of the internalization of environmental considerations directly into financial decision-making irrespective of the real economy context.

These two hypotheses build on the empirical approach taken by BIS and IMF with respect to economic productivity and growth, and may to some make intuitive sense. However, they are not the outcome of quantitative, empirical analysis, and so remain essentially a framing device for research to come. Whilst systematic data to readily test these hypotheses may be absent, however, the use of case material to further explore aspects of the proposed relationship is possible. In particular, the UNEP Inquiry's casework across 15 countries highlights the thinking and practice by financial system rule setters in seeking to improve its alignment with a range of social and environmental, as well as economic development, outcomes (UNEP, 2015). There are four interconnecting reasons for taking account of sustainable development in financial system design and development:

1. *Valuing externalities*: Action may be justified where markets systematically misprice the impact of externalities on financial returns, and thereby create negative spill-over impacts on third parties or society in general.

2. *Promoting innovation*: Action may be justified to stimulate "missing markets," generating positive spill-overs, for example, through common standards that improve liquidity in embryonic areas.

3. *Managing systemic risks*: Action may be justified where the stability of parts of the financial system may be affected by environmental impacts, or by associated policy, technological and social responses.

4. *Ensuring policy coherence*: Action may be justified to ensure that the rules governing the financial system are consistent with wider government policies.

These four reasons all need to be considered alongside the potential negative impacts and unintended impacts of action on the financial system or real economy outcomes. Such negative outcomes can arise for a number of reasons, each leading to the implementation of a flawed measure, either because of system complexities, conflicting objectives, or political interference. The converse can also be the case, that technical or political reasons make financial economy preferable to real economy interventions. The logic of why needs to be complemented by a logic that sets out the intended effects associated with broad approaches to how. The UNEP Inquiry provided a framework of five distinct *approaches to alignment*. Each approach is made up of multiple possible specific instruments, and is associated with expected links between the impact on financial returns and the delivery of public goods, such as environmental benefits:

1. *Enhancing market practice*, for example through better disclosure, aiming to increase financial returns, and their alignment to the delivery of public goods.

2. *Leveraging private capital with public finance*, for example through public subsidies or the use of central bank balance sheets, aims to increase financial returns in return for public goods.

3. *Directing finance through policy*, for example priority-sector lending and enhanced liabilities, can have varied effects on financial returns in requiring the delivery of public goods.

4. *Encouraging cultural transformation*, for example through oversight of conduct and through social compacts, can have varied effects on financial returns.

5. *Upgrading governance architecture*, for example through principles, mandates, and performance metrics, at national and international levels is an essential enabler of the measures above.

THE WAY FORWARD: A "QUIET REVOLUTION"

The Inquiry's core case material comprised the results of case-based work across 13 countries and regions: Bangladesh, Brazil, China, Colombia, the European Union, France, India, Indonesia, Kenya, the Netherlands, Switzerland, the UK, and the US, and in addition the consideration of several specialist topics set out in over 30 working papers, from green bonds to electronic trading, the future of stock exchanges, fiduciary responsibilities of pension funds, and the nexus between financial market development and human rights.

The Inquiry's core finding is that what it refers to as a "quiet revolution" is underway, seeking to increase the internalization of sustainable development outcomes into financial decision-making. This quiet revolution is particularly apparent in developing and emerging economies, where they face more immediate social and environmental challenges, and are less constrained by prevailing norms and interests. In China and elsewhere, air pollution has been a powerful driver in encouraging financial regulators, notably the China Banking Regulatory Commission, from advancing green credit guidelines for licensed banks. In Kenya, on the other hand, financial inclusion was the principle driver that resulted in the Central Bank of Kenya; it was also the main driver for the Bangladesh Bank. In Indonesia and Brazil, the core dependence of the domestic economy on the integrity of biodiversity, notably forests, has led the Central Bank of Brazil and the Indonesian financial regulator to establish stricter environmental risk management requirements, and invest significantly in capacity development and awareness across the financial community.

Notably, institutions responsible for governing developing country financial and capital markets are more accustomed than their developed country peers to responding to policy signals and national development priorities. South Africa's post-Apartheid "Financial Charter," an agreement between the financial community and major institutional stakeholders across the country, provides a case in point where broader national policy goals and development priorities have guided a generation of financial policies and regulations, as well as ongoing voluntary practice. Some developing countries are explicitly building sustainable development factors into the design of financial and monetary policies, regulations, and standards. The Bangladesh Bank, for example, has argued that supporting rural development and green energy through concessionary refinancing is a means of addressing its monetary policy targets by reducing over the longer term the destabilizing effects of inflation driven by imported food and fossil fuels. China will embed green finance considerations into the financial market development track of its 13th Five-Year Plan, similarly arguing that it is integral to improving financial market efficiency and effectiveness.

A number of champions are also emerging in the developed world, seeking to complement market initiatives with policy frameworks on risk, disclosure, and capital markets. The lenses through which developed countries view their financial systems' sustainable development outcomes are broadly comparable, but at times these are blended into an alignment with policy measures (Caruana, 2015). The Bank of England is progressing the first systematic analysis of the impact of climate on the UK's insurance sector, largely as part of its core prudential responsibilities, and in part as a response to the UK Climate Change Act. The French Government's 2010 Grenelle II requirements on corporate sustainability reporting were advanced further in November 2013 with the launch of a White Paper on Financing the Ecological Transition, a joint initiative of the Ministry of Ecology and the Treasury (Dron and Francq, 2013). The follow-up to the White Paper has been galvanized by the approach of the COP21 climate conference in Paris. New disclosure requirements were agreed in May 2015 so that investors need to include in their annual report how they manage sustainability factors, including the risks of climate change and their contribution to the international goal of limiting climate change.

The Inquiry also concluded, however, that the quiet revolution is both incomplete and fragile. Developed countries' financial systems are adaptive and highly innovative in some respects, but continue to trend towards greater levels of "financialization," where financial returns increasingly arise from trading that is disconnected from long-term value creation in the real economy. Despite, and in some respects because of, major regulatory developments in the wake of the financial crisis, financial and capital markets are today delivering even less investment in long-term infrastructure, and instead continue to reward highly liquid, leveraged trading over the prospects of greater, but less liquid, longer-term returns (Bassanini and Reviglio, 2011; Thimann and Zadek, 2015). Notwithstanding the limits owing to data inadequacies, the Inquiry's exploration of practice, combined with broader engagement and desk-based research, allows for conclusions to be drawn as to the potential for each of the five approaches as summarized in Table 14.1.

The approaches do not only have differing potential impacts but also differ by ease of implementation. For example, *enhancing market practice*, such as through improved disclosure, are easier measures to implement, being relatively low cost and often acceptable to market actors. *Public financing* is also comparatively easy to execute and attractive to market actors, but is, at the same time, limited in scope by scarce public finance. *Guiding finance directly*

Table 14.1. Comparative potential for the five approaches

Approach	Current practice	Potential impact	
Enhancing market practice	Widely adopted as relatively straightforward and relevant to all countries' financial systems	Aims to increase financial returns and their alignment to the delivery of public goods	Likely to have a slow, modest impact unless undertaken with additional measures
Harnessing balance sheets	Widely adopted, but limited by cost	Aims to increase financial returns in return for public goods	Can be very effective where deployed, but is likely to be limited in impact because of scarcity of public finance
Directing finance through policy	A long history of use, now being adapted for sustainability goals	Varied effects on financial returns in requiring the delivery of public goods, and relatively high risk of unintended consequences	Can be successful but with a greater potential for unintended consequences
Encouraging cultural transformation	Not widely practiced, but potential for wide application and positive signs emerging post-crisis	Can have varied effects on financial returns	Can be effective, especially when linked to policy direction and incentives and aligned to broader societal expectations
Upgrading governance architecture	Least practiced	Is an essential enabler of the measures above	

Source: UNEP, 2015; reproduced with permission by the copyright holder (UNEP)

through policy, by contrast, is likely to experience more pushback from the market and, crucially, may have higher likelihood for unintended consequences. In drawing lessons from experience, therefore, policymakers and regulators will need to strike a balance between ease and potential impact, as shown in Figure 14.3.

More broadly, integrating sustainable financing innovations into the evolution of their financial systems provides developed and developing countries with both short- and long-term potential benefits. In the short to medium term, developing economies have the opportunity to draw on international practice in increasing financial access, reducing environmental pollution with associated public health gains, and improving financial flows to clean energy. Developed countries, likewise, have short- to medium-term opportunities for improving market integrity, dampening less productive forms of trading,

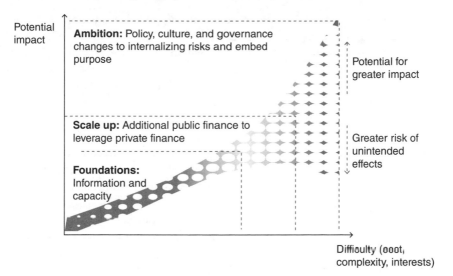

Figure 14.3. Ease and potential impact

Source: UNEP, 2015; reproduced with permission by the copyright holder (UNEP)

enhancing financial and monetary stability, and addressing higher-profile goals such as reduced carbon emissions. The longer-term opportunity for both developed and developing economies is to evolve efficient financial systems that are more effective in serving the needs of inclusive, sustainable economies and societies. The shared opportunity is to shape a financial system more suited to the 21st century, during which all economies must go through profound transitions towards sustainable development.

CONCLUSION: TOWARDS A SUSTAINABLE FINANCIAL SYSTEM

Conventional and some unconventional measures adopted in the wake of the financial crisis have, by some measures, both saved the day and increased the resilience of the financial system in the face of future, broadly comparable, crises. Tomorrow's financial crises may, however, have different root causes, including environmental, and moreover more significant, and potentially fatal consequences. Alongside this "red alert" is the simple fact that tomorrow's successful economies will hopefully as a source of inclusive prosperity be those that have a dramatically higher level of natural resource productivity and negligible pollution.

A financial system is needed that can both survive new sources of turbulence, and that will invest in the transition to an inclusive green economy.

Needed then is a financial system that can support a transition that has to unleash future wealth creation to enable inclusive development while protecting and restoring natural assets. That means more finance for some enterprises, and less for others that might remain profitable for some time but are ultimately not assets fit for creating a viable future. Many of today's businesses, markets, products, and broader institutional arrangements, including finance, will need to be reshaped for this transition to be possible in the necessary timescales. As Lord Nicholas Stern remarks: "We are at a remarkable point in history. We have a chance to combine the profound structural changes we are seeing in the world economy and extraordinary technological change on the one hand with a rapid transition to a low-carbon economy on the other" (Stern, 2015).

This is the context in which financial system development needs to be understood, and the basis on which design and execution should be guided. Sustainable development above all requires changes in the deployment and relative value of financial assets and their relationship to the creation, stewardship, and productivity of real wealth. A "sustainable financial system" is therefore one that "creates, values and transacts financial assets in ways that shape real wealth to serve the long-term needs of an inclusive, environmentally sustainable economy" (UNEP, 2015).

Finally, the twin hypotheses presented at the outset of the paper can be revisited. Both the suggested "Business-as-Usual" and "Desired" scenarios clearly need to be subjected to empirical analysis. However, the core arguments underlying each, both a priori and on the basis of available evidence, seem like a reasonable starting point. Moreover, and drawing on the casework of the UNEP Inquiry, there is clearly a growing appreciation of both the unacceptability of the former and the possibility of moving towards the latter. Importantly, this appreciation is increasingly from the guardians of the financial system itself, the central bankers, financial regulators, and standard setters who have hitherto been reluctant to engage, let alone lead. Finally, in the context of broader geopolitical changes, it is perhaps not surprising, but nevertheless inspiring, that leadership from developing countries is playing a significant role in shaping the next generation of principles and practical design of tomorrow's financial and capital markets.

REFERENCES

Alexander, R., Ehrlich, P., Barnosky, A., García, A., Pringle R., and Palmer, T. (2015). "Quantifying Renewable Groundwater Stress," *World Resources Research*, 51(7): 5217–38. Available at: <http://agupubs.onlinelibrary.wiley.com/agu/issue/10.1002/wrcr.v51.7/>.

Bassanini, F. and Reviglio, E. (2011). "Financial Stability, Fiscal Consolidation and Long-Term Investment after the Crisis," *OECD Journal: Financial Market Trends*, 11(1): 1–45. Available at: <http://www.oecd.org/finance/financial-markets/48609330.pdf>.

Caruana, J. (2015). *Financial Reform and the Role of Regulators: Evolving Markets, Evolving Risks, Evolving Regulation*. Basel: Bank for International Settlements.

Cecchetti, S. and Kharroubi, R. (2012). "Reassessing the Impact of Finance on Growth," BIS Working Papers, July.

Coady, D., Parry, I., Sears, L., and Shang, B. (2015). "How Large Are Global Energy Subsidies?" IMF Working Paper.

DRC/IISD (2015). *Greening China's Financial System*. Geneva: Development Research Center of the State Council and International Institute of Environment and Development.

Dron, D. and Francq, T. (2013). *White Paper on Financing Econological Transition* (English translation). Paris: French Ministry of Ecology, Sustainable Development and Energy and Directorate General of the Treasury.

Greenhill, R., Hoy, C., Carter, P., and Manuel M. (2015). *Financing the Future: How International Public Finance Should Fund a Global Social Compact to Eradicate Poverty*. London: Overseas Development Institute.

ICESDF (2015). *Report of the Intergovernmental Committee of Experts on Sustainable Development Financing*. New York: UNDESA.

King, D., Schrag, D., Dadi, Z., Ye, Q., and Ghosh, A. (2015). *Climate Change: A Risk Assessment*. Cambridge: Centre for Science and Policy.

Norwegian Refugee Council (2014). *Global Estimates Report*. Oslo: Norwegian Refugee Council, Internal Displacement Monitoring Centre.

PBoC/UNEP (2015). *Greening China's Financial System*. Geneva: People's Bank of China and UNEP.

Stern, N. (2015). *Why Are We Waiting? The Logic, Urgency, and Promise of Tackling Climate Change*. Cambridge, MA: MIT Press.

Thimann, C. and Zadek, S. (2015). *New Rules for New Horizons: Report of the High Level Symposium on Reshaping Finance for Sustainability*. Geneva: UNEP Inquiry/Axa.

UNCTAD (2014). *World Investment Report 2014: Investing in Sustainable Development Goals*. Geneva: United Nations Conference on Trade and Development.

UNEP (2015). *The Financial System We Want: Aligning the Finance System with Sustainable Development*. Nairobi: United Nations Environment Programme.

WEF (2013). *The Green Investment Report: The Ways and Means to Unlock Private Finance for Green Growth*. Geneva: World Economic Forum.

WHO (2014). "Burden of Disease from the Joint Effects of Household and Ambient Air Pollution for 2012," World Health Organization, Press Release, March.

Wolf, M. (2014). *The Shifts and the Shocks: What We've Learned—and Have Still to Learn—from the Financial Crisis*. London: Allen Lane.

Yavrom, D. and Bernatkova, L. (forthcoming). "Subsidies to the Financial System: A Review of the Literature," UNEP Inquiry Working Paper, UNEP Inquiry/SAIS Johns Hopkins.

Zadek, S. (2012). "Shaping a Green Political Economy," Public Lecture on the Occasion of the Symposium and Biennial Public Lecture on Energy Solutions in the

Context of Sustainable Development, Green Economy and Poverty Eradication in Africa, University of Southern Africa (Unisa), October 26.

Zadek, S. (2013). "Greening Financial Reform," Project Syndicate, November 29.

Zadek, S., Merme, M., and Samans, R. (2005). *Mainstreaming Responsible Investment*. Geneva: World Economic Forum.

15

Integrated Reporting for a Re-Imagined Capitalism

Robert G. Eccles and Birgit Spiesshofer

INTRODUCTION

The essence of a re-imagined capitalism lies in resource-allocation decisions that go beyond short-term financial performance. Achieving this will require companies and investors to take a longer-term view and use a broader range of performance metrics. To do this, they will need information that goes beyond financial metrics, even as this information should be related to financial performance. Substantial changes in internal and external reporting will be required.

In this chapter, we make the case for integrated reporting as the type of corporate reporting necessary, although certainly not sufficient, to set the scene for a re-imagined capitalism. What, exactly, is an integrated report? A common misperception is that it is a single report that combines both financial and so-called non-financial, i.e., environmental, social, and governance (ESG) performance in a single report—a kind of fusion of the required financial report of any listed company and its (usually voluntary) sustainability report. Rather, an integrated report is how a company communicates to investors and other significant audiences its financial performance and how its performance on material ESG issues affects its financial performance. In contrast, the purpose of a sustainability report is to communicate about a company's performance and activities that are seen as of interest to important stakeholders but which are not core to its business strategy, at least at the present time. Thus, integrated reporting and sustainability reporting are complementary to each other since they are for different audiences.

The term "integrated reporting" dates back nearly 15 years in practice and 10 years in the literature. Nevertheless, only one country, South Africa, has mandated integrated reporting for all listed companies. All other companies, and they exist all over the world, who are publishing an integrated report are doing so on a completely voluntary basis. They are doing so because they believe there are both external (e.g., a better understanding of the company's strategy and performance) and internal (e.g., more "integrated thinking" across a company's many silos) benefits. Momentum for integrated reporting varies by country, but in general this movement is still in its early stages of getting the attention of the corporate and investor communities. Helping to spread this awareness and understanding of integrated reporting is the International Integrated Reporting Council (IIRC), formed in 2010, which "is a global coalition of regulators, investors, companies, standard setters, the accounting profession and NGOs. The coalition is promoting communication about value creation as the next step in the evolution of corporate reporting" (<http://integratedreporting.org/the-iirc-2/>; accessed August 25, 2015). The work of the IIRC and other organizations such as CDP, Global Reporting Initiative (GRI), and the Sustainability Accounting Standards Board (SASB) will play an important role in bringing about a new form of capitalism.

The next section describes three types of corporate reporting (financial, sustainability, and integrated) and classifies each in terms of corporate reporting's two functions: information and transformation. We then make the case for the central role integrated reporting can play in a re-imagined capitalism. Subsequently, we first discuss the feasibility of the US Securities and Exchange Commission (SEC) providing regulatory support for integrated reporting in the United States, and then analyze the implications of the *Directive 2014/95/EU of 22 October 2014 amending Directive 2013/34/EU as regards disclosure of non-financial and diversity information by certain large undertakings and groups* (Corporate Social Responsibility (CSR) Reporting Directive) for reporting in the European Union and, in particular, the paradigm shift to new functions of non-financial reporting. We conclude with some brief thoughts on what will be required for integrated reporting to become the prevailing practice.

THE TYPES AND FUNCTIONS OF CORPORATE REPORTING

An important element in any form of re-imagined capitalism is corporate reporting. To some, the question of how transparent companies should be about their activities and results is technical, arcane, and even boring. To the initiated, it is a hard-fought terrain defined by the tension between companies, who typically want less transparency, and stakeholders or audiences for the reporting, who want more.

Table 15.1. Three types of corporate reporting

Type of reporting	Content	Audience	Practice
Financial	Financial information	Investors	Mandated
Sustainability	Non-financial information	Stakeholders	Mostly voluntary
Integrated	Financial and non-financial information	Investors and significant audiences	Mostly voluntary

There are three basic types of corporate reporting: (1) financial, (2) sustainability, and (3) integrated. They vary in terms of content, audience, and practice (Table 15.1). Today's capitalism is based upon financial reporting, and we would argue that today's capitalism would not exist without financial reporting, which itself is based on accounting standards that must then be reviewed by independent audit firms to produce publicly reported financial performance metrics. Financial reporting should provide investors with information they need to make informed decisions, and listed companies are obligated to follow this practice in order to have access to public capital markets. A vast social infrastructure of securities regulators, e.g., the US SEC, accounting standard-setting bodies, primarily the US Financial Accounting Standards Board (FASB), and the International Accounting Standards Board (IASB), auditing firms, e.g., Deloitte, EY, KPMG, and PricewaterhouseCoopers, and oversight bodies of the accounting profession, e.g., the US Public Company Accounting Oversight Board, support the timely provision of high-quality financial information. This infrastructure has been developed over decades.

Sustainability reporting dates only back to the early 1990s. The purpose of sustainability reporting is to provide a broad range of stakeholders with information on a company's performance across a wide range of ESG performance dimensions. Although they can have financial implications, these dimensions are often referred to as "non-financial" information. The non-profit GRI, founded in 1997, played a central role in its development. CDP, originally called the Carbon Disclosure Project when it was formed in 2001, gave sustainability reporting critical teeth by developing measurement standards for greenhouse gas emissions and, more recently, water and forestry. Today over 5,000 companies issue sustainability reports, including 85 percent of the world's largest companies. Ten years ago, only 300 companies did so, as calculated by Arabesque Asset Management Ltd using the GRI reporting database for 2013, 2014, and 2015 (GRI, 2015).

Historically, most investors have had little interest in non-financial information, with the socially responsible investment community being an exception. Today more "mainstream" investors are showing interest in ESG performance. However, their interest lies in a relatively small subset of the total information available in a sustainability report: they want to know about a company's performance on material issues that affect its ability to create and preserve value. Although regulations around sustainability reporting are growing, it largely remains a voluntary practice by companies, although some recent EU legislation, discussed below, will change this. Even when regulations exist, they rarely specify which measurement standards should be used and what the format of the report should be. As a result, it is difficult for investors and other stakeholders to compare the performance of companies, even within the same sector, and to find the information of most interest to them.

The newest form of reporting—integrated reporting—dates back to the early 2000s, but has only received broad attention in the past five years. Defined by the IIRC's 2013 framework (IIRC, 2013: 4),

> [t]he primary purpose of an integrated report is to explain to providers of financial capital how an organization creates value over time. An integrated report benefits all stakeholders interested in an organization's ability to create value over time, including employees, customers, suppliers, business partners, local communities, legislators, regulators and policy-makers.

Along with GRI, the IIRC, started in 2010, and SASB, started in 2011, are the two key organizations seeking to spread awareness about and adoption of integrated reporting. Integrated reporting is completely voluntary with the exception of South Africa, where it is required of all companies listed on the Johannesburg Stock Exchange on an "apply or explain" basis (for a fuller discussion of the South African case see Eccles et al., 2015: chapter 1).

In addition to content, audience, and practice, each type of corporate reporting can be understood in terms of the function it fulfills (Table 15.2). Eccles and Serafeim (2015) have argued that corporate reporting has two functions: information and transformation. The information function refers to corporate reporting's duty to provide counter-parties to the corporation with the information they need to make an informed decision on whether to transact with the company and, if so, on what terms. In a corporate reporting context, these counter-parties include providers of capital, both equity and debt, as well as vendors, customers, employees, and regulators who are interested in assuring that this information is accurate and provided on a timely basis. The information function is "one-way" in that the company provides the information and the counter-party makes its decision, but with

Table 15.2. The functions of corporate reporting

Type of reporting	Function
Financial	Information
Sustainability	Transformation
Integrated	Transformation

no intent to affect the behavior of the company. In contrast, the transformation function involves feedback from the counter-party with the intent of changing the company (Eccles and Serafeim, 2015: 157):

> While the information function assumes no feedback from counterparties, the transformation function relaxes this assumption, allowing for engagement and activism from the counterparties. The counterparties receive and evaluate the information. Where they see opportunities to influence corporate behavior to their benefit, and potentially to the benefit of the corporation, they actively try to bring about change. This engagement, activism, and change process enables a company to transform.

The transformation function is a two-way street: the company must be open to the feedback it is getting from its counter-parties and willing to engage with them. Yet information is an end in and of itself in the information function; it is a necessary, but not sufficient, condition for the transformation function. While this two-way street is conceptually independent of the information's content, the types of corporate reporting are broadly distinctive in their intended function. The primary application of financial reporting is to provide investors with information to make investment decisions. In providing financial information, the company is not looking for feedback, perhaps other than to verify that it has met the expectations of its investors. It is not seeking input from its investors on how the company can be managed better to improve its financial results. For the most part, investors do not see this as their role. In investor briefings and conference calls, they ask questions—sometimes leading questions—but do not give advice. Some investors may use financial information to attempt transformation, as an activist investor does, who takes a large position in the company and then looks to make changes by putting its own representatives on the board and pressuring the company in other ways.

Current practices in financial reporting in the context of earnings guidance and quarterly conference calls that focus almost solely on short-term financial performance is a defining feature of capitalism as we know it today. Companies take decisions behind corporate castle walls and report on their performance outcomes to satisfy the information function of corporate reporting, and the main feedback the company receives is whether its stock price goes up or down. Sell-side analysts' quarterly and annual earnings estimates and relative indifference to ESG issues reinforce today's capitalism.

Whereas financial reporting is mandated by the state for all listed companies, sustainability reporting originates in the demands of civil society for more transparency by companies about their position and performance on ESG issues. Financial information can be taken for granted; the same is not true for non-financial information. Its seekers want information so that they can decide whether to engage with a company in an attempt to change its practices and behavior. Typically, the focus is on companies seen as underperforming on the topic of interest to the stakeholder. When the company responds to these entreaties, the transformation process begins. Yet, the outcome depends on resources invested by each side of the engagement, which itself is a function of the perceived importance of the issue. Companies must also consider the fact that different stakeholders' interests may be in conflict with each other. Trade-offs exist. Most often, stakeholders are so focused on their own issues that they are indifferent to this reality.

Sustainability reporting has played an important role in laying the groundwork for a new conception of capitalism since it explicitly recognizes the growing importance of stakeholders focused on ESG issues that matter to society. Because its function is one of transformation, it also opens up companies to engagement, which is a key tenet of any new form of capitalism (see also Chapter 9, this volume). Sustainability reporting's main limitation is that it does not distinguish between ESG issues material for the company—the province of capitalism—and the socially significant ones—the province of civil society. Capitalism resides within broader civil society, and changing social expectations will have implications for how it is practiced, but the relative indifference of investors to the information contained in a sustainability report indicates that simply pairing sustainability reporting with financial reporting will not contribute to a re-imagined capitalism.

Integrated reporting's primary interest is transformation, albeit from a somewhat different starting place. Sustainability reporting is an "outside-in" approach to transformation. Civil society puts pressure on the company to disclose information that it uses to enact an engagement process that leads to transformation. Integrated reporting is more of an "inside-out" approach: advocates for integrated reporting argue that companies should, in the beginning, practice it for their own good. Integrated reporting is argued to be a way of fostering "integrated thinking" so that the company operates in a holistic way, taking account of material ESG issues across the six capitals (financial, manufactured, natural, intellectual, human, and social and relationship) that affect financial performance. It will lead to a better-managed company that is more able to create value over the short, medium, and long term, and in doing so, provide the information necessary for its investors to take a longer-term view and to attract more who do. It is a kind of "reverse activism" in which the company is influencing its investor base rather than the other way around.

HOW INTEGRATED REPORTING SUPPORTS A RE-IMAGINED CAPITALISM

Today many people are seeking to re-imagine capitalism. All such concepts have certain characteristics in common: (1) greater attention to the negative externalities produced by a company and what it is doing to mitigate them, (2) greater attention to the interests and expectations of other stakeholders, especially for very large companies, since society increasingly looks to them and not just governments to contribute to sustainable development, (3) striking the proper balance between meeting the expectations of shareholders and other stakeholders, (4) institutional investors factoring in a company's sustainability performance in investment decisions, and (5) a longer-term outlook on the part of both companies and investors.

Integrated reporting supports all of these characteristics. In terms of (1), the "Value Creation Process" in "The International <IR> Framework" (Figure 15.1) emphasizes that companies use the six capitals as inputs into their business model and have outcomes that impact these capitals. These outcomes are both positive and negative. The framework further notes that the company should explain "the interdependencies and trade-offs between the capitals, and how changes in their availability, quality and affordability affect the ability of the organization to create value" (IIRC, 2013: 17). While the framework does not specify how the uses and outcomes of these capitals should be measured, it makes clear that the company should take all of them into account. Organizations like CDP, GRI, and SASB are developing measurement and reporting standards to provide guidance to companies for doing this.

Addressing (2), the framework lists "stakeholder relationships" as one of its seven Guiding Principles: "An integrated report should provide insight into the nature and quality of the organization's relationships with its key stakeholders, including how and to what extent the organization understands, takes into account and responds to their legitimate needs and interests" (IIRC, 2013: 5). Stakeholder engagement is essential for understanding stakeholders' interests and expectations. Striking the proper balance between stakeholders and shareholders, and amongst stakeholders themselves, requires recognizing that trade-offs often exist due to interdependencies across choices. With proper engagement and a full and transparent explanation for why the company made the choices it did, stakeholders will accept the legitimacy of the decision even if they do not agree with it.

Key to (3), balancing the many and often competing interests of shareholders and a broad range of stakeholders, is the Guiding Principle of "connectivity of information": "An integrated report should show a holistic picture of the combination, interrelatedness and dependencies between the factors that affect the organization's ability to create value over time" (IIRC, 2013: 5). What distinguishes an integrated report from a "combined report" is that the former shows the relationships, positive and negative, over specific time frames, between financial and non-financial performance. A combined report simply provides financial and non-financial information in a single document. Also key to (3) is the Guiding Principle of "materiality": "An integrated report should disclose information about matters that substantively affect

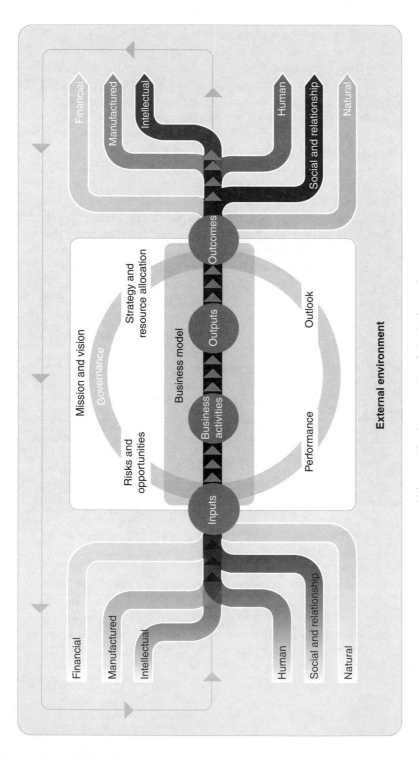

Figure 15.1. The value-creation process

the organization's ability to create value over the short, medium and long term" (IIRC, 2013: 33).

Materiality is a central, albeit somewhat elusive, concept in all three types of reporting. It is entity specific, audience and time frame-dependent, and based on human judgment. It is ultimately grounded in the judgment of the company's board of directors about whom it regards as the company's most significant audiences and the time frames it uses to evaluate the impact the company has on them (for a fuller discussion of materiality see Eccles et al., 2015: chapter 6). Materiality is different from what is "socially significant," although the two are often confused—as when a company produces a "Materiality Matrix." A company can only determine what is material for itself—not for others—even as it can and should form a view about the absolute and relative level of importance different stakeholders accord ESG issues.

Materiality raises one of the central questions about integrated reporting: its relationship to sustainability reporting. Many have the mistaken notion that integrated reporting will lead to a single report that contains both financial and non-financial information and that sustainability reporting will no longer be necessary. This is not true. The integrated report contains information that is material based on the company's designated significant audiences and time frames. The sustainability report contains information on the company's non-financial performance that it believes to be of importance to society, as represented by the stakeholder groups it deems as important but not significant—at least for now—to its value-creation process.

In terms of (4), an increasing number of investors, although still a minority, are seriously working to incorporate ESG issues and a company's performance on them into their own decision-making processes. This has always been true for socially responsible investment funds, but now "mainstream" investors, such as large pension funds and institutional asset managers, are starting to do so as well—even if they do this from a value rather than values perspective (see also Chapter 17, this volume). One complaint typically made by investors interested in "ESG integration" is that they are not getting the data they need from the company to do so. Integrating it into decisions involves struggling with finding the material information relevant to them in a separate sustainability report and then combining it with the voluminous information found in the company's financial report. A well-done integrated report, based on the Guiding Principle of "conciseness," solves this problem: "An integrated report includes sufficient context to understand the organization's strategy, governance, performance and prospects without being burdened with less relevant information" (IIRC, 2013: 21). The integrated report is the way in which the company communicates its performance across all relevant financial, environmental, social, and governance dimensions so that investors can take an integrated view as well.

Finally, there is the issue of time frame—of the need for longer-term thinking on the part of both companies and investors. The shorter the time frame under consideration, the greater the trade-offs between different types of performance and the interests of shareholders and other stakeholders are. With longer-term thinking, companies can make the investments necessary to improve both financial and non-financial performance, but they need patient investors in order to do so. Companies routinely complain about their obligation to operate under short-term earnings pressure from their investors, while simultaneously reinforcing this attitude by providing guidance on quarterly earnings targets. Investors complain that companies do not provide them with sufficient information to be comfortable taking long-term positions, while eagerly anticipating the next earnings call. The Guiding Principle of "strategic focus and future orientation" is relevant here: "An integrated report should provide insight into the organization's strategy, and how it relates to the organization's ability to create value in the short, medium and long term and to its use of and effects on the capitals" including "how the organization balances short, medium and long term interests" (IIRC, 2013: 16).

While conceptually integrated reporting appears to be the right type of corporate reporting for a re-imagined capitalism, it can only play this role if it is practiced by virtually all companies. At the least, all large, publicly listed ones must practice it. Making this a reality is no simple feat. As noted, the only country to require integrated reporting is South Africa, and the rigor with which this is enforced falls far below what is required for financial reporting. One explanation for this relative lassitude is the lack of a consensus on frameworks and non-financial measurement standards. Another is the understandable unwillingness of regulators to specify standards at this early stage of the development of this new type of corporate reporting. Even if South Africa and other countries were to mandate integrated reporting as prescriptively as financial reporting is mandated, there would be the additional challenge of reconciling the reporting model across countries. It was not that long ago that each country had its own version of generally accepted accounting principles (GAAP). Two major ones now dominate: the more rules-based US GAAP under FASB, and the more principles-based International Financial Reporting Standards under the IASB. The "convergence" initiative to create one global set of accounting standards has been a long, difficult, and as of yet an unfinished process.

In the short term, it is best to let market forces work—for investors to demand integrated reporting by companies, in whatever form it comes, and for companies to respond to these demands. During this time, further work will be done to improve frameworks and standards for measuring and reporting on non-financial information. Ultimately, the state will have to intervene in some fashion in order to ensure broad-based adoption. Broadly speaking, this could happen in two ways. Regulators responsible for financial reporting could expand their mandate to integrated reporting. In the US, this would be the SEC. The alternative is for new legislation to be enacted, such as the EU's CSR Reporting Directive. We will consider each of these in turn.

THE SEC AND INTEGRATED REPORTING

The Securities Act of 1933 and the Securities Exchange Act of 1934 established the Securities and Exchange Commission (SEC). Its mission is to promote the public interest by protecting investors, facilitating capital formation, and maintaining fair, orderly, and efficient markets. Transparency is the main regulatory mechanism to ensure the correct evaluation and pricing of securities in the marketplace—the information function of reporting—which is the primary intent of the SEC. But there is also a modest transformation function, since reporting is intended to steer business behavior by exposing corporate conduct to public supervision. We say "modest" because financial reporting, the province of the SEC, is intended to spur companies to better performance as financial results are, more or less, reflected in their stock price.

The SEC has well-established standards for transparency, including monitoring and enforcement mechanisms. Its definition of materiality is consistent with that of integrated reporting. More recently, it has extended its traditional focus on financial information to include selected types of non-financial information. Thus, it is not inconceivable that the SEC could support the adoption of integrated reporting in the US. That said, since the SEC defines its role primarily in terms of the information function, the transformational aspects of integrated reporting would depend on how shareholders and other stakeholders react to the SEC's support of integrated reporting and, in turn, how companies respond to their desire for engagement.

The disclosure requirements for registered securities are contained in Regulation S-K (see <http://www.ecfi.gov/cgi bin/text-idx?node=pt17.3.229>) or Regulation S-B for small businesses. For securities' reports, information must be disclosed that is: (1) specifically *required* under Regulation S-K or necessary to ensure that required disclosures are *not misleading*, and (2) *material* to investors' or shareholders' decision-making processes in accurately valuing securities (emphasis added). The Supreme Court of the United States defined what shall be considered "material" for securities reporting. A fact is material if "there is a substantial likelihood that a *reasonable investor* would consider it important" and would have viewed the information "as having significantly altered the 'total mix' of information made available" (US Supreme Court, 1988, *Basic Inc.* v. *Levinson*, emphasis added). This "requires delicate assessments of the inferences a 'reasonable shareholder' would draw from a given set of facts and the significance of those inferences to him." Note that the Supreme Court's definition is not restricted to financial information; if a "reasonable investor" thinks quantitative or even qualitative non-financial information is important in the "total mix" of information, it should be disclosed. Regarding contingent and forward-looking information, the Supreme Court requests to balance "the indicated *probability* the event will occur and the anticipated *magnitude* of the event in the light of the totality of company activity" (US Supreme Court, 1988, emphasis added). Changing social expectations may thus influence this assessment of "materiality," just as it is changing social expectations that have created the call to re-imagine capitalism. The Supreme Court's definition of materiality can clearly accommodate this.

The SEC has already provided guidance on specific types of non-financial information in its "Commission Guidance Regarding Disclosure Related to Climate Change" (SEC, 2010) and the Division of Corporation Finance drafted in its CF Disclosure Guidance: Topic No. 2 Cyber-Security (SEC, 2011) interpretive guidance on how existing securities regulations, in particular Regulation S-K, may require disclosure of information relating to climate change or cyber-security matters where they are material to the issuer or any of its business segments. Each piece of guidance discusses how the costs of compliance with laws and regulations to prevent and mitigate risks related to climate change and cyber-security may result in material expenses to be included in the financial disclosures. Both detail how the descriptions of items 101 (description of business), 103 (legal proceedings), 303 (management's discussion and analysis), 307 (disclosure controls and procedures), and 503(c) (risk factors) may compel issuers to address climate change or cyber-security risks or incidents. The International Corporate Accountability Roundtable has requested that the SEC promulgate similar interpretive guidance or rulings for human rights issues.

It is clear that under Regulation S-K, and with its definition of materiality, the SEC has the authority to potentially provide strong support for integrated reporting. Exactly what form this would take and when it would (and should) happen is not clear. While the mission of the SEC is to protect investors through, among other things, transparent corporate disclosures, it also has to balance the costs these disclosures impose on companies with the benefits to investors, who ultimately bear these costs. In general, the corporate community resists additional disclosures for both valid (rarely are required disclosures eliminated even when they are no longer relevant) and self-serving (more disclosure creates more accountability) reasons. For example, there was a strong negative reaction against the guidance on climate change although the SEC really just said "go reread Regulation S-K and think about it in the context of climate change."

Thus, it is highly unlikely that the SEC would do anything like revising its instructions on the Form 10-K (Form 20-F for foreign registrants) filing to be based on the International <IR> Framework. Instead, it would issue guidance in the spirit of integrated reporting within its existing regulatory regime. For example, it could issue a guidance statement on the six capitals, or perhaps one on natural capital and one on the intangible assets of intellectual, human, and social and relationship capital. Similarly, it could issue a guidance statement reminding companies that "material" includes non-financial information and cite SASB as one source for input since its standards have been specifically designed for the Form 10-K filing. Should this happen, it is our view that a big step would be taken in the US towards the practice of "pure" integrated reporting. Since the requirements for what information should be included in the Form 10-K (Form 20-F) are detailed and prescriptive, few meet the framework's Guiding Principle of "conciseness." However, the company could accomplish this by simply making its annual report, which is not an official filing document, an annual integrated report that more closely follows the framework. Once a company has crossed the Rubicon of including all material ESG issues in its Form 10-K (Form 20-F), based on, say, SASB guidance, it will have substantially laid the groundwork for turning its annual report into an integrated report. The latter will require a more narrative discussion about "connectivity of information" and perhaps a bit more "strategic focus and future orientation."

THE EU AND INTEGRATED REPORTING

The alternative to an existing regulatory body providing support for integrated reporting is new regulation or even legislation from the domain of "sustainability" that is not tied to the complex apparatus of financial reporting regulations. To some extent this is already happening. In a joint 2013 report called "Carrots and Sticks," KPMG, the Centre for Corporate Governance in Africa, Global Reporting Initiative, and the United Nations Environment Programme considered some 180 policies in 45 countries. The study reported finding that, by 2013, 72 percent of the policies had become mandatory, as compared with 62 percent of the policies in 32 countries examined in 2010, and 58 percent of the policies in 19 countries in 2006 (KPMG, 2013).

The most important example of legislation in support of the disclosure of non-financial information is Directive 2014/95/EU ("CSR Reporting Directive") of 22 October 2014 amending Directive 2013/34/EU as regards disclosure of non-financial and diversity information by certain large undertakings and groups (European Council, 2013). It follows up on EU Directive 2013/34/EU of 26 June 2013 on the annual financial statements, consolidated financial statements and related reports of certain types of undertakings which concerns country-by-country reporting of company payments to governments in resource-rich countries. Directive 2014/95/EU has to be implemented by the member states by December 6, 2016 (Spiesshofer, 2014a). The CSR Reporting Directive expands the reporting requirements to a wide range of enterprises and subjects: it requires companies concerned to disclose in their management report information on policies, risks, and outcomes as regards environmental matters, social and employee aspects, respect for human rights, anti-corruption and bribery issues, and diversity in their board of directors. This will provide investors and other stakeholders with a more comprehensive picture of a company's performance (European Commission, 2014). The information is to be included in the company's annual report. The directive has high expectations for the benefits of this legislation (European Commission, 2014: FAQs):

> Each individual company disclosing transparent information on social and environmental matters will realise significant benefits over time, including better performance, lower funding costs, fewer and less significant business disruptions, better relations with consumers and stakeholders. Investors and lenders will benefit from a more informed and efficient investment decision process. Society at large will benefit from companies managing environmental and social challenges in a more effective and accountable way.

The European Commission (2014) argues that the above benefits cannot be realized by relying solely on voluntary reporting by companies. It states that only around 10 percent (2,500) of large EU companies are reporting on their environmental and social performance. This number will rise to some 6,000 companies under the new directive.

The reporting on non-financial and diversity issues is not entirely new. Large enterprises have already been required to include non-financial performance indicators like information on environmental and employment issues in the annual report to the extent they are necessary for the evaluation of the company. The new CSR Reporting Directive goes beyond value assessment and shareholder and investor information and financial performance. It is a paradigm shift insofar as it is designed to direct business conduct by introducing due diligence and "knowing and showing" requirements, not only with regard to the CSR compliance of the company or group, but also with regard to the supply chain (see Spiesshofer, 2014b). Targets include economic stakeholders like shareholders, investors, and creditors, as well as civil society and the general public, which shall be enabled to supervise and eventually enforce proper business reporting and conduct. Thus, the CSR Reporting Directive does not only serve the information function, but focuses also on transformation.

The purpose of the directive is not only risk assessment and risk management for the company and proper description of value-relevant factors. It also includes the avoidance of negative "impacts"—the soft steering of business conduct below the threshold of a violation of laws and regulations. The regulatory function of reporting is "know and show," i.e., to learn about causally linked negative impacts, to develop avoidance or mitigation strategies, and to show this to the general public and stakeholders. In its considerations, the directive recommends to member states to enable all persons and organizations having a "legitimate interest" to enforce compliance with this directive. Although it is not spelled out in the directive, this could include citizen lawsuits and private enforcement actions by potentially affected parties or NGOs—all examples of the engagement process inherent in the transformation function. The other purpose of the directive is to enhance consistency and comparability of non-financial information disclosed throughout the European Union, albeit respecting the diversity of CSR guidelines and approaches taken by enterprises—which is tantamount to trying to square the circle. The reporting on diversity in the Corporate Governance Declaration will, in a kind of "self-name-and-shame exercise," force companies to diversify the whole top management level—a particular target of transformation.

The requirement to measure impact raises yet another category of reporting in addition to activities and results. Activities lead to results that have impacts on an audience outside the company. Stock price is an example of the impact of financial performance on investors. Impacts can be positive (e.g., the social wealth created by new jobs) or negative (e.g., global warming caused by carbon emissions). Impacts are typically even more difficult to measure than are the results of non-financial performance. For example, those in the field of "impact investing" struggle to set standards for measures just as others are working to establish standards for non-financial information (see also Chapter 17, this volume). Impact measurement can have both an information (e.g., by influencing the decisions of others regarding the company, such as buying its stock or products or taking a job there) and transformation (e.g., when a group mobilizes around impacts to reward or punish a company for the impacts it is creating) function.

Consideration 7 of the directive contains differentiated guidance concerning the *materiality* of information, introducing a certain amount of ambiguity regarding which information should be reported. The report *shall* describe the actual and foreseeable impacts on the environment and on health and safety, and on energy and water consumption. It *can* describe with regard to social and employee matters the implementation of essential ILO-Conventions, respect for trade union and workers' rights, social dialogue, and dialogue with local communities. With regard to human rights and anti-corruption, the report *could* contain information regarding the avoidance of human rights violations and corruption (emphasis added). Consideration 8 classifies the issues with respect to risk intensity: adequate information is required with regard to those factors which will lead most probably to the realization of essential risks with significant impacts. The materiality depends on the magnitude and severity of the negative impacts. This qualification is similar to the stipulation of the US Supreme Court. Although the urgency to report is differentiated, the purpose is impact and thus transformation oriented.

According to the directive, the member states shall provide that enterprises may base their reporting on national, EU, or international guidelines such as the UN Global Compact, the UN Guiding Principles on Business and Human Rights, the OECD-Guidelines for Multinational Enterprises, ISO

26000 Guidance on Social Responsibility, GRI, or other recognized international guidelines like those of the IIRC. Although not mentioned by name, SASB would qualify and this directive provides an opportunity to spread the adoption of these standards. Enterprises shall describe which guideline they have used for the reporting. As these guidelines vary widely in terms of scope, specification, issues covered, and methodology, it is not evident how consistency and comparability of the reports across the EU will be achieved (Spiesshofer, 2014a). We note that comparability is more important for the information function for the same reasons it is important for financial reporting. Investors want to compare the performance of companies, at least within a sector, in choosing if and how much to invest in any of them. In the transformation function, effective engagement can take place simply based on targeting performance improvements in a company, however it chooses to measure an activity, outcome, or impact.

The directive has been criticized for a number of reasons: reporting requirements are introduced without developing homogenous substantive standards of "expected behavior" first. Consistency and comparability are hard to achieve with substantial flexibility for the member states regarding opt-out possibilities, the report-or-explain approach, and a variety of possible guidelines on which the reporting can be based. The reporting of negative "impacts" encompassing the whole supply chain is potentially endless and connected with potentially significant costs (Spiesshofer, 2014a). The directive emphasizes that it is not about integrated reporting but clearly acknowledges that it could be a step in that direction (<http://europa.eu/rapid/press-release_MEMO-14-301_en.htm>, accessed August 25, 2015):

> The Directive focuses on environmental and social disclosures. Integrated reporting is a step ahead, and is about the integration by companies of financial, environmental, social and other information in a comprehensive and coherent manner. To be clear, this Directive does not require companies to comply with integrated reporting. The Commission is monitoring with great interest the evolution of the integrated reporting concept, and, in particular, the work of the International Integrated Reporting Council.

However, one of the challenges the EU will face should it decide to do so is in clarifying the question of audience. The current directive is a kind of "all things for all people," failing to distinguish between material issues for integrated reporting versus the socially significant ones for sustainability reporting. As noted above, the directive is ambiguous regarding the underlying concept of materiality on which it is based. Nevertheless, nothing in the legislation would preclude a company from making its own definition of materiality. Furthermore, since the detailed implementation of the directive will be determined by each member state, individual countries could decide to recommend the International <IR> Framework as the basis for complying with this directive. We regard this as unlikely, at least in the short term, for the same reasons as discussed regarding the SEC, if the member state chooses its securities regulator as the entity responsible for implementing the directive in its own country. However, how the implementation occurs and which entity is responsible for it will be decided by each member state, and this could result in substantial variation. Despite these qualifications, the CSR Reporting Directive could turn out to be an important step towards integrated reporting in the EU over the long term and perhaps more quickly in certain member states should they decide to do so.

CONCLUSION: TOWARDS THE UNIVERSAL ADOPTION OF INTEGRATED REPORTING

We conclude this chapter facing a dilemma. On the one hand, it is clear that integrated reporting can play a central, even pivotal, role in bringing about a re-imagined capitalism. This can only happen at a system level through nearly universal adoption of integrated reporting—at least amongst the largest companies in the world that control the vast bulk of economic activity. Voluntary adoption is unlikely to achieve this objective in a meaningful time frame. This would suggest a regulatory solution: the other side of the dilemma. Our discussion of the US and the EU makes it clear that such regulation is unlikely to happen. Even if it did, the result could become a mere "tick-the-box" compliance exercise, achieving in only a minimalist way the information function of reporting and losing the transformation function so vital to achieving a re-imagined capitalism.

So what can be done? We begin by noting again that integrated reporting is not a silver bullet. Many other things must happen as well, including integrated asset management, asset ownership, investment legal duties, proxy voting, corporate governance, corporate brokerage, investment consulting, financial literacy, and financial regulation (Waygood, 2015; see also Chapters 9, 12, 16, and 17, this volume). All of these can help spread the adoption of integrated reporting; integrated reporting, in turn, can contribute to each of these. The causal relationships are many and complex; there is no simple, single linear path to take. Furthermore, the most promising paths will vary by country. In some countries regulatory forces will play a stronger role. In others, it will be market forces. Both will be necessary in all countries. From this perspective we have four common-sense incremental recommendations relevant all over the world. We say incremental because these recommendations are based on existing regulatory regimes. However, we believe that ultimately, a non-incremental outcome can be achieved once the proper groundwork has been laid.

First, companies should strive to implement the concepts in the framework, leveraging the work of SASB, into their relevant official filing documents, such as the Form 10-K or Form 20-F, the new Strategic Report now required of UK listed companies, and the annual report. The old adage, "don't let the perfect be the enemy of the good" applies here. Rather than focusing on an integrated report as a particular type of report that needs to be structured in a particular way, companies should start to practice integrated thinking in the context of the five characteristics of a re-imagined capitalism described above. They should simply adapt their existing reporting practices as best they can.

Second, asset owners, asset managers, and sell-side analysts should encourage companies to practice integrated thinking in their communications with them. They should also, and again on an incremental basis, start practicing more integrated thinking themselves. This means they need to go beyond having separate "ESG teams" to having their sector specialists develop a view on what the material ESG issues are and how they can affect financial performance.

Third, the accounting community should move from mere advocacy for integrated reporting to actually helping to spread its adoption. This means that the audit professionals, not simply the advisory or consulting professionals (which is largely the case to date), need to have proactive conversations about integrated reporting with the CEO, CFO, and board of directors of the companies they audit. The auditors also need to become better informed about what information investors want, since they are the ultimate clients.

Fourth, the International Organization of Securities Commissions (IOSCO), "the international body that brings together the world's securities regulators and is recognized as the global standard setter for the securities sector," should establish a task force to publish a report on how securities commissions can support integrated reporting within their existing regulatory regime (IOSCO, 2015). These recommendations will support the first three recommendations as they lay the groundwork for the timing and nature of new legislation and regulation to support integrated reporting.

The road to universal adoption of integrated reporting is a long one, but it is one that must be traveled. Our desire is that we achieve this objective by 2025. We will play whatever part we can to make that happen.

REFERENCES

Eccles, R. G. and Serafeim, G. (2015). "Corporate and Integrated Reporting: A Functional Perspective," in S. Mohrman, J. O'Toole, and E. Lawler (eds), *Corporate Stewardship: Organizing for Sustainable Effectiveness*. Sheffield: Greenleaf Publishing.

Eccles, R. G., Krzus, M. P., and Ribot, S. (2015). *The Integrated Reporting Movement: Meaning, Momentum, Motives, and Materiality*. Hoboken, NJ: John Wiley and Sons.

European Commission (2014). *Disclosure of non-financial and diversity information by large companies and groups—Frequently asked questions*, Brussels, April 15. Available at: <http://europa.eu/rapid/press-release_MEMO-14-301_en.htm> (accessed August 25, 2015).

European Council (2013). *EU Directive 2014/95/EU of 22 October 2014 amending Directive 2013/34/EU as regards disclosure of non-financial and diversity information by certain large undertakings and groups ("CSR Reporting Directive")*, adopted by the Council of the European Union on September 29, 2014, OJ L 330, 15.11.2014, p. 1–9.

GRI (2015). "Sustainability disclosure database," Global Reporting Initiative. Available at: <http://database.globalreporting.org/search>.

International Integrated Reporting Council (IIRC) (2013). *The International <IR> Framework*. Published December, Copyright 2015.

IOSCO (2015). *IOSCO: About IOSCO*. Available at: <https://www.iosco.org/about/? subsection=about_iosco> (accessed August 25, 2015).

KPMG (2013). "Carrots and Sticks: Sustainability Reporting Policies Worldwide: Today's Best Practice, Tomorrow Trends," *Global Reporting Initiative*, Unit for Corporate Governance in Africa, pp. 1–96.

Securities and Exchange Commission (SEC) (2007). *Securities Act Rule 408 and Exchange Act Rule 12b–20*. Available at: <https://www.sec.gov/rules/final/2007/33-8876.pdf> (accessed August 25, 2015).

Securities and Exchange Commission (SEC) (2010). "Climate Change Guidance," 17 CFR PARTS 211, 231 and 241 (Release Nos. 33–9106; 34–61469; FR-82, Commission Guidance Regarding Disclosure Related to Climate Change, February 8. Available at: <https://www.sec.gov/rules/interp/2010/33-9106.pdf> (accessed August 25, 2015>.

Securities and Exchange Commission (SEC) (2011). "Cyber Security Guidance," *CF Disclosure Guidance: Topic No. 2 Cyber-Security*. Available at: <https://www.sec.gov/divisions/corpfin/guidance/cfguidance-topic2.htm> (accessed August 25, 2015).

Spiesshofer, B. (2014a). "Die neue europäische Richtlinie über die Offenlegung nicht-finanzieller Informationen—Paradigmenwechsel oder Papiertiger? [The New European Directive on the Disclosure of Nonfinancial Information: Paradigm Shift or Paper Tiger?]," *Neue Zeitschrift für Gesellschaftsrecht* 33/2014 (A): 1281–7.

Spiesshofer, B. (2014b). "Wirtschaft und Menschenrechte—rechtliche Aspekte der Corporate Social Responsibility [Business and Human Rights—Legal Aspects of CSR]," *Neue Juristische Wochenschrift* 34/2014 (B): 2473–9.

US Supreme Court (1988). *Basic Inc. v. Levinson*. 485 U.S. 224, 238.

Waygood, S. (2015). "A Roadmap for Sustainable Capital Investments: An Aviva White Paper," *Aviva Investors*: 1–60.

16

Reasonable Expectations and Fiduciary Obligations

Legal Pathways to Longer-Term Thinking

Edward Waitzer and Douglas Sarro

INTRODUCTION

Our market system has achieved tremendous successes and remains critical to serve the common good. But its continued vitality is threatened by increasingly urgent challenges—from income inequality to human rights abuses, to the depletion of our planet's natural capital (OMCFG, 2013). While these challenges may appear to be solely social or environmental in nature, they are economically important as well. The development of markets depends on the continued availability of natural resources and on stable political systems that respect human dignity. In this sense, the interests of firms and stakeholders are intertwined (see also Chapters 9 and 10, this volume).

The financial and corporate sectors' ability to mobilize capital, allocate risk, and generate wealth empowers them to make substantial contributions to addressing these challenges. Traditionally, legislatures have helped to define the nature of this contribution, through taxation and other forms of legislation and regulation. However, they have become increasingly constrained by the inability of governments to tackle long-term, systemic policy issues because of the short-term incentives that motivate political processes. This challenge is reinforced by the ever increasing degree of interdependence and interconnectedness—trends that have left us with a world in which domestic regulation no longer provides adequate instruments to deal with public stewardship challenges.

As the tension between public expectations and legislative responsiveness becomes more severe, a growing role has emerged for our courts and independent regulatory bodies to use open-ended concepts like "reasonableness," when attached to nouns such as "expectations," "person," or "doubt" to create and modify legal standards and forge new and often radical legal pathways. A role has also emerged for private institutions to help shape these legal pathways. As Henderson and Ramanna (2015) argue, when society lacks a robust political market to address the negative consequences of self-interested profit seeking, private institutions have a duty to fill the resulting gap by playing a more active role in maintaining the conditions that sustain capitalism.

In this chapter, we focus on two legal concepts—reasonable expectations and fiduciary duties—which have evolved into powerful tools by which courts and regulators can require private actors to treat stakeholders fairly and consider the long-term effects of their actions on society as a whole. In recent years, these concepts have broadened—both in scope and in the range of potential claimants—and have become bellwethers for the trajectory of the law. Because both concepts are highly flexible and adaptable, their expansion creates an opportunity for private institutions. By proactively changing their behavior to reflect the principles underlying these concepts, they can create "best practices" that may ultimately be adopted by courts and regulators as examples of "reasonable" behavior.

The transition we have observed towards more robust regulatory and legal regimes, rooted in reasonable expectations and a broader understanding of fiduciary duty, can be viewed as a movement away from rules that merely encourage *rationality*, towards those that encourage *reasonableness* (Lydenberg, 2014). Philosopher John Rawls illustrated the distinction between these two concepts, noting that a group could take a stance that "was perfectly rational given their strong bargaining position, but [that] was nevertheless highly unreasonable, even outrageous" (Rawls, 1971: 290). Whereas "rationality" focuses on the maximization of self-interest, "reasonableness" supposes that decision makers act with reference to others in society and to agreed-upon principles and norms—i.e., show concern with the protection and enhancement of the common good.

This chapter seeks to describe what we believe is an accelerating trend, and explore some of its implications. The first section discusses the nature of reasonable expectations and explains the main objectives of the doctrine: to ensure the fair treatment of others and to prevent behavior that undermines the effectiveness of legal institutions. The second section discusses how fiduciary obligations have evolved to require financial and corporate sector professionals to actively pursue the long-term best interests of their beneficiaries, viewed not only as economic actors, but also as responsible citizens. The third section suggests some areas of the law that we expect will be informed by reasonable expectations and fiduciary duties. The fourth section proposes proactive measures that private actors could take to anticipate and help shape how these concepts develop. A brief conclusion follows.

NATURE OF REASONABLE EXPECTATIONS

Protecting reasonable expectations is a central organizing principle for many (if not most) legal rules in common law systems (Pound, 1922). The standard is applied unevenly—private law generally emphasizes the more subjective aspect of expectations (i.e., the expectations of particular stakeholders), while public law tends to focus more on objective "reasonableness" (viewed from the perspective of society as a whole). By definition, reasonable expectations mean more than the current law. As the Supreme Court of Canada stated in *BCE Inc.* v. *1976 Debentureholders* (hereafter *BCE*, 2008), the doctrine "looks beyond legality to what is fair, given all of the interests at play" to address conduct that is "wrongful, even if it is not actually unlawful" (*BCE*, 2008: ¶71). Contextual and dynamic, reasonable expectations can be thought of as legal polyfilla—molding around other structures to plug the gaps. This engenders reasonable expectations in and of itself.

Despite the wide range of contexts in which courts make use of reasonable expectations (discussed below), the doctrine has been used to achieve object-ives that are remarkably consistent. Two objectives appear to be the most salient. First, to require powerful public and private actors to treat others fairly, i.e., with honesty and avoiding actions that would impose unnecessary or disproportionate costs on others. Second, to uphold the integrity of legal regimes (and, through them, social institutions), i.e., sanctioning tactics that frustrate the purpose of a legal, regulatory, or social norm by allowing an actor to avoid the obligations associated with that norm.

Fair Treatment of Others

The "reasonable expectation of privacy" test used in search and seizure law seeks to ensure that police treat individuals fairly by restricting the use of investigative tactics that interfere with individual privacy. It holds that, where an investigative tactic significantly impinges on society's interest in individual privacy, that tactic must be classified as a "search" that is subject to constitu-tional oversight by the courts; this means that police are required to minimize the costs the use of the tactic imposes on society (e.g., by using the tactic only after obtaining a warrant that confirms that there are reasonable grounds to believe that its use will yield evidence of a crime).

In *BCE*, 2008, the Supreme Court of Canada held that reasonable expect-ations also inform a "duty of fair treatment" in corporate law, which requires boards of directors to consider the effects their decisions have on stakeholders, and to avoid actions that "unfairly maximize a particular group's interest at the expense of other stakeholders" (*BCE*, 2008: ¶64). The interests that must be considered in this context are not limited to legal interests; they include the economic and social interests of the affected stakeholders (*BCE*, 2008: ¶102).

While the reasonable expectation of privacy test considers the interests of society as a whole, the duty of fair treatment focuses on the interests of corporate stakeholders. The practical difference between these standards will likely erode over time, as courts lend greater recognition to the interests of the full range of corporate stakeholders (*BCE*, 2008: ¶¶39–40). For example, a court could hold that, where a board of directors pursues a course of action that harms the environment, and the board had an alternative course of action available to it that would have avoided these harms without imposing an undue burden on the corporation as a whole or on other stakeholders, the board acted contrary to reasonable expectations and should be liable for oppression. Though the statutory provisions governing oppression claims require a showing that there be an act or omission that "is oppressive or unfairly prejudicial to or that unfairly disregards the interests of [a] security holder, creditor, director or officer" (see, e.g., Canada Business Corporations Act, s. 241(2)), an institutional investor with a long-term investment horizon could argue that corporate action that needlessly harms the environment unfairly disregards the interests of that investor.

Tort law provides another example of how reasonable expectations have been used to prevent the imposition of unnecessary costs on others. In *T. J. Hooper v. Northern Barge Corp.*, a leading US tort case, "reasonable prudence" was held by Judge Learned Hand to require a tugboat operator to carry radio sets (a then relatively new technology), even though they were not required to do so by statute, on the basis that doing so had become a nearly universal safety practice. The court held that the duty of care is a concept that adapts to new technology, and that the operator should have weighed the risk of injury created by its lack of "compliance," and the gravity of the possible injury, against the costs that would have been associated with adhering to the general practice that would have mitigated this risk (*T. J. Hooper v. Northern Barge Corp.*: 740).

In addition to imposing a duty to minimize the costs one imposes on others, fair treatment also entails standards of honest conduct. In *Bhasin v. Hrynew* (hereafter *Bhasin*, 2014), the Supreme Court of Canada, citing the "reasonable expectations" of commercial parties, recognized a "general duty of honest contractual performance" (*Bhasin*, 2014: ¶92). The Court was careful to explain that this duty does not require contracting parties to "put the interests of the other contracting party first" or to "forego advantages flowing from the contract" (*Bhasin*, 2014: ¶93). Rather, it simply requires that the party to a contract not "lie or otherwise knowingly mislead [the other party] about matters directly linked to the performance of the contract" (*Bhasin*, 2014: ¶93). While *Bhasin* is regarded as a landmark case in Canada, the principles enunciated in *Bhasin* would hardly be viewed as controversial in the United States or Europe, where a duty of honest contractual performance has long been recognized

(*Restatement (Second) of Contracts*, 1981: §205; Whittaker and Zimmerman, 2000). For example, according to Whittaker and Zimmerman (2000: 25), the German Civil Code prevents contractual parties from "proceeding ruthlessly and without due consideration to the reasonable interests of the other party"— in other words, parties must act reasonably, rather than merely rationally.

Reinforcing the Integrity of Social Institutions

Courts also use reasonable expectations to address tactics that threaten to frustrate the purpose of a legal regime by allowing an actor to avoid obligations that ordinarily come with that regime, and accordingly undermine the social institutions the regime was intended to uphold. Consider, for example, *Hodgkinson* v. *Simms* (hereafter *Hodgkinson*, 1994), in which a financial advisor left his client with the impression that he was giving advice that served the client's best interests, but sought to avoid the obligation by sending the client a letter with lengthy, complicated disclaimers. The Supreme Court of Canada held that, because the advisor held himself out as independent and as an expert on the particular subject matter on which the client sought advice, i.e., real estate tax shelters, and effectively chose his client's investments for him, the advisor had invited a reasonable expectation that he would act in his client's best interests, and accordingly was subject to fiduciary obligations notwithstanding his disclaimers (*Hodgkinson*, 1994: 428–9, 431, 433–4). The Court noted that allowing the advisor to solicit clients' trust, but then avoid fiduciary obligations through the use of disclaimers, would likely undermine the public trust and confidence in financial advisors and other professional services that fiduciary law seeks to encourage.

In sum, reasonable expectations, by "look[ing] beyond legality to what is fair" and addressing conduct that is "wrongful, even if it is not actually unlawful" (*BCE*, 2008: ¶71), operate to close gaps in the law by requiring individuals and organizations entrusted with public or private power to consider the interests of others before exercising that power, and to minimize the costs they impose on their stakeholders as well as on society as a whole. The doctrine also empowers courts to reinforce the integrity of legal relationships and regimes, along with the social institutions that rely on them, by sanctioning attempts to avoid the obligations imposed by these relationships and regimes.

THE NATURE OF FIDUCIARY DUTIES

Fiduciary duties provide a second legal pathway towards longer-term thinking that considers the interests of stakeholders. The increasing importance of fiduciary duties in common law jurisdictions can be viewed as a response to changes in how society is organized, and the effects these changes have had on the effectiveness of other areas of law in controlling conduct. In particular, a legal consequence of the growth of specialization and interdependence has been that the traditional tools available in common law jurisdictions for supervising counter-parties, available through the law of contract, no longer guarantee the effective delivery of specialized services. In 1983, Frankel (1983: 802) noted that the United States was undergoing a transition from being a "contract society," which values economic independence and bargaining between equal parties, to a "fiduciary society," which values interdependence and reliance on the services of specialists. In a fiduciary society, legal regimes must, in the absence of any practical mechanism by which laypersons can supervise the work of the specialists they hire, provide protections that encourage individuals to *trust* that the specialists they rely upon will keep their best interests at heart (Frankel, 1983: 802).

Fiduciary law aims to promote this trust by providing that, when one party to a relationship (a fiduciary) gains discretionary power over another party (the beneficiary), in circumstances in which both parties would "reasonably expect" that the fiduciary will exercise this power in the best interests of the beneficiary, the fiduciary must exercise its powers with prudence and in the best interests of the beneficiary (Waitzer and Sarro, 2012). Like the concept of reasonable expectations, fiduciary duties are not a rigid code that can be addressed through "check box" compliance. Rather, they are open-ended and contextual, prescribing broad principles, the content of which can vary depending on the circumstances and can change over time. Below, we discuss the evolution of two central duties owed by fiduciaries—the duties of care and loyalty—with a focus on how these duties apply to financial professionals.

The Duty of Care

The duty of care illustrates how the duty has evolved to keep pace with developments in our understanding—in this instance, of what it means to be a prudent investor. Financial crises have often served as a trigger for changes in the content of the duty of care. For example, in response to the collapse of the South Sea Bubble in 1720, which caused significant losses to the beneficiaries of trusts that invested in the South Sea Company, the English courts of equity sought to discourage trustees from investing in speculative investments by redefining the meaning of trustees' fiduciary duty of care. They adopted a "legal list" approach, whereby a prescribed list of "safe" investments, including government bonds, were presumptively viewed as prudent, while other investments such as equities were presumed to be imprudent (Langbein, 1996: 643).

Over time the market environment made this approach impractical. Fixed-income investments deemed "safe" by the courts left investors vulnerable to inflation risk, and trustees learned that, over the long run, equities outper-formed the "legal list" investments. Modern Portfolio Theory (MPT) offered a new approach to investment, holding that, rather than weighing the risk of a portfolio by looking at each individual investment in isolation, investors should weigh risk by looking at the portfolio as a whole. It was therefore prudent for investors to give some weight in their portfolio to high-risk investments—and thus achieve some exposure to the high returns these investments offered. By assuming efficient capital markets and substituting portfolio-level diversification and risk control for judgment-based securities selection as the basis for prudent investment, MPT enabled trustees to pursue investment policies that promised less risk and better returns. During the 1990s, MPT provided the theoretical foundation for signifi-cant reforms in the duties of fund fiduciaries. These reforms redefined trustees' duty of care as a duty to invest "prudently," with reference to the portfolio as a whole, and to ensure that the portfolio is designed to generate a suitable rate of return without creating an undue risk of loss (Langbein, 1996). In recognition of the complexity of the task of analyzing the risk of a portfolio as a whole, these rules also permitted the delegation of responsibility for investment management to third parties (Hawley et al., 2011).

MPT has, however, produced some perverse effects. Trustees, seeking to protect their interests by mitigating their exposure to liability, took pains to avoid "underperforming" the market in the short term. They relied on the assumption, which forms a part of MPT, that price is always the best guide to value, as well as the resulting belief that those who fell behind the market, even on a quarterly basis, could face liability for failing to generate appropriate returns. As a result, they pursued a number of tactics intended to help them "beat the markets" in the short term, including (i) taking advantage of informational asymmetries (e.g., insider trading, high frequency trading, or other ways of trading "ahead" of others), and (ii) engaging in passive investing, i.e., "buying the market" and keeping costs as low as possible to ensure that one doesn't underperform the benchmark indices. In addition, in an effort to shield themselves from liability, trustees adopted a third tactic of taking full advantage of the delegation rule, relying heavily on an ever expanding chain of advisors, managers, and consultants (Stewart and Antolin, 2009).

These approaches, while "rational" tactics, have tended to disconnect the investment process from the real economy (see also Chapters 8 and 14, this volume). The first tactic ignores the fact that investment "has to be a positive-sum game to some extent, or else no one would play" (Bernstein, 2005: 120–1). The second increases systemic risk through herding behavior and the short termism of markets (IMF, 2015: 93). While passive investors think of themselves as "long term," they are, in fact, invested in largely index-linked funds, which are constantly adjusting to the relevant index, hence, as Zadek et al. (2005: 19) suggest, making them perpetual investors in short-term investments. Herding behavior amplifies the volatility created by speculators, and high-frequency traders, who are left to set market prices (Hawley et al., 2011). It erodes long-term value, makes markets less efficient, and impedes efforts to improve corporate governance by misaligning asset owner and investor goals (Krehmeyer and Orsagh, 2006). It also ignores the arbitrage opportunities available to those with a longer investment horizon (Roherge et al., 2013). These effects have become matters of concern for society as a whole and for the interests of future generations, because of the dislocations and imbalances they create (Lydenberg, 2014). The third tactic increases the complexity and the cost of sustaining the financial ecosystem without furthering the interests of beneficiaries—fostering a "food chain [that] operates in reverse, with service providers at the top and clients at the bottom" (Rajan, 2008).

It is now broadly accepted that most investment returns come from general exposure to the market, or "beta," rather than from seeking market benchmark outperformance strategies, or "alpha" (Ibbotson, 2010). As a result, systemic factors have become critical to fiduciary responsibility. Yet the mismatch between heightened expectations and suboptimal results persists. One of the likely reasons for this is that so many players in the investment chain benefit from the *status quo*. Managers of actively managed funds collect high fees in return for their promise to help investors beat the market, even when they consistently fail to deliver (Malkiel, 2013). Financial advisors and brokers receive incentives from third parties to recommend high-cost investment strategies to their clients based on short-term performance metrics (Frankel, 2010). In a sense, we have drifted away from the most fundamental meaning of fiduciary duty, which is to preserve the assets entrusted to the fiduciary. If one thinks of preserving assets as meaning to protect them from inflation, it's but a small step to include protecting them from a degenerating environment, society, or trust in fiduciaries. In formulating new norms to govern the financial sector, legislators, regulators, and courts are increasingly relying on this broader view of investor "prudence"—a view that by necessity entails a longer-term approach to investment.

The Duty of Loyalty

The duty of loyalty—to act in the best interests of beneficiaries—has long been recognized as the "cardinal duty" in the fiduciary relationship (Miller, 2011: 270), such that, where a conflict arises between the duty of care and the duty of loyalty, the conflict must be resolved in favor of the duty of loyalty (Laby, 2004: 75). This duty has historically been described narrowly, as implying only a duty to avoid conflicts of interest or to disclose such conflicts to the beneficiaries. It has also been argued, however, that this duty is best framed as a broad, positive duty to "actively pursue" the best interests of beneficiaries (Hanrahan, 2013: 220). The narrower view of the duty of loyalty is incapable of achieving fiduciary law's goal of encouraging trust in specialized service providers. Disclosure has been shown to be an imperfect tool for managing conflicts, with Cain et al. (2005), for instance, showing that when a service provider discloses a conflict of interest to a consumer, that consumer is likely to either ignore or insufficiently discount for the conflict. And while Sah and Loewenstein (2014) suggest that disclosure requirements may lead service providers to avoid conflicts of interest, particularly if service providers are motivated to develop and maintain a reputation for ethical behavior, such an avoidance of conflicts is only a necessary step towards reinforcing trust in financial markets, not a sufficient one.

Regulators and courts have increasingly taken notice of these facts. For example, in *Rural Metro* (2014), the Delaware Court of Chancery described corporate directors' fiduciary obligations as a duty to "act prudently, loyally, and in good faith to maximize [the company]'s value over the long-term for the benefit of its stockholders." And in *CDX Liquidation Trust* v. *Venrock Assocs.* (2011), Judge Posner of the US Court of Appeals for the Seventh Circuit made clear that disclosure of a conflict of interest does not release a corporate director from his or her duty to act in the best interests of the corporation, noting that "[i]f having been informed of the conflict the disinterested directors decide to continue to trust and rely on the interested ones, it is because they think that despite the conflict of interest those directors will continue to serve the corporation loyally" (*CDX*, 2011: 219). In *F.R.C.* v. *Deloitte and Einollahi* (2015), the Appeal Tribunal of the UK Financial Reporting Counsel emphasized that auditors must take into account the "public interest" by "act[ing] with integrity, honesty, objectivity and competence" (p. 72). In *BCE*, 2008, the Supreme Court of Canada held that, in executing its duty of loyalty to the corporation, the board was required to reflect on the interests of the corporation both as an economic actor and as a "good corporate citizen," which means having regard not only for the interests of shareholders and creditors, but also broader social interests, including those of the environment (*BCE*, 2008: ¶40).

When a fiduciary invests on behalf of, or provides advice to, a client, it must treat that client—and everyone who invests or otherwise has an interest in that client—fairly and equitably. This "duty of impartiality" requires fiduciaries to consider and balance the divergent interests of these beneficiaries (*Edge* v. *Pensions Ombudsman*, 1998; *Restatement (Third) of Trusts*, 2007:

§78). As a result, fiduciaries charged with managing and advising investment vehicles that encompass multiple generations of beneficiaries (such as defined benefit pension plans or sovereign wealth funds) must consider the long-term implications of their decisions or advice (Richardson, 2013b: 129; *Withers* v. *Teachers' Retirement System*, 1978; *Varity Corp.* v. *Howe*, 1996). Similarly, it has been suggested that, because a corporation has perpetual existence, corporate directors must consider the effects their decisions will have on both current and future generations of stakeholders of that corporation, as the corporation will rely on current and future generations to sustain its continued operation (Stout, 2015). This, in effect, imports the principles of impartiality and intergenerational equity into the duty of loyalty.

MAPPING THE TRAJECTORY OF THE LAW

Having described the principles that have given content to the doctrine of reasonable expectations and a dynamic conception of fiduciary duties, we explore some of the implications of these principles for those in the corporate and financial sectors. In particular, we believe that regulators' and courts' enhanced understanding of the link between private law and the public interest will lead them to use the principles that motivate the doctrines of reasonable expectations and fiduciary obligations as a basis for extending the scope of legal protections available to stakeholders, including future generations and the environment. We highlight the following as illustrative implications of this legal trajectory: (i) the broadening of rules relating to standing and intervenor status to make it easier for environmental and other groups to challenge harms to stakeholders caused by powerful actors; (ii) the expansion of materiality and corporate reporting requirements relating to environmental and other social issues; (iii) the adoption of intergenerational equity as a paradigm for assessing whether defined benefit plan pension fund trustees have met their fiduciary duties to their beneficiaries; and (iv) the continued evolution of the test for piercing the corporate veil to hold parent companies liable for environmental and human rights harms caused by their subsidiaries.

Broadening Standing

Reasonable expectations, and in particular, the principle that powerful actors should consider and seek to minimize the negative effects their decisions will have on others, will likely lead courts to continue to extend standing or intervenor status in private law cases to a broader range of stakeholders and their representatives (including groups representing the environment and future generations), so that failures to consider the interests of these stakeholders can be identified and remedied. Courts have increasingly recognized that private law has a public dimension, noting, for example, that it is prudent to consider the "social and economic" consequences of bankruptcy before making orders in insolvency proceedings (*Comstock*, 2014: ¶38), that fiduciary law's "underlying purpose" is to "reinforc[e] the integrity of social institutions and enterprises" that are of significant public importance (*Hodgkinson*, 1994: 422), and that a corporate director's fiduciary duties give rise to a responsibility to consider the interests of "employees...consumers, governments and the environment," as well as other corporate stakeholders (*BCE*, 2008: ¶40). The acknowledged link between these areas of private law and the public interest would appear to provide an opening for public interest groups to intervene in corporate or insolvency cases that have environmental, labor, human rights, or other societal implications. As is suggested below, the link between pension law and the goal of intergenerational equity may similarly provide an avenue by which advocates for future generations could obtain standing in pension cases that raise issues that have implications for multiple generations of beneficiaries.

Materiality

Materiality and corporate reporting requirements relating to environmental and other social issues will, we believe, continue to expand in response to a growing consensus that market participants are under an obligation to consider and report the effects their activities have on the environment and other stakeholders (see also Chapter 15, this volume). Information is generally regarded as "material" if a "reasonable investor" would view that information as significant in making an investment decision (*TSC Industries* v. *Northway, Inc.*, 1976: 449; *Sharbern Holding Inc.* v. *Vancouver Airport Centre Ltd.*, 2011: ¶44), and it would be hard to argue that a "reasonable investor" seeking to maximize long-term risk-adjusted returns in today's environment would not have regard for a variety of environmental, social, reputational, relational, governance, and other non-financial information. There is a growing body of research suggesting that consideration of such factors tends to enhance a firm's economic performance (Chapter 17, this volume).

There remains considerable distance between current regulatory and accounting frameworks and changing expectations, creating a situation in which a broad range of non-financial information is material but not yet mandated or consistently reported on. Regulators are catching up, with new rules and guidance on disclosure of information on issuers' impacts on issues such as climate change, as well as environmental, social, and governance issues more broadly. Examples include the US Securities and Exchange Commission's guidance regarding disclosure related to climate change, issued in 2010, initiatives by a number of stock exchanges to launch sustainability indices and to require or encourage listed companies to publish corporate social information—or explain why they are not doing so, and legislation passed by the European Parliament requiring publicly traded companies with more than 500 employees to report on non-financial sustainability factors by 2017. The private sector has also made considerable progress on its own. For instance, approximately US$62 trillion in assets are managed by institutions that are signatories to the UN Principles for Responsible Investment, and a majority of the companies in the S&P 500 and the Fortune 500 indices now report voluntarily on their environmental, social, and governance impacts (Clark and Master, 2012; see also Chapter 15, this volume).

Intergenerational Equity

The duties of defined benefit plan pension fund trustees will increasingly be framed in terms of intergenerational equity. As noted above, we have seen a dramatic and rapid shift from a narrow focus on short-term movements in price to legal standards based on reasonable expectations. The former approach was rooted in beliefs about efficient markets and the importance of rational (i.e., self-interested) behavior, both at the individual and systemic levels. In contrast, *reasonableness* supposes that decision makers act with reference to others in society and to agreed-upon principles and norms, i.e., show concern with the protection or enhancement of the common good. It also recognizes that the actual benefit of financial returns depends on the circumstances of individual investors (e.g., whether these returns can be used to purchase the same quality of health care and education as investors in other jurisdictions, or as investors in the same jurisdiction could a decade ago), and that, as a result, fund fiduciaries should be concerned with the question of whether their investment decisions will leave beneficiaries objectively better off. In this vein, the "duty of impartiality" requires fund fiduciaries to consider and balance the divergent interests of current and future beneficiaries, and in particular, to invest in a way that serves the well-being of present beneficiaries without endangering the well-being of future generations (Hawley et al., 2011).

Piercing the Corporate Veil

Notwithstanding the clear articulation in virtually every corporate law statute of the principle of limited liability, common law courts have developed the concept of piercing the corporate veil to address concerns about abuse of the corporate form. Motivated by the goal of ensuring that the corporate form is not used to avoid the obligations imposed by environmental, human rights, or other legal and regulatory regimes, courts will continue to prove increasingly willing to "pierce the corporate veil" in response to corporate conduct that undermines the purpose of these regimes and, in doing so, violates reasonable expectations or fiduciary obligations. While courts have traditionally "pierced the corporate veil" in response to a perceived abuse of the corporate form that amounts to a "deliberate" or "fraudulent" evasion of the law (Heintzman and Kain, 2013: 338), a series of recent Canadian and American decisions (e.g., *Sun Capital Partners III, LP* v. *New England Teamsters*, 2013; *Pension Benefit Guar. Corp.* v. *Asahi Tec Corp.*, 2013; *Alcoa*, 2014) appear to have taken the principle of anti-avoidance even further, by imposing personal liability not only in response to instances in which the corporate structures at issue were created for the *purpose* of undermining a legal or regulatory regime, but also in response to instances in which these structures merely had the *effect* of undermining the purposes of the legal regimes alleged to have been infringed. These decisions serve as precedents that may encourage courts and regulators in other jurisdictions to take similar action, to the extent that they have not done so already. The jurisdiction to pierce the corporate veil can be thought of as a particular application of the principle that one should not be permitted to act in a way that undermines the integrity of legal relationships and institutions, a principle that responds to "reasonable expectations." In this manner, it has become an instrument to accelerate the legal legitimization of social norms and encourage good citizenship.

PROACTIVE RESPONSES

Henderson and Ramanna (2015) argue that the traditional view of the corporate directors' role as fiduciaries—to maximize profit within the bounds of the law—may be compelling when there is a robust political market to check the consequences of self-interested profit seeking that distorts the underlying conditions for capitalism. However, they argue that when political markets are "thin," private institutions have a duty to fill the resulting gap by playing a more active role in maintaining the conditions that sustain capitalism, even when this requires subverting the short-term profit interests of the institution. This logic conforms to that reflected in the judicial and regulatory activism outlined above—using "reasonable expectations" and fiduciary standards to import social norms into most aspects of the law. In this section, we propose adaptive mechanisms which might reinforce this dynamic: (i) collaboration between issuers and institutional investors to respond to shared challenges; (ii) the introduction of legal mechanisms to protect future generations;

(iii) re-orienting regulation to respond to emerging risks and opportunities rather than solely responding to past failures; and (iv) developing financial products that respond to social as well as market needs. By working proactively to develop mechanisms for implementing the principles discussed, the corporate and financial sectors can create "best practices" that will influence how courts and regulators interpret the scope of reasonable expectations and fiduciary duties, as well as the principles that underlie these concepts.

Collaboration

Collaboration is essential to solving the challenges that threaten our economy and our society. To some extent, coalitions seeking to achieve better govern-ance already exist, particularly on the "buy side," and fulfill an important role. These groups include the International Corporate Governance Network, as well as investor-led coalitions that operate on a regional level, including Eumedion in Europe, the Collective Engagement Working Group in the United Kingdom, the US-based Council of Institutional Investors, the Canadian Coalition for Good Governance, and the Australian Council of Superannuation Investors. The efforts of these organizations should be supplemented by more robust models for collaboration between investment intermediaries and issuers. Too much of the dialogue over good governance has been one sided: asset owners telling issuers how they ought to act. It is easy to understand why managers would respond defensively. The result is that a relationship that ought to be cooperative is too often seen by both sides as antagonistic or adversarial. It is only by seating both sides at the same table, as equal partners with a common agenda, that we can forge the kind of trust necessary to effect collaborative change. To some extent, this work is occurring already—with promising initiatives including the Conference Board's Task Force on Cor-porate/Investor Engagement or the Shareholder-Director Exchange and the Focusing Capital on the Long Term initiative (see also Chapter 21, this volume).

Legal Mechanisms to Protect Future Generations

Designing public institutions to counteract the short termism that pervades our political systems and that amplifies market short termism (OMCFG, 2013) is another challenge that must be addressed. One model might be to establish a commissioner or ombudsperson for future generations, with the task of thinking about, consulting, and speaking up for those who cannot speak for themselves in the struggle to define public policy and regulatory mechanisms. Such a commissioner could also have legal standing to challenge government actions that fail to take the interests of future generations into account (SEHN, 2008). One can also envision broader reforms throughout government that seek to minimize the influence short-term political interests have on government planning and priorities. For example, independent "public-value" rating agencies have been proposed as a mechanism to assist political systems and societies to assess the value and legitimacy of reform proposals advanced by interest groups and thus create incentives for such groups to focus on win-win rather than rent-seeking requests (Hausmann, 2015). There may also be merit in exploring the use of existing legal instruments. For example, a public express trust is a charitable trust established to further a specific public goal or to help the community in general. One can imagine concepts such as the gradual transfer of a significant minority ownership interest in private institutions to such a public trust with a future-oriented remit—much like the focus of many sovereign wealth funds today (Richardson, 2013a).

Rethinking Regulation

Instead of focusing on emerging problems, regulators often become mired in a backward-looking, highly politicized and adversarial process. In response, many regulated institutions focus on defending their incumbency—from regulatory intervention or in court. The result is a vicious cycle—complex rules breed complex systems and an "is it legal" approach to product design and institutional cultures that can put consumers at risk. Regulators have a number of tools available that can allow them to reverse this dynamic and focus on emerging risks, particularly for those most vulnerable. "Big data" promises to make available to regulators a wealth of searchable data that could be used to help identify emerging problems before a crisis strikes. One recent study indicated that, just as epidemiologists can use trends in web searches to detect outbreaks of infectious diseases in real time, so can regulators use trends in big data to identify emerging problems in the financial sector (Mitts, 2014). The migration of "soft law"—consensual norms that reflect "reasonable expectations"—into enforceable legal standards provides another opportunity to develop rules for emerging issues in cooperation with the private sector (Goodman and Jinks, 2004). Perhaps the most important lesson—one consistent with "reasonable expectations"—is to eschew elaborate regulatory responses in favor of simplicity. For one, given the possibilities for arbitrage and manipulation, simpler solutions tend to be more robust (Zingales, 2015). Simpler rules also reduce lobbying costs and distortions and facilitate public accountability, because they are easier to explain and enforce. For example, a simple way to deal with unwary investors being taken advantage of is to impose liability (i.e., fiduciary duties) on their advisors.

Developing Financial Products that Respond to Social Needs

There are extraordinary opportunities for the financial sector to develop—and better explain—products, services, and markets that help mobilize capital and allocate risk to address pressing social needs. Consider, for example, work underway on environmental, longevity, and social enterprise asset classes (Sandor et al., 2014; OSFI, 2014). These new asset classes promise to use market dynamics to reward socially purposeful enterprise and risk shifting, penalize socially harmful activities, and encourage the private sector to take proactive steps to minimize the costs they impose on others. Accelerating this process presents a chance for the financial sector and regulators to work together to increase public awareness of the vital role of financial services in creating sustainable wealth. Likewise, leadership by financial sector regulators and policymakers to encourage the development of these products demonstrates that financial regulation is about more than protecting consumers from deceptive products and practices. Rather, it should be about ensuring, more broadly, that society is well served and that consumers get a "fair deal."

CONCLUSION

Courts and regulators have and, we believe, will continue to use the concepts of reasonable expectations and fiduciary duties as a basis for penalizing and deterring actions by powerful private actors that tend to undermine the integrity of the legal regimes and social institutions on which these actors rely, or that disclose a failure to consider the interests of those who are significantly affected by the decisions these actors make. As discussed above, this trend reflects a movement away from rules that merely encourage rationality, towards rules that encourage reasonableness (Lydenberg, 2014). It also reflects an understanding that the market system has achieved tremendous successes, and continues to have enormous potential to serve the common good, but that this potential can be achieved only if the corporate and financial sectors are guided by a sense of social purpose.

The private sector has a choice. It can be proactive and collaborative, by acting in a "reasonable" manner that embraces the social utility of private enterprise and financial services. Or it can resist this dynamic and face an unsustainable status quo—an approach that may seem "rational" in the short run (to the extent that it avoids the costs associated with the initial steps necessary for change), but that will ultimately prove both unreasonable and irrational, leading to higher compliance and foregone opportunity costs, higher penalties, diminished public trust, a less effective market system, and potentially far more severe environmental, social, and financial consequences in the long run (WEF, 2014: 23). This is the inflection point our corporate and financial sectors will either respond to as an opportunity to help shape the emerging regulatory norms or will have such norms emerge—and ultimately imposed—in a reactive manner.

ACKNOWLEDGMENTS

This chapter draws from Waitzer and Sarro (2014) as well as Waitzer and Sarro (2016). The authors thank Matthias Kipping and Stephen Aylward for their helpful comments.

REFERENCES

Judicial Decisions and Statutes

Alcoa Inc., Securities and Exchange Commission Release No. 34–71261, 2014 WL 69457 (January 9, 2014).

BCE Inc. v. *1976 Debentureholders* ("*BCE*"), 2008 SCC 69, 2008 3 S.C.R. 560.

Bhasin v. *Hrynew*, 2014 SCC 71, [2014] 3 S.C.R. 495.

Canada Business Corporations Act, R.S.C. 1985, c. C-44.

CDX Liquidation Trust v. *Venrock Assocs.*, 2011 640 F.3d 209 (7th Cir. 2011).

Comstock Canada Ltd (Re), 2013 ONSC 4756.

Edge v. *Pensions Ombudsman*, [1998] Ch. 512, aff'd. [1999] EWCA Civ 2013, 4 All E.R. 546 (C.A.).

F.R.C. v. *Deloitte and Einollahi*, Report of the Appeal Tribunal (January 30, 2015). Available at: <https://www.frc.org.uk/Our-Work/Publications/Professional-Discipline/Report-of-the-Appeal-Tribunal-Deloitte-Touche-M-Ei.pdf>.

Hodgkinson v. *Simms*, [1994] 3 S.C.R. 377.

In re Rural Metro Corp. Stockholders Litig., 88 A.3d 54, 80 (Del. Ch. 2014).

Pension Benefit Guar. Corp. v. *Asahi Tec Corp.*, 2013 No. 10–1936 (ABJ), 2013 WL 5503191 (D.D.C. October 4, 2013).

Sharbern Holding Inc. v. *Vancouver Airport Centre Ltd*, 2011 SCC 23, [2011] 2 S.C.R. 175.

Sun Capital Partners III, LP v. *New England Teamsters and Trucking Indus. Pension Fund*, 724 F.3d 129 (1st Cir. 2013).

T. J. Hooper v. *Northern Barge Corp.*, 60 F.2d 737 (2d Cir. 1932).

TSC Industries v. *Northway, Inc.*, 426 U.S. 438 (1976).

Varity Corp. v. *Howe*, 516 U.S. 489 (1996).

Withers v. *Teachers' Retirement System of City of New York*, 447 F. Supp. 1248, 1257–78 (S.D.N.Y. 1978).

Secondary Literature

Bernstein, P. L. (2005). *Capital Ideas: The Improbable Origins of Modern Wall Street.* Hoboken, NJ: John Wiley and Sons.

Cain, D. M., Loewenstein, G., and Moore, D. A. (2005). "The Dirt on Coming Clean: Perverse Effects of Disclosing Conflicts of Interest," *Journal of Legal Studies*, 24: 1–25.

Clark, L. and Master, D. (2012). *Corporate ESG/Sustainability/Responsibility Reporting: Does It Matter?* New York: Governance and Accountability Institute, Inc.

Commission Guidance Regarding Disclosure Related to Climate Change, Securities and Exchange Commission Release No. 33-9106 (February 2, 2010).

Frankel, T. (1983). "Fiduciary Law," *California Law Review*, 71: 795–836.

Frankel, T. (2010). "Fiduciary Duties of Brokers-Advisors-Financial Planners and Money Managers," Boston University School of Law Working Paper, No. 09-36.

Goodman, R. and Jinks, D. (2004). "How to Influence States: Socialization and International Human Rights Law," *Duke Law Journal*, 51: 621–703.

Hanrahan, P. F. (2013). "The Fiduciary Idea in Financial Services Law," in J. O'Brien and G. Gilligan (eds), *Integrity, Risk and Accountability in Capital Markets: Regulating Culture.* Oxford: Hart Publishing, pp. 203–28.

Hausmann, R. (2015). "Building Agencies to Rate Public Policy," McKinsey Global Institute. Available at: <http://www.mckinsey.com/industries/public-sector/our-insights/building-agencies-to-rate-public-policy>.

Hawley, J., Johnson, K., and Waitzer, E. (2011). "Reclaiming Fiduciary Duty Balance," *Rotman Journal of International Pension Management*, 4: 1–16.

Heintzman, T. G. and Kain, B. (2013). "Through the Looking Glass: Recent Developments in Piercing the Corporate Veil," *Banking and Finance Law Review*, 28: 526–48.

Henderson, R. and Ramanna, K. (2015). "Do Managers Have a Role to Play in Sustaining the Institutions of Capitalism?" Brookings Institution Center for Effective Public Management. Available at: <http://www.brookings.edu/~/media/research/files/papers/2015/02/managers-sustainable-capitalism-henderson-ramanna/brookingsinstitutionsofcapitalismv5.pdf>.

Ibbotson, R. (2010). "The Importance of Asset Allocation," *Financial Analysts Journal*, 66: 18–20.

IMF (2015). *Global Financial Stability Report: Navigating Monetary Policy Challenges and Managing Risks.* Washington, DC: International Monetary Fund.

Krehmeyer, D. and Orsagh, M. (2006). *Breaking the Short-Term Cycle.* Charlottesville, VA: CFA Centre for Financial Market Integrity and Business Roundtable Institute for Corporate Ethics.

Laby, A. B. (2004). "Resolving Conflicts of Duty in Fiduciary Relationships," *American University Law Review*, 54: 75–149.

Langbein, J. H. (1996). "The Uniform Prudent Investor Act and the Future of Trust Investing," *Iowa Law Review*, 81: 641–69.

Lydenberg, S. (2014). "Reason, Rationality and Fiduciary Duty," *Journal of Business Ethics*, 81: 365–80.

Malkiel, B. G. (2013). "Asset Management Fees and the Growth of Finance," *Journal of Economic Perspectives*, 27: 97–108.

Miller, P. (2011). "A Theory of Fiduciary Liability," *McGill Law Journal*, 56: 235–88.

Mitts, J. (2014). "Predictive Regulation," unpublished manuscript. Available at: <http://papers.ssrn.com/sol3/papers.cfm?abstract_id=2411816>.

OMCFG (2013). *Now for the Long Term.* Oxford: Oxford Martin Commission for Future Generations.

OSFI (2014). "Longevity Insurance and Longevity Swaps," Office of the Superintendent of Financial Institutions, Policy Advisory No. 2014-002. Available at: <http://www.osfi-bsif.gc.ca/eng/docs/longins.pdf>.

Pound, R. (1922). *An Introduction to the Philosophy of Law.* New Haven, NJ: Yale University Press.

Rajan, A. (2008). *DB and DC Plans: Strengthening Their Delivery.* Tunbridge Wells: CREATE-Research.

Rawls, J. (1971). *A Theory of Justice.* Cambridge, MA: Harvard University Press.

Restatement (Second) of Contracts (1981).

Restatement (Third) of Trusts: Prudent Investor Rule (2007).

Richardson, B. J. (2013a). "Sovereign Wealth Funds and Socially Responsible Investing: An Emerging Public Fiduciary," *Global Journal of Comparative Law,* 1: 125–62.

Richardson, B. J. (2013b). *Fiduciary Law and Responsible Investing: In Nature's Trust.* London: Routledge.

Roherge, M. W., Flaherty, J. C., Jr, Almeida, R. M., Jr, and Boyd, A. L. (2013). "Lengthening the Investment Time Horizon," MFS White Paper Series.

Sah, S. and Loewenstein, G. (2014). "Nothing to Declare: Mandatory and Voluntary Disclosure Leads Advisors to Avoid Conflicts of Interest," *Psychological Science,* 25: 575–84.

Sandor, R. L., Clark, N. J., Kanakasabai, M., and Marques, R. L. (2014). *Environmental Markets: A New Asset Class.* CFA Institute Research Foundation. Available at: <http://www.cfapubs.org/doi/pdf/10.2470/rf.v2014.n1.1>.

SEHN (2008). *Models for Protecting the Environment for Future Generations.* Science and Environmental Health Network and the International Human Rights Clinic at Harvard Law School. Available at: <http://hrp.law.harvard.edu/wp-content/uploads/2013/02/Models_Future_Generations.pdf>.

Stewart, F. and Antolin, P. (2009). "Private Pensions and Policy Responses to the Financial and Economic Crisis," International Organization of Pension Supervisors Working Paper No. 8.

Stout, L. A. (2015). "The Corporation as Time Machine: Intergenerational Equity, Intergenerational Efficiency, and the Corporate Form," *Seattle University Law Review,* 38: 685–723.

Waitzer, E. J. and Sarro, D. (2012). "The Public Fiduciary: Emerging Themes in Canadian Fiduciary Law for Pension Trustees," *Canadian Bar Review,* 91: 163–209.

Waitzer, E. J. and Sarro, D. (2014). "Fiduciary Society Unleashed: The Road Ahead for the Financial Sector," *Business Lawyer,* 69: 1081–116.

Waitzer, E. J. and Sarro, D. (2016). "Protecting Reasonable Expectations: Mapping the Trajectory of the Law," *Canadian Business Law Journal,* 57: 285–313.

WEF (2014). *Global Risks Report,* 9th ed. Geneva: World Economic Forum.

Whittaker, R. and Zimmerman, S. (2000). "Good Faith in European Contract Law: Surveying the Legal Landscape," in R. Whittaker and S. Zimmerman (eds),

Good Faith in European Contract Law. Cambridge: Cambridge University Press, pp. 7–62.

Zadek, S., Merme, M., and Samans, R. (2005). *Mainstreaming Responsible Investment*. Geneva: World Economic Forum.

Zingales, L. (2015). "Does Finance Benefit Society?" Available at: <http://faculty. chicagobooth.edu/luigi.zingales/papers/research/Finance.pdf>.

17

Corporate Social Responsibility

The Case for Active Ownership by Institutional Investors

Gordon L. Clark and Michael Viehs

INTRODUCTION

The past two decades have seen a significant increase in interest in responsible investment products from both individual and institutional investors. As the Global Sustainable Investment Alliance reports, the total assets under management devoted to sustainable investment assets have increased to US$21.4 trillion in 2014 (GSIA, 2014). At the time of writing, the United Nations Principles for Responsible Investment had more than 1,300 signatories with US$59 trillion assets under management (PRI, 2015), also alluding to the growing importance of sustainable and responsible investing. But not only financial markets are witnessing a growing interest in sustainable and responsible investment products; the number of academic research articles and studies that investigate the motives for investors' interest in responsible investment products has also risen markedly over the last several years. Many of the underlying research questions addressed by scholars have thus far focused on whether there is a monetary benefit towards responsible investment, i.e., the extent to which it is possible to earn superior risk-adjusted investment returns over the long run by devoting funds towards responsible investment products.

Responsible investment products can be considered to be products that, in one way or another, incorporate information on the corporate social responsibility (CSR) practices and the environmental, social, and governance (ESG) qualities of the companies invested in. The most common responsible investment approaches for institutional and individual investors are either inclusion or exclusion strategies, whereby companies with good ESG practices are included in the investment portfolio, and companies with very poor ESG and sustainability practices are excluded from the portfolio. Amongst the underlying motivations for investors to pursue responsible investment strategies are morals and values (see, e.g., Derwall et al., 2011; Hong and Kacperczyk, 2009) but also the potential to achieve superior risk-adjusted investment performance, or "alpha."

At the center of the research discussion about CSR lies the debate about whether companies should pursue CSR activities in the first place (see also Chapters 9 and 11, this volume). That is, should companies ensure that their ESG practices are well designed to accommodate non-financial stakeholders, or only serve the shareholders and maximize the company value (see, e.g., Friedman, 1970)? These two, often conflicting views are also known as the stakeholder and shareholder views regarding a company's main objectives. In this chapter, we take the standpoint that companies' main objective is the maximization of shareholder value (cf. Chapter 12, this volume), but that they should also ensure that reasonable ESG practices are in place and thereby serve stakeholder groups other than their most important stakeholders, namely the shareholders and other capital providers.

Against the backdrop of a growing interest in responsible investment products that take into account CSR and ESG information, the question remains: How can companies be incentivized to ensure that they have, for example, environmental management systems in place, proper human rights and worker safety standards installed, or an efficient corporate governance structure? More precisely, what—if not regulation—can ensure that companies do not recklessly focus on shareholder value maximization? We argue that institutional investors, such as pension funds, mutual funds, and insurance companies can be seen as drivers of change who monitor corporations' CSR and ESG practices closely, motivating them to adhere to best practice ESG standards in particular industries. By following an active ownership approach, institutional investors become truly responsible investors who not only design their investment products to reflect the current state of the art of ESG practices, but also take into account the underlying dynamics of CSR and ESG, which require a continuous updating of investment and screening approaches. Ultimately, investors that pursue these active ownership strategies will be able to realize longer-term benefits such as risk-adjusted outperformance and an overall reduced risk level of their investment portfolio.

The remainder of this chapter is structured as follows. In the next section we first give a brief overview of the literature on CSR and ESG to showcase the monetary benefits for companies to implement good ESG practices and for investors to pursue responsible investment strategies and then briefly discuss traditional responsible investment approaches. Subsequently, we present our arguments for the case of active ownership, and describe the major active ownership tools available to shareholders in this respect. Lastly, we outline what we think the future of truly responsible investment will look like.

THE SUSTAINABILITY OF RESPONSIBLE INVESTMENT APPROACHES

Responsible Investment Research: An Overview

As previously stated, the responsible investment literature has grown significantly over the last few years. A detailed review of this literature is beyond the scope of this chapter and hence, this section briefly summarizes the findings of our meta-study "From the Stockholder to the Stakeholder" (Clark et al., 2015) where we reviewed the literature on ESG, CSR, and sustainability in collaboration with Arabesque Asset Management. The purpose of this brief review is to highlight the clear benefits to corporations and investors that arise out of good CSR and ESG practices.

The more than 200 papers and studies covered in Clark et al. (2015) emanate from several topical backgrounds, such as the organization, accounting, management, environmental economics, financial economics, and corporate finance literature. We reviewed the extant literature and industry reports and determined the effect of superior ESG and CSR practices on: (i) the corporate cost of capital, (ii) the company's operational performance, and (iii) the company's financial performance. The underlying motivation for this study was the lack of consensus, either in the literature, or in industry, about the relationship between sustainable business practices and firm performance and the cost of capital. Taking into account methodological differences of studies and measurement practices of ESG and CSR, we concluded the following:

- 90 percent of the studies that investigated the costs of capital of companies found that proper ESG practices, i.e., more sustainable business practices, reduced the cost of capital.
- 88 percent of the studies on operational company performance documented that sustainable business practices were positively associated with company performance.
- 80 percent of the studies covering the financial performance of companies found a positive association between sustainable business practices and stock market performance.

Overall, we posited a clear business case for sustainable business practices: companies can do well by doing good and enjoy better financing conditions that allow their investors to realize better returns through investing in companies that have proper ESG policies in place. But how exactly can investors, in particular institutional investors, implement practices that take into account the sustainability features of investee companies? This is discussed in the following section.

Responsible Investment in Practice

The financial services industry has come up with several approaches towards responsible investment to exploit the aforementioned monetary effects of superior ESG and sustainability practices of investee firms. These can be divided into two broad categories: exclusion approaches or inclusion strategies.

In its most basic form, responsible investment is conducted by implementing *exclusionary screens* to investment portfolios. By applying those screens, firms from particular industries are shunned from the investment portfolio because they violate the institutional investor's norms and moral values. Such an approach is thus also often called "norms-based investing." This responsible investment approach is driven solely by non-financial parameters that emphasize social norms and moral standards. Often, the religious beliefs of the investor or the institutional investor's beneficiaries also play a role. Heinkel et al. (2001) and Hong and Kacperczyk (2009) have documented the drawbacks and pitfalls of exclusionary approaches towards sustainable or responsible investment. If a sufficient amount of large institutional investors exclude companies from the equity investment portfolios, stock prices of those companies will decrease, driving up their expected rates of return. Accordingly, these companies experience severe effects on their costs of capital from systematically applied exclusionary screens. In the event that multiple institutional investors with large stakes exclude certain firms from their investment portfolios, there is limited risk sharing amongst the residual institutional shareholder base (see, e.g., Heinkel et al., 2001), which in turn may cause them to ask a higher price for the capital they provided, for example higher interest rates or higher expected rates of return on stocks. Thus, institutional investors have to be aware that by excluding companies from their equity investment portfolios, they might actually forego potentially valuable investment opportunities (see, e.g., Hong and Kacperczyk, 2009).

The second widely adopted responsible investment approach are *inclusionary screens*—or best-in-class approaches, whereby companies are selected for the investment portfolio based on extra-financial information on their ESG performance. Often, investors adopt best-in-class approaches, selecting only those companies for the investment portfolio that score high on ESG dimensions. However, different investors might attach unequal weight to environmental, social, and governance subcategories so that the final investment portfolios could look quite unalike. With that approach, institutional investors "screen out" lagging companies, which might in fact have the greatest scope for improvements along the different ESG dimensions, focusing instead on the industry leaders.

In our opinion, these two approaches do not constitute truly responsible investment. By simply excluding certain companies that do not meet the investors' moral beliefs on ESG quality, such corporations will not improve their business practices because enough investors will still be prepared to absorb the shares of these shunned companies. Also, by underweighting the ESG laggards in investment portfolios, institutional investors do not use their economic power to improve companies and thereby do not contribute to a more sustainable society and responsible capitalism. Consequently, we argue, large institutional investors, such as pension funds and insurance companies, should pursue a different, complementary responsible investment approach, namely active ownership.

Learning Effects in Financial Markets: Implication for Inclusion Approaches

Another important reason why investors should pursue active ownership as their major responsible investment approach is the learning effect in financial markets. Earlier in this chapter, we described the positive effects that arise out of superior ESG and sustainability standards. In particular, firms with better ESG practices tend to perform better and have lower costs of capital. However, the observed effects of corporate social responsibility measures on firm characteristics are of course not static, but dynamic. These effects are observed at a single point in time, and are subject to changes when markets become aware of particular relationships. That is, when "learning effects" begin to materialize in financial markets. There exists a plethora of research that investigates these learning effects. Most of this focuses on the governance (G) dimension of the ESG universe. However, we believe that the evidence on the learning effects within the governance dimension represents a meaningful example for the future evolution of pricing effects of corporate social and environmental performances as well.

One of the earliest and most influential studies on the performance differential between poorly and well-governed firms was the ground-breaking study by Gompers et al. (2003). This work concluded that well-governed firms—defined as those with few anti-takeover defenses in place—significantly outperformed their poorly governed counterparts on a risk-adjusted basis, in turn suggesting a positive correlation between good corporate governance and financial outperformance. Since its publication, several scholars have investigated whether the observed relationship in Gompers et al. (2003) also holds for subsequent time periods. For example, Core et al. (2006) and Bebchuk et al. (2013) found that during extended time periods in the years following Gompers et al.'s original sample period it was no longer possible to realize abnormal returns from investment strategies that focused on well-governed firms. The authors attributed this finding to an ongoing learning effect present in financial markets: market participants, researchers, and the media became increasingly aware of governance issues, which in turn led to the incorporation of governance information into a firm's stock price (Bebchuk et al., 2013).

Similar results have been obtained by Borgers et al. (2013) for the social dimension of ESG: the authors demonstrated that it was possible to earn significant abnormal risk-adjusted returns by investing in firms with good stakeholder relations over the period from 1992 to 2004. However, these significantly abnormal returns ceased to exist subsequently from 2004 to 2009 (Borgers et al., 2013), suggesting once again the learning effects in financial markets. One manifestation of these learning effects has been the increasing awareness of the importance—for financial markets and scholars—of extra-financial information. This phenomenon was observed in a study by Eccles et al. (2011), which demonstrated the tremendous current interest of analysts and market participants in relevant E, S, and G information.

Such results indicate that financial markets are subsequently pricing extra-financial information on ESG issues. Eventually, trading strategies on these factors cease to deliver superior financial returns because market participants pick up the additional value stemming from superior ESG practices. This in turn has important implications for the responsible investment strategies of institutional investors: eventually, engagement with investee firms on ESG issues, and active ownership, will remain the only way for institutional investors to invest in a sustainable and responsible manner. The following section will address this argument.

MAKING A CASE FOR ACTIVE OWNERSHIP

The preceding section makes two important points. First, proper ESG standards, i.e., more sustainable business practices, are correlated with better performance and a company's reduced cost of capital. Second, financial markets will eventually become aware of these positive effects of sustainability practices, leading to securities prices that reflect extra-financial information on ESG practices. Thus, in order to continue to benefit from superior sustainability practices of investee companies, investors will have to move into a new responsible investment direction, namely *active ownership*. We argue that, in the long run, active ownership will be the only suitable way for institutional investors to credibly signal to financial markets that they are pursuing responsible and sustainable investment strategies. Hence, to become a truly responsible investor, shareholders will have to actively raise their voice and engage with companies on ESG and strategy-related issues—especially with the laggards on ESG quality. In doing so, shareholders will overcome the barrier towards truly valuable responsible investment.

What Is Active Ownership?

Stock ownership in publicly listed corporations carries with it a monitoring function. That is, the shareholders of corporations not only provide the capital for corporations to sustain their operations, but also elect the board of directors—the most important monitoring body in corporations in one-tier corporate governance systems as compared to the supervisory board in two-tier systems. By actively participating in corporate governance, shareholders also ensure that the company is managed in their interests, and that value is created in a responsible and sustainable manner. However, the relationship between corporate management and shareholders is often prone to conflicting interests (see, e.g., Jensen and Meckling, 1976), with managers sometimes pursuing their own goals and maximizing their private benefits first.

To attenuate these—sometimes significant—conflicts of interest, shareholders can take on a more active ownership position. That is, they can actively monitor companies and also intervene if the company is not managed in their best interests. This holds true for large institutional shareholders, such as pension funds, mutual funds, and insurance companies. Additionally, shareholders can interfere with management if the corporation's ESG standards do not meet industry standards. These shareholders often have in mind a responsible investment approach when they start to actively own corporations to monitor its incumbent ESG policies. Consequently, active ownership can be defined as the proactive execution of ownership rights by the shareholders of publicly listed companies, be it in the form of exercising voting rights at the annual general meeting (AGM), filing shareholder resolutions, or direct shareholder engagement activities with investee firms. All of these approaches enable institutional shareholders to employ their economic power and actively engage with firms to improve their ESG practices—and thus their sustainable business practices—which in turn lead to long-term financial success.

The Role of Institutional Investors in Active Ownership

Conceptually, all shareholders can become active owners of companies. However, we feel that a particularly important role should be attributed to large institutional investors such as pension funds, mutual funds, and insurance companies. Institutional investors should actively engage with firms on strategy-related topics, provide advice to boards and managers, and ensure that corporations have reasonable ESG policies in place. Evidence on these initiatives by institutional investors is scarce, but exists, for example in Bauer et al. (2013), Clark et al. (forthcoming), Dimson et al. (2015), and McCahery et al. (2015). Institutional investors are of particular importance in active ownership because they are currently the largest and most powerful shareholder group. Institutional ownership—in particular in the United States—has been steadily increasing over the last decades (see, e.g., Gillan and Starks, 2007). At the same time, stock ownership by households and retail investors has decreased significantly over the last 50 years in all major capital markets around the world (see, e.g., Rydqvist et al., 2011).

Against this backdrop, the incentives are almost non-existent for small retail shareholders and households to actively monitor firms and to engage with them on ESG issues. For that group of investors, the costs of active ownership clearly exceed the benefits, which would have to be shared with other investors as well. Thus, large institutional shareholders are in our view suitable corporate monitors as they have substantially more incentives to surveil corporations (see, for example, Shleifer and Vishny, 1986, and Burkart et al., 1997). They also have the potential to overcome the well-known free-rider problem inherent in any corporation with a dispersed ownership structure (see, e.g., Grossman and Hart, 1980). Based on these arguments, it is of utmost importance that large institutional investors, such as pension funds and insurance companies, consider the concept of active ownership as an integral part of their responsible investment framework in addition to the commonly adopted inclusion and exclusion approaches. In doing so, these active investors benefit financially from active ownership activities: returns are generated in a much more sustainable and responsible fashion, giving rise to competitive and reputational advantages within the "mainstream" financial industry.

Active Ownership Tools

Which specific active ownership tools do institutional investors have at their disposal? In our view, there are at least six major ways in which institutional investors can become active owners of publicly listed corporations, namely through (i) proxy voting, (ii) private engagements, (iii) shareholder resolutions, (iv) media campaigns, (v) class action lawsuits, and (vi) divestment or the "Wall Street walk." These active ownership tools are also often referred to as *shareholder engagement tools* or *shareholder activism devices*, since they are only relevant to shareholders of publicly listed corporations. For other types of

investment classes, similar active ownership tools exist, thus the aforementioned list of active ownership tools is not complete and may likewise encompass engagement tools relevant to bondholders, private equity investors, and
other capital providers. However, for the remainder of this section, we focus
on active ownership tools for shareholders and discuss their functioning and
effectiveness in promoting more sustainable business practices from a shareholder's perspective. We will now provide a short overview of each of these
active ownership tools.

Proxy Voting

Each shareholder has a very straightforward active ownership tool at their
disposal: exercising voting rights during the AGM. More precisely, shareholders can actively vote at investee firms' AGMs, for or against management
and shareholder proposals, and thereby directly influence the company's
business strategy and ESG policies. In doing so, especially institutional investors fulfill their fiduciary duties, and ensure that investee firms have reasonable
business and ESG strategies in place. Though proxy voting can be a straightforward active ownership tool for institutional investors, the literature thus far
provides only limited evidence of its efficacy in promoting proper ESG
standards or creating superior financial performance at investee firms (see,
e.g., Gillan and Starks, 2000 or Bauer et al., 2010). At the center of the
discussion whether proxy voting is an effective engagement tool is the fact
that—at least in the US—the voting outcomes of resolutions at the AGM are
not binding for managers. That is, managers can refuse to implement any
resolution, even if this resolution received more than 50 percent of the votes at
the meeting. Against this backdrop, many institutional investors have
launched "just-vote-no campaigns," where they basically withhold their vote
in order to signal their discontent regarding certain corporate policies with
managers and directors. The evidence indicates that these campaigns are
effective in improving the governance structures of corporations (see, e.g.,
Del Guercio et al., 2008). Though the direct impact on corporations might not
be measurable in terms of a high voting outcome, we propose that active proxy
voting should be part of every institutional investor's responsible investment
strategy because low voting turnouts at AGMs definitely signal investors'
discontent with managerial performance, company performance, or ESG
standards.

Private Engagements

Alongside exercising voting rights, private engagements are another important
active ownership tool available to institutional investors. Private engagements
are any direct contact or dialogue between (institutional) investors and their

portfolio firms. These engagements can take the form of management meetings, on-site visits, regular phone calls with executives, or letter writing regarding strategic issues or ESG policies. The aim of these activities is to keep close contact with the investee firms and thereby ensure that the strategic focus of firms is long-term oriented, and that their ESG practices are reasonable. Private engagements generally take place continuously and result in institutional investors building up relatively close relationships with their investee firms. Continuous private dialogue between large institutional investors and their corresponding investee firms should be seen as an important active ownership tool.

Empirical evidence sheds light on the presence and success of private engagements. Dimson et al. (2015), for example, studied the private engagement activities of a large institutional investor, revealing that successful private engagements at US companies resulted in significant positive abnormal returns, relative to matched peers. Similarly, Bauer et al. (2013) have documented that institutional investors are actively engaging with investee firms on a global scale. The authors studied a global set of engagement activities carried out by a UK-based asset manager at almost 400 international firms. They bring into sharper focus the presence and effectiveness of these private engagement activities at international firms and conclude that private engagements on ESG policies take place more frequently nowadays than in the past and, in addition, that environmental and social topics are now on the institutional investor's agenda when engaging with firms. Moreover, the authors document that institutional investors should be aware of certain "home bias" effects when outsourcing their engagement efforts to a foreign engagement service provider, which most of the time comprises another institutional asset manager. Specifically, Bauer et al. (2013) demonstrate that, even though the engagement efforts of a UK-based asset manager are relatively more successful in the US and Japan, most engagements take place with domestic, UK-based investee firms, giving rise to a home bias within the geographical distribution of engagements. Hence, institutional investors should decide carefully to which asset managers they outsource the engagement activities, and may even consider conducting engagements on ESG and strategic issues themselves in-house by setting up a responsible investment team.

Our overall conclusion from the albeit scarce literature on private engagements is that by building up a close and trustworthy relationship with their portfolio firms, institutional investors can leverage this relationship to effectively advise portfolio firms on ESG and strategy-related issues. This development could incentivize firms to adopt a longer-term business perspective that also takes ESG parameters into account. Private engagements are strongly correlated with shareholder resolutions (discussed next) and proxy voting, on the basis that shareholder resolutions can, at times, entail private negotiations between shareholder and corporations and proxy voting as a result of unsuccessful private engagements (see, e.g., Bauer et al., 2015).

Shareholder Resolutions

Alongside proxy voting at AGMs, shareholders can also directly shape the agenda of the AGM by filing shareholder resolutions on, for example, ESG-related topics. Shareholder resolutions can be filed by any (larger) shareholder to corporations, and include requests for corporate change either with respect to ESG standards or strategic-related issues that are not directly related to ordinary business issues. In the United States, for example, shareholders require a stake of US$2,000 in market value in a firm in order to be eligible to file a resolution (Bauer et al., 2015). These shareholder resolutions are generally filed in order to have a vote during the AGM. Filed resolutions also have the potential to raise public awareness; as such, their power to alter corporate behavior—even if the voting outcome of resolutions is relatively low—should not be underestimated. However, as has been pointed out by Bauer et al. (2015), not all filed shareholder resolutions eventually go to a vote during the AGM; some may be omitted, or even withdrawn, after private negotiations between the filing shareholder and the corporate directors. Often, shareholder resolutions are withdrawn before the AGM, because management wants to avoid certain resolutions being put to a vote, fearing adverse effects on their own managerial power or pay practices, thus providing the filing shareholder with a compromise to achieve a withdrawal (Bauer et al., 2015). Shareholder resolutions should be seen as a last-resort active ownership tool after the efforts to influence corporate ESG behavior and strategy by proxy voting and private engagement have failed. Resolutions are quite confrontational vis-à-vis portfolio firms, and might undermine the effectiveness of collabora-tive and friendlier private engagements that institutional investors undertake with their investee firms. However, we argue that they should still be viewed as part of the overall shareholder engagement arsenal for their potential to promote change at corporations regarding ESG policies.

Media Campaigns

One way for institutional investors to raise public awareness about ESG failures in corporations is to launch a media campaign. Core et al. (2008) as well as Dyck et al. (2008) have demonstrated the potential of media campaigns to change corporate behavior and trigger negative publicity. It should be noted, however, that this is probably the most aggressive strategy for institu-tional investors to voice their concerns. For long-term investors, such as pension funds, insurance companies, and many asset management firms, it might therefore be preferable to start with a collaborative media campaign in order to underpin their efforts to change corporate behavior and ESG practices. Notwithstanding, institutional investors should be mindful that media campaigns could be perceived by investee corporations as a bellicose form of shareholder engagement that could in turn imperil long-term relations with their investee company. To ensure a constructive dialogue with firms, institutional investors should therefore view media campaigns only as a last resort.

Class Action Lawsuits

Class action lawsuits are considered to be important (ex-post) governance mechanisms in relation to ESG behavior of companies. The most prominent research examples in this area are by Romano (1991) and Karpoff et al. (2005), who investigated the financial market implications of class action lawsuits. More specifically, Karpoff et al (2005) explored the losses in market value for corporations, which violate environmental regulations. The authors estimated that the loss in market value is quite similar to the legal fines and fees imposed on corporations for environmental wrongdoing. Hence, financial markets are aware of the adverse ESG behavior of firms, and price this behavior and potential further externalities accordingly. It is therefore important for investors to be aware that adverse ESG events could lead to legal implications and fines which in turn impact the market value of investee firms. Also, investors could consider the threat of a class action lawsuit as an effective way to make managers aware of unsatisfying ESG policies, and thereby prevent adverse ESG events and catastrophes.

Divestment, or the "Wall Street Walk"

As mentioned earlier, one of the most common approaches to responsible investment is the exclusion of particular firms or entire industries. Exclusion, or divestment, is probably the most direct way for investors to express their discontent with managerial actions and corporate ESG practices—a behavior termed in the financial and economic literature as "walking the Wall Street walk." Existing evidence on the "Wall Street walk" indicates that, in general, the mere threat of divesting from a company makes managers exert greater effort (see, e.g., Admati and Pfleiderer, 2009; Edmans, 2009; Edmans and Manso, 2011). There is also empirical evidence on the "Wall Street walk" by Parrino et al. (2003) that highlights the importance of this active ownership device. However, it is important to realize that not all institutional investors can pursue this path of least resistance and simply liquidate their ownership positions in certain firms. For one, investors might be "indexed," which means that their investment portfolio is supposed to mirror a major stock market index. This requires that these index investors hold particular stocks and cannot sell these ownership positions. Second, some investors might hold relatively large positions which make it impossible to liquidate the stake at once, unless the market for these stocks is very liquid. Hence, institutional investors who cannot easily sell their positions because of an unsatisfactory ESG strategy or managerial performance may find themselves having to adopt different active ownership tools to raise their voice.

At the time of writing this chapter, the debate as to whether institutional investors, in particular endowments, should divest from less sustainable companies—or even whole industries—has gathered momentum. Traditionally, this discussion has focused on firms that operate in industries considered to be sinful, such as alcohol, tobacco, or military defense. More recently, however, interest groups, such as the 350.org network, have claimed that institutional investors should also divest from firms in the fossil fuel industry in order to raise awareness amongst investors about climate change, pollution, and renewable energy. However, divestment from whole industries, as part of an active ownership approach, is widely debated. Our argument in this chapter is that any institutional investor considering divestment as part of their long-term investment strategy should be aware of the economic implications of divestments noted in the theoretical and empirical financial economics literature (see, e.g., Heinkel et al., 2001 or Hong and Kacperczyk, 2009): if a sufficiently large number of institutional investors exclude these companies, the expected rates of return of these companies go up, as do the costs of capital of these corporations. In effect, investors might forego profitable investment opportunities. Conceptually, these economic effects are significantly related to the effects from exclusionary responsible investment approaches, as outlined previously.

Thus, we argue that outright divestment approaches will not make corporations more sustainable and will also not improve their ESG standards. Eventually, outright divestment campaigns will not enable the longer-term survival of companies' affected industries. We claim that prior to adopting divestment strategies, institutional investors should first make use of their economic power, and engage with corporations' ESG issues, especially with those from industries that might become severely affected by future climate change. Institutional investors have the ability to raise awareness on these issues and can advise companies on how they can best prepare themselves for the challenges of newly introduced regulations regarding climate change, pollution, carbon emissions, and renewable energies. Recent evidence has clearly shown the eagerness of institutional investors to adopt an array of engagement strategies to influence corporate environmental, social, or governance behaviors (see, e.g., Bauer et al., 2015; Dimson et al., 2015; McCahery et al., 2015). Only if these engagements fail over a longer period of time should divestment become a viable, responsible investment strategy for institutional investors.

A Blueprint for a Credible Responsible Investment Strategy by Institutional Investors

Based on the discussion in this chapter and on our previous research (esp. Bauer et al., 2013; Viehs et al., 2013), we now postulate a theoretical yet credible responsible investment strategy for large institutional investors. In our opinion, a responsible investment strategy for institutional investors should comprise at least the following items:

- *Sign up to responsible investment initiatives or networks* such as the United Nations Principles for Responsible Investment (UNPRI), the Carbon Disclosure Project (CDP), or the International Corporate Governance Network.
- *Proactively exercise voting rights* during AGMs according to pre-specified voting guidelines.
- *Pursue a shareholder engagement strategy*, including a continuous dialogue with investee firms on ESG and strategy-related topics, management meetings, and on-site visits. Engagement can be conducted by specialized shareholder engagement service providers or in-house.
- *Introduce a shareholder resolutions policy* and, in the event that proxy voting and/or the shareholder engagement policy do not cause a change in company behavior, consider the *filing of own shareholder resolutions*, again according to pre-specified internal guidelines.
- *Consider divestment and exclusion as part of your strategy*, however, only as the final mechanism to be used and, also, depending on your clients' demands.

Any responsible investment strategy should comprise continuous dialogue as an overarching umbrella engagement tool, underpinned by structured proxy voting guidelines and a shareholder- resolution filing strategy. Depending on the nature of the institutional investor and its client base, exclusion policies—or divestments—should only be implemented with the consent of clients and beneficiaries, and as a last-resort mechanism towards responsible investing. In doing so, institutional investors will be able to benefit financially from seeking investments in socially responsible companies. This will shape the financial market in the years to come.

CONCLUSION: THE FUTURE OF RESPONSIBLE INVESTMENT

The future of responsible investment will be active ownership made up of institutional investors engaging with companies on ESG policies and strategy-related topics. To sustain long-term financial outperformance, capital providers will have to ensure that sustainable business practices become the norm in the industry in order to tackle society's most urgent challenges, such as climate change, pollution, hunger, and water scarcity.

Academic research, key players in the responsible investment industry, together with non-government organizations such as the UNPRI or CDP can push the topic of responsible investment into the mainstream financial world, creating awareness amongst corporations, and making capital markets and economic systems more stable and sustainable for future generations. In doing so, it is important that these key interest groups make the case that sustainable business practices and good corporate ESG standards do not necessarily preclude healthy financial returns. Even at this stage, research demonstrates that it is still financially beneficial to invest in a responsible and sustainable manner (see, e.g., Eccles et al., 2014; Clark et al., 2015).

Stated differently, the primary objective of the corporation remains to maximize profits and shareholders remain the most important stakeholder group. However, profit maximization can be pursued in a sustainable fashion, along with good ESG practices which, in addition, create non-monetary benefits for non-financial stakeholder groups as well (in the spirit of Jensen, 2002). Profit maximization does not mean that profits cannot be maximized sustainably, nor do sustainable business practices imply that profits cannot be maximized. Over the long run, only those companies that balance shareholder value maximization with the implementation of sustainable business practices will survive. In order to remain competitive, companies will have to generate profits sustainably. Institutional investors play a key role in this process through helping companies to find the right balance between profits and sustainability by implementing constructive active ownership strategies.

This chapter does not claim that institutional investors should change the world for the better—this is not its objective. As we have argued, "institutional investors cannot, and also do not have the responsibility to change the world. But they can make a difference where no proper ESG standards are in place" (Clark and Viehs, 2014: 45). It is important to stress that legislation and customers also have a key role to play in this process. Only if consumers, the beneficiaries of institutional investors, and legislation realize that the implementation of sustainable business practices does not imply sacrificing financial returns, will the financial industry fully transition into a sustainable one (see also Chapter 14, this volume).

ACKNOWLEDGMENTS

This chapter summarizes and builds on our previous work, in particular, Clark et al. (2015) and Clark and Viehs (2014).

REFERENCES

Admati, A. R. and Pfleiderer, P. (2009). "The 'Wall Street Walk' and Shareholder Activism: Exit as a Form of Voice," *Review of Financial Studies*, 22(7): 2645–85.

Bauer, R., Braun, R., and Viehs, M. (2010). "Industry Competition, Ownership Structure and Shareholder Activism," ECCE Working Paper, Maastricht University.

Bauer, R., Clark, G. L., and Viehs, M. (2013). "The Geography of Shareholder Engagement: Evidence from a Large British Institutional Investor," Working Paper, Maastricht University and University of Oxford.

Bauer, R., Moers, F., and Viehs, M. (2015). "Who Withdraws Shareholder Proposals and Does It Matter? An Analysis of Sponsor Identity and Pay Practices," *Corporate Governance: An International* Review, 23(6): 472–88.

Bebchuk, L., Cohen, A., and Wang, C. C. Y. (2013). "Learning and the Disappearing Association between Governance and Returns," *Journal of Financial Economics*, 108: 323–48.

Borgers, A., Derwall, J., Koedijk, K., and ter Horst, J. (2013). "Stakeholder Relations and Stock Returns: On Errors in Investors' Expectations and Learning," *Journal of Empirical Finance*, 22: 159–75.

Burkhart, M., Gromb, D., and Panunzi, F. (1997). "Large Shareholders, Monitoring, and the Value of the Firm," *Quarterly Journal of Economics*, 112(3): 693–728.

Clark, G. L. and Viehs, M. (2014). "The Implications of Corporate Social Responsibility for Investors: An Overview and Evaluation of the Existing CSR Literature," Working Paper, University of Oxford.

Clark, G. L., Feiner, A., and Viehs, M. (2015). "From the Stockholder to the Stakeholder: How Sustainability Can Drive Financial Outperformance," Working Paper, University of Oxford and Arabesque Asset Management. Available at: <http://papers.ssrn.com/sol3/papers.cfm?abstract_id=2508281>.

Clark, G. L., Saito, Y., and Viehs M. (forthcoming). "Institutional Shareholder Engagement with Japanese Firms: Culture, Process, and Expectations, 2006–2012," *Annals in Social Responsibility*.

Core, J. E., Guay, W. R., and Rusticus, T. O. (2006). "Does Weak Governance Cause Weak Stock Returns? An Examination of Firm Operating Performance and Investors' Expectations," *Journal of Finance*, 61(2): 655–87.

Core, J. E., Guay, W., and Larcker, D. F. (2008). "The Power of the Pen and Executive Compensation," *Journal of Financial Economics*, 88(1): 1–25.

Del Guercio, D., Seery, L., and Woidtke, T. (2008). "Do Boards Pay Attention When Institutional Investor Activists 'Just Vote No'?" *Journal of Financial Economics*, 90(1): 84–103.

Derwall, J., Koedijk, K., and ter Horst, J. (2011). "A Tale of Values-Driven and Profit-Seeking Social Investors," *Journal of Banking and Finance*, 35(8): 2137–47.

Dimson, E., Karakas, O., and Li, X. (2015). "Active Ownership," *Review of Financial Studies*, 28(12): 3225–68.

Dyck, A., Volchkova, N., and Zingales, L. (2008). "The Corporate Governance Role of the Media: Evidence from Russia," *Journal of Finance*, 63(3): 1093–135.

Eccles, R. G., Krzus, M. P., and Serafeim, G. (2011). "Market Interest in Nonfinancial Information," *Journal of Applied Corporate Finance*, 23(4): 113–27.

Eccles, R. G., Ioannou, I., and Serafeim, G. (2014). "The Impact of Corporate Sustainability on Organizational Processes and Performance," *Management Science*, 60(11): 2835–57.

Edmans, A. (2009). "Blockholder Trading, Market Efficiency, and Managerial Myopia," *Journal of Finance*, 64(6): 2481–513.

Edmans, A. and Manso, G. (2011). "Governance through Trading and Intervention: A Theory of Multiple Blockholders," *Review of Financial Studies*, 24(7): 2395–428.

Friedman, M. (1970). "The Social Responsibility of Business Is to Increase Its Profits," *New York Times Magazine*, September 13. Available at: <http://www.colorado.edu/studentgroups/libertarians/issues/friedman-soc-resp-business.html> (accessed June 16, 2015).

Gillan, S. L. and Starks, L. T. (2000). "Corporate Governance Proposals and Shareholder Activism: The Role of Institutional Investors," *Journal of Financial Economics*, 57: 275–305.

Gillan, S. L. and Starks, L. T. (2007). "The Evolution of Shareholder Activism in the United States," *Journal of Applied Corporate Finance*, 19(1): 55–73.

Gompers, P. A., Ishii, J., and Metrick, A. (2003). "Corporate Governance and Equity Prices," *Quarterly Journal of Economics*, 118(1): 107–56.

Grossman, S. J. and Hart, O. D. (1980). "Takeover Bids, the Free-Rider Problem, and the Theory of the Corporation," *Bell Journal of Economics*, 11(1): 42–64.

GSIA (2014). *Global Sustainable Investment Review*, Global Sustainable Investment Alliance. Available at: <http://www.gsi-alliance.org/members-resources/global-sustainable-investment-review-2014/> (accessed June 24, 2015).

Heinkel, R., Kraus, A., and Zechner, J. (2001). "The Effect of Green Investment on Corporate Behavior," *Journal of Financial and Quantitative Analysis*, 36(4): 431–49.

Hong, H. and Kacperczyk, M. (2009). "The Price of Sin: The Effect of Social Norms on Markets," *Journal of Financial Economics*, 93(1): 15–36.

Jensen, M. C. (2002). "Value Maximization, Stakeholder Theory, and the Corporate Objective Function," *Business Ethics Quarterly*, 12(2): 235–56.

Jensen, M. C. and Meckling, W. H. (1976). "Theory of the Firm: Managerial Behavior, Agency Costs, and Ownership Structure," *Journal of Financial Economics*, 3(4): 305–60.

Karpoff, J. M., Lott, J. R., Jr, and Wehrly, E. W. (2005). "The Reputational Penalties for Environmental Violations: Empirical Evidence," *Journal of Law and Economics*, 48(2): 653–75.

McCahery, J. A., Sautner, Z., and Starks, L. T. (2015). "Behind the Scenes: The Corporate Governance Preferences of Institutional Investors," Working Paper, Tilburg University, University of Amsterdam and University of Texas.

Parrino, R., Sias, R. W., and Starks, L. T. (2003). "Voting with Their Feet: Institutional Ownership Changes around Forced CEO Turnover," *Journal of Financial Economics*, 68(1): 3–46.

PRI (2015). *About the PRI Initiative*. Principles for Responsible Investment. Available at: http://www.unpri.org/about-pri/about-pri/ (accessed July 6, 2015).

Romano, R. (1991). "The Shareholder Suit: Litigation without Foundation," *Journal of Law, Economics, and Organization*, 7(1): 55–87.

Rydqvist, K., Spizman, J., and Strebulaev, I. (2011). "The Evolution of Aggregate Stock Ownership," CFS Working Paper, University of Frankfurt.

Shleifer, A. and Vishny, R. W. (1986). "Large Shareholders and Corporate Control," *Journal of Political Economy*, 94(3): 461–88.

Viehs, M., Hummels, H., and Bauer, R. (2013). "Shareholder Engagement: An Alternative Way to Invest Responsibly," ECCE Research Paper, commissioned by Kempen Capital Management. Available at: <http://www.kempen.nl/uploadedFiles/Kempen/01_Asset_Management/Producten_en_diensten/VerantwoordBeleggen/Research%20paper%20ECCE.pdf> (accessed June 24, 2015).

18

Building the Right Long-Term Approach

The Power of Aligning Leadership, Strategy, and Execution

Bruce Simpson and Tiffany Vogel

INTRODUCTION

From the first joint-stock company in the 17th century, to the birth of the insurance market in the 18th century, and the formalization of rules for stock exchanges in the 19th century, it is clear that capitalism has been re-imagined many times and over many centuries (see also Chapter 1, this volume). This evolutionary process continues today and has been explored in many chapters of this book. In this chapter we argue that, for business, sustainability over the long term stems from change *within*. Therefore, we turn our attention to internal organizational transformation since we believe that one of the largest and most important evolutionary leaps of the 21st century will be the shift toward developing strategies for the long term.

Corporate social responsibility (CSR) has been a long-standing approach to responsible corporate engagement and viewed as an entry point into long termism. Strategic and operational planning for the long term, however, is relatively new to organizations, since most CEOs face relentless pressure from markets, shareholders, and boards to deliver short-term results (see also Chapters 2 and 12, this volume). Getting CSR right has become a major piece of the answer to tap fully into the value of investing and building companies for the long term. Done right, CSR bridges successfully from vision to strategy and execution at all levels of an organization and its suppliers and customers. CSR also enables those stakeholders to reap environmental and societal benefits in addition to economic success, driving value against an organization's triple bottom line.

This chapter highlights the importance of building the right long-term approach, as the need to re-imagine CSR is more urgent than ever before.

Drawing on external and McKinsey-based research and reflecting on our own experiences, the chapter contains four additional sections. The context for corporate social responsibility is first set, and builds a compelling case for change. Subsequently, we analyze this case for change through an organizational lens and articulate the benefits of a long-term view in driving both shareholder and stakeholder value. The main section of the chapter then examines "typical" modes of CSR and, based on a variety of company case studies, argues that the "trinity" of visionary leadership, mindful strategy, and flawless execution must co-exist simultaneously to sustain long-term transformations. The final section offers lessons in long-term capitalism and charts a path forward—a new corporate frontier—as the key to progress and sustainable change.

PRESSURES FOR CHANGE

Today, the need to realize the triple bottom line through Michael Porter and Mark Kramer's articulation of "shared value" (Porter and Kramer, 2011) and Ian Davis' "social contract" (Davis, 2005) over the long term has never been more compelling. And the bar is rising faster than ever, due to four major forces.

First, *shareholders' and stakeholders' expectations are at record heights*, because capitalism can hardly keep pace with the rapidly changing shifts in the global economy. One of the biggest global forces at work today is the rise of emerging markets. By 2030, more than 3 billion people in Asia and Africa will move into the middle class, creating a new population of consumers at an unprecedented scale. As a result, growing resource constraints will be a significant challenge, testing the limits of human ingenuity to close the gap between demand and supply of key resources like food and water. A McKinsey study estimated that demand for water will exceed supply by 40 percent within 20 years (Addams et al., 2009). Resource shortages such as these will have far-reaching business, political, and societal implications and are likely to exacerbate tensions and conflicts between competing users.

The shift in demographics toward an aging population is placing new pressures on capitalism, as society will be forced to spend more on health care and social security. There has also been a rise in income inequality, and these disparities are growing. In 1970, the top 1 percent of the population in the Organisation for Economic Co-operation and Development countries earned about 7 percent of income. By 2009 this same group had doubled its share to 14 percent. Meanwhile, the bottom 10 percent slid from having 4 percent of total income to 3 percent (OECD, 2014).

When we consider these external pressures—a rising middle class, growing resource constraints, shifting demographics, and increased inequality—it is easy to place government at the center of programs to address these challenges. Yet, as these pressures intensify across political boundaries, public sector players can only do so much to provide the necessary resources and put the right mechanisms in place for success. Companies now need to share responsibility for longer-term solutions, and expectations for them to deliver more than short-term returns are growing (see also Chapter 9, this volume).

Second, *transparency is greater than ever* given the speed of technological change and communications, raising the bar for business engagement in society. In the past decades, technological innovation and complexity has increasingly outpaced management and global governance response efforts. Massive developments in technology have created an unprecedented level of global interconnectedness which, while bringing great gains, also brings significant risks to companies as they race to stay ahead of their competitors (Goldin and Vogel, 2010; Goldin and Mariathasan, 2014). In this ecosystem of rising uncertainty and increased complexity, it is not surprising company lifespans continue to contract: the average S&P company lifespan was 90 years in 1930; today that average is 18 years; not particularly conducive to long-term thinking (Innosight, 2012).

Transformation in our communication technologies has also resulted in unprecedented levels of transparency, where corporations increasingly find themselves under a global media microscope. Individuals and non-government organizations (NGOs) can now observe almost all actions of business in real time, and they can mobilize quickly with global campaigns at almost zero cost (Browne and Nuttall, 2013). Any perceived management missteps are widely scrutinized and published globally. Recently, there have been several well-documented examples of companies' share prices dropping precipitously after these organizations were suspected of anti-CSR practices—even before the full facts were known. At the same time, companies frequently do not get full credit and media exposure for the responsible actions they *do* take. For example, a mining company that has launched numerous high-impact community initiatives in developing countries where it operates continues to be one of the leading targets for negative press on human rights, corruption, and environmental damage. And although it invests more in CSR than its competitors, it does not rank as one of the top-50 socially responsible Canadian extractive companies (Corporate Knights, 2015).

As companies begin to focus on a broader community of stakeholders, many have successfully pursued co-branding strategies with NGOs to accelerate shifts in public perception (see also Chapter 9, this volume). For instance, WWF and Lafarge entered a global partnership on environmental conservation, Lululemon has partnered with the Dalai Lama and, at one point, Alcan was the only Canadian company participating in the US Climate Action Partnership and the UN Global Compact. Still, forging successful partnerships with the right NGOs has become more difficult. Increased transparency means there is now reticence on both sides: NGOs fear associating with the wrong corporate partner; and partnering with the wrong NGO can do a company more harm than good. The mutual challenge is to ensure such partnerships extend beyond a mere public relations exercise and reflect deeper organizational change. Given the stakes, business needs to find a way to reframe this increased level of transparency from a source of disadvantage to a source of advantage.

Third, while transparency is at its highest, *trust in business is declining*. As more traditional business and economic models begin to fail parts of society, it comes as no surprise that trust in business, particularly in the West, has been steeply declining and is now at cataclysmic lows. In 1966, Gallup polled the American public and trust in business stood at 55 percent. By 2012, this trust had plummeted to 21 percent, a drop that accelerated after the financial crisis (Gallup, 2015). Conversely, in many parts of Asia, conditions are more conducive to long-term planning because of government interventions to stimulate economic development, as well as the presence of more family-run businesses that take a long-term view (see also Chapter 4, this volume). Interestingly, and perhaps not coincidentally, in Asia trust in business has increased and is as high as 65 percent in some countries (Edelman, 2014). In short, businesses in the West need to rebuild the trust between them and the public if they are to ensure prosperity and longevity in the future (see also Chapter 2, this volume). As Richard Edelman, President and CEO of Edelman public relations, writes, "Trust is no longer earned by quantitative operational metrics—such as company profits—but by the values the company or country exhibits through its actions" (Edelman, 2014: 12).

Finally, *the talent gap is widening while the next generation seeks careers with a broader mission and purpose* (see also Chapter 7, this volume). As demographics shift to an aging population, the ratio of workers to non-workers is falling out of balance. In Asia, for example, there were ten workers for every retiree in 2000. By 2050, that ratio will drop to three workers per retiree (OECD, 2011). The gap between the supply and demand for talent is widening and, as a result, the "war" for talent and productivity is tougher than ever. At the same time, millennials are placing new expectations on their employers: they are more fickle, less loyal, and are seeking a mission and purpose in their careers. In the past, the average employee tenure at a given company was at least 10 years. Today, in the United States, that number has dropped to approximately four years (Bureau of Labor Statistics, 2013). For this generation, it is more about lifetime employability than lifetime employment.

How will companies attract the best and the brightest—*and* retain them? According to Meister and Willyerd (2010: 69),

> Millennials view work as a key part of life, not a separate activity that needs to be "balanced" by it. For that reason, they place a strong emphasis on finding work that's personally fulfilling. They want work to afford them the opportunity to make new friends, learn new skills, and connect to a larger purpose. That sense of purpose is a key factor in their job satisfaction; according to our research, they're the most socially conscious generation since the 1960s.

And a recent survey revealed that the millennials' view of businesses' role and purpose is changing: 36 percent feel that the purpose of business is to improve society, and 75 percent believe that businesses are focused on their own agendas rather than on helping improve society (Deloitte, 2015). These results signal that the corporate world requires a paradigm shift toward increased social accountability and engagement. Free the Children (FTC) is a fast-growing non-profit organization that fueled a new wave of social engagement, mobilizing youth and their families across 5,000 schools in Canada and soon 25,000 schools across North America. FTC encourages, measures, and celebrates the social engagement of participants. Eighty-four percent of FTC alumni know they "can make a positive impact on society" (Mission Measurement, 2014), and they are 3.9 times more likely "to mobilize others to solve a social problem" than non-FTC youth. This engaged group expects more social impact from their employers and they are also 2.4 times more likely to buy products from companies they perceive to invest in social issues (Mission Measurement, 2014).

What does all of this mean when, in today's world, urgency and expectations are higher, transparency is unprecedented, trust levels are at their lowest, and talent is searching for careers with greater purpose? Firms can no longer afford to do nothing. Getting it right is more important than ever. And while the downside of getting it wrong has never been more damaging, the upside potential is growing. Engaging in corporate social responsibility is quickly becoming a must, and can drive enormous value if wisely embedded into a core part of a firm's mission and strategy. We can no longer operate according to Milton Friedman's conventional view that "the business of business is business" (Friedman, 1970). Witness the exponential growth in CSR reporting over the past decade. In 1999, fewer than 500 companies published reports. As of 2010, almost 3,500 companies measured their environmental footprints and set targets (Bonner and Friedman, 2012). The same authors also examined how CSR has now expanded to encompass environmental, social, governance, health, diversity, labor, and safety issues—"almost any issue or concern that affects the operations and reputation of the company."

THE BENEFITS OF A LONG-TERM VIEW

A commitment to a longer-term strategy will drive shareholder as well as stakeholder value in several ways, namely by:

- *Avoiding operational and reputational risks and crises*: According to Simpson (2007), "a corporation that strategically integrates social responsibility develops an early warning system." This may not prevent pitfalls, but it helps management respond more quickly and creatively and with greater flexibility when it does encounter challenges. We explore examples later in this chapter, but we recognize that an approach to drive economic value alone, while valuable, has its limitations and may be less rooted in long-term business strategy (see also Chapter 12, this volume).

- *Launching new business models that drive competitive advantage and commercial gain*: This form of shareholder value creation "sees the social and political dimensions not just as risks—areas for damage limitation— but also as areas for opportunity." Developing a new business model with a long-term strategy at its core requires that organizations "scan the horizons for emerging trends and integrate their responses across the organization, so that the resulting initiatives are coherent rather than piecemeal" (Bonini et al., 2006: 21). Hewlett-Packard, for example, has stated a new agenda: "putting purpose at the heart of strategy" to inspire the company to think about innovative solutions that go beyond incremental improvements, while connecting customer needs with human, economic, and environmental impact (Hewlett-Packard, 2014).

- *Attracting, motivating, and retaining the best employees*: The traditional focus on performance is no longer enough to attract and retain the best employees. In the war for talent, an organization's commitment to social responsibility is becoming increasingly important in not only attracting, but retaining the best and the brightest. The best organizations have a bold mission, clear strategy, and focused execution on three levels: (i) the mission and purpose quotient (MQ), which is seen to be credible to employees, and to have societal impact over and above corporate performance goals; (ii) the emotional quotient (EQ), i.e., company behaviors and team norms that explicitly deliver apprenticeship and an open environment of trust and collaboration that encourages all employees to speak up, make a difference, and "be all they can be"; and (iii) the IQ, i.e., clear goals and objectives that show exactly how employees deliver value on the broader goals above, as well as traditional performance objectives, which pull the goals and mission together into focused and measurable execution.

Organizations that deliver along all of these dimensions encourage employees to bring more than their discipline and rigor to work, adding attributes like creativity, collaboration, and initiative that employees choose to bring, and which increase productivity and company loyalty. McKinsey research indicates that companies ranking in the top quartile for motivation, external orientation, environment, and values were 1.8 times more likely than those in the bottom quartile to have above-average margins for their industry, as measured by earnings before interest, taxes, depreciation, and amortization (De Smet et al., 2007). Finding meaning and purpose in work was also found to have the strongest impact on a person's overall life satisfaction. In fact, it is five times more influential than any other of the core elements of centered, high-performance leadership, i.e., connecting, framing, engaging, energizing (Barsh and De Smet, 2009; McKinsey, 2010a).

Research from the Hay Group finds that highly engaged employees are on average 50 percent more likely to exceed expectations than the less engaged. Companies with highly engaged people outperform those with the most disengaged employees—by 54 percent in employee retention, 89 percent in customer satisfaction, and by 400 percent in revenue growth (Goffee and Jones, 2013). To retain employees, organizations will need to better manage their business objectives and broader social and environmental commitments. In so doing, they will benefit the community *and* reap the rewards of their highly motivated employees, who are inspired by contributing to causes deeply meaningful to them. Even more important, however, is linking these commitments to the organization's purpose and values.

Ranked the "Happiest Company in the World" for caring for its employees, Costco "recognizes that in the long run, the interests of employees mirror those of the company." Costco outlines a compelling business case: paying its workers above the industry standard results in lower employee turnover, higher productivity, and better customer service than industry peers, which ultimately drives profit (Sisodia et al., 2014). Southwest Airlines engages stakeholders by hosting an annual Diversity Summit, where executives, human resource practitioners, employees, and leaders in the community meet to discuss diverse perspectives on inclusion. Southwest's purpose is to create an authentic and welcoming environment for employees and communities alike, which has driven positive business performance and employee satisfaction, innovation, and community engagement (Southwest Investor Relations, 2013).

Case studies throughout the book, *Firms of Endearment: How World-Class Companies Profit from Passion and Purpose* (Sisodia et al., 2014), reinforce that the social responsibility of business is not only to drive shareholder value and innovate, but also to create benefits for all stakeholders, including local communities, governments, and social organizations. But what is the robustness and magnitude of the underlying business case for transformational change toward long termism? The creation of shared value from solely profit driven to purpose driven is material: empirical studies support findings that the quality of a company's environmental, social, and governance practices positively correlates with market-based outperformance in the form of better returns on equity, cash flow, and dividend growth (Deutsche Bank, 2012; Hermes, 2014; see also Chapter 17, this volume). For example, GMI ratings research finds that for the ten-year period ended August 31, 2012, a portfolio of companies with top-decile accounting and governance risk ratings would have outperformed the lowest-decile portfolio by 54 percent. Similarly, *Firms of Endearment* highlights that in a 15-year longitudinal study (1998–2013), corporations operating on a model to benefit all stakeholders versus a maximize-return-to-shareholders model outperformed the S&P 500 by a factor of 14 times, and "Good to Great" companies by a factor of 6 times (Sisodia et al., 2014).

McKinsey, too, has found what's good for society is, in many cases, also what's better for business. Much of our work with clients has revealed a strong link between profits and organizational *performance* (De Smet et al., 2007), but it has also determined organizational *health* is key to long-term competitive advantage (Keller and Price, 2011a; McKinsey, 2010b). A 2010 McKinsey survey revealed that companies committed to addressing social issues in emerging markets boost their profits as well as their social impact. According to the survey, the vast majority of companies believe that macroeconomic growth in developing markets is key to their business strategies, and more than two thirds of companies are engaged in that growth, whether through education (22 percent currently engaged), private sector development (15 percent), or technological advancement (16 percent). So then, what is the key to getting it right?

LEADERSHIP, STRATEGY, AND EXECUTION AS THE "TRINITY" TO LONG TERMISM

For long-term capitalism to thrive, a company must ensure it has three key elements in place: visionary leadership to inspire change; long-term strategy to embed change; and then, above all, flawless execution. A natural question emerges: what happens when all three elements are not in place? We argue that four typical failure modes plague organizations and prevent them from realizing their potential in terms of capturing full economic benefit, securing stakeholder buy-in, and garnering reputational acknowledgment for their efforts. Only when leadership, strategy, and execution act in parallel do the full benefits of long termism bear material impact (see Figure 18.1).

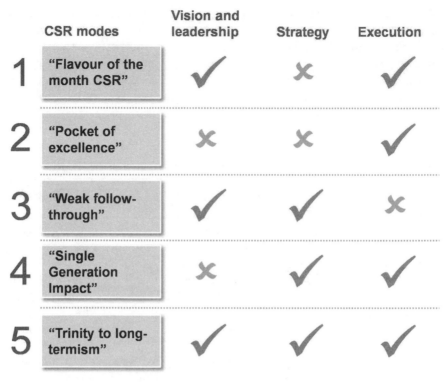

Figure 18.1. Typical modes of CSR across the trinity of leadership, strategy, and execution

Flavor of the Month CSR

Leadership and top team alignment are critical to an organization's long-term success. "Redefining the way a company thinks about itself requires leaders to promote their vision again and again with unremitting energy, both internally and externally" (Browne and Nuttall, 2013). But even when backed by supportive leadership poised to enact change, CSR can fail to deliver on its core purpose. Indeed, leadership can often skip the strategic planning process for long-term change and accelerate into execution mode. This often results in small-scale, short-term solutions that commonly reflect classical philanthropic efforts with "flavor of the month" impetus behind them. Here, well-intentioned leaders set a vision, but Michael Porter and Mark Kramer summarize the result as: "A hodgepodge of uncoordinated CSR and philanthropic activities disconnected from the company's strategy that neither make any meaningful social impact nor strengthen the firm's long-term competitiveness" (Porter and Kramer, 2006). In these cases, we witness the failure of traditional CSR to deliver real impact, despite growing investment in these initiatives, because of two underlying flaws in the strategic planning process.

First, companies might suffer from a *lack of professionalization of CSR*. Thus, in many cases, the effects of centralized CSR initiatives are unclear at best, with 9 percent of CSR professionals responding "no effect" to shareholder value by implementing programs and 53 percent "not sure" (Riddleberger and Hittner, 2009). This is because companies put little focus on resources or capabilities for CSR and centralize the function, instead of embedding it into business unit strategic planning. The result can be initiatives that lack the full support of the business, local cultural context, and effective stakeholder engagement, which are critical for operational delivery of the work. At the centralized level, focus is often placed on more superficial "shows" of CSR, such as voluminous CSR reports or mitigating media scandals.

Second, some companies have developed a *focus on short-term, light-touch engagement models with partners*. Examples of this can be seen broadly, where well-intentioned executives become impassioned by a certain cause or theme, which is divorced from the underlying economic drivers of their business operations. Often, with typical NGO partnerships, leaders will attach their organizations to advocacy campaigns to drive awareness about a cause, philanthropic donations to foundations, or community/environment efforts that provide financial support to local educational programs for employees. For example, to protect value and secure their licenses to operate in local countries, many mining companies focus on community improvement initiatives. While deeply beneficial to the local communities, these programs are vulnerable to the flavor of the month whims of senior executives because they are not deeply embedded into the business (e.g., changing supply and distribution chains). They are tough to sustain as long-term strategies and may fade away once their impact wanes, when their reputational capital has been fully enjoyed, or when management changes hands.

Pocket of Excellence

The organizational pocket of excellence is different to the flavor of the month. Here, we commonly observe great bottom-up ideas that typically originate on the front lines but rarely scale or become fully embedded across the rest of the organization. In heavy industrial, manufacturing, and resource-based organizations, an effort is quite often compartmentalized and, in many cases, overlooked within and beyond the organization. Often, there is a strong bottom-up business case for operational change, and these decisions have been taken at a small scale—for example, energy efficiency improvements implemented by front-line workers to improve productivity.

With visionary leadership and the drive to scale this into a broader strategy, pockets of excellence can present great business opportunities for the long term. We have found that organization-wide energy efficiency transformations in manufacturing, for example, can identify total savings potential of 10 to 12 percent, all of which is typically implementable within 18 months and with payback below two years. An additional 5 percent of savings is usually possible with a two- to five-year payback (McKinsey, 2013). But all too often, these initiatives fail to gain traction because of a lack of top-level leadership to drive change. Duke Energy's Keith Trent (now retired) emphasized that "[w]hether it's the CEO or his or her senior leaders, the biggest job is creating that vision for the company." Without the right leaders who are willing to take on significant personal risk and rally others behind them, incumbents, who benefit from the status quo, may resist the leader and suppress opportunities for broader organizational change (Browne and Nuttall, 2013).

Beyond capturing suboptimal economic benefits from small-scale solutions, pockets of excellence also have a poor reputational return on investment. In the case of a global mining company, analysis showed that its negative media hits increased as CSR spend increased, which means the risk-reward profile is highly skewed to mistakes. Pockets of excellence rarely get broader stakeholder credit for what they do right, and any misfires are broadcast widely. Instead, companies should capitalize on digital communications to improve transparency and showcase worthy bottom-up initiatives. As discussed earlier, millennials have an appetite to see measurable impact even at the micro level. Technology can help firms share these wins. Telus partnered with Free the Children (FTC) to build a free, cause-agnostic app (We365) to create user profiles and connect with other like-minded agents of change. FTC's Track Your Impact word app is a digital platform that attaches a unique social impact to an individual consumer purchase. Furthermore, FTC measures the benefits for corporate partners of social programs. RBC's "We Create Change" penny drive with FTC led to 140 million pennies being delivered via 55,000 unique walk-ins to branches—and 56,000 people received clean water for life as a result. Moreover, in comparison to a control group, FTC participants were two times more likely to believe RBC is an innovative company, were 1.5 times more likely to recommend RBC to others, and considered RBC products/services 1.7 times more frequently (RBC, 2013).

Pockets of excellence are certainly not the panacea for long-term change, but with proper stewardship and leadership, they can become ideas that can deliver high-value returns, scale, and, potentially, even transform an organization. And improved measurement of the impact increases their traction, credibility, and sustainability.

Weak Follow-Through

Companies fall short most frequently on execution, and CSR is no exception. In this third failure mode, the leader has set a compelling vision for the organization and taken the subsequent step to embed this vision into the strategic planning process. However, these priorities do not have a supporting operational plan to ensure their sustained execution. With expectations rising and increased transparency, this failure mode can be particularly damaging to an organization's reputation and to the level of trust enjoyed by its stakeholders.

To retain a focus on outcomes, companies should set metrics and targets to measure progress and link incentives to their achievements. But organizations often struggle with Louis Lowenstein's aspiration to "manage what you measure," both in the management of operational results and the performance management of their people. Despite recent achievements in big data analytics, there is a marked lack of data aggregation and analysis upon which to make sound decisions. In fact, research from IBM indicates that 70 percent of companies do not collect data frequently enough to make strategic decisions that could address inefficiencies across eight major categories, including CO_2, waste, and labor standards (Riddleberger and Hittner, 2009).

Other critiques in this area stem from global frameworks or mechanisms that aim to encourage business to adopt long-term-oriented practices. For example, even though the UN Global Compact and the UN CEO Water Mandate are credited for their aspirations and principles, they have been widely critiqued for being "too flexible and vague" in their failure to pressure the translation of their principles into real operational and measurable change for their signatories (Hoessle, 2014: 34). The UN Principles for Responsible Investment (PRI), for example, have been praised for their ability to define and legitimize the responsible investment ideology, but their challenges to render the approach actionable and implementable into mainstream financial markets have also been noted (Gray, 2009). When organizations fail to execute against their strategic priorities, we commonly see phrases like "green washing" or "glossy CSR brochures" appear so it becomes particularly important for businesses to ensure an appropriate level of rigor for transparency, accountability, and reporting in the operational execution of their strategic plans.

Here, the CEO's leadership also comes into play, whose role it should be to ensure shared value and long-term thinking is reflected in operational execution. One of the key caveats in design thinking is that designing for everyone can ultimately result in designing for no one. The same can be said for corporate strategies that aim to please all stakeholders: the result is often sluggish progress and analysis paralysis of operations.

Single Generation Impact

Our final failure mode of single generation impact is closest to charting a new corporate frontier: where long-term priorities have been deeply embedded into the strategic planning process and where operations are executed to deliver on these priorities. In most cases, this transformation would be at the behest and bold vision of an initial leader. However, how do we ensure irreversibility of this organizational transformation over several generations, when research shows that 70 percent of transformation efforts fail over the long term (Keller and Price, 2011b)? In many cases, the question becomes one of talent: how does an organization maintain its momentum during a critical leadership change to sustain the long-term transformation within the company? Moreover, how can leaders go beyond their organizations to transform their industries and chart new boundaries on the corporate frontier?

One of the limitations to multi-generational impact derives from the traditional but imperfect corporate structure of board of directors. Boards, by their mandate, should be invested in longer-term strategy of an organization and should adopt a longer-term view than even the CEO (see also Chapters 19 and 21, this volume). A constructive tension should exist between the CEO and board, where the short-term responsibilities of the CEO should be challenged against the longer-term and more diverse management priorities of the board. Many boards, however, are currently subject to unique structural challenges, where decision-making is dependent more on short-term shareholder returns, and where risk-averse members aim to maintain their own personal reputations with status quo decisions.

Future corporate structures and hierarchies should evolve to reflect the importance of leaders today, while the next generation will need to think about ensuring a transformation sustains beyond any one individual to embed itself into the culture and values of the organization.

Trinity to Long Termism

It has been said that companies are victims of their own good deeds. The more common or required a practice is, the less credit a company will get for it. Simply complying with international labor or environmental standards will never be enough because over the past decade acting in a socially responsible manner has become the *sine qua non* of a global brand. Instead, a firm must show that it's on the *frontier of change* (Martin, 2002). So which companies are

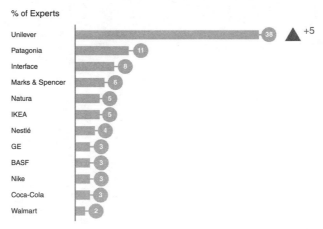

Figure 18.2. Leading companies on corporate social responsibility

Source: GlobeScan/SustainAbility Survey, 2015: 13. Reproduced with permission

truly on the frontier of change by getting visionary leadership, strategy, and execution right for the long term?

According to the 2015 GlobeScan/SustainAbility Leaders Survey (2015), which surveys over 800 influential thought leaders on sustainability across 80 countries, Unilever remains the top-ranking corporate sustainability leader for the fifth year in a row (see Figure 18.2). Even across geographies, there is general consolidation around leading companies (see Figure 18.3), a few of which we examine as examples of the trinity to long termism. Unilever is the pre-eminent example of a brownfield business transformation (see also Chapter 2, this volume), and Patagonia is one of greenfield business transformation.

The President and CEO of Campbell Soup, Denise Morrison, has said: "You can lead the change or be a victim of change" (Wang, 2013). In all of the top-performing organizations, leadership asserted the former—a new and bold vision for the organization. CEO Paul Polman of Unilever articulated himself as a visionary leader from the beginning: "We are finding out quite rapidly that to be successful long term we have to ask: what do we actually give to society to make it better? We've made it clear to the organization that it's our business model, starting from the top" (Browne and Nuttall, 2013). In 2004, Patagonia's founder, Yvon Chouinard, started the "Don't buy this t-shirt" campaign and followed it up years later with its 2011 Black Friday ad: "Don't buy this jacket." Chouinard made a conscious decision to inspire a responsible economy where customers think before they buy. Chouinard also carefully appointed the right CEO to carry out his specific vision for Patagonia, ensuring this would not become an example of "single generation impact" (Patagonia, 2014).

Adopting a historical view of leadership can also reveal some of the major shifts in long-term strategic planning. Over a decade ago, strategies subscribed

% of Experts, by Region

Figure 18.3. Leading companies on corporate social responsibility by region

Source: GlobeScan/SustainAbility Survey, 2015: 14. Reproduced with permission

more frequently to the precautionary principle of "do no harm," where risk management was the dominant framework. In the past, "[t]he alignment between far-sighted business practices and enduring social ideals has remained largely implicit" (Simpson, 2007). The complexity of the challenges businesses face today requires a stronger, deeper, and more explicit social contract. Strategies are now focused on integrating change deeply within the business practices, where leading firms exert influence either upstream or downstream through their operations. As a result, leaders in 1997—such as those in the extractive and chemicals industries—have seen center-stage recalibrate to industries more typically in consumer packaged goods, food, and retail by 2015 (Figure 18.4).

Patagonia, however, could be viewed as an example of a greenfield business transformation. From its inception, founder Yvon Chouinard embedded sustainability and responsible business as core to the culture and so the strategy decisions taken by the business always grew out of a consistent mission and vision: "Build the best product, cause no unnecessary harm, use business to inspire and implement solutions to the environmental crisis" (Patagonia, 2015). Early on, in 1986, Chouinard invested in sustainability efforts, imposing an "earth tax" of 1 percent of sales and 10 percent of profits to be donated to environmental organizations. Employee health concerns in the early 1990s led to the switch to organic cotton and eventually a complete examination of Patagonia's supply chain—the post-consumer recycled (PCR) program uses plastic bottles to make fabric for the majority of the company's products. Patagonia's ability to consistently innovate at the edge of the corporate frontier has had clear strategic benefits. Although the industry standard is near 44 percent employee attrition, Patagonia reports it has only a 25 percent turnover rate (Patagonia, 2014). It also receives an estimated $5 million to $7 million a year in free media coverage as a result of its sustainability program (Patagonia, 1999).

Finally, we have seen how these organizations have led the way not only in terms of leadership and strategic thinking, but also in operational execution. Unilever's Sustainable Living Plan lays out the business case, the associated measures of success—about 60 targets for 7 metrics, including total water consumption and greenhouse gas emissions—as well as a plan of execution. Unilever is still growing at 4.3 percent per year ahead of markets and despite reporting massive growth in production volumes. It also reports a 40 percent CO_2 emissions reduction and 65 percent water reduction from 2008 levels, as well as total waste reduction of 73 percent (Roos, 2010). Unilever's zero-waste-to-landfill facilities have saved the company $200 million, and energy-use reduction has resulted in an additional $150 million in savings since 2008 (Unilever, 2013).

Patagonia has transparently reported on its impact from the beginning: Patagonia's initial switch to organic cotton resulted in a 15 to 40 percent

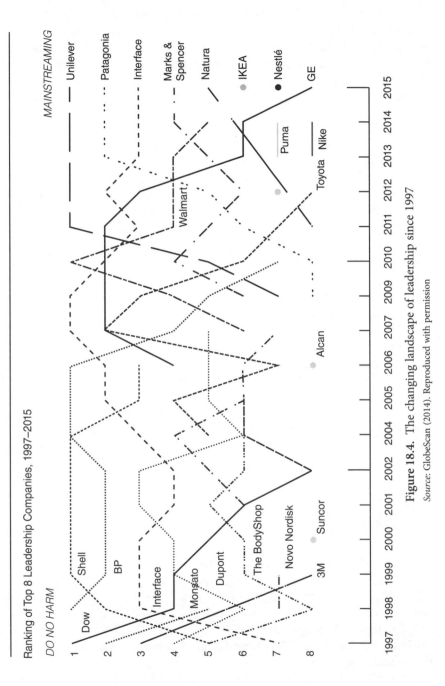

The changing landscape of leadership since 1997

Ranking of Top 8 Leadership Companies, 1997–2015

Figure 18.4. The changing landscape of leadership since 1997

Source: GlobeScan (2014). Reproduced with permission

increase in cotton costs, and it reported passing 20 percent of that on to the customer. Despite the increase in price, Patagonia's sales rose 25 percent (Patagonia, 2014). It also closely tracks the impact of its initiatives: it reports 86 million plastic bottles saved from landfill sites, and the oil saved to date by using PCR in lieu of virgin materials is enough to power a city the size of Atlanta for a year. It still donates 1 percent of sales or 10 percent of profit—whichever is greater—annually to environmental causes, which totaled $61 million in 2014.

Of course, we could have outlined many other cases in this chapter. IKEA recently announced the strong sustainability progress against its People and Planet Positive Strategy and is regarded by many CSR industry experts to be the next Unilever (IKEA, 2014). Marks & Spencer's sustainability strategy, Plan A—"since there cannot be a Plan B"—has been recognized by CSR experts not only for its innovative and expansive approach (over 180 com mitments), but also for its honest declaration of its plans and achievements—as well as its shortcomings (Marks & Spencer, 2015). Marks & Spencer fully integrates CSR metrics into store-level key performance indicators and embeds the philosophy of Plan A into the daily work of employees at all levels.

In all these cases—Unilever, Patagonia, IKEA, and Marks & Spencer, as well as the many other industry leaders—the trinity of long termism was clearly evident in the form of compelling leadership, a long-term strategy that embedded new business practices in the organization, and a plan for execution that holds itself accountable to targets for operational excellence.

CHARTING THE NEW CORPORATE FRONTIER: LESSONS FOR LONG-TERM CAPITALISM

The trailblazers charting the new corporate frontier can teach us a number of lessons for the long term. Indeed, although capitalism's problems seem daunting, they can be addressed by taking actions that improve leadership, strategy, and execution.

Leadership

Drive long-term change from the top and reward active owners of long termism. Change starts with leaders who are willing to fight the status quo and articulate their vision with clarity and conviction throughout the organization. Given the need for bold leadership, the selection of that leader is critical to the success of an organization. Moreover, once a leader has been installed, incentive and reward systems should be put in place to ensure decision-making is re-oriented to focus on the long term. Bold leaders have the opportunity to shift away from linking compensation and evaluation to quarterly earnings in favor of longer-term metrics.

Reposition, redesign, and rewire board governance as active stewards of long termism. Executive leadership cannot implement a bold vision alone—it needs the support and push from boards to think longer term. Structural changes are also needed at the board level to shift incentives away from risk-averse, short-term decision-making toward longer-term strategic planning. Board members should also be devoting more hours to their role and, relatedly, increasing the number of hours they commit to the organization's strategy.

Strategy

Embed long-term strategies into the core business. Typical CSR departments need to be dismantled and decentralized into the business lines to ensure strategy discussions are relevant, actionable, and appropriately long term. Long-term strategies also need to be vetted constantly against the organization's initial mission and vision to ensure it is remaining faithful to its core values.

Shift from shareholders to stakeholder engagement. Improved shareholder value will not be sustained if we do not create benefits for all stakeholders, including local communities, governments, and social organizations. A business ultimately needs a community's license to operate in it, and it will only get this license if its operations benefit that community. Organizations need to engage in active dialogue with the appropriate stakeholders and incorporate their inputs into the strategic planning process.

Execution

Establish clear metrics and targets to manage what you measure. Organizations must adopt a "manage what you measure" mindset and set bold targets for organizational health as well as performance. These metrics are the first step in building trust both within and outside of the organization, and they also signal to stakeholders that the organization is holding itself accountable for achieving real operational execution against the vision.

Turn transparency into a pillar of success and rebuild trust—communicate down, communicate up, communicate out. Once the organization is aligned on the right long-term targets and metrics, they then need to be cascaded throughout the organization. Employees at the front line should clearly understand the organization's objectives and why they are being asked to change/work differently. In addition, structural changes should be made to reinforce accountability, including incorporating expectations into job descriptions and performance management processes.

In addition to communicating down through the organization, leadership must also communicate up to the board level differently. It needs to ask more of its board members and more openly share the challenges the business faces. Board members should be increasingly engaged as thought partners to long termism. This will involve re-orienting institutional investors to improve the investor-corporate dialogue, and some key players are taking action to improve the communication of long-term corporate strategies to their investors. Finally, communicating out is a crucial final pillar in rebuilding public awareness, trust, and brand loyalty.

In sum, the challenges faced by capitalism are formidable, but they will only get worse if we do not begin to address them and actively solve them. The "gambling culture" we engage in places too many bets on immediate outcomes but, as the world becomes more transparent, interconnected, and fast-paced, these short wins come at a greater cost to more people. It is time to meet our commitments to future generations and society as a whole, to broaden our perspectives and embrace a longer-term view. This change must stem from multiple industries, institutions, and geographies. Most important, it must sustain the belief that through unwavering vision, mindful strategy, and flawless execution—as well as relentless optimism and openness to change—the benefits of long termism can be realized.

REFERENCES

Addams, L., Boccaletti, G., Kerlin, M., and Stuchtey, M (2009). *Charting Our Water Future*. 2030 Water Resources Group. Available at: <http://www.mckinsey.com/client_service/sustainability/latest_thinking/charting_our_water_future> (accessed March 4, 2015).

Barsh, J. and De Smet, A. (2009). "Centered Leadership through Crisis: McKinsey Survey Results." Available at: <http://www.mckinsey.com/insights/leading_in_the_21st_century/centered_leadership_through_the_crisis_mckinsey_survey_results> (accessed February 20, 2015).

Bonini, S. M. J., Mendonca, L. T., and Oppenheim, J. M. (2006). "When Social Issues Become Strategic," *McKinsey Quarterly*, 2: 20–31. Available at: <http://www.beitberl.ac.il/centers/iserc/articles/documents/when%20social%20issues%20become%20startegic.pdf> (accessed March 23, 2015).

Bonner, J. and Friedman, A. (2012). "Corporate Social Responsibility: Who's Responsible? Finding an Organizational Home for an Increasingly Critical Function," unpublished paper, New York University. Available at: <http://www.prsa.org/intelligence/partnerresearch/partners/nyu_scps/corporatesocialresponsibility.pdf> (accessed March 19, 2015).

Browne, J. and Nuttall, R. (2013). "Beyond Corporate Social Responsibility: Integrated External Engagement," McKinsey & Company, March. Available at: <http://www.mckinsey.com/insights/strategy/beyond_corporate_social_responsibility_integrated_external_engagement> (accessed March 22, 2015).

Bureau of Labor Statistics (2013). "Spotlight on Statistics: Tenure." Available at: <http://www.bls.gov/spotlight/2013/tenure/> (accessed July 12, 2015).

Corporate Knights (2015). "2015 Best 50 Results," *Corporate Knights Magazine*, Summer. Available at: <http://www.corporateknights.com/reports/best-50/2015-best-50-results-14333042/> (accessed July 10, 2015).

Davis, I. (2005). "The Biggest Contract," *Economist*, May 26. Available at: <http://www.economist.com/node/4008642> (accessed March 8, 2015).

De Smet, A., Loch, M., and Schaninge, B. (2007). "The Link between Profits and Organizational Performance," *McKinsey Quarterly*. Available at: <https://solutions.mckinsey.com/catalog/media/TheLinkBetweenProfitsAndOrganizationalPerformance.pdf> (accessed March 12, 2015).

Deloitte (2015). "The Deloitte Millennial Survey." Available at: <http://www2.deloitte.com/content/dam/Deloitte/global/Documents/About-Deloitte/gx-wef-2015-millennial-survey-executivesummary.pdf> (accessed November 2, 2015).

Deutsche Bank (2012). "Sustainable Investing: Establishing Long-Term Value and Performance." Available at: <https://institutional.deutscheawm.com/content/_media/Sustainable_Investing_2012.pdf> (accessed March 5, 2015).

Edelman, R. (2014). "Restoring Trust in an Era of Change," in Focusing Capital on the Long Term (ed.), *Perspectives on the Long Term*, Canada Pension Plan Investment Board and McKinsey & Company, pp. 12–15. Available at: <http://www.fclt.org/en/ourthinking/perspectives.html> (accessed February 5, 2016).

Friedman, M. (1970). "A Friedman Doctrine: The Social Responsibility of Business Is to Increase Its Profits," *New York Times*, September 13.

Gallup (2015). "Confidence in Institutions." Available at: <http://www.gallup.com/poll/1597/confidence-institutions.aspx> (accessed July 12, 2015).

GlobeScan (2014). "Unilever Maintains Sustainability Leadership Amid Change." Available at <http://www.globescan.com/news-and-analysis/blog/entry/unilever-maintains-sustainability-leadership-amid-change.html> (accessed June 12, 2015).

GlobeScan/SustainAbility (2015). "The 2015 Sustainability Leaders: A GlobeScan/SustainAbility Survey," May. Available at: <http://www.globescan.com/component/edocman/?view=document&id=179&Itemid=591> (accessed June 12, 2015).

Goffee, R. and Jones, G. (2013). "*Creating the Best Workplace on Earth*." Available at: <https://hbr.org/2013/05/creating-the-best-workplace-on-earth> (accessed June 10, 2015).

Goldin, I. and Mariathasan, M. (2014). *The Butterfly Defect: How Globalization Creates Systemic Risks, and What to Do about It*. Princeton, NJ: Princeton University Press.

Goldin, I. and Vogel, T. (2010). "Global Governance and Systemic Risk in the 21st Century: Lessons from the Financial Crisis," *Global Policy*, 1(1): 4–15.

Gray, T. (2009). "Investing for the Environment? The Limits of the UN Principles of Responsible Investment," University of Oxford. Available at SSRN: <http://dx.doi.org/10.2139/ssrn.1416123> (accessed February 5, 2016).

Hermes Global Equities (2014). "ESG Investing: Does It Just Make You Feel Good, or Is It Actually Good for Your Portfolio?" Available at: <https://www.governance.co.

uk/resources/item/667-esg-investing-does-it-make-you-feel-good-or-is-it-actually-good-for-your-portfolio> (accessed March 23, 2015).

Hewlett-Packard (2014). "HP 2014 Living Progress Report." Available at: <http://h20195.www2.hp.com/V2/GetPDF.aspx/c04152740.pdf> (accessed July 25, 2015).

Hoessle, U. (2014). "The Contribution of the UN Global Compact towards the Compliance of International Regimes: A Comparative Study of Businesses from the USA, Mozambique, United Arab Emirates and Germany," *Journal of Corporate Citizenship*, 53: 27–60.

IKEA (2014). "IKEA Sustainability Report." Available at: <http://www.ikea.com/ms/en_US/pdf/sustainability_report/sustainability_report_2014.pdf> (accessed March 22, 2015).

Innosight (2012). "Creative Destruction Whips through Corporate America." Available at: <http://www.innosight.com/innovation-resources/strategy-innovation/upload/creative-destruction-whips-through-corporate-america_final2015.pdf> (accessed August 10, 2015).

Keller, S. and Price, C. (2011a). "Organizational Health: The Ultimate Competitive Advantage." Availabe at: <http://www.mckinsey.com/insights/organization/organizational_health_the_ultimate_competitive_advantage> (accessed March 23, 2015).

Keller, S. and Price, C. (2011b). *Beyond Performance: How Great Organizations Build Ultimate Competitive Advantage*. Hoboken, NJ: Wiley.

McKinsey (2010a). "The Value of Centered Leadership: McKinsey Global Survey Results." Available at: <http://www.mckinsey.com/insights/leading_in_the_21st_century/the_value_of_centered_leadership_mckinsey_global_survey_results> (accessed February 20, 2015).

McKinsey (2010b). "Rethinking How Companies Address Social Issues: McKinsey Global Survey Results." Available at: <http://www.mckinsey.com/insights/winning_in_emerging_markets/rethinking_how_companies_address_social_issues_mckinsey_global_survey_results> (accessed March 14, 2015).

McKinsey (2013). "Sustainability and Resource Productivity Cases: Part 2: Green Operations," internal McKinsey Green Operations Practice (accessed on March 12, 2015).

Marks & Spencer (2015). "Marks and Spencer's 2015 Plan A Report." Available at: <http://planareport.marksandspencer.com/> (accessed March 22, 2015).

Martin, R. (2002). "The Virtue Matrix: Calculating the Return on Corporate Responsibility," *Harvard Business Review*, March. Available at: <https://hbr.org/2002/03/the-virtue-matrix-calculating-the-return-on-corporate-responsibility> (accessed March 20, 2015).

Meister, J. C. and Willyerd, K. (2010). "Mentoring Millenials," *Harvard Business Review*, 88(5): 68–72.

Mission Measurement (2014). "FTC Social Impact Study Fact Pack," copy provided by Free the Children. Used with permission.

OECD (2011). "Sizing up the Challenge Ahead: Future Demographic Trends and Long-Term Care Costs." Available at: <http://www.oecd.org/els/health-systems/47884543.pdf> (accessed August 20, 2015).

OECD (2014). "Income Inequality Update." Available at: <http://www.oecd.org/els/soc/OECD2014-Income-Inequality-Update.pdf> (accessed August 20, 2015).

Patagonia (1999). "Patagonia: First Ascents: Finding the Way towards Quality of Life and Work." Available at: <http://www.greenleaf-publishing.com/content//pdfs/pata.pdf?productid=2130> (accessed March 19, 2015).

Patagonia (2014). "Patagonia: A Sustainable Outlook on Business." Available at: <https://danielsethics.mgt.unm.edu/pdf/patagonia.pdf> (accessed March 19, 2015).

Patagonia (2015). "Patagonia's Mission Statement." Available at <http://www.patagonia.com/us/patagonia.go?assetid=2047> (accessed March 20, 2015).

Porter, M. and Kramer, M. (2006). "Strategy and Society: The Link between Competitive Advantage and Corporate Social Responsibility," *Harvard Business Review*, 84: 78–92.

Porter, M. and Kramer, M. (2011). "Creating Shared Value," *Harvard Business Review*, 89(2): 62–77.

RBC (2013). "Free the Children/RBC 'We Create Change' Penny Drive." Available at: <http://www.rbc.com/newsroom/news/2013/20130627-wcc-closing.html> (accessed March 12, 2015).

Riddleberger, E. and Hittner, J. (2009). "Leading a Sustainable Enterprise: Leveraging Insight and Information to Act." Available at: <http://www-01.ibm.com/common/ssi/cgi-bin/ssialias?infotype=PM&subtype=XB&appname=GBSE_GB_TI_USEN&htmlfid=GBE03226USEN&attachment=GBE03226USEN.PDF> (accessed March 21, 2015).

Roos, G. (2010). "Unilever to Cut Environmental Impact of Products by 50%." Available at: <http://www.environmentalleader.com/2010/11/15/unilever-sets-aggressive-environmental-goals/> (accessed March 12, 2015).

Simpson, B. (2007). "Elevating Our Vision of Social Responsibility," *Corporate Social Responsibility Review*, Autumn: 7–10. Available at: <http://www.globescan.com/pdf/CSRReviewAutumn07.pdf> (accessed March 10, 2015).

Sisodia, R., Wolfe, D., and Sheth, J. (2014). *Firms of Endearment: How World-Class Companies Profit from Passion and Purpose*. Upper Saddle River, NJ: Pearson Education.

Southwest Investor Relations (2013). "Southwest Airlines Announces Speaker Lineup for Fourth Annual Award-Winning Diversity Summit on August 1." Available at: <http://southwest.investorroom.com/2013-07-10-Southwest-Airlines-Announces-Speaker-Lineup-For-Fourth-Annual-Award-Winning-Diversity-Summit-On-August-1> (accessed March 31, 2015).

Unilever (2013). "Unilever Sustainable Living Plan 2013: Marking Progress Driving Change." Available at: <http://www.unilever.com.au/Images/ANZ%20USLP%203rd%20Year%20Update_tcm72-389984.pdf> (accessed November 2, 2015).

Wang, U. (2013). "Campbell Soup CEO: 'You Can Lead the Change or Be the Victim of the Change,'" *Guardian*, October 25. Available at: <http://www.theguardian.com/sustainable-business/campbell-soup-ceo-business-social-responsibility> (accessed July 10, 2015).

19

A New Way of Thinking about Resource Development

A Values-Based Approach

Richard A. Ross and D. Eleanor Westney

INTRODUCTION: DIVERGING EXPECTATIONS

The products of mining are essential to daily life in the 21st century. Whether it is the alarm clock that coaxes you from slumber; the coffee machine that brews that wake-up call for your body, the car, bus, or train that transports you to your daily activities, the buildings where you work, study, or play, the computers and cell phones that keep you connected—all originate from the mining of metals and minerals. There is a saying, "If it's not grown, it's mined," but even our food would not be possible without the steel machines that plant and harvest our crops. Wooden chairs, fabricated from trees that are grown in our forests, could not be shaped and assembled without metal tools.

However, open the pages of your local newspaper or surf the internet and you will see that mining-development projects are the focal point of significant concerns and even outright opposition from communities, governments, and non-government organizations (NGOs) globally (Ernst and Young, 2014). These reactions to mining development are not limited by either the geography or stage of economic development of the country in which that development is taking place; mining developments are as likely to meet opposition in the United States as in Peru or Melanesia (Bebbington and Bury, 2013; Horowitz, 2010; Wilshire et al., 2008). Multibillion-dollar mining-development projects, such as Pascua Lama that straddles the Argentina-Chile border, have experienced lengthy delays or have been indefinitely deferred due to local concerns and opposition (Nolen, 2014). Even in Canada, a country with a rich history of mining development, these same concerns and opposition have surfaced over mining development projects, such as the Ring of Fire in Northern Ontario (Talaga, 2013).

This contradiction between societies' need for metals and minerals and their resistance to mining operations originates in the divergence in expectations between the mining industry, including public, private, and government-controlled mining companies, and its stakeholders, including communities, governments, NGOs, and shareholders, when it comes to (a) the acceptable impacts of mining on the environment and (b) the equitable distribution of wealth from mining. Environmental impact and wealth distribution are not only contentious issues in the engagement of mining companies with their stakeholders; they are also, more generally, among the central drivers of the quest for more responsible, long-term capitalism. The challenges that mining companies face in developing common ground with stakeholders, and the new ways of thinking this requires, therefore have relevance not only for this extremely important industry, but also for the broader search for a new model of capitalist enterprise.

This chapter first addresses the diversity and complexity of stakeholders with whom a mining company must engage in building and operating a mine, and then examines more closely the challenges of finding common ground with stakeholders on the issues of acceptable environmental impact and wealth distribution. These two issues cannot be resolved objectively by scientific or economic formulae, because they go well beyond questions of interests and trade-offs. As we will argue, the resolution can only be found through understanding and accepting the wide diversity of fundamental values of the mining enterprise and the individuals, communities, organizations, states, shareholders, and other investors who all have a vested interest in its business. They therefore require a new way of thinking about the roots of the great diversity of stakeholder perspectives, and a different type of conversation between the mining company and its stakeholders. The chapter closes with a discussion of the leadership and management changes that will help a mining company engage more effectively with its stakeholders.

CHALLENGES IN BUILDING AND OPERATING A MINE

Stakeholders in Mines and Mining Companies

The mine site is the key to a mining company's interactions with stakeholders, because the stakeholders are different at each mine. A mine, obviously, must be located where there are mineral resources below the surface. That site may be on agricultural land, or close to towns and villages, or in a remote site far from the transport and energy infrastructure needed to build and operate the mine. Mining companies have long been preoccupied with the technical challenges of efficiently developing the mine, but increasingly their success depends on the relationships they develop with those who live close to the mine, those with some claim on the land (who may or may not live in close proximity to the site), those whose livelihood will be affected by the mine, and the different levels of government with jurisdiction over resource development. Mining companies often refer to local communities and government as *local* stakeholders, whose focus is on the individual mine rather than on the company as a whole.

Anthropologists studying the impact of mining on communities have identified these groups—local communities and the various levels of government—as the *core stakeholders* in the mine, along with the mining company itself (Ballard and Banks, 2003). This identification of the mining company as a stakeholder in the mine highlights the fact that each mine is the equivalent of a business unit: that is, an organizational subunit with a relatively high level of responsibility and resource control to make decisions affecting its performance (Strikwerda and Stoelhorst, 2009). Therefore the corporate headquarters can be viewed as a key internal stakeholder in the mine. In addition to the mining company and the local core stakeholders, a mine also faces a growing number of *auxiliary stakeholders*, particularly NGOs, who are engaged by virtue of their connections to one or more of the core stakeholders (Ballard and Banks, 2003). Auxiliary stakeholders are more likely to seek interactions with the company as a whole, rather than with the individual mines. They deserve attention, but for the mining company, the successful development and operation of a mine is more dependent on the local core stakeholders.

The local core stakeholders are different at each mine not only in terms of who they are, but also their interests, expectations, and values. Both the stakeholders and their perspectives on the mine differ at a mine in Finland from those at a mine in Zambia, and those in British Columbia from those in northern Quebec. A mining company with mines in several locations therefore has different sets of local core stakeholders in each location, and each category of stakeholder can encompass significant diversity. The state, for example, has multiple levels of administration (local, provincial, national) and at each level there are usually multiple departments with jurisdiction over different aspects of the mine, with significant differences among them: the finance ministry perspective often differs from that of departments in charge of labour or environmental regulations (Poulton et al., 2013). Communities are often deeply divided over the development of a mine (Campbell and Roberts, 2010), and even over who should be counted as members of the community. Indeed, as Ballard and Banks (2003) have pointed out, a mining project can create or define a community among social groups with little or no previous connection, and anthropologists have found in the community dynamics around mining projects a rich research venue for understanding local societies.

As mining companies try to understand and work with this diversity of stakeholder perspectives, they must also take into account their financial stakeholders, who are central to the capitalist system old or new, and whose focus is on the company as a whole, not just on one of its mines. Whereas the immobility of the resource defines the local stakeholders, it is the high level of risk in the mining business that shapes the expectations of financial stakeholders. This risk comes from the long and uncertain identification of the resource and the development of the mine, and the price volatility of the products of mining.

The risk-return equation is made particularly challenging in the mining industry given the time from the first dollar invested in a mineral prospect to the first dollar returned. The odds of finding a mineral reserve from the multitude of prospective mineral properties are extremely low: numerous studies suggest that only one out of 1,000 potential sites will eventually become a productive mine (MacDonald, 2002: 42). This high risk has shaped the industry structure. The term "the mining company" in fact covers two distinct types of companies: those that explore for and discover mineral deposits, and those that build and operate mines. The former—often referred to as "juniors"—are usually very small, and very few of them ultimately undertake to develop a mine at the discovery site (MacDonald, 2002). Juniors will more often sell their interest in the undeveloped resources or reserve to a senior company with the capacity to build and operate the mine. Historically, juniors interacted much less intensively with local stakeholders than did the companies that undertook the much more visible and consequential activities of building and operating mines. But even juniors are now realizing the importance of establishing good relationships with local stakeholders, since this can have a significant impact on subsequent development (Matten, 2013). The junior companies conduct most of the exploration in the mining industry and attract the high-risk financial stakeholders; they have been described as funneling the equivalent of "venture capital" into the industry (MacDonald, 2002).

Financial stakeholders in operating companies, however, also assume a high level of risk. Even when a discovery is made, the mineral reserves lie hidden below the surface of the earth, and even with the most advanced technology available today, this severely constrains the ability of geologists to identify and delineate a mineral prospect. This process has to be done gradually and in stages. Gathering sufficient data to form an assessment of the quantity, grade, and distribution of a mineral reserve requires drilling a mineral prospect and extracting core samples of the mineralization. This requires a significant investment that still does not bring with it a guarantee of success. Developing the mine once the scope of the reserves has been ascertained is a lengthy process, which has been growing longer as the requirements for environmental and social impact assessments and consultation with local stakeholders have become more demanding. The companies that develop and operate mines are those that most stakeholders and the general public—and this chapter—have in mind when they refer to the mining industry.

Moreover, mines are wasting assets. Although the life of a mine is measured in decades, every ounce of gold or pound of copper extracted leaves a shrinking reserve. Financial stakeholders invest in a company, and the value of that company depends on its reserves; therefore mining companies are driven to replace their reserves. This replacement process is complicated by the second major factor making mining a high-risk industry: the volatility of commodity prices. Mining companies cannot set the price they get for their product. The market determines the price of the commodity and the mining industry is a price taker. If metal prices stayed somewhat constant, this would make decisions to invest in finding new reserves somewhat easier. However, commodity prices are volatile and cyclical, and subject to "boom-and-bust" swings, which in metals have become particularly difficult to predict in recent years (Jacks, 2013). It is therefore understandable that financial stakeholders' expectations for returns are high. Often they have suffered through mediocre, if not negative returns, for extended periods of waiting for metal prices to rebound, and they often earn their returns during very short windows when metal prices spike.

Finding ways to respond to the very diverse expectations of stakeholders and managing to maintain consistency at individual mines and across the company are difficult challenges. The challenges are especially difficult in the context of two issues that are distinctively salient in the mining industry: environmental impact and wealth distribution.

The Acceptable Impacts of Mining on the Environment

No matter how much care is taken, the extraction of metals and minerals cannot take place without having some impact on the air, water, and land. The heavy equipment used in the mining process produces greenhouse gases and dust emissions that impact the quality of air. The waste rock dumps and tailings impoundments constructed to store the residual waste from mining have the potential to create significant adverse water quality and land impacts. These air, water, and land impacts also affect species biodiversity within the mine's footprint and potentially farther afield. The technological advances that have made possible the mining and processing of lower-grade ores, including increased resort to open-pit mining, have over the past two decades increased the potential environmental impact of mining operations, with growing volumes of tailings and a much more dramatic transformation of the landscape than experienced with underground mines (Poulton et al., 2013).

Even so, the standards of environmental practices in the mining industry have improved over the past decade, as even its critics are willing to admit (Hart and Coumans, 2013). Mining companies are well aware of the environmental impacts arising from their activities and are taking measures to mitigate these impacts to the extent that current technology and financial constraints allow. However, in spite of the progress in environmental performance, the environmental impacts of individual mining operations vary widely. This in part is a result of the legacy of the environmental impacts from past mining practices. In the United States, for example, 156 abandoned mine sites are sources of pollution and have been targeted for federal clean-up, at an estimated cost of $15 billion (Kirsch, 2014). Many mines in operation today, as well as mines abandoned by previous owners, were constructed when environmental standards were less rigorous than they are today. In many, remediating the environmental impacts after decades of mining would be prohibitively costly. An example is the Ok Tedi mine in Papua New Guinea where hundreds of millions of tons of waste rock and tailings have been discharged into the Fly River system since the mine's operations commenced in 1984 (Tinguay, 2007). This material is so widely dispersed throughout the 1,000 km Fly River system that remediation is impossible (Kirsch, 2014). It is estimated that it will take over 200 years for the river system to naturally flush itself out before it returns to its pre-mine condition.

Legacy mines are not the only challenges for the reputation of the mining industry. The improved standards of today's environmental practices are still not consistently applied. There are too many examples of individual mining operations that have not applied the more rigorous environmental mitigation measures endorsed by much of the mining industry. Moreover, both the foci of concern for local core stakeholders and their number and diversity have broadened in recent years, with growing recognition of the potential impact of mining not only on the local site but also on the larger watershed ecology. The wide-reaching impact of tailings dam collapses, such as that which occurred at Mount Polley in British Columbia in 2014, has engaged communities who live at considerable distances from the mine site to see themselves as stakeholders in the mine. Moreover, as concerns about water resources have grown in recent decades, the growing demands of mine operations on water usage with the processing of lower-grade ores has raised the anxiety of local stakeholders about the effects of mining on water supplies in the wider regional ecology (Poulton et al., 2013; Li, 2015).

Local stakeholders increasingly begin their interactions with a mining company with considerable skepticism about whether that company is prepared to meet their expectations and adequately mitigate environmental risks from its operations. Studies of mining conflicts have shown that local core stakeholders often feel that the mining company does not understand their perspectives and therefore cannot adequately respond to their concerns

(Horowitz, 2010; Kemp and Owen, 2013). Local anxieties about environmental impact are all too often addressed with very general assurances that make light of the potential impact in order to get agreement (Velásquez, 2012: 236), or with very detailed technical specifications that local stakeholders perceive as excluding them from any dialogue (Poulton et al., 2013: 365). Both types of response fail to comprehend and respect the perspectives of local stakeholders trying to balance the potential economic and social benefits of the mine with environmental impacts that could affect the quality of their lives and those of their children for decades to come. Local stakeholders judge the integrity and reliability of the mining company based on these interactions: as one case study points out, "[t]rust depends not simply upon qualities inherent in trustor or trustee, but on the reciprocal perceptions of and interactions between the parties" (Velásquez, 2012: 617).

On the other hand, the mining company must reassure its financial stakeholders that the investments required will create more financial value than would be generated by following less than "best in class" standards that might be legal under local regulations but unacceptable to local communities. This process of aligning and demonstrating values may require a mining company to act beyond the requirements of local environmental legislation, particularly where that legislation falls below the more advanced standards of developed countries. The growing value that institutional shareholders and financial institutions place on ethical investing, added to the potential costs that could be generated by conflicts with local stakeholders once the mine begins operations, can help the company to align its financial stakeholders with its local core stakeholders.

In some cases, the perspectives of the local core stakeholders may be such that there is no outcome in which they are prepared to accept the environmental impact of a mining development project. In these cases, the mining company and its stakeholders must accept the likelihood that there may not be an alignment of values and that therefore the development of certain mineral prospects are unlikely. The development of the New Prosperity Mine in British Columbia has been effectively halted due to local First Nations opposition, as well as Environment Canada's assessment that the mine's environmental impact would be too adverse, given the company's current waste disposal plans (Canada Newswire, 2014). The diverging expectations in this case appear too significant for the parties involved to overcome.

The Equitable Distribution of Wealth from Mining

Some of Canada's most highly esteemed philanthropists, including Seymour Schulich, Pierre Lassonde, and Robert McEwan, accumulated their wealth through mining. However, the generous acts of such individuals do little to still the rising chorus of anxiety about the concentration of wealth and the disparities within and across societies today. The distribution of wealth in capitalist economies is increasingly an issue that raises conflicts over values as well as over value.

Issues of wealth distribution are particularly salient for the mining industry, in part because of the great disparities in the perspectives of its stakeholders. For the purposes of this chapter we define wealth to include not only the financial returns but also the social benefits arising from the extraction of minerals, such as employment, training, community development, and infrastructure development. Mining generates wealth from non-renewable resources under the soil, and therefore in many countries there is a feeling that all citizens, not just local communities, should benefit from the wealth they generate—but how much should they benefit? Financial stakeholders who have provided the resources for the high levels of investment over long periods of time before a mine begins productive operations are likely to have very different perspectives on how the wealth from that operation should be distributed from those held by local and national governments, for example. Local communities often differ from national governments in what they view as a fair distribution of the wealth created by a local mine. These differences are often particularly acute for mining projects located in poor and less-developed countries, where mining developments have been a major source of foreign direct investment.

The upswings of mining's boom-and-bust cycles exacerbate stakeholder disagreements on wealth distribution. Most recently, the dramatic rise in commodity prices through the first decade of the 21st century greatly increased profits accruing to mining companies. Copper prices, which are indicative of the performance of many metals, rose from a low of US$0.65 per pound in 1999 to over US$4.60 per pound in 2011. This translated into a significant increase in wealth accruing to financial stakeholders. A case in point is Inmet Mining Corporation, whose share price rose from a low of $1.60 per share to a high of over $110 per share during this period. Although there were other factors also contributing to this share price increase, rising copper prices were not an insignificant factor.

Many governments have seen the dramatic increase in the wealth generated by the mining industry during this period and have come to feel that they have not adequately shared in this wealth generated from the non-renewable resources under their soil. In spite of the recent cooling of the commodity boom of the first decade of this century, many countries have changed, or are considering changes to, their tax and royalty laws to ensure a more equitable distribution of wealth generated by mining. Many of these countries, such as Peru, Argentina, Zambia, and Australia, are areas of significant mining investment; their governments are trying to find the right balance between sharing in the wealth generated from mining while continuing to encourage future investment. A case in point is the change in the 30 percent mining royalty imposed by Zambia's government in late 2014, to which Barrick Gold responded by announcing that it would suspend operations at its Lumwana copper mine. When the government reduced the royalty to 9 percent Barrick rescinded its decision (Hill, 2015).

How the economic benefits from mine development are shared within a country can also be a challenge. Mining communities have not been blind to the dramatic rise in metal prices and feel that their fair share of wealth from resources development may have not accrued to their local economies. For example, Mongolia has recently seen significant mining developments. According to the World Bank, the GDP per capita in Mongolia grew from US $2,650 in 2010 to US$4,418 in 2013. How the sudden and significant change in wealth is equitably distributed between the mining companies involved, local communities, and the Mongolian people is creating challenges, particularly as there have been little in the way of formal processes in place to address the equitable distribution of wealth (Osborne et al., 2015).

Some developed countries, such as Canada, have in place mechanisms which attempt to address the equitable sharing of wealth through Impacts and Benefits Agreements (IBAs). These agreements are used in new mining developments to formalize the distribution of wealth between mining companies and their local communities. IBAs, however, are not required by law in every case. Even where IBAs are used, they have been criticized as not being sufficiently transparent and not directly tied to the environmental assessment process (Poulton et al., 2013). Often local communities must rely solely on the common law duty of the mining company to consult with them. This vagueness in the law has not made it easy for mining companies or their core stakeholders to find a mechanism to bridge their expectation gaps.

In some cases, the expectations of local core stakeholders are such that they cannot foresee an equitable distribution of the wealth from a mine development. This is particularly understandable if the mine development risks significant environmental impacts. Although such projects can create significant employment and other economic benefits, this is not always the perception or even the reality for many local core stakeholders. An interesting example of how difficult it is to find a balance between the environmental impacts and the equitable sharing of wealth is the arrangement between BHP Billiton ("BHP") and the Government of Papua New Guinea in 2002 regarding the Ok Tedi mine. BHP turned over their 52 percent interest in the Ok Tedi mine to a corporation whose mandate was to support sustainable development initiatives in Papua New Guinea. The motivation for BHP was to mitigate the potential environmental liability associated with the Ok Tedi mine by ensuring that the wealth from the mine benefited Papua New Guineans, particularly those in the Western Province where the mine is located. These agreements have been in effect for over ten years. However, following a recent change in the governing party in Papua New Guinea, these agreements have been cancelled. This now brings back into question how the wealth from that mine will be equitably shared, particularly with the communities in the Western Province most affected by the mine's environmental impacts. In this case, the values and expectations of the government have changed and what was once determined to be an equitable trade-off between environmental impacts and the equitable sharing of wealth has been brought into question.

THE RESPONSE OF THE MINING INDUSTRY

The mining industry has recognized the need to respond to the growing power of local core stakeholders and their capacity for influencing the future development of mines. This power has been enhanced by the advent of social media and the growing array of auxiliary stakeholders, such as NGOs, who provide information and support for local core stakeholders, such as community groups, local governments, and national regulators even in the poorest and most isolated regions of the world. The primary response has been to develop frameworks and standards for addressing local stakeholder concerns.

The Canadian mining industry has been a leader in these developments, beginning with the Whitehorse Mining Initiative (WMI) in 1993. Led by the Mining Association of Canada (MAC), the WMI was an innovative multi-stakeholder approach to crafting strategies and policies for sustainable mining by bringing together leaders from the mining industry, labor, federal and provincial mining departments, the Aboriginal community, and the environmental movement (McAllister and Alexander, 1997). The WMI was concerned with broad issues of resource management and cooperation in national and provincial policies, regulations, and processes across the key industry stakeholders, and became a model for similar multi-stakeholder initiatives in other countries (Fitzpatrick et al., 2011).

In response to ongoing criticisms of the global mining industry and pressures from NGOs on financial institutions such as the World Bank, International Finance Corporation, and the European Bank for Reconstruction and Development to stop financing extractive industry projects, a group of mining industry executives met at Davos in 1999 and launched the Global Mining Initiative (GMI) to assess and guide the mining industry towards sustainable development practices. The process led to the formation of the International Council Mining and Minerals (ICMM) in 2001, which, at its global conference in Toronto a year later, produced the Toronto Declaration, that committed member companies to continue the work started by the GMI and the ongoing development of reporting standards for the industry. Those Global Reporting Initiative (GRI) standards have been updated twice since their launch, and are widely used in sustainability/corporate social responsibility reports issued by mining companies (Fonseca et al., 2013; see also Chapter 15, this volume).

MAC is an associate member of the ICMM, but has developed its own widely admired initiative, called "Towards Sustainable Mining" (TSM). This program was established in 2004 and provides member companies with a set of tools to drive performance and ensure that mining operations are managed more responsibly. In contrast to the GRI, whose indicators are focused at the company level, this program also addresses performance at the level of the mine, and covers aboriginal and community outreach, energy and greenhouse gas emissions, tailings management, biodiversity conservation, health and safety, crisis management, and mine closure (Fitzpatrick et al., 2011). TSM not only provides management tools to the industry but also requires regular disclosure and independent verification of a company's progress. Thirty-eight mining companies are full members of MAC and must meet the requirements of TSM as a condition of their membership in MAC.

Two criticisms can be made of the GRI and TSM initiatives. One, frequently articulated by NGOs, is that adherence to the standards is voluntary, and companies can withdraw from the process. The second is that the membership of ICMM and MAC covers only a small proportion of the world's mining companies. The ICMM currently lists 23 mining companies as members; MAC has 38. The Toronto stock exchanges have over 1,600 listed mining companies. Even if we were to eliminate the junior exploration companies from our expectations that adhere to TSM, most mining companies are absent from this leadership effort. Moreover, MAC currently requires that its member companies implement TSM at their Canadian operations—but members with operations outside Canada are not required to comply with TSM at their international facilities. Some are doing so voluntarily but these are the exception, even though the merits of TSM equally apply to any mining operation in any country.

This does not mean that Canadian mining companies who are not members of MAC are blind to their stakeholders' expectations or do not have their own sustainability-related programs. Many mining companies in Canada have some level of commitment to improving their environmental impacts and addressing their local core stakeholders' concerns. Even so, it is understandable if stakeholders are confused whether the Canadian mining industry is serious about addressing their expectations if it cannot even achieve widespread support for a common set of standards of responsible performance within Canada, let alone globally.

Regarding expectations from its financial stakeholders, the mining industry has been reactive to their concerns rather than proactive in establishing shared perceptions and expectations. The mining industry has rushed into the equity and bond markets at the top of the metal price cycle, when financing is readily available. They have used those funds to acquire new resources or developed existing resources to meet the growth expectations of financial stakeholders during that phase of the metal price cycle. When the metal price cycle reverses direction, the mining industry responds by writing off those same investments, laying off employees, decreasing investment in exploration, deferring development projects, and trimming back sustainability-related initiatives. The mining industry has not yet been able to find a more sustainable business model to manage itself more effectively through the metal price cycle.

The mining industry is also reacting slowly to financial stakeholders' struggle to understand the role of sustainability in their decisions to invest in mining. Many investors are left with the decisions to hold or sell their investments after hearing news that the value of a mining project was significantly eroded due to local core stakeholder opposition. Communicating and understanding both the risks and opportunities surrounding the equitable sharing of wealth and environmental impacts has been a challenge for both the mining industry and its financial stakeholders.

If the mining industry is to get ahead of the diverging expectations with its local core stakeholders and achieve the financing it needs from its financial stakeholders, it must move from a reactive response to a leadership position. If the mining industry's response is simply reactive, it will forever lag or even fall further behind the expectations of its local and financial stakeholders. Every mining company in the industry should by now see how much wealth can be destroyed for all concerned through the misalignment of expectations. Local core stakeholders are clearly telling the mining industry that there has to be a better balance between the equitable distribution of wealth that mining can generate and its impacts on the environment. The financial stakeholders are clearly telling the mining industry that it cannot continue to make significant upfront commitments of capital without more assurance that conflicts with local stakeholders will not put their returns at risk.

Clearly, the current business model for the mining of metals and minerals is not working. Only a shift in approach across the industry will succeed in finding a sustainable business model for mining in order to meet society's needs. We need a new way of thinking about resource development.

A NEW WAY OF THINKING

As Freeman et al. (2004: 364) have pointed out, "Stakeholder theory begins with the assumption that values are necessarily and explicitly a part of doing business" (see also Chapter 10, this volume). Bridging the divergence on perspectives and values among mining company stakeholders requires the company's strategy and actions to be grounded in the core value of respect. This means respect for the planet and the environment and respect for the basic needs of society and for the value of the resources that the industry has been given the privilege to mine. It also means respect for the perspectives of each core stakeholder, including both local core stakeholders at each mine and the company's financial stakeholders. This value of respect is the foundation for a partnership model in the mining industry that recognizes that all stakeholders have a vested interest in the wealth that can be created and shared from mining developments and that all stakeholders are ultimately affected by the environmental impacts of mining.

This new way of thinking would ensure that no new mining development proceeds before the mining company and its local core stakeholders have reached agreement on the responsible development of the mining project, and specifically its environmental impacts and the maximization of the value of the project and equitable distribution of wealth for all. These agreements would be a condition for any financing provided by the financial stakeholders, and the mining company would have to explain clearly to those stakeholders how rushing into construction without this agreement runs unacceptable risks of destroying value. The mining industry can no longer invest significant amounts into a mine development without some assurance that it has the acceptance of its core stakeholders. These agreements would hold the mining company and its stakeholders accountable over the long term for the commitments they make. These agreements would also require each party to invest in the project. This investment could be financial but it also could be technical, human capital, supply chain contributions, local business development, infrastructure, and the mineral reserves.

This new way of thinking would demand that planning for any mining project would start at the end of the mine life. What is sustainable about mining is what is left at the end of the mine life cycle, when it closes and the last ounce of metal is extracted. The legacy of the mine includes not only the environmental impacts of the extraction of ore but the human capital of the workers whose skills can be transferable to other jobs and the wealth generated from the mine that has found its way into government treasuries through taxation and royalties. The legacy also includes dividends paid to shareholders and re-invested in new mining ventures, and company revenues that have been invested in developing new mines and improving the technologies and techniques of sustainable mining. This new way of thinking has to have long-term goals that are transparent to all. These goals must be tracked and reported on over the life of the mine. All stakeholders would then share in the value created from the mine commensurate with the investment they make. The local core stakeholders would agree upon the process to allocate value from the project and acknowledge the returns required by the mining company to meet the expectations of its financial stakeholders. This allocation of value would reflect the realities of the metal price cycle and result in a sharing of the wealth in the good times and hunkering down in the bad.

As a result, this new way of thinking would create the most value for everyone while significantly reducing the risks for everyone involved.

The implications of this new way of thinking are significant for mining companies, their local and financial stakeholders, and to society as a whole. One implication is a slower pace in the rate of new mining developments, because building shared perspectives based on common values and developing a clear understanding of expectations from all stakeholders takes time. Another implication is that certain mining projects will not proceed, as expectations will not always be met. As a result it will also most likely result in an increase in metal prices. This increase of metal prices would reflect the full costs of the products. The costs to mitigate the environmental impacts and to achieve support from individual local core stakeholders would therefore be more fairly borne by society.

This new way of thinking may also change the industry structure, making it more difficult for smaller mining companies with minimal resources to participate in future growth. Achieving a fair outcome will require management depth, a breadth of resources to replenish reserves, and the financial capacity to take the time to achieve long-term value-creating outcomes for all stakeholders. A mining company must be in a position to walk away from a development prospect if it cannot achieve the support from all stakeholders. Even the very small-scale exploration juniors of the industry are finding that they can get a better price for their discoveries if they invest time and attention in developing positive relationships with local stakeholders in the course of their activities (Matten, 2013).

Finally, this new way of thinking will require a significant degree of leadership from mining companies, from the mining industry, and from stakeholders, as well as a new level of multilateral cooperation that the mining industry has struggled to achieve in the past. Although the mining industry has made considerable progress in addressing stakeholder expectations, there is an opportunity today for the mining industry to get ahead of these expectations by taking the lead on this new way of thinking.

TOWARDS THE NEW WAY OF THINKING

Articulating the core value of respect is only the first step in building the responsible mining company. Ensuring that actions at each mine consistently follow all the company's core values is a major challenge, given the significant geographic distance between the mine sites and the company headquarters and the great variation in the local contexts of the mines. This challenge can only be met by a new way of leading by the CEO, senior management team, and board of directors. They must work together to develop the systems, processes, and company culture grounded on the fundamental shared belief that the company's goal is to create value for all stakeholders and that doing this requires mutual respect, both within the company and in dealings with external stakeholders. Leaders shape the company culture not only by what they say but also by how they act and what they pay attention to, and by the systems and processes they put in place (Schein, 2010).

The company's leaders must spend time at the mine sites, interacting with the local mine leadership team and the local employees and with local core stakeholders, demonstrating in these interactions the value of respect. By paying visible attention to the local mine employees charged with local community relations and development, top executives can give them a stronger voice in decision-making at the mine. By the performance measures they put in place, the company leaders can ensure that the local leadership team understands the need to balance the traditional output measures with performance on environmental and social responsibility. These behaviors must be understood and promoted by the board of directors, charged with the governance of mining companies. Under Canadian corporate law, the board has a duty to act in the best interest of the corporation. The traditional interpretation of this duty seemed to focus predominantly on acting in the best interest of shareholders. In today's world, however, the ability of a mining company to create value is as much determined by its local core stakeholders as its financial stakeholders. Boards can change their perspectives to ensure that their governance processes consider the perspectives of all stakeholders and thereby truly meeting their duties to the corporation.

Although the journey towards this new way of thinking will take many years, there are concrete steps that boards can implement now to demonstrate leadership and make progress. These include the following:

- Boards can move out of the boardroom for their meetings and into the communities in which they operate to ensure that they have an understanding of the values and expectations of both their local core and financial stakeholders. Boards can report annually on the number and nature of their interaction with stakeholders to demonstrate that they are seeking an awareness of the values and expectations of all stakeholders.

- Boards can disclose the values that they believe are core to the success of the company and illustrate how these values translate into the strategy of the company and the execution of that strategy. This will include clear and concise expectations regarding environmental impacts and equitable sharing of wealth as well as other core measures of operating and financial performance.

- Boards can approve clear performance metrics for their senior executives on measures that are within their control and are clearly focused on creating wealth for all stakeholders. These measures will be incorporated into five-year plans that would be publicly disclosed with interim annual steps to track progress.

- Boards can ensure their senior executives have sufficient time to execute their five-year plans by providing five-year employment contracts. Boards will acknowledge their approval for the recommendations made by their senior executives and hold themselves as accountable for the outcomes as they do their senior executives.
- Boards can change the compensation practices for their senior executives with a significant weighting of compensation to the later part of these contracts. This compensation will be tied to the five-year plans and be based on measures that are within the control of the senior executives which includes environmental, social, and other sustainability-related factors as much as financial and operational performance.
- Boards can only approve the development of new mining projects following the execution of agreements between the company and its local core stakeholders that clearly outline how they have adequately addressed the expectations surrounding environmental impacts and equitable sharing of wealth.

Even with this progress in individual mining companies, it cannot be left solely to individual mining companies and their boards to make progress. The mining industry as a whole must move toward a more consistent application of standards and management systems that support sustainable outcomes. The leading mining companies are already organized into well-respected industry associations, such as MAC. Mining companies and their associations can lobby financial regulators to encourage them to establish, as a condition precedent to equity and bond market financings, evidence that mining companies are adhering to internationally accepted sustainability standards. Institutional investors have a role to play, as they tend to be longer term in their orientation than at least some of the individual shareholders, and have significant influence that can be used to encourage more clear disclosure in mining company's sustainability-related risks and opportunities (see also Chapter 17, this volume).

Finally, the mining industry and all stakeholders can support the education, attraction, and retention of the next generation of leaders in the mining industry with individuals who see the execution of values as a key measure of success. Curricula in business, mining and geology, environmental management, social development, and political science programs can provide courses that help our young leaders to have these conversations in school before they enter the workforce. Upon graduation they can continue these discussions in their careers and continue to work to evolve this new way of thinking so it can become a set of standards and practices acceptable to all. For the foreseeable future, society will continue to rely on metals and minerals for its existence. Mining has a role to play, not only in providing these products, but also in the generation of significant wealth for all stakeholders and in its responsible stewardship of the environment.

REFERENCES

Ballard, C. and Banks, G. (2003). "Resource Wars: The Anthropology of Mining," *Annual Review of Anthropology*, 32: 287–313.

Bebbington, A. and Bury, J. (eds) (2013). *Subterranean Struggles: New Dynamics of Mining, Oil, and Gas in Latin America.* Austin: University of Texas Press.

Campbell, G. and Roberts, M. (2010). "Permitting a New Mine: Insights from the Community Debate," *Resource Policy*, 35: 210–17.

Canada Newswire (2014). *New Prosperity Gold-Copper Mine Project: Environmental Assessment Decision,* February 26. Available at: <http://search.proquest.com. ezproxy.library.yorku.ca/docview/1502041188?accountid=15182> (accessed July 23, 2015).

Ernst and Young (2014). *Business Risks Facing Mining and Metals 2014–15.* Available at: <http://www.ey.com/Publication/vwLUAssets/EY-business-risks-in-mining-and-metals-2015-2016/$File/EY-business-risks-in-mining-and-metals-2015-2016.pdf> (accessed July 22, 2015).

Fitzpatrick, P., Fonseca, A., and McAllistair, M. L. (2011). "From the Whitehorse Mining Initiative towards Sustainable Mining: Lessons Learned," *Journal of Cleaner Production*, 19: 376–84.

Fonseca, A., McAllister, M. L., and Fitzpatrick, P. (2013). "Measuring What? A Comparative Anatomy of Five Mining Sustainability Frameworks," *Minerals Engineering*, 46/47: 180–6.

Freeman, R. E., Wicks, A. C., and Parmar, B. (2004). "Stakeholder Theory and 'the Corporate Objective Revisited,'" *Organization Science*, 15(3): 364–9.

Hart, R. and Coumans, C. (2013). *Evolving Standards and Expectations for Responsible Mining, a Civil Society Perspective.* Paper presented at the 2013 World Mining Congress, Montreal (August 11–15, 2013), Canadian Institute for Mining, Metallurgy, and Petroleum. Available at: <http://www.cbern.ca/kr/One.aspx?objectId=19522326&contextId=677979&lastCat=10539789> (accessed July 20, 2015).

Hill, M. (2015). "Barrick Rescinds Plan to Halt Operations at Lumwana Mine, Zambia Says," *Globe and Mail*, 23 April. Available at: <http://www.theglobeandmail.com/report-on-business/industry-news/energy-and-resources/barrick-rescinds-plan-to-halt-operations-at-lumwana-mine-zambia-says/article24072670/> (accessed August 2, 2015).

Horowitz, L. S. (2010). "'Twenty Years Is Yesterday': Science, Multinational Mining, and the Political Ecology of Trust in New Caledonia," *Geoforum*, 41: 617–26.

Jacks, D. S. (2013). *From Boom to Bust: A Typology of Real Commodity Prices in the Long Run.* National Bureau of Economic Research, w18874.

Kemp, D. and Owen, J. R. (2013). "Community Relations and Mining: Core to Business but Not 'Core Business,'" *Resources Policy*, 38: 523–31.

Kirsch, S. (2014). *Mining Capitalism: The Relationship between Corporations and Their Critics*. Oakland, CA: University of California Press.

Li, F. (2015). *Unearthing Conflict: Corporate Mining, Activism, and Expertise in Peru*. Durham, NC: Duke University Press.

McAllister, M. L. and Alexander, C. J. (1997). *A Stake in the Ground: Redefining the Canadian Mining Industry*. Vancouver: University of British Columbia Press.

MacDonald, A. (2002). *Industry in Transition: A Profile of the North American Mining Sector*. Winnipeg: International Institute for Sustainable Development.

Matten, D. (2013). *Corporate Social Responsibility in Junior Mining Companies*, Impakt Consulting White Paper Series. Available at: <http://www.dirkmatten.com/Papers/HL/Impakt%20Schulich%20WP%202013.pdf> (accessed August 2, 2015).

Nolen, S. (2014). "High and Dry," *Report on Business Magazine*, April: 42–51. Available at: <http://www.theglobeandmail.com/report-on-business/rob-magazine/high-and-dry/article18134225/> (accessed July 31, 2015).

Osborne, D., Cane, I., Cousins, M., and Chuluunbaatar, E. (2015). *Integrated Report: An Integrated Analysis of Economic, Political and Social Issues that Support or Hinder Growth and Poverty Reduction in Mongolia*. Available at: <http://dfat.gov.au/about-us/publications/Documents/mongolia-economic-political-social-analysis-report.pdf> (accessed September 5, 2015).

Poulton, M. M., Jagers, S. C., Linde, S., Van Zyl, D., Danielson, L. J., and Matti, S. (2013). "State of the World's Nonfuel Mineral Resources: Supply, Demand, and Socio-Institutional Fundamentals," *Annual Review of Environment and Resources*, 38: 345–71.

Schein, E. H. (2010). *Organizational Culture and Leadership*, 4th ed. San Francisco, CA: Jossey-Bass.

Strikwerda, S. and J. W. Stoelhorst. (2009). "The Emergence and Evolution of the Multidimensional Organization," *California Management Review*, 51(4): 11–31.

Talaga, T. (2013). "American Mining Giant Pulls out of Ring of Fire," *Toronto Star*, November 22.

Tinguay, A. (2007). "The Ok Tedi Mine, Papua New Guinea: A Summary of Environmental and Health Issues," unpublished report sponsored by Ok Tedi Mining Ltd.

Velásquez, T. A. (2012). "The Science of Corporate Social Responsibility: Contamination and Conflict in a Mining Project in the Southern Ecuadorian Andes," *Resources Policy*, 37: 233–40.

Wilshire, H. G., Nielson, J. E., and Hazlett, R. W. (2008). *The American West at Risk: Science, Myths, and Politics of Land Abuse*. New York: Oxford University Press.

20

Restoring the Capitalist Promise

Opportunities in the US Youth Labor Market

Shawn Bohen and Gerald Chertavian

INTRODUCTION

With an estimated 73 million 15–24 year olds unemployed worldwide, one of the most visible failings of modern capitalism has been its inability to create economic opportunity for many young people. By 2018, global youth unemployment is projected to reach nearly 13 percent, with wide regional variation (ILO, 2015). Ninety percent of the global youth population lives in the developing world where stable, quality employment is particularly scarce. Indeed, in some countries, two thirds of the youth population is out of work and out of school (ILO, 2013). The highest rates of youth unemployment are in the Middle East and North Africa, but even among the advanced economies of the European Union where the expectation of finding secure employment was the norm for generations, current trends show extended job searches and increasing rates of part-time and temporary employment among large numbers of youth.

The global youth employment crisis is a two-dimensional supply–demand mismatch. On the one hand, deficiencies in education and training leave too many youth without the skills demanded by employers, with heavy costs for both. There is also a mismatch on the other end of the spectrum, when labor demand is weak and youth are employed intermittently, if at all, or in roles for which they are overqualified. Underutilized talent deflates a given nation's economic growth and greatly disadvantages youth with the lowest educational attainment. These mismatches in the youth labor market form what we call the "opportunity divide" and have serious implications for many nations. In many parts of the world, the affected youth population has the acronym NEET: Not in Education, Employment, or Training. In the US, this population has historically been described as "disconnected youth." We prefer the descriptor "opportunity youth" because although these young adults may not currently be contributing to national economic growth and productivity, they have enormous potential to bring skills and leadership to workplaces, communities, and families and become recognized as the economic assets they are—such a shift from negative to positive and empowering language being a central tenet of the perception change we seek to catalyze.

In addition to the clear economic and human costs of youth disconnection, there are daunting implications for the capitalist system itself should a significant portion of the next generation become nervous or cynical about their prospects in the existing socio-economic and political systems. Among other hazards, disillusioned youth are susceptible to ideologies that seem to promise more economic security in exchange for certain freedoms. Versions of this disenchantment have already been expressed in events such as the recent anti-austerity movements in Greece and Spain, the political upheaval of the Arab Spring, the youth riots in Paris, and the growing concern about income inequality in the United States (Hoffman and Jamal, 2012).

Although the opportunity divide has global resonance, effective interventions require in-depth understanding of individual country's conditions. This chapter therefore illuminates the particular conditions in the United States, which are detailed in the next section. In the main section of the chapter we first summarize our own experience in creating and leading an intensive one-year education and training program for young adults in the US called "Year Up." This experience has allowed us to identify three key roles for businesses to tap into the latent, powerful national resource of opportunity youth—essential not only for long-term national growth and prosperity but also for a restoration of the capitalist promise for the current and future generations. The remainder of the section presents each of these suggestions in some more detail: (i) informing education and training systems about labor market needs, (ii) transforming traditional education and training pathways, and (iii) shifting private sector human resource management beliefs and behaviors. In a brief concluding section, we discuss how the US case might also inform decision makers elsewhere.

THE OPPORTUNITY DIVIDE AND ITS COSTS
IN THE UNITED STATES

The fact that one in seven young adults aged 16 to 24 in the United States is not in school and not working is a crushing reality for those individual lives, creating daily deprivations, psychic damage, and blemished employment histories (Measure of America, 2015). Even the steeliest among us must be troubled, if not out of empathy, then out of economic anxiety. Young adults who are neither in school nor working cost US taxpayers an estimated

$93 billion annually in lost revenues and increased social services (Belfield et al., 2012). More important even than these costs, however, opportunity youth represent an enormous underutilized natural resource, and one that the nation cannot squander if we are to prosper in the global economy.

In the US, we cannot disregard these throngs of disengaged youth because they coexist paradoxically with a growing number of unfilled "middle-skills" jobs, positions that require some education beyond high school but not necessarily a college degree. In fact, "middle-skills" jobs account for the majority (54 percent) of US jobs, but only 44 percent of the country's workers are trained to the middle-skill level, leaving a yawning labor market gap (National Skills Coalition, 2014). Already many employers in industries that offer the highest promise for family-supporting wages are acutely attuned to the scarcity of key workers needed to drive contemporary enterprises. Businesses with these hard-to-fill jobs face high turnover, diminished worker-to-worker transfer of firm-specific knowledge, increased overtime, and other competitive disadvantages. Indeed, the growing skills gap is forcing employers to spend more on training employees, 15 percent more in 2014 (Bersin, 2014). In addition to the economic costs of these labor market failures, there are weighty social costs. Recent anxiety about rising income inequality in the US has highlighted that too often zip code dictates destiny (Chetty et al., 2015). Presently, only 6 percent of children born into low-income families become high earners (Measure of America, 2015). And we know that poverty disproportionately affects people of color and women and constrains their educational opportunities (National Center for Law and Economic Justice, 2013). This is a direct challenge to the "American dream" which imagines that every citizen has an equal opportunity to achieve prosperity through hard work and initiative.

The opportunity divide in the US results to a large extent from our systems of education and training not meeting either employers' or workers' needs. In truth, "systems" is a grossly inaccurate description of the patchwork of education and workforce training entities in the US. These include public and private primary schools, i.e., kindergarten through grade 8, and secondary schools, i.e., grades 9 to 12, two- and four-year public and private colleges, and a wide range of non-profit credentialing and workforce development agencies, as well as many for-profit training intermediaries. All these organizations seek to prepare workers, yet they do so with little or no coordination with one another or with employers. One of the fundamental inefficiencies of the US systems is that they are not well connected to employer demand. This may be at least in part because government, a third-party payer, picks up the lion's share of the tab: $923 billion in total federal/state/local education expenditures in 2015 (Chantrill, 2015). In addition, while private sector spending on employee training outstrips public spending—$100 billion versus $3.4 billion—these investments are generally focused on the advancement of upper-level employees once they have already been hired, not on strengthening the supply of entry or middle-skills workers (Lennon, 2015).

As imperfect as US educational systems may be, post-secondary degrees and credentials have historically had real economic value, especially for lower-income individuals (Leonhardt, 2015). Indeed, having some post-secondary education, even without a degree, adds an estimated quarter of a million dollars to lifetime earnings, and a bachelor's degree, on average, is estimated to be worth $2.8 million over a lifetime (Carnevale et al., 2011). Current US post-secondary completion rates are abysmal, however, with only 58 percent of students in public four-year colleges graduating in six years, and an average two-year public college graduation rate of only 19 percent (Chronicle for Higher Education, 2013).

Ironically, even as low-income men and women of color are collectively struggling for educational and economic advancement, recent research has established the competitive advantage of workforce diversity. Companies with the greatest gender, racial, and ethnic diversity are found to be more likely to have financial returns above industry averages, and diversity is "probably a competitive differentiator that shifts market share toward more diverse companies over time" (Hunt et al., 2015). It is also important to recognize that "minority" populations will soon become the majority in the US, so this is not a problem confined to the margins. Demographic trends alone provide a powerful reason to redouble our investments in preparing opportunity youth to meet our human capital needs.

While US businesses have engaged with the education system at least since *A Nation at Risk* was published in the early 1980s (National Commission on Excellence in Education, 1983), the current labor market mismatch necessitates a more profound involvement than most employers have attempted to date. In order to recruit, hire, train, and grow the human capital required to drive our national economic engine towards a healthy future, the private sector needs to bring "supply chain management" techniques to the domestic development of middle-skill workers. Through our work at Year Up, we have discerned key ways that US businesses can improve this supply of workers by focusing on the untapped potential of opportunity youth.

SUGGESTIONS FOR MOBILIZING THE POTENTIAL OF OPPORTUNITY YOUTH

Background: Our Experience at Year Up

Our organization, Year Up, was born from the belief that talented, motivated young adults deserve support, training, and opportunities to succeed, and that our country needs to better utilize *all* its human capital. Year Up provides an intensive one-year program for urban young adults, aged 18 to 24, who have either a high school diploma or the General Education Development credential and yet are detached from work or school. Year Up has become a premier workforce training solution for more than 250 companies at 18 sites across the United States since its inception in Boston in 2000.

Year Up students spend six months learning technical and professional skills in the classroom and then apply those skills during six-month internships with employers in high-growth industries such as information technology and financial operations. Students earn college credits and a stackable credential, as well as a weekly stipend. Throughout this "high expectations, high support" program, students are supported by staff advisors, mentors, dedicated social services staff, and a powerful network of community partners. Nearly all Year Up students are low income, and 95 percent are young men and women of color. Year Up is funded through a combination of contributions from employers, private philanthropic support, individual donations, and, to date, a small amount of public funding through grants and contracts.

In sharp contrast to average US high school and college completion rates, Year Up consistently retains 75 percent of students, and 85 percent or more of alumni are employed or in school within four months of graduation. Those who go directly into the workforce earn an average of $18 per hour (or $36,000 per year), more than double the current federal minimum wage. Year Up also has an unmatched record of employer engagement; our corporate partners contribute an average of $25,000 for each Year Up student they host during the internship phase, which speaks volumes about the return on investment they find in this partnership. What these employers learn is that with the right training and support, formerly disengaged youth can become vital business assets and a viable talent pipeline for myriad entry-level, career-pathway jobs.

While Year Up is one of many "intermediary" suppliers of talent, it distinguishes itself in two important ways. First, unlike many workforce development programs, employer demand both drives and sustains the Year Up model, from the market-driven skills which form the core curriculum to the corporate underwriting of the internships which sustain its operations. This tight linkage to employer demand—combined with research-based program design and strong business accountability practices—helps account for Year Up's extraordinary results. Second, Year Up is different from most workforce training programs in that it has a deliberate "systems change" agenda through which it seeks to scale impact beyond direct service. Specifically, Year Up works to leverage our expertise by: changing public perceptions of urban young adults from social liabilities to economic assets; shifting employer practices in talent sourcing and hiring; and influencing public policy to support innovative pathways for youth that lead to career wages that grow over time. These insights from our experience, we believe, can inform broader changes to the way businesses can come to play a key role in closing the opportunity gap and tap into the national resource of opportunity youth.

Improving Information about Labor Market Needs

Imperfect information is perhaps the greatest contributor to labor market inefficiency, especially current information about available jobs and the requirements for those jobs. The US secondary and post-secondary education systems are woefully out of touch with the needs of modern-day employers. Sadly, many workforce development programs are also not well attuned to current industry trends, and most individual job seekers also lack this knowledge (Holzer, 2011). Despite the earnings boost of a post-secondary credential, the connection to workforce preparation is so weak that most workers today cannot assume that academic degrees will necessarily lead to employment (Accenture, Burning Glass Technologies, and Harvard Business School, 2014). Many large employers do not engage with workforce pipelines other than traditional, four-year colleges, and even then it is a limited engagement with a narrow slice of talent. Employers should work with a variety of third party partners or "intermediaries"—schools, non-profits, unions, for-profit trainers, etc.—to *inform them about labor market needs* and transform the information inefficiencies at the root of these labor market failures.

As a first step to address the information gaps, employers need to find ways to provide greater transparency about desired capabilities and do so in a timelier manner. Big data offers new, more efficient access to information that can be aggregated and shared, not only with schools and training entities but with students, parents, and workers (Altstadt, 2011). As an example, Year Up recently partnered with LinkedIn to understand employment trends by geography. Among other revelations, the analysis showed that demand for workers with cyber-security skills vastly outstripped supply in the Bay Area. This pointed Year Up towards a whole new training focus for that location ensuring that participants are being trained for jobs and careers that exist. With accessible online job databases and demographic data, educators and trainers can be much more strategic in understanding current and future employment trends and can use that information to shape programs. Businesses such as LinkedIn, Burning Glass, and others are primed to share their expertise in data mining and analytics to drive better information towards education and training providers, especially community colleges which serve more than 11 million students and are specifically geared towards workforce development.

The second information improvement lies in employers articulating the importance of specific proficiencies that enable individuals to succeed in the workplace. While some of these are technical skills, many are so-called "soft skills" which are not traditionally emphasized in schools or captured in achievement tests and grades, yet are critical to success in the workplace (Heckman and Kautz, 2012). Communication skills, facility at working in groups or teams, ethics, time management, and an appreciation for diversity are among the top skills valued by employers (Carnevale and Smith, 2013). Efforts such as the Partnership for 21st Century Learning have started the conversation, but more must be done to promote the skills that are crucial to post-industrial jobs. Employers need to ensure that education and training systems keep these critical capacities front and center by bringing a "customer" mindset to hiring and explicitly seeking and rewarding the desired skills.

Transforming Educational and Training Pathways

The second way that employers can play a vigorous role in closing the opportunity divide is by *transforming traditional education and training pathways* to help students achieve market-relevant, post-secondary credentials. Although high school graduation rates have increased over the last 50 years and recently reached an all-time high, more than 25 percent of all American youth, and 40 percent of American minority youth, are still not finishing secondary school (Balfanz et al., 2012; US Department of Education, 2015). Given the growing demand for middle and higher skills, even an increased high school graduation rate, while important, is a hollow victory unless we couple it with additional post-secondary education and training required for middle-skills jobs.

One of the key ways that employers can transform traditional pathways is by offering more "work-based" learning experiences for young people by partnering with middle and high schools to provide career awareness, exposure, and immersion experiences. Workplace learning provides one of the most effective ways to learn and apply both technical and soft skills (Symonds et al., 2011). Early college high schools are one of the more exciting ways that employers are partnering to combine rigorous coursework with work-based learning. These alternative approaches are showing improved student outcomes, especially for low-income and minority students, as well as payoffs for engaged employers.

IBM's partnership with the New York City Department of Education and City University of New York, dubbed P-TECH for Pathways in Technology Early College High School, is one excellent example of this approach (see also Chapter 7, this volume). In P-TECH's model, the diverse, unscreened student population begins in 9th grade and, after six years, graduates with a high school diploma and an associate's degree in applied science. The partnership is deep and multi-faceted, with high school technology teachers emailing college professors, and IBM's human resources professionals informing teachers about hiring trends. In addition to its active engagement with curriculum design and student mentoring, IBM guarantees job interviews to qualified P-TECH graduates. There are 27 schools currently operating under the P-TECH model in the US.

ROXMAPP, a partnership between Roxbury Community College, Madison Park High School, and several local employers in Massachusetts, is another newer, promising effort to offer students six-year career pathways. The program enables high school students to earn college credits, complete an associate's degree or non-credit industry certification, and gain real-world experience including: job shadowing, worksite visits, internships, mock job interviews, and paid summer internships. Employers such as JPMorgan Chase, Starbucks, Citibank, Accenture, Microsoft, and Bank of America have all made major investments to create new pathways to help low-income youth and other vulnerable populations increase their employability. These employer-led initiatives include: entrepreneurship training, mentorships, summertime employment, and civic engagement opportunities for young people, as well cross-sector gatherings to formulate strategies to strengthen and scale the most effective alternate pathways.

As awareness has grown about the shortcomings of current workforce preparation, it has become clear that credentials are no guarantee that students possess the skills and knowledge they need to be effective work-place contributors. Another promising way to strengthen the supply of skilled workers is the movement towards competency-based teaching and assessment, away from "seat-time" and credit accumulation. Though the competency-based training and assessment field is still nascent, there is wide agreement on basic tenets: students advance based on demonstrated skills and content knowledge; students advance at individual rates rather than on a teacher-driven, class-wide schedule; and students receive customized supports to ensure they are able to reach mastery (Le et al., 2014). For the competency movement to gain traction, employers need to be active participants in ensuring proper focus on relevant skills—technical, problem solving, and interpersonal. A case in point: Google's website indicates they are looking for candidates with the ability not only to think and lead but "for engineering candidates in particular, we'll be looking to check out your coding skills and technical areas of expertise."

It is worth clarifying that the focus on competency should not be mistaken for an abandonment of broad-based education in which students are exposed to literature, history, arts, science, and more. Exposure to arts and sciences will produce the flexible, creative, ethical problem solvers we need. In the words of Fareed Zakaria (2015),

> American routine manufacturing jobs continue to get automated or outsourced, and specific vocational knowledge is often outdated within a few years. Engineering is a great profession, but key value-added skills you will also need are

creativity, lateral thinking, design, communication, storytelling, and, more than anything, the ability to continually learn and enjoy learning – precisely the gifts of a liberal education.

The key to the competency approach, however, is that students do not have to learn in lock step with their age group, or at an "average" pace set by the teacher, or even in a classroom per se. Rather they need to learn through methods that keep them engaged and give the subjects real-world meaning.

Changing Employer Attitudes and Practices

In spite of economic theory positing "rational actors," new insights in the last two decades of brain science and behavioral economics, not to mention research on implicit bias, have taught us that hiring decisions are not always made from a position of logic or rationality (Banaji and Greenwald, 2013; Kahneman, 2011). The final and critical area in which employers must act is in terms of *shifting their own hiring, training, and human resource development practices*. Given demographic trends, unless US employers start to act differently, they will simply not be able to address the dire shortage of "middle-skills" workers and will experience significant economic consequences. It is insufficient to exhort or even assist the education and training systems—the "suppliers"—to change. Businesses must change their own outmoded "supply management" practices as well, and not just for opportunity youth. Our human capital machine is not effective at retraining those who need it whatever their age, nor is it flexible enough to take advantage of the talents of those who want to work less than full time. If the 152 million Americans living at or below twice the poverty level were employed and earning family-supporting wages, we would all do better. More employers need to change their current hiring, training, and human resource development practices to get us there.

The bachelor's degree as a minimum requirement provides a good illustration of the problem and the potential cure for outdated practices. Many employers advertise a bachelor's degree as a minimum requirement for entry-level positions. However, a bachelor's degree requirement automatically excludes 82 percent of African Americans and 87 percent of Latinos over 25, dramatically shrinking the pool of considered talent, curtailing opportunity for these populations, and obscuring the substantial capabilities they potentially bring to employers (Ogunwole et al., 2012). Upon examination, some employers have realized that many jobs can be performed by someone with a high school diploma, minimal additional training, and/or a market-relevant credential. Coupled with "competency-based" assessments, the elimination or modification of this requirement could open up opportunities to many low-income men and women of color who have disproportionately low educational attainment but plenty of aptitude.

At every step of the hiring process, too often the ways employers define and evaluate merit are skewed to favor job applicants from economically privileged backgrounds (Rivera, 2015). Another practice in need of revisiting has to do with resume screening practices. Whether it is due to unconscious bias of human resource professionals shaped by their own education and training backgrounds, or software algorithms programed to screen for certain degrees or other proxies, too often the traditional screening systems have built-in preferences that imprudently shrink the pool of considered talent. To help overcome some of these systemic biases, Year Up has partnered to create the first-ever employer-focused, national public service announcement (PSA) campaign, Grads of Life (GoL). Launched in the fall of 2014, the GoL campaign showcases young adults with atypical resumes who bring unique talents, determination, resilience, and loyalty to forward-thinking employers. The campaign includes TV, print, and outdoor advertisements, radio segments, digital and mobile banners, and a website to encourage employer action: GradsofLife.org. As with PSA campaigns about smoking, seatbelt safety, and drunk driving, the goal is to influence public attitudes and behavior over time.

Professional development is another opportunity for employers to examine and shift their practices. Conventionally, it was considered foolish to invest in the development of low-wage workers because they were likely to leave and take any skills-upgrade investments with them to another employer. Recently, a small but growing number of US employers are seeking to move away from a "procurement" approach to entry and mid-level jobs towards a "talent acquisition and development" approach, and applying it to their entire workforce, not just the traditional upper tiers of management. In 2014, Starbucks created a program to allow any of its 135,000 employees who work 20 hours per week or more to receive 100 percent tuition reimbursement to earn a bachelor's degree through Arizona State University's online program. The program is unusual in that Starbucks is not seeking to upgrade its employees' skills to improve their performance as, say, baristas, but rather to upgrade their life opportunities, helping them "access the American dream" as their promotional flyers put it. CEO Howard Schultz and Arizona State's president Michael Crow are partnering to overcome the abominably low college-completion rates for low-income students, one of the biggest barriers to professional opportunity for individuals, and a contributor to the skills gap for employers.

Another example of an employer investing in entry-level, low-skill employees is from Southwire, a leading manufacturer of electrical wire located in Carroll County, Georgia. In the 1980s, in recognition of its growing need for more skilled workers, Southwire committed to only hiring high school graduates. By the 2000s, the company was increasingly concerned about the high school graduation rates in its community, as well as the skills and preparation of students who did graduate. To help ensure that it had the workforce it needed, Southwire pursued a "vertical integration" approach to talent supply by developing a program in cooperation with the school system starting in 2007. Through its "12 for Life" program, Southwire provides students the chance to mix classroom learning and workplace training at a specially built facility within its manufacturing plant, simultaneously offering young people education, a paycheck, and key work and life skills. "12 for Life" is not a vocational or technical training program; rather, it enables students to graduate on time with a regular high school diploma while also giving the company access to workers with the skills it desires. Though it was not designed with money making in mind, the program broke even after just three months and generated $1.7 million for the company in its first six years (Rivkin and Lee, 2013).

Both Starbucks and Southwire understand that it is in their short- and long-term interest to invest in individuals who have not been well served by traditional approaches. As Starbuck's website proclaims, "Supporting our partners' [employees'] ambitions is the very best investment Starbucks can make" (<https://www.washingtonpost.com/news/answer-sheet/wp/2014/06/15/starbucks-to-offer-employees-free-tuition-to-complete-online-bachelors-degree/>). Investing in the "underserved" is more than just corporate social responsibility or philanthropy for these employers. They understand that their fortunes are inextricably linked to the well-being of the communities in which they operate and the life prospects of their employees. Their vision aligns with that of legendary Henry Ford who reputedly sought to pay his factory workers well enough that they could also be his customers.

CONCLUSION: WORKING TOGETHER TO RESTORE THE CAPITALIST PROMISE

Countries with economies as diverse as Saudi Arabia, Chile, Brazil, Rwanda, and Kenya have been in touch with Year Up to learn from our work and translate our lessons to their context. They share an understanding that providing opportunities for youth and skilled talent for employers is not solely a public sector problem, or something that the private sector can solve unaided. No matter the locale, it is critical to align business, government, and non-government organizations behind improvements in education and training to prevent labor market mismatches, ease school-to-work transitions, and shift beliefs and behaviors to tap into the potential of opportunity youth.

As understanding in the US grows about just how important this agenda is to our collective economic interests, a diverse and multi-sector group of actors has begun working together to address the opportunity divide. The Business Roundtable, the US Chamber of Commerce, the National Governors Association, the US Conference of Mayors, and the Society for Human Resource Management are just a handful of the players that are becoming vocal and effective advocates for ways that businesses can address their own self-interest in transforming opportunities for young people who have been left out of the current workforce.

Smart public policy can also incentivize private investments in workforce development, with bipartisan support. For example, a temporary additional category for "disconnected" youth within the Work Opportunity Tax Credit was passed in 2009—though it expired before the private sector was able to widely utilize it, and members of Congress from both parties have supported strong tax credits for employers offering apprenticeships. A new, expansive employment pathways tax credit would be beneficial for both business and the public, and given the high cost of youth disconnection could essentially pay for itself. State and federal governments should also align inducements for companies to retain and develop human capital over time. This could include creating tax incentives for companies to assist their employees in pursuing further education which has significant impact on long-term earnings.

Similarly, to spur the development of alternative pathways that align closely with business needs, Congress should consider competitive grant programs for creating internships, apprenticeships, and mentorships. The National Fund for Workforce Solutions, a partnership among leading foundations, the Boeing Company, and the federal Social Innovation Fund, provide an excellent model for multi-sector innovation. Likewise, Skillworks, a multi-year initiative in Massachusetts, brings together philanthropy, government, community organizations, and employers to address the twin goals of helping low-income individuals attain family-supporting jobs and businesses find skilled workers.

While these specific recommendations apply to the US, they exemplify a critical re-imagining that is needed not only for the benefit of youth lacking opportunity, but to sustain the capitalist system as a whole from the dangers inherent in significant swaths of young people disengaged from economic opportunity. Employers, government, and the third sector must work together to retool educational systems, hiring practices, and human capital development methods to unlock the assets we need to meet the challenges of the 21st-century global economy. Overcoming the opportunity divide will build our shared prosperity on the eternally humbling promise of youth.

ACKNOWLEDGMENTS

The authors would like to thank the thousands of extraordinary Year Up students and alumni whom they have had the privilege of learning from over the years. They also wish to acknowledge the dedication and vision of their many colleagues who have shaped the ideas in this chapter and, in particular, for their close input on this piece: Savan Kothadia, Charlie Mangiardi, Elyse Rosenblum, and Catie Smith. And finally, they are grateful to Kim Bohen for shaping the learning into lucid prose.

REFERENCES

Accenture, Burning Glass Technologies, and Harvard Business School (2014). *Bridge the Gap: Rebuilding America's Middle Skills.* Available at: <http://www.hbs.edu/competitiveness/Documents/bridge-the-gap.pdf>.

Altstadt, D. (2011). *Aligning Community Colleges to Their Local Labor Markets: The Emerging Role of Online Job Ads for Providing Real-Time Intelligence about Occupations and Skills in Demand.* Washington, DC: Jobs for the Future.

Balfanz, R., Bridgeland, J., Bruce, M., and Fox, J. F. (2012). *Building a Grad Nation: Progress and Challenge in Ending the High School Dropout Epidemic.* Washington, DC: Civic Enterprises.

Banaji, M. and Greenwald, A. (2013). *Blindspot: Hidden Biases of Good People.* New York: Delacorte Press.

Belfield, C., Levin, H., and Rosen, R. (2012). *The Economic Value of Opportunity Youth.* Washington, DC: Civic Enterprises.

Bersin, J. (2014). "Spending on Corporate Training Soars: Employee Capabilities Now a Priority," *Forbes*, February 4. Available at: <http://www.forbes.com/sites/joshbersin/2014/02/04/the-recovery-arrives-corporate-training-spend-skyrockets/>.

Carnevale, A. and Smith, N. (2013). "Workplace Basics: The Skills Employees Need and Employers Want," *Human Resource Development International,* 16(5): 491–501.

Carnevale, A., Rose, S., and Cheah, B. (2011). *The College Payoff: Education, Occupations, Lifetime Earnings.* Washington, DC: Georgetown University Center on Education and the Workforce.

Chantrill, C. (2015). *Government Spending Details.* Available at: <http://www.usgovernmentspending.com/year_spending_2015USbn_16bs2n_2024#usgs302>.

Chetty, R., Hendren, N., and Katz, L. (2015). "The Effects of Exposure to Better Neighborhoods on Children: New Evidence from the Moving to Opportunity Experiment," National Bureau of Economic Research, Working Paper, No. w21156. Available at: <http://www.nber.org/papers/w21156.pdf>.

Chronicle for Higher Education (2013). *College Completion.* Available at: <http://collegecompletion.chronicle.com>.

Heckman, J. and Kautz, T. (2012). "Hard Evidence on Soft Skills," *Labour Economics,* 19(4): 451–64.

Hoffman, M. and Jamal, A. (2012). "The Youth and the Arab Spring: Cohort Differences and Similarities," *Middle East Law and Governance,* 4(1): 168–88.

Holzer, H. (2011). *Raising Job Quality and Skills for American Workers: Creating More Effective Education and Workforce Development Systems in the States.* Washington, DC: Brookings Institute.

Hunt, V., Layton, D., and Prince, S. (2015). "Why Diversity Matters," *McKinsey & Company*, January. Available at: <http://www.mckinsey.com/insights/organization/why_diversity_matters>.

ILO (2013). *Global Employment Trends of Youth 2013: A Generation at Risk.* Geneva: International Labour Organization.

ILO (2015). *Youth Unemployment.* Geneva: International Labour Organization. Available at: <http://www.ilo.org/global/topics/youth-employment/lang–en/index.htm>.

Kahneman, D. (2011). *Thinking, Fast and Slow.* London: Macmillan.

Le, C., Wolfe, R., and Steinberg, A. (2014). *The Past and the Promise: Today's Competency Education Movement.* Washington, DC: Jobs for the Future.

Lennon, C. (2015). "Private and Public Investment in Training Is Needed," *New York Times*, March 19. Available at: <http://www.nytimes.com/roomfordebate/2015/03/19/who-should-pay-for-workers-training/private-and-public-investment-in-training-is-needed>.

Leonhardt, D. (2015). "College for the Masses," *New York Times*, April 24. Available at: <http://www.nytimes.com/2015/04/26/upshot/college-for-the-masses.html>.

Measure of America (2015). *The Opportunity Index 2015.* Available at: <http://www.measureofamerica.org/opportunity-index/>.

National Center for Law and Economic Justice (2013). *Poverty in the United States: A Snapshot.* Available at: <http://www.nclej.org/poverty-in-the-us.php>.

National Commission on Excellence in Education (1983). *A Nation at Risk: The Imperative for Educational Reform.* Washington, DC: US Department of Education.

National Skills Coalition (2014). *United States' Forgotten Middle: State-by-State Snapshots.* Available at: <http://www.nationalskillscoalition.org/resources/publications/file/middle-skill-fact-sheets-2014/NSC-United-States-MiddleSkillFS-2014.pdf>.

Ogunwole, S., Drewery, M., and Rios-Vargas, M. (2012). *The Population with a Bachelor's Degree or Higher by Race and Hispanic Origin: 2006–2010.* Washington, DC: US Census Bureau.

Rivera, L. A. (2015). *Pedigree: How Elite Students Get Elite Jobs.* Princeton, NJ: Princeton University Press.

Rivkin, J. and Lee, R. (2013). *Southwire and 12 for Life: Scaling Up? (A).* HBS case no.714-434. Boston, MA: Harvard Business School Publishing.

Symonds, W., Schwartz, R., and Ferguson, R. (2011). *Pathways to Prosperity: Meeting the Challenge of Preparing Young Americans for the 21st Century.* Report prepared for the Harvard University Graduate School of Education, Cambridge, MA.

US Department of Education (2015). *U.S. High School Graduation Rate Hits New Record High.* Available at: <http://www.ed.gov/news/press-releases/us-high-school-graduation-rate-hits-new-record-high>.

Zakaria, F. (2015). *In Defense of a Liberal Education.* New York: Norton.

21

Conclusion

Capitalism Re-Imagined

Dezső Horváth and Dominic Barton

INTRODUCTION

Contrary to the dire predictions of some, the sun is not setting on capitalism: capitalism is here to stay. Whatever its critics might say, whatever its inherent limitations or flaws, capitalism has been an incredibly successful engine of innovation and wealth creation, improving the quality of life for billions of people throughout the world. And it will continue to be a source of economic growth and prosperity for many decades to come. Yet, despite this, capitalism has not gone unchallenged—particularly since the economic meltdown of 2008 and the onset of the Great Recession. Triggered by the lending of highly leveraged subprime mortgages and a lack of sufficient oversight of financial institutions, the meltdown cast capitalism in a particularly bad light.

One of the fallouts of the financial crisis is that public trust in capitalism has sunk to an all-time low in many developed countries (see also Chapter 2, this volume). One reason for this growing lack of public trust in capitalism lies in the loosened ties between business and society. Over the last three decades, businesses and business leaders have shifted toward an increasingly isolated, narrow and short-sighted view of capitalism—one built on the idea that the interests of shareholders take precedence over those of all other stakeholders, including society, and that the overriding mandate of a business is to deliver quarterly results. This trend has been to the detriment of both business and society (see also Chapter 10, this volume). Another reason for this erosion in public trust is the slow but steady rise in income inequality. The Organization for Economic Cooperation and Development (OECD) has shown that the gap between rich and poor has grown in most OECD countries over the last 30 years (OECD, 2011: 1; see also Piketty, 2014; OECD, 2015). Public distrust and animosity over income inequality reached a boiling point with the emergence several years ago of the Occupy Wall Street movement (see also Chapter 13, this volume).

If capitalism has lost its way, then which direction should it take? This chapter makes specific suggestions how capitalism should be re-imagined both at the macro level in terms of maximizing national wealth and well-being and at the micro level in terms of businesses maximizing their long-term value. In what follows, we will first highlight the persistence of significant variety *within* capitalism, which became increasingly apparent after the fall of the Berlin Wall in 1989, but also existed earlier. We then use the comparisons between countries to identify promising models going forward, in terms of both economic performance and well-being, which—perhaps not surprisingly—are those that take into consideration a broader set of stakeholders. With respect to the micro level, we argue that executives, asset managers, and boards must refocus on long-term value creation. We conclude by stressing that to make such a re-imagined capitalism a reality requires collaboration by many, including governments, but with businesses and investors called upon to take a particularly active, catalytic role.

DRAWING ON THE VARIETIES OF CAPITALISM OVER SPACE AND TIME

There have probably been different models of capitalism as long as there have been systems where ownership was predominantly private, where incentives and rewards were mainly geared towards individuals, and where most exchanges took place through markets. But for much of the 20th century, these differences were obscured by the much more fundamental opposition between capitalism and communism—free enterprise and a planned economy. It is only when the latter failed, symbolized by the fall of the Berlin Wall in 1989, that the differences within capitalism became more apparent.

One of the first to highlight these differences was the French economist and businessman Michel Albert in a book entitled *Capitalism Vs. Capitalism*, originally published in French in 1991 (Albert, 1993). Albert distinguished two models of capitalism. On the one hand, there is what he called "Rhine capitalism," since its main examples are located along the river Rhine: Switzerland, Germany, and the Netherlands. One should also include the Nordic countries, i.e., Denmark, Finland, Norway, and Sweden, and, to a lesser extent, Japan, in this group. This type of capitalism—which some have referred to as the *"stakeholder model"*—is marked by a long-term vision, namely in terms of savings and investment, cooperative relations between management, labor, and other stakeholders, and a more redistributive tax regime. On the other hand, there is what Albert calls "neo-American capitalism" and what is sometimes referred to as the "*shareholder model.*" Prevalent in the United States and the United Kingdom, this model is marked by a strong shareholder-first orientation, more fluid labor contracts, and a weaker social safety net.

Albert's differentiation was followed by many academic treatments, which ultimately arrived at largely identical groupings of countries and very similar characterizations of the differences between them. British sociologist Ronald Dore, for example, contrasted welfare capitalism and stock market capitalism. He portrayed the former, embodied by Germany and Japan, as under threat by the increasing prevalence of the latter, emanating from the "Anglo-Saxon countries" (Dore, 2000). Probably most influential was the distinction between "liberal" and "coordinated market economies" introduced by political economists Peter Hall and David Soskice in their volume on *Varieties of Capitalism* with the US and the UK once again as the main examples for the former and Germany and the Nordic countries as examples of the latter (Hall and Soskice, 2001). Among the many differences they identified were higher income inequality in the former and more collaborative relations between all stakeholders in the latter.

Why does this matter? It matters because variety means choice and that in turn means we are *not bound by a single model of capitalism.* But while the ability to draw on an alternative model of capitalism is important, it is also necessary to see to what extent countries and—by extension—businesses are locked into their particular model or, put differently, whether they can change. History provides a clear and positive answer on the ability of countries and businesses to change.

Albert (1993) did not call the shareholder model *Neo*-American by accident. It only became the model of choice in the US and the UK in the 1970s and then spread around the world in the decades that followed, in particular after the fall of the Berlin Wall (Davis, 2013). While difficult to imagine today, until then the American model was much more akin to the stakeholder one—going back to the reforms introduced during the 1930s in response to the Great Depression by President Franklin D. Roosevelt under the "New Deal." And unbeknownst to many, *this* American model also influenced developments in Germany and Japan following their defeats in World War II—contributing to the introduction of what the Germans, for instance, call "social market economy" and to the subsequent economic boom in both countries (Kudo et al., 2004).

So, there is no reason why—following the recent Great Recession—countries cannot re-examine and retool their models of capitalism. The following sections will outline what such a reformed model should look like both at the macro and micro levels and suggest how we might get there.

BUILDING AN INCLUSIVE AND COMPETITIVE MODEL OF CAPITALISM

Enhancing Performance and Well-Being through Stakeholder Orientation

As a first step, we can begin by looking at the macro-economic level and assess how national economies are performing. And what we discover is that the countries where more inclusive, stakeholder models of capitalism prevail tend to rank higher on various measures of overall economic performance, and in particular within the broader context of national well-being and sustainability.

The latest evidence indicates a clear and compelling correlation between the long-term outlook and stakeholder orientation built into a particular capitalist model and enhanced competitiveness. Put differently, an inclusive, stakeholder-oriented model of capitalism makes countries more competitive. For example, Switzerland, Finland, Sweden, and Germany—all of which are considered so-called stakeholder-model countries—are ranked among the top six globally by the World Economic Forum's *Global Competitiveness Reports* over a five-year period, from 2010–11 to 2014–15 (WEF, 2015). Not surprisingly, these countries also do very well in subcategories such as innovation, which is partially driven by a long-term investment horizon. Sweden, for instance, routinely ranks among the world's top innovators, placing 2nd in the Bloomberg Rankings (2014) of the most innovative countries in the world and 3rd in *The Global Innovation Index 2015* put together by Cornell University, INSEAD, and the World Intellectual Property Organization (Cornell University, INSEAD, and WIPO, 2015).

The United States has been—and continues to be—the world's leading innovator, producing many of the advances driving the digital revolution and creating breakthroughs in areas as diverse as cloud technology, next-generation genomics, and advanced materials. Yet some more recent studies show that the US may be losing ground. For instance, a discussion paper emanating from the Stanford Institute for Economic Policy Research, which examines the macro-economic impact of short-term behavior by firms concludes that the intense focus on quarterly earnings at many of America's largest publicly held companies may be reducing research and development spending, which in turn could reduce US growth (Terry, 2015: 35).

The Nordic countries in particular—Sweden, Norway, Finland, and Denmark—have all surged to the top of the major global competitiveness rankings in recent years, prompting many to ask whether the rest of the free-market world should be adopting more of the features of their variety of capitalism, which typically include low corporate tax rates and efficient public spending combined with innovative policies that allow private companies to deliver public services. Describing this injection of "market mechanisms into the welfare state to sharpen its performance," the *Economist* (2013) went as far as heralding what it called "Viking capitalism" as the "next supermodel" of capitalism. It also pointed out, as have we, that the Nordic countries ranked highly on a wide range of measures covering both *economic criteria*, such as productivity, competitiveness, innovation, and ease of doing business, and *social criteria*, ranging from corruption to human development.

These stakeholder-oriented countries also fare very well when it comes to sustainability. Thus, a recent survey of sustainable governance, which included a wide range of economic, social, and environmental indicators, found that the Nordic countries, together with Switzerland and Germany, are the "most successful countries with regard to sustainable policy outcomes" in terms of improving the quality of life of their citizens (Bertelsmann Stiftung, 2015: 3). Furthermore, countries with similar growth rates but different models of capitalism produced different rates of improvement in the quality of life of their citizens. The US and Germany, for example, posted similar growth rates, but stakeholder-oriented Germany performed much better in terms of converting that growth into national well-being (Beal et al., 2015: 10).

Reducing Income and Educational Inequality

As we noted earlier, income inequality has been one of the primary causes for an erosion of public trust in capitalism. However, the problem with income inequality may be more far-reaching. A growing number of studies have shown that income inequality, which tends to be much lower in countries adhering to the stakeholder model, may actually impede economic growth and competitiveness. Reducing income inequality, therefore, should be a key objective when moving towards a re-imagined capitalism.

The link between high-income inequality and lower growth was borne out by an International Monetary Fund report published in June 2015. The report found that "if the income share of the top 20 percent (the rich) increases, then GDP growth actually declines over the medium term, suggesting that the benefits do not trickle down." The report also found that, conversely, "an increase in the income share of the bottom 20 percent (the poor) is associated with higher GDP growth" (Dabla-Norris et al, 2015: 4; see also OECD, 2015). Perhaps not surprisingly, the countries that are among the most globally competitive are also the countries that have the lowest rates of income inequality, which, according to the World Bank, include Norway, Denmark, Sweden, Finland, and Iceland (World Bank, 2015). The 2014 OECD Income Distribution Database showed nearly identical results, with the Nordic countries among those with the lowest income inequality among OECD members (OECD, 2014a). We can conclude, therefore, that those countries with the smallest disparities in income—countries that have a strong and stable middle class—tend to outperform countries with more extreme levels of income inequality.

Income inequality is especially pronounced in the United States, which ranks near the bottom of the latest OECD survey of income disparities among industrialized nations (OECD, 2014b: 1). According to a *New York Times* analysis, 35 years ago, an American family at the 20th percentile of the income distribution in the US made more than their counterparts in Sweden, Norway, or Finland. Today, the reverse is true (Leonhardt and Quealy, 2014). The growing gap between the wealthiest Americans and those at the bottom of the income ladder is being driven by a number of factors, including educational inequality, where the authors of the *New York Times* analysis found that "educational attainment in the United States has risen far more slowly than in much of the industrialized world over the last three decades, making it harder for the American economy to maintain its share of highly skilled, well-paying jobs" (Leonhardt and Quealy, 2014; see also Chapter 20, this volume). In 2014, the OECD issued a report that showed the US lagging behind other developed economies when it comes to educational equality, and this in turn has contributed to income inequality (Porter, 2014). The comparison with Sweden is once more very instructive here: the large increase in college-level graduates in Sweden over the last 30 years is probably one of the reasons why Sweden not only had lower income inequality but also higher per-capita growth rates than the US (Leonhardt and Quealy, 2014).

And while some may view income inequality and the related problem of educational inequality as being primarily political or socio-economic issues, there are concrete steps that companies can take to address income disparity. Later in this chapter we show how equipping investors and board members with an owner mindset can place companies on the path toward long-term value generation. Providing employees with a share of ownership in the business can not only mitigate the problem of growing income inequality but also create a powerful mechanism for enhancing a company's productivity and long-term competitiveness.

Improving Quality of Life through Inclusion

There is also another intriguing correlation between countries that practice a more inclusive stakeholder model of capitalism and the quality of life enjoyed by their citizens, as measured through tangible areas such as education, health, housing, safety, and work-life balance.

Take Switzerland for example. The country ranked first in the 2015–16 World Economic Forum's Global Competitiveness Report (WEF, 2015). But the country also does extremely well in terms of quality of life, as measured by the OECD's 2014 Better Life Index (OECD, 2014c). Another study showed a correlation between well-being and happiness as measured by the World Happiness Report, a ranking published by the United Nations-affiliated Sustainable Development Solutions Network. The report found that well-being and happiness measures were generally aligned—in other words, citizens of countries that experienced sustainable and more inclusive economic growth were for the most part also the happiest (Beal et al., 2015: 27).

There is substantial evidence, therefore, that a broader stakeholder model of capitalism can provide benefits both for society and business, and that this advantage is symbiotic: more globally competitive businesses create greater wealth and, when a portion of that wealth is re-invested into human development and social well-being, it generates enhanced employee productivity and creativity.

RECALIBRATING THE CORPORATION FOR THE LONG TERM

We have reviewed some of the issues involved in reforming capitalism at the macro-economic level. But what sort of changes need to happen at the level of the corporation itself? To begin with, we need to fundamentally rewire the ways that we govern, manage, and lead corporations and business leaders must recognize that serving stakeholders—not just shareholders—is essential to maximizing corporate value. For this to happen, business leaders need to first break free from the tyranny of short-term thinking and begin managing for the long-term performance and health of their companies. Second, investors and boards of directors need to act like owners. And third, we need to create new management tools and metrics to orient behavior towards a re-imagined capitalism.

Integrating Long-Term Thinking and Stakeholder Orientation

So how do business leaders move from ingrained short-term thinking to long-term managing? The drivers pushing executives and boards toward a short-term focus vary but are often interconnected. For executives, these drivers include compensation structures, ever shortening job tenure, perceptions about legacy, and the business necessities involved in meeting quarterly targets. For board members, the factors influencing short-term thinking include fear of failing to fulfill their legal duties, a fear that often turns them into a kind of "compliance police" instead of focusing on the long-term interests of company owners. As a result, the relentless focus on short-term performance—the quarterly heartbeat of modern business—diverts attention required of executives and boards away from the long-term health of the organization and it undermines long-term value realization for institutional investors as well. The new mantra must be: long-term thinking is essential for long-term success.

Moreover, companies need to integrate stakeholder management into all decision-making. To begin with, executives must understand that taking care of all stakeholders is vital to taking care of shareholders and, moreover, essential to maximizing corporate value over the long term. Short-term pressures, however, make it difficult to prioritize the complicated job of balancing stakeholder interests. These pressures also frequently allow share-holder concerns to trump other stakeholder interests. But in the final analysis, companies need to realize that the issue of shareholders and stakeholders is not an either/or proposition.

Developing an Owner Mindset

Most large public companies have extremely dispersed ownership. As a result, CEOs often end up listening to trading-oriented investors, who tend to be the least committed to the long-term health and success of the company. Several studies, including a 2004 study at the National Bureau for Economic Research, find that when shareholders are ready to sell at the slightest change in stock price, companies tend to manage for the near term, forgoing investments in profitable long-term projects due to worries that the near-term stock price will fall (Graham et al., 2004: 4). But it takes time to build, strengthen, and grow a successful business—and investors need to give companies that breathing room. We know from years of data generated by the Dow Jones Sustainability Index, for example, that companies that have a long-term focus and strong stakeholder orientation create greater shareholder value on average over the mid-to-long term (see also Chapter 17, this volume).

While dispersed ownership can be a contributing factor to short-term management, the opposite, i.e., a more active ownership model for large institutional investors such as pension funds, insurance companies, and wealth funds, might provide a solution for ingraining a longer-term focus in businesses. These massive funds typically invest on behalf of long-term clients with a time horizon measured in decades rather than months, giving them a built-in mandate to focus capital on the long term.

In addition to investors, boards also need to act more like owners by serving as agents of long-term value creation. But for this change to happen, board members must devote more time to their roles, become more engaged with the business, interact more with management, and work with management to develop and implement a long-term strategy. And boards also need to give the senior management team the time and space required to build long-term value, rather than adding to the already intense pressure that exists to maximize short-term profits. In a 2013 global survey of senior executives conducted by McKinsey & Company and the Canada Pension Plan Investment Board, boards were the most cited source of short-term pressure (Barton and Wiseman, 2014).

Creating New Management Tools and Metrics

What else do we need to make this shift to longer-term, broader capitalism work? Generation Investment Management LLP, a London-based investment firm dedicated to long-term investing, recommends the adoption of several common-sense practices to help ensure longer-term value creation (Generation Investment Management, 2012). Some of the suggested practices include the following: mandated integrated reporting of environmental, social, and financial performance (see also Chapter 15, this volume); ending the practice of issuing quarterly earnings guidance; aligning compensation structures for asset managers and corporate executives with the company's long-term performance; and encouraging innovations such as loyalty-based securities that promote long-term investing—based on the logical premise that short-term capital engenders short-term management thinking. L'Oréal, for example, offers a loyalty bonus to registered shareholders that grants a 10 percent incremental dividend to all shareholders that hold registered shares for at least two years.

One of the key recommendations focuses on encouraging investors to take a longer-term perspective by ending the practice of issuing quarterly earnings guidance. Companies such as Unilever, Merck, GE, AT&T, and Coca-Cola have all taken this step, while some newer companies, such as Google, have never provided quarterly earnings guidance from the outset. Others have taken a different approach: IBM, for example, has created five-year roadmaps so long-term investors can see the company's growth over a longer time horizon. Either way, the trend toward not issuing quarterly earnings guidance is gaining momentum. Recent surveys by the National Investor Relations Institute of their members show that the percentage of companies providing guidance dropped from 85 percent in 2009 to 76 percent in 2012 (cited by Karageorgiou and Serafeim, 2014: 10). In addition, recent sweeping changes to regulations governing publicly traded companies operating in the UK have loosened reporting requirements.

Companies also need to begin adopting a broader set of performance measures, or big-picture compasses, that contribute to their longer-term success. These metrics could include measures such as the depth and quality of talent within the firm, as well as the company's innovation rate or patent pipeline, and the company's environmental footprint. Other tools that could include formal mechanisms to measure corporate reputation with all key stakeholders, not just a selected few such as investors or customers. And lastly, companies need to give greater attention to environmental, social, and governance measures since these measures inherently focus management attention on long-term performance.

Finally, we need to consider the compensation structures governing asset managers. Typically, fund managers' pay is tied to outperforming various yearly stock market benchmarks, which in turn reinforces short termism. But if compensation were linked to performance over longer periods, then we would have a greater likelihood of growing funds that delivered long-term value.

FROM IMAGINATION TO REALITY: THE WAY FORWARD

We began this chapter by talking about the growing public distrust of capitalism and the loosening of the traditional bonds between business and society over the past several decades. The notion of bonds between business and society is as old as capitalism itself. Adam Smith, considered by many to be the founding philosopher of capitalism, often wrote about the profound interdependence between business and society, and how that symbiosis helps to foster long-term value creation.

Clearly, capitalism has been a force for tremendous good—and it can continue to be. We need to move beyond the severely limited and short-term focused model of capitalism—away from "quarterly capitalism"—and toward a broader-based, long-term capitalism. In addition, we need to revise our thinking in regard to the value of business and the critical role it plays in society. Fortunately, there is growing momentum for change. Corporations today increasingly realize that business issues cannot be isolated from social, political, and environmental considerations. Growing concerns about climate change, environmental degradation, and income disparity are making it imperative for companies to deal seriously with broad-based social, environmental, and economic issues in a way they never used to. Adopting a long-term focused, stakeholder-oriented approach to business is more than just good corporate citizenship: it is good business management.

So how do we get there and who exactly will initiate and implement the necessary changes? One place to start is with the world's largest asset owners—pension funds, mutual funds, insurance firms, and sovereign wealth funds. In the same way that investors and board members need to act more like owners, so too do these asset funds. They need to do this by engaging corporate executives and by building long-term relationships with the companies in which they invest.

Business leaders are another natural source for initiating change. In the past, business leaders have often taken the lead in implementing broad-based, far-reaching change (see also Chapter 1, this volume). Consider Henry Ford, widely credited with developing the mass production of automobiles with his Model T. But Ford did something perhaps even more significant: he decided to share the resulting productivity gains with his workers by paying them higher wages, convinced that this would better enable them to buy his cars. Simply put, Ford not only developed mass production, but also mass consumption through higher incomes. This combination of high productivity with high wages (and high quality) is still an important feature of the stakeholder model of capitalism today, with Germany being a prime example. As other contributions to this volume have shown, some trailblazing business leaders have already taken up the challenge—but many more need to do so.

And finally, political leaders would be another source for bringing about widespread changes. Historically, several major changes to the capitalist model have been linked to political leaders, such as Franklin D. Roosevelt's New Deal. Governments throughout the developed world have begun making some changes following the global financial crisis, most notably on the regulatory side. But large-scale changes in the prevailing capitalist model have typically resulted from the actions of many individuals beyond the government. This will undoubtedly be the case today if we are to bring about meaningful and long-lasting changes.

Whichever direction capitalism ends up taking, it is increasingly apparent that the narrow shareholder model is being gradually eclipsed by a model that is more closely attuned to the complexity and diversity of the world we live in— a model that is more stakeholder oriented and more guided by principles of long-term value creation and sustainability. It is a model where boards and executives act more like owners, and asset owners and managers invest for the long term; where employees are increasingly treated as partners in the profitability and success of the business; where consumers and suppliers are increasingly engaged as co-creators in shaping the products and services that businesses provide; and where corporations are fully integrated into the communities and countries in which they operate.

If there is anything we have learned from history, it is that capitalism is incredibly resilient. The current crisis of faith in capitalism, fueled by the Great Recession, has compelled leaders in business, government, NGOs, and academia to rethink the way we do business—to re-imagine capitalism. We believe we are heading in the right direction. And although a lot of progress has been made, there is still much more that needs to be done if we want to ensure that capitalism continues to be an engine of growth and prosperity in the 21st century.

ACKNOWLEDGMENTS

We would like to thank Paul Pivato for assisting with the original draft of this chapter as well as Andrew Cedar and Matthias Kipping for their helpful editorial suggestions. As is customary, the ultimate responsibility for its content remains ours.

REFERENCES

Albert, M. (1993). *Capitalism Vs. Capitalism: How America's Obsession with Individual Achievement and Short-Term Profit Has Led It to the Brink of Collapse*. New York: Four Walls Eight Windows.

Barton, D. and Mark Wiseman (2014). "Focusing Capital on the Long Term," *Harvard Business Review*, 92(1/2): 44–51.

Beal, D., Rueda-Sabater, E., and Heng, S. L. (2015). *Why Well-Being Should Drive Growth Strategies: The 2015 Sustainable Economic Development Assessment*, Boston Consulting Group, May. Available at: <https://www.bcgperspectives.com/Im ages/BCG-Why-Well-Being-Should-Drive-Growth-Strategies-May-2015.pdf>.

Bertelsmann Stiftung (2015). *Policy Performance and Governance Capacities in the OECD and EU: Sustainable Governance Indicators 2015*. Available at: <http:// www.sgi-network.org/docs/2015/basics/SGI2015_Overview.pdf> (accessed October 21, 2015).

Bloomberg Rankings (2014). "Most Innovative in the World 2014: Countries." Available at: <http://images.businessweek.com/bloomberg/pdfs/most_innovative_coun tries_2014_011714.pdf> (accessed September 9, 2015).

Cornell University, INSEAD, and WIPO (2015). *The Global Innovation Index 2015: Effective Innovation Policies for Development*, Ithaca, Fontainebleau, and Geneva. Available at: <https://www.globalinnovationindex.org/userfiles/file/reportpdf/gii-full-report-2015-v6.pdf>.

Dabla-Norris, E., Kochhar, K., Suphaphiphat, N., Ricka, F., and Tsounta, E. (2015). "Causes and Consequences of Income Inequality: A Global Perspective," International Monetary Fund, Staff Discussion Notes No. 15/13, June 15. Available at: <https://www.imf.org/external/pubs/ft/sdn/2015/sdn1513.pdf>.

Davis, G. F. (2013). "After the Corporation," *Politics and Society*, 41(2): 283–308.

Dore, R. (2000). *Stock Market Capitalism: Welfare Capitalism. Japan and Germany versus the Anglo-Saxons*. Oxford: Oxford University Press.

Economist (2013). "The Nordic Countries: The Next Supermodel," *Economist*, February 2. Available at: <http://www.economist.com/news/leaders/21571136-politicians-both-right-and-left-could-learn-nordic-countries-next-supermodel> (accessed October 21, 2015).

Generation Investment Management (2012). "Sustainable Capitalism," Generation Investment Management LLP, London, February 15. Available at: <https://www. genfound.org/media/pdf-generation-sustainable-capitalism-v1.pdf>.

Graham, J. R., Harvey, C. R., and Rajgopal, S. (2004). "The Economic Implications of Corporate Financial Reporting," National Bureau of Economic Research, Working Paper No. 10550, June.

Hall, P. A. and Soskice, D. (eds) (2001). *Varieties of Capitalism. The Institutional Foundations of Comparative Advantage.* Oxford: Oxford University Press.

Karageorgiou, G. and Serafeim, G. (2014). "Earnings Guidance: Part of the Future or the Past?" Generation Foundation and KKS Advisors, January 30. Available at: <https://www.genfound.org/media/pdf-earnings-guidance-kks-30-01-14.pdf> (accessed September 9, 2015).

Kudo, A., Kipping, M., and Schröter, H. (eds) (2004). *German and Japanese Business in the Boom Years: Transforming American Management and Technology Models.* London: Routledge.

Leonhardt, D. and Quealy, K. (2014). "The American Middle Class Is No Longer the World's Richest," *New York Times*, April 22. Available at: <http://www.nytimes. com/2014/04/23/upshot/the-american-middle-class-is-no-longer-the-worlds-richest. html?_r=0>.

OECD (2011). *Divided We Stand: Why Inequality Keeps Rising.* Paris: OECD Publishing.

OECD (2014a). "OECD Income Distribution Database (IDD): Gini, Poverty, Income, Methods and Concepts." Available at: <http://www.oecd.org/social/income-distribution-database.htm> (accessed October 21, 2015).

OECD (2014b). "United States: Tackling High Inequalities, Creating Opportunities for All," June. Available at: <http://www.oecd.org/unitedstates/Tackling-high-inequal ities.pdf>.

OECD (2014c). "OECD Better Life Index." Available at: <http://www. oecdbetterlifeindex.org/> (accessed October 21, 2015).

OECD (2015). *In It Together: Why Less Inequality Benefits All.* Paris: OECD Publishing.

Piketty, T. (2014). *Capital in the Twenty-First Century.* Cambridge, MA: Belknap Press of Harvard University Press.

Porter, E. (2014). "A Simple Equation: More Education = More Income," *New York Times*, September 10.

Terry, S. J. (2015). "The Macro Impact of Short-Termism," Stanford Institute for Economic Policy Research, Discussion Paper 15-022, June. Available at: <http:// siepr.stanford.edu/research/publications/macro-impact-short-termism> (accessed September 9, 2015).

WEF (2015). "Competitiveness Rankings," World Economic Forum, Geneva. Available at: <http://reports.weforum.org/global-competitiveness-report-2015-2016/ competitiveness-rankings/> (accessed October 21, 2015).

World Bank (2015). "GINI Index (World Bank Estimate)." Available at: <http://data. worldbank.org/indicator/SI.POV.GINI> (accessed October 21, 2015).

Index